International Development

NEW APPROACHES TO INTERNATIONAL HISTORY

Series Editor: Thomas Zeiler, Professor of American Diplomatic History, University of Colorado Boulder, USA

Series Editorial Board:

Anthony Adamthwaite, University of California at Berkeley (USA)
Kathleen Burk, University College London (UK)
Louis Clerc, University of Turku (Finland)
Petra Goedde, Temple University (USA)
Francine McKenzie, University of Western Ontario (Canada)
Lien-Hang Nguyen, University of Kentucky (USA)
Jason Parker, Texas A&M University (USA)
Glenda Sluga, University of Sydney (Australia)

New Approaches to International History covers international history during the modern period and across the globe. The series incorporates new developments in the field, such as the cultural turn and transnationalism, as well as the classical high politics of state-centric policy-making and diplomatic relations. Written with upper level undergraduate and postgraduate students in mind, texts in the series provide an accessible overview of international diplomatic and transnational issues, events, and actors.

Published:

Decolonization and the Cold War, edited by Leslie James and Elisabeth Leake (2015)
Cold War Summits, Chris Tudda (2015)
The United Nations in International History, Amy Sayward (2017)
Latin American Nationalism, James F. Siekmeier (2017)
The History of United States Cultural Diplomacy, Michael L. Krenn (2017)
International Cooperation in the Early 20th Century, Daniel Gorman (2017)
Women and Gender in International History, Karen Garner (2018)
International Development, Corinna R. Unger (2018)

Forthcoming:

The International LGBT Rights Movement, Laura Belmonte
Reconstructing the Postwar World, Francine McKenzie
The Environment and International History, Scott Kaufman
The United States and Latin America in the Contemporary World, Stephen G. Rabe
The History of Oil Diplomacy, Christopher R. W. Dietrich
The Nineteenth Century World, Maartje Abbenhuis and Gordon Morrell
Global War, Global Catastrophe, Maartje Abbenhuis and Ismee Tames

Series Editor Preface

New Approaches to International History takes the entire world as its stage for exploring the history of diplomacy, broadly conceived theoretically and thematically, and writ large across the span of the globe, during the modern period. This series goes beyond the single goal of explaining encounters in the world. Our aspiration is that these books provide both an introduction for researchers new to a topic, and supplemental and essential reading in classrooms. Thus, *New Approaches* serves a dual purpose that is unique from other large-scale treatments of international history; it applies to scholarly agendas and pedagogy. In addition, it does so against the backdrop of a century of enormous change, conflict, and progress that informed global history but also continues to reflect on our own times.

The series offers the old and new diplomatic history to address a range of topics that shaped the twentieth century. Engaging in international history (including but not especially focusing on global or world history), these books will appeal to a range of scholars and teachers situated in the humanities and social sciences, including those in history, international relations, cultural studies, politics, and economics. We have in mind scholars, both novice and veteran, who require an entrée into a topic, trend, or technique that can benefit their own research or education into a new field of study by crossing boundaries in a variety of ways.

By its broad and inclusive coverage, *New Approaches to International History* is also unique because it makes accessible to students current research, methodology, and themes. Incorporating cutting-edge scholarship that reflects trends in international history, as well as addressing the classical high politics of state-centric policy-making and diplomatic relations, these books are designed to bring alive the myriad of approaches for digestion by advanced undergraduates and graduate students. In preparation for the *New Approaches* series, Bloomsbury surveyed courses and faculty around the world to gauge interest and reveal core themes of relevance for their classroom use. The polling yielded a host of topics, from war and peace to the environment; from empire to economic integration; and from migration to nuclear arms. The effort proved that there is a much-needed place for studies that connect scholars and students alike to international history, and books that are especially relevant to the teaching missions of faculty around the world.

We hope readers find this series to be appealing, challenging, and thought-provoking. Whether the history is viewed through older or newer lenses, *New Approaches to International History* allows students to peer into the modern period's complex relations among nations, people, and events to draw their own conclusions about the tumultuous, interconnected past.

Thomas Zeiler, University of Colorado Boulder, USA

International Development

A Postwar History

CORINNA R. UNGER

BLOOMSBURY ACADEMIC
LONDON • NEW YORK • OXFORD • NEW DELHI • SYDNEY

BLOOMSBURY ACADEMIC
Bloomsbury Publishing Plc
50 Bedford Square, London, WC1B 3DP, UK

BLOOMSBURY, BLOOMSBURY ACADEMIC and the Diana logo are trademarks of
Bloomsbury Publishing Plc

First published in Great Britain 2018
Reprinted by Bloomsbury Academic 2019, 2020

A catalogue record for this book is available from the British Library.

A catalog record for this book is available from the Library of Congress.

ISBN: HB: 978-1-4725-7630-9
           PB: 978-1-4725-7629-3
         ePDF: 978-1-4725-7631-6
        eBook: 978-1-4725-7632-3

Series: New Approaches to International History

Typeset by Integra Software Services Pvt. Ltd
Printed and bound in Great Britain

To find out more about our authors and books visit www.bloomsbury.com
and sign up for our newsletters.

CONTENTS

ABBREVIATIONS

APDB	Agricultural Production Development Bureau
ARA	American Relief Administration
BMZ	Bundesministerium für wirtschaftliche Zusammenarbeit
CARE	Cooperative for American Remittances to Europe
CIEC	Conference for International Economic Cooperation
COMECON	Council for Mutual Economic Assistance
CTA	Commission for Technical Assistance
DAC	Development Assistance Committee
DG	Directorate General
EC	European Community
ECLA	Economic Commission for Latin America
ECOSOC	United Nations Economic and Social Council
EDF	European Development Fund
EEC	European Economic Community
EPTA	Expanded Program for Technical Assistance
ERP	European Recovery Program
FAO	Food and Agriculture Organization
FIDES	Fonds d'Investissement pour le Développement Économique et Social des Territoires d'Outre-Mer
FLN	Front de Libération Nationale
FRG	Federal Republic of Germany
GATT	General Agreement on Tariffs and Trade
GDR	German Democratic Republic
IADP	Intensive Agricultural District Programme
IBRD	International Bank for Reconstruction and Development
IDA	International Development Association
IIA	International Institute of Agriculture
IIT	Indian Institute of Technology
ILO	International Labor Organization
INCAP	Central American Institute of Nutrition
IMF	International Monetary Fund
IRDP	Integrated Rural Development Programme
IRRI	International Rice Research Institute
NDB	New Development Bank
NGO	Non-governmental organization

NIEO	New International Economic Order
ODA	Official Development Assistance
OECD	Organization for Economic Cooperation and Development
OEEC	Organization for European Economic Cooperation
ONUC	United Nations Operation in the Congo
OPEC	Organization of Petroleum Exporting Countries
PL	Public Law
SAP	Structural Adjustment Policy
SEWA	Self Employed Women's Association
SIDA	Swedish International Development Authority
SUNFED	Special United Nations Fund for Economic Development
TAA	Technical Assistance Administration
TANU	Tanganyika African National Union
TVA	Tennessee Valley Authority
UNCTAD	United Nations Conference on Trade and Development
UNDP	United Nations Development Program
UNESCO	United Nations Educational, Scientific, and Cultural Organization
UNICEF	United Nations Children's Fund
UNIFEM	United Nations Development Fund for Women
UNO	United Nations Organization
UNRRA	United Nations Relief and Rehabilitation Administration
US	United States
USAID	United States Agency for International Development
USSR	Union of Soviet Socialist Republics
VISTA	Volunteers in Service to America
WHO	World Health Organization
WTO	World Trade Organization
YMCA	Young Men's Christian Association

ACKNOWLEDGMENTS

Writing this book has been a rewarding opportunity to engage, either in person or in thought, with many colleagues from whom I have learned much about the history of development. Marc Frey has been most generous in taking the time to comment on a first draft of the manuscript, and has kindly provided suggestions on many issues (development and other) over the years. I am grateful for his friendship and collegiality. Several other colleagues have given me valuable feedback on chapters and kindly shared literature and source material. Thank you, Giuliano Garavini, Artemy Kalinovsky, Steffi Marung, Kevin O'Sullivan, and Martin Rempe.

The students in the course "Histories of Development" at Jacobs University Bremen gave me a first opportunity to systematically think about where the history of development begins, where it ends, and why it matters. Aleksandar Pelovski provided helpful research support. Working with Dienabou Barry, Karin Bugow, Verena Kröss, Smriti Sharma, and Aliya Tonkobayeva on the research project "International History of Rural Development since 1950," generously funded by the Volkswagen Foundation, has been a unique opportunity to look at development across geographical, cultural, and temporal divides. At the European University Institute in Florence, I have benefited from discussions with the participants of the seminars "Decolonization and Development" and "International History," and the numerous exchanges with my colleagues at the Department of History and Civilization have been a source of inspiration and motivation.

I am grateful to the readers who reviewed the book proposal and the manuscript and provided me with helpful suggestions and comments. I would also like to thank the editors of the series *New Approaches to International History* for inviting me to contribute a volume, and the editors at Bloomsbury Press for their efforts in producing this book. Finally, and crucially, I would like to thank Ulrike Schulz, who has accompanied me through the various stages of conceptualizing, writing, and finishing the book, for her continuous support.

CHAPTER ONE

Introduction

The challenges of development

In 2016, the Bill and Melinda Gates Foundation decided to give 100,000 chickens to poor people in so-called less-developed countries.[1] The goal of this initiative, according to Microsoft founder Bill Gates, was to help overcome individual poverty. "It's pretty clear to me that just about anyone who's living in extreme poverty is better off if they have chickens," Gates stated. According to Gates and an anthropologist on whose research the program is based, the advantages of having chickens are numerous: chickens are "easy and inexpensive to take care of"; they are a "good investment" because they breed fast and can be sold, which adds to household income; they can "keep children healthy" due to the nutrients eggs contain, and because the income from selling chickens can be used to buy better food for the children; and they "empower women" by giving them access to the market in societies in which they are otherwise excluded from the formal economy.[2] The point on women's empowerment contains a link to a separate blog post by Melinda Gates, who has a particular interest in the role of women in development. She argues that chickens, which men usually consider as economically or symbolically irrelevant, can be a valuable resource for women, who can use them to secure an income and improve their own social standing.[3]

The blog includes the image of a chicken separated into different parts, labeled education, empowerment, financial security, nutrition, health, and entrepreneurship.[4] Together, these key words reflect a highly popular contemporary approach to overcoming poverty and promoting development—an approach that emphasizes the ability of individuals to leave poverty behind when given the necessary assistance. Instead of expecting governments to conduct investment programs to reduce inequality and improve the living conditions of the population through central interventions, an internationally active, non-governmental organization (NGO) takes on the responsibility of affecting change through measures like the donation of 100,000 chickens. Education is considered essential for the success of the project, as are access to resources and health care. Since women are believed to be more responsible than men in spending money, they stand at the center of the development project—a novelty compared to most development approaches of the twentieth century, which saw development, by and large, as a monopoly of male expertise and activity. The chicken project is an expression of a particular understanding of development, one that is characterized by the belief that it is important to take into consideration the structural differences on the ground and the ability of individuals to change their own lives within those boundaries. The primary goal of this type of development is not to radically change social and economic structures in order to reduce inequalities but to identify niches in which economic growth can be stimulated. Economic growth in turn is expected to create opportunities for individuals to improve their own lives in terms of income, health, and education. It is an essentially liberal model that prizes knowledge, entrepreneurship, and individuality.

The approach promoted by the Gates Foundation seems to meet many of the criteria development projects are currently judged by. It is sensitive to gender inequalities, it avoids bureaucratic and hierarchical top-down mechanisms, focusing instead on local settings and grassroots participation, and it is geared toward encouraging economic independence instead of creating structural dependencies. Yet for all these apparent advantages, not everyone shares the foundation's enthusiasm for the project. The government of Bolivia, which was supposed to participate in it alongside several African countries, was offended by the foundation's assumption that what Bolivia needed was chickens—as if Bolivians were so poor and backward that they did not have the means to breed chickens on their own, or as if the country's problems could be solved by importing American birds. Bolivia's minister of land and rural development, César Cocarico, was quoted as saying that Gates should not talk about Bolivia's needs before having gained a better understanding of the country.[5] His rejection of American philanthropic support for Bolivia's rural poor produced much publicity because the offer from the Gates Foundation was considered a political provocation. According to the description of the Bolivian government, the foundation is part of a US effort to use development assistance to spread capitalism and accelerate globalization in order to strengthen American power in the world—in other words, development aid is seen as a Trojan horse for Western capitalism and imperialism. Apart from this ideological critique, the Bolivian response to the Gates initiative is a reaction to the assumption that Bolivia's economy is primarily agricultural, and that therefore development, instead of accelerating high-tech industrialization and modernization, should focus on small-scale rural projects. Bolivia's national pride was clearly hurt by this perception, which seemed to reproduce the (real or imagined) dichotomy between the developed (male) and the less-developed (female) world, between North and South, between the West and the Rest.

The chicken episode reflects many of the problems practitioners and supporters of development assistance face. They have to explain to a skeptical public why tax money should be spent on helping others far away while poverty in one's own country or region is on the rise; why granting large credits to authoritarian governments is supposed to have positive effects that justify immense financial risks, high levels of corruption, and a lack of political transparency; and why, after having witnessed thousands of seemingly failed development projects that cost much more than expected and had unforeseen and highly problematic ecological, social, and cultural consequences, we should continue to put trust in the promise of development.[6] The chicken project seems to support those who are convinced that development assistance is economically misguided and morally irresponsible. They argue that aid is paternalistic in that it takes away responsibility and agency from those living in poverty, that it destroys markets and has negative economic effects, and that, despite all efforts to promote equality, it actually reinforces notions of difference and hierarchy.

Yet it would be shortsighted to interpret the chicken anecdote exclusively from a contemporary political perspective. In many ways, the Gates Foundation's initiative is a reaction to decades of criticism of various types, models, and forms of development assistance and the result of trying to learn from past mistakes and frustrations. Instead of continuing to work with established approaches, the foundation tries to find new ways of promoting development. The fact that it is an NGO taking on what, for decades, used to be the task of governments and international organizations, is important in this context. It challenges established political patterns and practices but also produces questions about political legitimacy. Similarly, the Bolivian government's refusal to accept chickens from the foundation should not be reduced to a momentary expression of anti-Americanism. Rather, it has to be understood against the background of the so-called developing countries being treated as helpless and grateful recipients of Western aid while remaining structurally dependent on the fully industrialized, or post-industrial, countries. The fact that the Gates Foundation offers chickens, not technology, could be interpreted as yet another expression of the attempt by the industrial countries to keep the Global South in a state of underdevelopment compared to the Global North.

If we want to understand why some development approaches are hailed as a universal formula to overcome poverty while others are considered unacceptable or unfeasible, we have to identify their particularities and their respective positions in the field of development. Specifically, we need to study the historical roots of the various approaches, the agendas of their proponents and opponents, the political and ideological settings in which they were anchored, the ways in which they were implemented, the practical effects they had, and the lessons that were drawn from those experiences. That is what this book aims to do: it offers an overview of historical thinking about and experiences with development over the course of the twentieth century in different political, economic, cultural, and geographical settings. The following questions serve to define the book's guiding interests: when and where did the notion of development originate? How did it evolve into the professional, highly competitive policy and business field we know today? Who were the key players involved, and how did they influence the discourses and practices that continue to shape development approaches today? How did international, global, and regional political and economic changes affect development policies and projects? And what is the historical meaning of development as a political and cultural practice from a long-term perspective?

Historiographical and conceptual considerations

The book's focus is on development in the decades after the end of the Second World War, when, against the background of the end of the European overseas empires and decolonization and in the context of the Cold War, development aid became established as a professional field and as a diplomatic tool. However, ideas about developing economies and societies that were considered backward or underdeveloped did not suddenly appear in 1945.[7] Enlightenment thinking about human improvement had already imprinted itself on European perceptions of differences between countries and societies. Even prior to the Enlightenment, John Locke (1632–1704) had proposed that working a piece of land and thereby improving its quality gave the worker property rights toward the land; this implied that economically developing a place, region, or country justified the claim of ownership.[8] Adam Smith (1723–1790) and John Stuart Mill (1806–1873) made influential arguments about the importance of economic growth for a country's progress. Karl Marx (1818–1883), when analyzing the process of economic development within a society, highlighted the importance of capitalism as a system that, while exploitative and unequal in character, contained a progressive historical momentum and drove history forward.[9] Political and intellectual elites in the mid-nineteenth century became increasingly interested in comparisons between countries and their respective states of development. Among the most famous examples was Japan's Meiji Restoration of the late 1860s, whose goal was to strengthen Japan vis-à-vis China and the Western powers by modernizing the country's military, economy, and administration. Famously, Sun Yat-sen (1866–1925), the founder and first president of the Republic of China, in his 1918 *International Development of China*, called for international financial support to allow China to modernize economically and socially.[10]

The implicit idea of catching up suggests that there was an understanding of developmental differences that gained importance in the context of an increasingly globalizing economy, which was, in part, driven by imperial competition as it came to characterize the late nineteenth and early twentieth centuries. Many supporters of imperialism believed that overseas colonies offered unique economic opportunities as well as the chance to strengthen the nation by mastering the challenges of the frontier experience. At a time when technological and scientific advancements were taking place at rapid speed, imperial conquest and colonial rule became closely entangled with notions of scientific progress as an expression and a tool of civilizational superiority and political power.[11]

At the same time, many academics and administrators argued that, as societies were becoming more complex, social relations and structures had to be planned systematically, and that scientific experts were better placed to do so than politicians.[12] The support for planning and technocracy became one of the emblems of early ideas about how to develop and modernize societies. The Soviet Union provided one of the most radical examples in this regard. The USSR's leaders proclaimed the construction of the so-called new Soviet person as the starting point for a new, better type of society, one which was organized and planned according to scientific principles (although not everyone agreed that Marxism qualified as a scientific method).[13] Less radically inclined, but no less ambitious was the American New Deal of the 1930s, a response to the socioeconomic effects of the Great Depression but also an effort to overcome what was seen as underdevelopment in the southern parts of the United States. The effort to use public resources to stimulate the economy and to employ governmental instruments to modernize socioeconomic structures gave social reformers an opportunity to try out their ideas in practice. They advocated solutions to the perceived problems resulting from the transformation from agrarian to industrial society, ranging from programs to strengthen local communities to new types of housing to efforts at increasing the efficiency of rural economies.[14] Similarly, in many European countries programs were conducted in the interwar period to design more rational societies.[15]

The effort to modernize social life was not limited to the domestic sphere. Colonialism and imperialism produced a setting in which interventions into the social and economic structures of foreign countries constituted an everyday practice. The notion of difference, so central to imperialism, was reflected in the effort to adapt the colonized societies to the norms of the so-called mother country by changing what was considered problematic about them. French administrators in Algeria, American missionaries in the Philippines, Soviet officers in Central Asia—all of them had a particular understanding of what made the specific regions within their countries' empires backward and what had to be changed in order to meet their domestic and imperial standards.[16] Of course, theirs was a different kind of thinking from what we, today, associate with development assistance.

The goal was not to improve the standards of living in the colonies but to increase their productivity and to legitimize colonialism. The case of the Netherlands is telling in this regard: in 1901, after several years of debates about colonial practices, the Dutch queen declared the so-called Ethical Policy, which emphasized the Netherlands' responsibility for the welfare of the Dutch Southeast Asian colonies. Agricultural and technological improvements as well as educational measures were supposed to lift up the populations of the Dutch East Indies. Arguing that interventions into existing socioeconomic structures were necessary as part of a civilizing mission, and that improvements could be achieved by systematically addressing the causes of poverty with the help of modern technology, the Dutch Ethical Policy was an early example of colonial development policy.[17]

In many cases members of the colonial elites agreed with colonial officials about the problems they believed existed in a particular country and how to best solve them. What united them was the belief that some form of intervention was necessary to modernize what they considered backward structures and practices.[18] Some focused on the need for education of the indigenous inhabitants who could serve the colonial system. Others called for the improvement of health care and for better research and training structures, which would have a positive effect on productivity. Yet again others believed in the transformative power of labor and trade.[19] While many of these ideas were in line with imperial power interests, others gained a subversive quality when a growing number of anti-colonial actors demanded changes in colonial policies. Many pointed out that the colonial administrations did not live up to their promises of uplifting the societies under foreign rule. The call for more active development efforts gained traction both in the colonies and internationally throughout the 1920s and 1930s, and some of the colonial governments reacted to them by establishing development funds. This decision reflected the assumption that living conditions and welfare were responsibilities of the government, a trend that was underlined by new economic approaches to dealing with crises. The interwar period witnessed the establishment of a growing number of non-governmental and international organizations concerned with these issues. The League of Nations and its various committees early on identified the standard of living as a key concept in trying to balance regional economic disparities.[20] Similarly, the language of development was prominent in the preparations for the Bretton Woods organizations in the early 1940s.[21]

As these examples suggest, when studying the history of postwar international development it is important to be aware of the direct and indirect forerunners of development-related ideas and practices. Furthermore, one should not assume that the established caesuras of twentieth-century political history are valid for the history of development, too. The periodization necessarily varies according to the questions asked.[22] In addition to keeping in mind the long, pre-1945 history of development it is crucial to remember that development as a field was distinctly international and interdisciplinary in character. Individual experts, many of them academics—engineers, economists, sociologists, geographers, anthropologists, demographers, historians, urban planners, agronomists—produced the knowledge and wrote the textbooks that became the theoretical basis of development practice. In doing so, some were very aware of their role as representatives of a specific nation and tried to contribute to the formulation of their governments' foreign policies. Others conducted their research primarily for academic reasons or because they wanted to help find solutions to the problems they believed they had identified, whether it was building a bridge, establishing a community development program, or advising a government on economic planning. Not every development expert would have identified as a concerned citizen, although many tried to convince governmental and non-governmental bodies to support their work by including references to its political relevance.

Undoubtedly, there was no such thing as apolitical development research. Studying a development problem necessarily implied a specific understanding of the challenges of the present and the future—for example, why the agricultural sector of a certain country was not productive enough and how it should be reorganized to increase its productivity. Research of this kind included ideas about what type of economy the country in question should have, which technology was appropriate to change existing agricultural practices, what role the rural inhabitants should play in the national economy, and how their living patterns had to be changed for that reason. In those cases where development experts tried to translate their knowledge into policy advice, the political quality of the underlying assumptions intensified. Whether their advice was taken up depended on a number of factors, among them the experts' ability to translate complex findings into clear messages, a political climate that valued academic knowledge, and an interest in and perceived need for advice on the part of governments and non-governmental organizations.

The best known example of academics acting as development policy advisers are the American historians and social scientists who, in the postwar years, formulated modernization theories and suggested them as the basis for development policies. Individuals like Max F. Millikan (1913–1969), Walt W. Rostow (1916–2003), Daniel Lerner (1917–1980), and Lucian Pye (1921–2008) felt that they had a contribution to make beyond academic research, and that their knowledge could help to improve and strengthen the position of the United States in the Cold War.[23] Liberal anti-communism was at the heart of their thinking. In what might have been a historically unique moment, they succeeded in making themselves heard vis-à-vis the White House. Particularly the Kennedy administration was eager to recruit academic advisers, giving them privileged access to policy-making bodies. Their scientific optimism and their personal self-confidence greatly contributed to their rise as public intellectuals. Based, at least in part, on their recommendations, economic, technical, and military development aid gained enormous prominence as a foreign policy tool as the United States replaced the former European colonial powers in the so-called Third World and entered into a competition with the Soviet Union.[24]

Because scholars like Rostow and others were so visible, and because their success in being acknowledged as political experts was so unusual, historians have been attracted to studying their personas and ideas in great depth. Historical studies have paid close attention to the intellectual history of American modernization theories, to the ways in which those concepts were linked to development thinking, and to the foreign policy recommendations the experts formulated.[25] For all their benefits, these studies have tended to present modernization theory as a genuinely American product of the Cold War. Yet many of the ideas and assumptions on which modernization theory rested were not entirely new when Rostow and his colleagues began to popularize their arguments. "Rather than a conceptual revolution, modernization might be better understood as the reformulation of an older discourse, a process whereby older models of social change were reworked and blended together into an holistic pattern."[26] Colonial officers had been thinking about social change in the colonies for decades; when the problems they identified seemed to become more complex, they requested academic advice which would help them to justify their decisions.[27] For that reason, the emphasis on the American fathers of modernization theory needs to be balanced by including the other actors involved.

More generally, it is crucial to remember that politicians, scholars, and experts across the world believed in the power of science and planning to tackle problems perceived as expressions of underdevelopment. It is certainly true that "the development of economic assistance, welfare, and planning *within the borders of the national state* helped lay the foundations for international economic aid."[28] The nation state was a key political entity for much of the twentieth century. Yet we should not assume outright that citizenship and national identity defined individuals and organizations involved in development assistance and development projects. Experts were socialized in specific national settings, of course, but their knowledge was rarely confined to or completely defined by national concerns precisely because development was transregional and transnational in scale.

What made the idea of development so attractive for many people of very different cultural, intellectual, political, and geographical backgrounds was its promise that poverty could be overcome with constructive means, that individual nations or societies could be designed in better, improved ways, and that regional inequalities could be leveled. For those in favor of socialist ideas, development could help to overcome class differences by giving the poor access to resources, and by establishing social structures that prevented economic imbalances from increasing. To those in favor of liberal capitalism, development provided a way of accelerating economic growth and keeping the political radicalism of the left at bay. This kind of instrumental thinking about development gained particular relevance in the context of the Cold

War, when the Soviet Union and the United States as well as their respective allies and partners (national governments as well as non-governmental and international organizations) used development aid to further their strategic and ideological goals. Meanwhile, for the leaders of the former colonies that were becoming independent in the postwar decades, the promise of development was an essential element of the *raison d'être* of the new nations and the legitimacy of their governments. Whereas the colonial powers had exploited their colonies economically, the leaders of the newly independent states wanted to follow development paths in line with their countries' authentic interests. With the help of development assistance from abroad, they would become modern, internationally recognized nations on a par with the industrial countries. This would allow them to discard the notions of racial, cultural, and civilization inferiority which had for so long defined relations between the colonies and the colonizers as well as within colonial societies. Development was seen as a promise of a better future, as a tool of liberation, and as a vision of a feasible alternative to the past and present.

This optimistic understanding of development tends to be forgotten today. Too many disappointments, ranging from supposedly failed projects to failed states, have challenged the belief that real progress under the label of development is possible. On a more abstract level, many critics portray the concept of development as a neo-colonial, neo-imperial, or neoliberal approach to maintaining Western dominance over the so-called developing countries. For them, development is a way for governments and companies to gain access to resources and markets, thereby contributing to processes of globalization and the privatization of public goods. They highlight the unequal power relations between so-called donors and so-called recipients of aid, and argue that development assistance reproduces Eurocentric and Western notions of difference.

There are many good reasons to be skeptical of development assistance, and it is crucial to study in detail the various interests and strategies that were and are tied to it. Development assistance is always accompanied by a range of expectations; it never is a pure aim. Yet by focusing solely on the hierarchical notion implicit in development thinking, and on the quality of development as a power tool used by an elite against the majority of the population, there is a danger of losing sight of the fact that for many individuals, social groups, and nations the promise of development was and is something very real.[29] To overcome the simplistic dichotomy between the arguments in favor of and against development and development aid, it is not sufficient to criticize ideological positions. What is needed is "historical analysis in place of metacritique."[30] Such an analysis has to pay attention to all sides concerned, not only to those in power or those contributing to an academic discourse. Specifically, it is important to include not only prominent foreign policy-makers and experts but also mid- and lower-level bureaucrats and officers, development workers in the field, and, perhaps most importantly, the different social groups affected by and reacting to development projects. Here, too, we have to differentiate—between women and men, urban and rural society, social status and class, ethnicity and religion. No history of development can ever be complete, but historians should try to include as many perspectives as possible. Only then will they be able to gain new insights that will bring new arguments to the discussion about the challenges and potential benefits of development and development assistance. To do so, it is important to reflect on some conceptual questions concerning the historical study of development.

Development can mean many things, and as a concept it suggests itself to a variety of political interpretations and arguments. A democratic movement can embrace the idea of development and find it useful with regard to describing its goals just as an authoritarian regime can use the term to give meaning to its political agenda. Similarly, an anti-colonial activist can call for development arguing that colonialism prevents the development of the colony and its economy, while the colonial power can make the case that it is precisely the need for development of the supposedly underdeveloped colony that makes its presence necessary. Because development is such an opaque term, it is important to position each understanding of development squarely in its specific historical, social, philosophical, and political context. The same is true of related terms like underdevelopment, modernization, improvement, progress, development aid, and development assistance. All of these terms carry multiple political connotations that have changed over time. For example, the term development aid has been replaced by the term development cooperation because it suggests a more equal relationship between donors and recipients. This case shows that contemporary semantics, too, are politically driven and cannot claim neutrality. Thus, instead of using quotation marks to signal a distance to the normative interpretations entailed in the various terms used by the historical actors, the book aims to historicize the perspectives that informed their use.

From an epistemological point of view, a specific understanding of development is rarely the result of purely theoretical thinking. Rather, it is influenced and shaped by particular experiences with development, be they real or imagined. For example, when development economists in the 1950s were writing about the problems of a country they considered to be underdeveloped, more often than not they did so with at least an implicit view on how and why another country had developed more quickly. Similarly, rural development experts drawing up a new scheme on how to solve a region's irrigation problems did not do so in a vacuum. They based their recommendations on what they knew about earlier attempts to establish irrigation systems in the same or a neighboring region, and they tried to include elements of programs in other places that they believed would be useful in their specific case. Being aware of the layered character of development ideas and concepts helps us to better understand the ways in which they played out in practice.

In recent years our knowledge of the history of development—of the different phases, actors, and forms of development aid in different moments of the twentieth century and in different parts of the world—has rapidly grown thanks to a large number of case studies.[31] What seems lacking is a more integrated perspective that brings together case studies from various regions and includes the history of development before 1945 as well as beyond the 1970s. This is not to say that the history of development could or should be written as a grand narrative. Such a construct would hide the complexity of the many small and large decisions, concerns, and actions involved in every development project. Yet it seems important to connect the different strands of research more systematically with each other in order to assess the ways in which the history of development is related to historical phenomena like decolonization, the Cold War, regional integration or disintegration, and the North–South divide. Specifically, it appears useful to bring the different fields of research into conversation with each other in order to arrive at a better understanding of the structures, patterns, and actors involved in development, which in turn might give us new insight into the international history of the twentieth century. What allows a history of development to do so is the fact that it provides a unique lens to study political, economic, social, and cultural constellations across time. Its multifaceted character makes it possible to study governmental decisions on a par with non-governmental ones; it offers insight into the power of cultural assumptions without neglecting economic and political aspects; it allows us to combine diachronic with synchronic perspectives, and to study discourses together with practices; and it lends itself to studying international and global phenomena like the South–North conflict, environmental problems, and the history of competing ideologies.

This book rests on two basic assumptions. One is the assumption that ideas matter and have real, effective consequences for the ways in which social orders are shaped. On this basis, the book aims to contribute to a more differentiated understanding of which social, intellectual, and political beliefs and interests have informed the decisions leading to different development approaches. The book's focus is on the interactive nature of the history of development, assuming that development policies and practices did not take place in a vacuum but were shaped by specific historical actors and situations. This research perspective differs from a more deterministic point of view according to which a region's or society's development is largely preconditioned by a specific arrangement of economic and natural resources, demographic and climatic phenomena, or cultural factors.[32] Specifically, the book is interested in how individuals, governments and organizations tried to implement their respective visions of development, how much room for maneuver they had to promote their development agendas, which aspects of those agendas they were able to realize, and which ones remained theory.

The book's second assumption is closely linked to the first one. It is the understanding that it is not sufficient to study the discursive and ideational levels of development thinking, and that we need to pay attention to the practical and material aspects of development, too. Physical and structural conditions matter, and they have to be included in the analysis to do justice to the importance and complexity of problems like poverty, economic and political inequality, ecological degradation, and perceptions of cultural or racial difference that can translate into discrimination and violence.[33] The book shares the understanding that "things, nature, technologies, labor, and commodities count, not just as cultural representations or referents in language, but in their own right."[34] It approaches historical perceptions of development and the material, political, economic, and social phenomena taking place not on their bases as separate entities but perceives them as interdependent. This is different from arguing that material structures (pre)determine ideas and actions as it leaves more room for individual and collective decisions and behavior.

Based on existing research, some parts of this agenda are easier to realize than others. The book predominantly draws on secondary literature, with some primary sources added in individual cases. The selection of the literature and, correspondingly, of the examples and regions discussed is necessarily prejudiced as it is defined by the author's language skills, knowledge of literature, and research experience. Other scholars would have selected other examples and included a different range of literature, and some readers will find particular cases and countries missing. Specifically, the book builds on works in English and German, and it reflects the dominance of Western European and North American publications and research projects in the field of international and global history. Within Europe, the biggest number of examples relates to the colonial powers, Great Britain and France, on whom much more has been written than on other countries. Something similar is true of the ratio between literature on the history of development in Asia and Africa compared to Latin America. Also, Eastern European development actors do not receive the same degree of coverage as do their Western counterparts. Similarly, access to sources and studies on the development field after the 1970s are still relatively scarce, resulting in a shorter chapter on this period of time. Rather than aiming for an encyclopedic account, this book is guided by the effort to point out key moments and recurring patterns in the history of development and to offer an interpretation and periodization of the history of development from a *longue durée* perspective.

Chapter outline

The book proceeds as follows: The second chapter introduces readers to different definitions and concepts of development and traces the history of economic ideas about inequality and economic growth. This leads to a discussion of the role of industrialization in the development process, the unequal development of different world regions, and the question of how economists in the early and mid-twentieth century interpreted these problems and which solutions they advocated, which in turn shaped the emerging field of development economics.

The third chapter focuses on the forerunners of development thinking and practice. It shows that development as it came to be understood in the postwar period had a variety of intellectual and political roots which, in part, challenged each other. The common denominator that tied the different roots together was an understanding of poverty and inequality as a challenge that could not be locally or regionally contained and therefore had to be addressed on a larger scale. This applied particularly to the situation in the colonies, but also to less developed regions in otherwise industrialized countries.

The fourth chapter analyzes the emergence of the concept of development in the period between the early 1930s and the early 1950s. It argues that in this prolonged moment a particular international constellation emerged that made it possible for proponents of development to gain public attention and political support. The key factors were the Second World War, its effects on the European empires, the onset of decolonization, and, in the early postwar years, the Cold War conflict. Heavily influenced by the experience of the economic crises of the interwar period and by the war, the political awareness of the power of inequality and poverty grew exponentially at this time. While the imperial powers tried to use development measures to rein in the challenges this implied to their empires, the United States embraced this perspective as an opportunity and endorsed it with its technological and economic power. American actors thereby popularized the idea of development and established it internationally, not least through the newly founded international organizations. It was against this background that development studies as a professional field became established.

The fifth chapter turns to the political meaning development was given in the postwar period. It shows how the so-called developing countries, among them many former colonies, advocated rapid economic development in the interest of improving their domestic situation and their international standing. This constellation opened up spaces for industrial countries to offer development assistance of different kinds, each of which reflected various political and economic interests. The Cold War accelerated the disbursement of development aid and pushed it into particular directions. At the same time, the recipients of technical, financial, and military support proved to be skilled in bargaining, helped by the fact that the number of possible providers of development assistance increased rapidly over time.

In the sixth chapter, the focus is on different development approaches and practices in the postwar decades. While large-scale industrialization, urbanization, and infrastructure projects left the most visible traces of development efforts in Asia, Africa, and Latin America, the chapter focuses on those areas of development that affected the largest number of individuals. These were community development, rural and agricultural improvement, education, health, and birth control. The different examples show that development models rarely translated into practice as imagined. Rather, most approaches were adapted and re-adapted and in turn triggered discussions about the need to change directions in a nation's or region's development. There was no universal formula that worked for all cases in the same way, development practitioners came to realize; the political, social, and cultural particularities of each case greatly affected the outcome of even the most meticulously planned project.

The seventh chapter turns to the growing critique of mainstream development thinking and practices as they had become established in the postwar years. The strongest critique in the late 1960s and 1970s came from the so-called developing countries themselves, whose leaders challenged the idea that development assistance from the industrial countries was sufficient for them to modernize. What they called for was a change in global economic structures that would allow them to overcome their dependence on the industrial centers. Their demands were echoed by critics of development in the Western world, who were uncomfortable with the various forms of inequality inherent in development assistance and who emphasized the need for more cooperative forms of practicing solidarity. Political events like the Vietnam War and Cold War détente as well as social processes like a generational change in international organizations made development ideas more vulnerable but also more susceptible to change. Consequently, many development actors began to experiment with new approaches, thereby opening up the formerly narrow definition of development.

The eighth chapter chronicles the search for new meanings of development after the challenge to mainstream development in the 1970s. It shows how the distance between those in favor and against development assistance grew and became entangled with discussions about the relations between the state and the market, as so-called neoliberals intensified their calls for more competition and less public investment to encourage economic growth and social mobility and thereby challenged the Western postwar consensus. The end of the Cold War accelerated this tendency as the socialist alternative to the capitalist development model lost credence.

The conclusion draws on the main findings of the different chapters. It provides a *longue durée* interpretation of the history of development, and it highlights similarities and differences between the different periods which can be identified. In a final step, the chapter discusses the possibility of drawing on historical insights to inform current and future development approaches.

CHAPTER TWO

Development in History: "Everyman's Road to Utopia?"

Politicians, administrators, scholars, journalists, and individuals in very different parts of the world and under very different circumstances have tried to find a convincing answer to the question of what development could and should mean. In order to gain insight into the hopes and concerns that are connected to the notion of development, it is useful to take a look at some of the definitions of development and the conceptual questions tied to them.

Defining and conceptualizing development

The number of definitions of development one can find is endless. Heinz W. Arndt, in his 1987 book on the history of the idea of economic development, listed some of the understandings of development that had been used since the mid-twentieth century:

> Higher living standards. A rising per capita income. Increase in productive capacity. Mastery over nature. Freedom through control of man's environment. Economic growth. But not mere growth, growth with equity. Elimination of poverty. Basic needs satisfaction. Catching up with the developing countries in technology, wealth, power, status. Economic independence, self-reliance. Scope for self-fulfillment for all. Liberation, the means to human ascent. Development ... appears to have come to encompass almost all facets of the good society, everyman's road to utopia.[1]

The order in which the understandings are listed reflects the fact that development is most often associated with growth, particularly (and sometimes solely) economic growth. The *Encyclopedia Britannica* describes economic development as "the process whereby simple, low-income national economies are transformed into modern industrial economies."[2] From this point of view, economic assistance serves as the tool to accelerate and enable this transformation process.[3] Other scholars focus on the social and political goals of development, such as securing individual freedom, producing social equality, and strengthening democracy.[4] This view of development is strongly normative in character: "Development means making a better life for everyone."[5] Others are much more critical about the idea of development and consider it an empty and potentially dangerous promise. In their eyes development is a Western ideological construct that helps to maintain the inequality between the so-called First World and the so-called Third World.[6] The latter perspective is closely connected to a critical trend in development studies that has gained in popularity since the 1990s. At the time, deconstructivist approaches, many of them inspired by Edward Said's and Michel Foucault's thinking about the nexus between power and knowledge, received a great deal of attention and were applied in many ways to criticize what was seen as orthodox development thinking.[7] More generally, it is important to remember that development thinking as we know it today started out as a concern of those living under privileged conditions to change economic, social, and sometimes political conditions elsewhere. Hence, development thinking was always based on an element of difference. Relatedly, the definition of what development means was never a fully egalitarian discussion. Actors from industrialized countries could usually claim more argumentative weight than actors from countries which were perceived to be in the process of developing.

What does this imply for the way in which development gains its meaning? The call for development indicates that, in the eyes of their contemporaries, a society or country seems to suffer from a lack of social progress, economic growth, or something else, and that this lack should be overcome. This alleged lack is measured against a specific ideal or standard. It is often connected to the notion of temporal difference, based on the view that some social groups, countries, or regions have made their path toward a certain level of industrialization, social order, or political system earlier or faster than others, or that the others are lagging behind. Consequently, while some have already reached the present, others seem to be caught in the past.[8] For example, the Bolivian minister opposing the Gates Foundation's chicken project referred to this perception by saying about Bill Gates: "He does not know Bolivia's reality to think we are living 500 years ago, in the middle of the jungle not knowing how to produce."[9] In other words, he accused Gates of portraying Bolivia as a backward country that had not yet made its way into modernity and was dependent on external donations because of its underdevelopment.

References to supposedly primitive economic, agricultural, and cultural practices are common in thinking about development phases. Historical precision is much less effective in emphasizing contrast than generalizations are. The "500 years" are not supposed to give the audience a refined understanding of Bolivia's situation in 1516. Rather, speaking of centuries serves to point toward the immense changes that, according to the minister's portrayal, have taken place in Bolivia since. Similarly, in descriptions of alleged backwardness, one often finds references to the Middle Ages to describe the difference in terms of political structures, economic behavior, and social norms that seem to characterize underdeveloped societies. These are reference to times many people consider to have been archaic.

In development thinking, one can find a distinct urge to accelerate the development process of a country by using some of the technologies and experiences of other countries, thereby saving time and energy. Here we see that development is a goal and a process at the same time: a country aims at becoming developed, and to do so its political leaders try to accelerate the development process.[10] Technology and expertise, themselves expressions of development, appear crucial in this context. The Great Leap Forward under Mao Zedong (1893–1976) in the People's Republic of China between 1958 and 1961 reflected the assumption that it was, indeed, possible to jump across phases of what was regarded as the natural process of development.[11] Teleological thinking about a country's path toward modernity also exists in the reverse direction. For example, US Air Force General Curtis LeMay (1906–1990), an influential military strategist in the Vietnam War, is said to have argued that the American Air Force had the ability to bomb North Vietnam "back into the stone age."[12] By this he supposedly meant undoing North Vietnam's economic development and reducing the country to a peasant economy that would not pose a threat to the United States.

As the quote suggests, the idea of development is closely entwined with a specific understanding of modernity, more specifically of industrial modernity. The synonymous use of the terms developed countries and industrial countries reflects this understanding, which implies that those countries which are not yet fully industrialized are underdeveloped or at least less developed. Although most of the countries which are usually considered the most developed ones by now rely on post-industrial economies that are dominated by the digital and service sectors, the specter of industrialization with its material and technological characteristics (factories, steel, and the mass production of capital goods and consumer goods) still serves as the implicit standard of measuring development. This brings us to debates from the early and mid-twentieth century about economic growth, the origins of industrialization, and the ways in which development thinking was linked to it in economic theories.

Debates about global inequalities, economic growth, and industrialization

The emergence of development economics and development studies more generally were shaped by the political events and academic debates of the twentieth century, as were the types of knowledge the new fields brought forth and planted in the public understanding of development. Academic thinking about economic development evolved rapidly in the first half of the twentieth century. In the late nineteenth and early twentieth centuries, economists had begun to study questions of economic growth in the context of the nation state, and governments became increasingly interested in using new tools of economic quantification to plan their activities. Of course, collecting information about economic resources, the number of inhabitants, production patterns and trade activities in a certain territory was not new. Rulers had always needed this kind of information, and they had begun to collect it more systematically in the eighteenth and nineteenth centuries.[13] Yet as economic research came to rely more and more on mathematical models and economic planning gained in prominence in many countries in the 1920s and 1930s, the need for systematic collections of economic and financial data grew. International organizations were at the forefront of this effort, often in close cooperation with national governments. The League of Nations collected different kinds of economic and financial data.[14] The International Institute of Agriculture (IIA), the forerunner of the Food and Agriculture Organization (FAO), focused on information about agricultural production patterns.[15] The International Labor Organization (ILO) was interested in gaining an overview of employment rates, wages, and working conditions across the globe.[16]

With the new kinds and amounts of data available, economists like Simon Kuznets (1901–1985) and Colin Clark (1905–1989) began to standardize "what was measured and how."[17] One of the most important results was the concept of national income accounting, which was developed in the early 1940s. Thanks to the new approach, the national incomes of different countries could be compared to each other, which allowed insight into national, regional, and global differences in terms of economic productivity and living standards defined by levels of income, spending, and saving.[18] What the comparisons showed was that those measures vastly differed across the globe. The most visible gap was the one between industrial and non-industrial countries. Today, scholars are still debating the question of why some countries and regions industrialized earlier than others, and why some have stayed comparatively poor for a long time.

Most historians agree that the process of industrialization, with its many economic, social, and cultural consequences, started in Europe, specifically in parts of England and Scotland, in the late eighteenth century and continued in other parts of Europe throughout the nineteenth century.[19] In recent decades, scholars have argued over whether one can compare the early beginnings of industrialization in other parts of the world with what happened in England. Specifically, in what is referred to as the Great Divergence debate, historians of China have challenged the underlying assumption that only European societies possessed the necessary combination of technology, productivity, legal and political conditions, and social resources to allow for the industrial revolution to happen. They have shown that the Yangzi Delta in China in the eighteenth century had reached a very high level of industrial development, and that the region was as likely to fully industrialize as comparable regions in England. However, rapid population growth in the delta together with the lack of coal created a comparative disadvantage. According to this interpretation, England's coal resources in combination with access to export markets, including the colonies, and the Atlantic slave economy were crucial in allowing industrialization to proceed.[20]

The debates about divergent developments in early modern Asia and Europe have made clear that the rise of what became seen as the West was not so much an expression of European genius but rather the result of a historically contingent (if unique) combination of factors which, in connection with the political and economic forces of imperialism and colonialism, allowed European countries to claim extremely powerful positions in the world in the nineteenth century. The emphasis on the particular historical context in which European industrialization happened needs to be taken into consideration when thinking about the reasons why countries or regions in Latin America, Asia, and Africa were, for a long time, not in a position to fully industrialize. It also means that it would be deeply ahistorical to assume that there was a linear path toward industrialization that all countries experienced sooner or later, and that when industrialization took place it happened in an identical fashion in all societies. This is an argument economic historian Alexander Gerschenkron (1904–1978) presented in the late 1950s and early 1960s.[21] His analysis of industrialization showed that there were distinct differences between countries like Great Britain and Russia, France and Germany. For example, Russia, as a latecomer to industrialization, could draw on technologies that had not been available when the Western European countries had industrialized. Furthermore, the way in which existing political structures encouraged industrialization or prevented it from happening depended on the state structures in place, Gerschenkron argued, pointing out the difference between the Russian and the French state, for example. Hence, Great Britain's industrialization experience could not serve as the model for all other countries, and the African and Asian nations which, in the 1950s and 1960s, aimed for industrialization could not be compared to European countries which had industrialized during the nineteenth century.[22]

This insight into the challenges of overcoming particular economic structures that made industrialization difficult was not new at the time. Already in the interwar period, representatives of the League of Nations'

Economic and Financial Organization had observed that "poor European countries were especially dependent on intra-European trade for their survival, whereas richer, predominantly industrialized European countries relied on their trading relationships beyond Europe's frontiers."[23] The poorer countries were those in Central, Eastern and Southern Europe whose economies were largely rural in character, while those countries in Western Europe which had industrialized earlier benefited from the cheap agricultural imports of their Eastern neighbors. At the time the predominant approach in reaction to this structural imbalance was to call for free trade. Many liberal economists in the 1920s believed that free trade would result in growth, and growth would provide the basis on which those who had less would be able to gain more. According to this logic, development was not a matter of redistribution in the interest of creating more equality but an issue of overall growth.[24]

One of the key questions related to mid-century economic thinking about poor countries was how growth should take place. Should it be planned and designed according to a master plan, or could it happen spontaneously? The Soviet Union had opted for a strictly planned development process to industrialize as quickly as possible. In doing so, the agrarian sector had been drawn upon heavily, resulting in an uneven development process.[25] Paul Rosenstein-Rodan (1902–1985), a Polish economist, in 1943 made a case in favor of balanced growth. By this he meant the planned transformation of an agrarian into an industrial economy, a process whereby the labor of those working in agriculture would be transferred to the industrial sector. The investment needed for setting up factories would have to come from foreign capital.[26] Rosenstein-Rodan's concept provided the basis for what became known as the big-push model: the idea that industrialization could be achieved in a short time if the necessary resources were provided and allocated correctly, and that industrialization was key to overcoming regional economic differences. This argument (which, notably, had its roots in an analysis of the economic situation of countries in Eastern and South-Eastern Europe) was complemented by the work of Roy Harrod (1900–1978) and Evsey Domar (1914–1997).[27] What became known as the Harrod-Domar model rested on the assumption that "a country's growth rate is directly proportional and strictly correlated to the investment rate, which depends in turn on the savings rate of that country."[28] A rather static formula, the Harrod-Domar model was soon criticized for not doing justice to the particularities of the economies of so-called underdeveloped countries.

Consequently, some economists began to call for more flexible approaches to growth, which, in response to the concept of balanced and planned growth, were summarized under the heading of unbalanced growth. Most prominently, German-American economist Albert O. Hirschman (1915–2012) argued that the resources of so-called developing countries could not be allocated in a planned manner as was possible in industrial economies, and that they could not be reduced to one essential factor like capital.[29]

Hirschman, who published his book *The Strategy of Economic Development* in 1958, emphasized that "development depends not so much on finding optimal combinations for given resources and factors of production as on calling forth and enlisting for development purposes resources and abilities that are hidden, scattered or badly utilized."[30] Similar to Gerschenkron, Hirschman stressed that the path toward economic development needed to be adapted to the specific conditions of each country, and that the ability to make collective development decisions was more important than technical and financial resources and expert planning.[31]

Gerschenkron's and Hirschman's arguments presented a challenge to modernization theory, which was immensely influential at the time in the United States. Its most famous representative was Walt Rostow, who in 1960 published his book *The Stages of Economic Growth*.[32] In the book, he presented a model of development through which every society would pass sooner or later: from traditional society to a transitional phase that prepared the pre-conditions for take-off to the take-off stage to the drive to maturity to the age of high mass-consumption. The last stage was a characterization of what Rostow believed the United States to be at the time of his writing— an industrial, capitalist, liberal democracy. The normative assumptions that informed *The Stages of Economic Growth* received much criticism, especially the idea that the American historical experience could serve as a model to the rest of the world. Yet Rostow was quite aware of the fact that his model reduced the complexity of development. In the introduction to his book, he wrote:

> I cannot emphasize too strongly at the outset, that the stages-of-growth are an arbitrary and limited way of looking at the sequence of modern history: and they are, in no absolute sense, a correct way. They are designed, in fact, to dramatize not merely the uniformities in the sequence of modernization but also—and equally—the uniqueness of each nation's experience.[33]

Hence, it would be wrong to assume that Rostow was not aware of social or cultural particularities or did not care for them. His explicit goal was not to document the world's complexity but to deduce patterns and structures from that complexity, and he saw industrialization as the crucial turning point in a society's history.

As Chapter 7 discusses in detail, the reductionist character of modernization theory with its trust in the transformative power of industrialization came under attack in the late 1960s and 1970s, and the promise of progress associated with it became widely considered as an illusion. Many development practitioners looked for approaches that paid more attention to cultural and geographical particularities, and some even questioned the need for industrialization per se, arguing that its ecological and economic costs were too high and that sustainable rural or small-scale development should be favored instead. Yet in practice the industrialization paradigm was never replaced; what changed over time were the policies on how to achieve industrialization and what to expect from it.

Conclusion

This brief overview of debates about the economic conditions favoring growth and about different strategies toward industrialization shows that the thinking about economic development which informs contemporary development theories and practices had many different origins and elements. It was not a monolithic bloc but rather an assemblage of very different, at times conflicting ideas about economic problems. The economists who later came to be seen as the fathers of development economics started out by studying problems that surrounded them, not knowing that development would become as prominent a field as we know it today. Their work was open-ended, and the solutions they formulated were influenced by contemporary academic debates, political discussions, and individual interests and perceptions. In other words, the ideas and theories about economic development were the product of very particular historical constellations and individual careers. When looking at the historical precedents of postwar development policies and practices in the following chapter, we find many examples of the ways in which contemporary events and changes influenced perceptions of economic, but also of social and political problems that seemed to demand interventions of the kind categorized as development today.

CHAPTER THREE

Forerunners of Development

Why did individuals in the nineteenth century begin to care about the fact that other societies than their own were poor and that people they did not know personally were suffering from poverty? Why did they start to advocate relief work and organize improvement schemes? To answer these questions, we need to look at those individuals and groups who called for and organized relief, humanitarian, and development projects; at the socioeconomic, political, and cultural processes taking place in their own societies and countries; and at the connections between them and other parts of the world in the form of exploration, travel, trade, colonialism, and imperialism.

Poverty, humanitarianism, and the civilizing mission

From an anthropological point of view, acts of charity, sharing, and helping are essential to produce a sense of communal belonging. Religious principles emphasize moral obligations toward others, and churches have served as centers of charity for centuries. In the eighteenth century, Enlightenment thinkers popularized the idea of public responsibility for those in need. Revolutionaries in France in the 1790s called it a duty of society to help its less fortunate members.[1] Early socialist thinkers identified poverty as a product of inequality originating from changes tied to the process of industrialization, resulting in what was perceived as the industrial proletariat, as Friedrich Engels (1820–1895) described it in his writings about Manchester in the mid-1840s.[2] Rulers and governments understood very clearly that if the number of those living in poverty reached a critical level this could threaten social stability and thus also the political order at large. Hence, they installed mechanisms to keep poverty at bay.

For example, in England and Wales, the first series of Poor Laws, which had their roots in the medieval period, was introduced at the end of the sixteenth century under Elizabeth I (1533–1603).[3] Parishes were given the task to provide basic relief to those who were unable to work. Poorhouses were set up to provide temporary shelter. The Poor Laws were revised in the mid-1830s following a series of popular upheavals. At the time, Britain was following a policy of strict economic liberalism, according to which public interventions in the economy were counterproductive. In contemporary thinking, poverty was a necessary and desirable element of social life because it served as an incentive for individuals to become more virtuous and to work harder. The state was not supposed to eliminate individual responsibility but rather to promote the value of labor, which was considered crucial to the nation's strength.[4] Hence, workhouses were set up in which the poor had to do manual labor to gain their stay. Living conditions in the workhouses allowed for mere survival, and daily life was strictly regimented; "the most important official tactic was to scare the destitute into not entering them."[5] Theoretically, the workhouses were expected to serve as places where individuals could be reintegrated into society by embracing Christian values and a what was considered a proper work ethic. Both aspects were closely connected to bourgeois gender roles, with men serving as breadwinners and women taking care of domestic and reproductive chores.[6] In everyday practice, the individual workhouses functioned in very different ways from the ideal, and full control over the inmates was probably rare. Still, the concept of the workhouse shows that contemporaries took poverty very seriously, and that they went to great lengths to try to regulate its most extreme forms and effects.

In the late nineteenth century, the idea of the workhouse as a tool to keep the poor and allegedly asocial members of society under control and to teach them how to behave according to social and economic norms made its way to the European colonies. Travel accounts, novels, and letters from missionaries, entrepreneurs, and colonial officials contributed to a growing sense among middle- and upper-class readers that the inhabitants of many African and Asian countries were living under conditions similar to those of the poor in Europe. Furthermore, they felt that, like the European paupers, the Africans and Asians they heard about lacked the ability to help themselves. They saw a need to intervene for religious reasons or because they felt that they, as members of a supposedly superior society or race, had a civilizing mission that involved changing the lives of others.[7]

For example, German social reformer Friedrich von Bodelschwingh (1831–1910) in the late nineteenth century argued that Africans were living in poverty because they lacked the kind of work ethic Europeans allegedly possessed.[8] Consequently, they needed to be taught how to work properly. This was an educational task Europeans were destined to take on because they were civilizationally advanced, he believed. In thinking about Africans, he drew on his experience with the poor in Germany, for whom he had established so-called work colonies, similar to the workhouses in Britain. The colonies offered room and board to homeless and unemployed people for a period of several months. Life in the work colonies was highly structured and controlled; there was no tolerance of idleness, and religious indoctrination was a constant. All of these measures aimed at re-socializing the poor through what Bodelschwingh and others believed was the healing power of work.[9]

The settlements in Germany served as models for the missions that were set up in Germany's African colonies in the 1880s and 1890s. Teachers, missionaries, and social workers who trained in German work colonies applied their experiences to the African context. The buildings, too, were modeled on those in Germany. Yet Christian social reformers were not race-blind: Bodelschwingh differentiated between German inhabitants of work colonies, who were theoretically allowed to leave, and their African counterparts, who were not given this choice. The sense of superiority that informed the different approaches was not necessarily defined by biological racism—the belief that race was a natural, essential category that defined individuals and their behavior. However, racist thought and ideology undoubtedly strengthened the notion of the civilizing mission and encouraged a degree of violence that seemed unacceptable toward members of one's own race.[10]

In the eyes of many Europeans, colonialism was not an end in itself but a means of improving the situation of Africans. Others used the concept of the civilizing mission to promote and intensify imperialism. For example, the Portuguese state in the early twentieth century justified the occupation and colonization of African territories with its alleged duty to help civilize seemingly primitive, racially inferior societies.[11] Europeans would guide and educate colonial societies—much like parents bringing up their children, who needed help until they could master life on their own. Despite its paternalistic bias, the belief in the ability of individuals and social groups to develop was informed by evolutionary and, at least theoretically, emancipatory thinking, which was close to the Enlightenment's emphasis on individual accountability and the importance of reason and education.[12] "However, once the colonized peoples were equal and in consequence could justly demand emancipation …, the basis of colonial rule would vanish, … destroying the foundation of self-legitimation."[13] Hence, the so-called civilizing mission was carried out within narrowly defined limits, with a focus on control and regulation that often translated into violence.

One of the most notorious examples of this logic was the effort of King Leopold II (1835–1909) of Belgium in 1884 to make Congo his personal property under the pretense of promoting abolitionism. The existence of slavery in African societies and the participation of African chiefs in the international slave trade had long concerned many European observers.[14] Leopold's promise of civilizing Congo by abolishing slavery served as a cover for the brutal exploitation regime he installed to secure a steady flow of ivory and rubber to Belgium. Rape, mutilations, labor camps, and many other forms of violence ruled the colony until international public protest grew too strong. In 1908, King Leopold's property was turned into a colony of Belgium.[15]

Meanwhile, US President William McKinley (1843–1901) in 1899 spoke of the duty to uplift the inhabitants of the Philippines, which the United States had conquered in 1898.[16] In the following years, many Americans became active in what they believed to be or presented as a national duty: bringing civilization to those regions which the United States considered its natural sphere of influence. The American military interventions in Cuba, Haiti, Nicaragua, and the Dominican Republic were driven by strategic and economic interests and complemented by efforts to remake the societies in question. It was in this context, too, that non-governmental organizations like the Young Men's Christian Association (YMCA) became a strong presence in East Asia, where they believed they had identified similar problems as in Latin America: a lack of individual ambition, team spirit, physical strength, and work ethic. The YMCA used team sports to try to anchor these concepts in Asian societies.[17] The fact that many of the objects of these interventions were not interested in or actively opposed to them was an essential part of the civilizing mission, whose proponents expected gratitude from the groups they addressed, yet were disappointed time and again.[18] As the examples show, the different civilizing missions, though claiming a universal quality, were strongly influenced by the specific beliefs and goals of their representatives. The same was true of early humanitarian activities, which overlapped in part with development thinking and practices.[19]

Over the course of the nineteenth century, individuals and governments began to pay more attention to the civilian victims of international and civil wars, and international humanitarian interventions steadily grew in number.[20] The number of newspapers, magazines, and news agencies increased rapidly, as did the number of individuals able to read and write. Simultaneously, the speed with which information could be exchanged via telegraph across continents and oceans multiplied, and public awareness of wars, natural catastrophes, and famines grew exponentially.[21] It was against this background that humanitarian activities became part of international political life. Think, for example, of Florence Nightingale's (1820–1910) efforts to offer medical help to soldiers wounded in the Crimean War (1853–1856), or J. Henry Dunant's (1828–1910) lobbying for the establishment of the Red Cross in the aftermath of the battle of Solferino (1859).[22] Famines, which occurred frequently in many regions of the world, became another rallying point of early humanitarian action.[23]

In many instances relief work was informed by religious motives.[24] The Quakers, who opposed the use of force and promoted peaceful means of intervention, became particularly active in humanitarian projects in the nineteenth and early twentieth centuries. The American Friends Service Committee was at the forefront of these efforts.[25] While Christian missionaries and church groups believed they had a religious duty to help and prosyletize, humanitarianism was far from being a Christian monopoly.[26] For example, in the late 1840s and early 1850s, individuals in the Ottoman Empire organized help for the victims of the Irish famine.[27] Red Crescent societies were established in many Muslim countries in the late nineteenth and early twentieth centuries, and the Chinese Red Cross was founded in 1904.[28] In 1914, the American Jewish Joint Distribution Committee was established to help Jews in Europe and the Middle East who were suffering from the effects of war.[29]

In the aftermath of the First World War, humanitarian organizations provided food, clothing, and medicine to civilians in Europe, many of whom were suffering from hunger and displacement, especially in those regions where civil wars continued after 1918. To help the millions of individuals who had lost their homes due to fighting and postwar border changes, and to support members of ethnic minorities who experienced repression, the League of Nations became active, as did the Red Cross.[30] Norway's Fridtjof Nansen (1861–1930) became the most famous spokesperson for refugee concerns. As the League's Commissioner for Russian Refugees, he lobbied European governments to accept refugees and to provide them with material support. He also issued Nansen passports to those who were stateless and thus could not legally leave or enter a country.[31] Meanwhile, American citizens donated thirty million dollars to the European Relief Council in 1920 and 1921.[32] Together, these individuals, groups, and organizations contributed to the evolution of a transnational network dedicated to helping those in need.[33]

Even the most benevolent humanitarian projects were accompanied by institutional, political, or economic interests. For example, the American Relief Administration (ARA) under the leadership of Herbert Hoover (1874–1964) provided food aid to Russians in the context of the civil war that had broken out after the Russian Revolution in 1917. Hoover and the Soviet government in 1921 negotiated an agreement that gave the ARA and its partner organizations access to and command of transport and distribution of supplies to the civilian population. While the main reason for providing food aid was to prevent the threat of mass starvation, the work of the ARA was also informed by the attempt to contain the spread of socialism and to open up markets for American agricultural surplus.[34]

As this overview of the history of humanitarianism demonstrates, public concern with problems of poverty and hunger, living conditions and economic security multiplied in the late nineteenth and early twentieth centuries, and new approaches to solving these problems were tried out by a variety of actors. The prominence and energy of non-governmental actors is striking in this regard. Private organizations could only do so much, however. Their resources were limited, and they could not prevent humanitarian crises, only react to them. The urgency of what was known as the social question and the call for more lasting welfare provisions came to influence the political discussions in many countries in the years after the First World War.

The social question was a conglomerate of problems related to the emergence of industrial society in the nineteenth and early twentieth centuries. The acceleration of industrialization, urbanization, and wage labor in factories was accompanied by growing public concern about the effects of the new social and spatial constellations and the ways in which they challenged the existing order. In the eyes of bourgeois elites, the crowded living conditions, lack of hygiene and education, and a decay of moral standards in the industrial centers made the so-called proletariat susceptible to radical political indoctrination. In the late nineteenth and early twentieth centuries, a growing number of governments in Europe began to react to the perceived social crisis by installing rudimentary welfare provisions.[35]

The First World War heightened public expectations toward the state and its services, as entire societies were mobilized and the economy was fully geared toward armament. Governmental and military bodies took on the organization of nearly every aspect of public life, and the number of expert committees to manage the prolonged state of emergency the war presented increased rapidly.[36] Against this background, governments promised their citizens—soldiers as well as the civilian population—a wide range of social and economic improvements for the future. When the war ended, governments were under immense pressure to keep their promises and provide welfare services to veterans and to families who had lost a family member in the war.[37] These expectations increased as several of the former authoritarian systems were replaced by democratic ones. Electoral logics gained tremendous influence over the provision of services for citizens and on approaches to solving problems which, by and large, had been considered private responsibilities in earlier years, like housing, health care, education, and welfare.[38]

A central event that sharpened governments' awareness of the political quality of the social question was the Russian Revolution of 1917. The revolutionary events highlighted the fact that the countryside was an extremely political space. It was where the majority of the population lived, where the agricultural economy had its center, and where access to land, labor, and resources were likely to fuel socioeconomic and political conflict.[39] Peasants could tip the balance and either accelerate or prevent a revolution against the existing order. This insight into the political power rooted in the countryside contributed to the establishment of numerous peasant parties in Central and South Eastern Europe in the interwar years.[40] On the other end of the political spectrum, the Russian Revolution inspired many leftist politicians and intellectuals. They realized that if they wanted to end the existing system they would have to win the support of the rural population first. Most famously, Mao Zedong in 1920s China propagated a communist revolution led by peasants. Instead of waiting for an industrial proletariat to rebel against its exploitation, the peasants would have to be awakened and become the revolutionary force to overthrow feudal lords or colonial rulers.[41] Somewhat less radically inclined, but no less determined, Indian nationalists in the 1920s and 1930s, most famously Mohandas Gandhi (1869–1948), advocated strengthening the village community as the nucleus of a future independent India. In doing so, they challenged the idea that India was unable to govern itself and needed colonial rule.[42]

The political developments described above, together with the economic crises of the post-1918 years, greatly increased the political and academic interest in rural socioeconomic conditions, agricultural production, and land issues in the early decades of the twentieth century. It is here that one sees the origins of what would later be called rural development.

Perspectives on agriculture and rural life

The effects of the First World War on agriculture were severe in many parts of the world.[43] During the war, agricultural production had been marginalized in many European countries in favor of their weapons industries, leading to severe food shortages and hunger. The war and the dissolution of the Russian, the Ottoman, and the Austro-Hungarian empires in its aftermath resulted in a highly unstable economic and political situation, which in turn led to hunger and starvation. Malnutrition and disease were rife.[44] Against this background, the relatively low productivity of agriculture in many of the affected countries came to be seen as a problem demanding state intervention.

Closely linked to the scarcity of food was the perception that in many of the poor regions of the world population density was high and the land available for farming was becoming scarce.[45] The Malthusian interpretation of the interdependence between population growth and food resources resulted in calls for land reform to create more efficient plots as well as for the improvement of agricultural techniques to increase yields. Apart from concerns about high population growth, agriculture's low productivity in many countries also meant that food was expensive, which in turn made it more difficult to feed the growing urban labor force staffing the factories. Hence, rural and agricultural problems had effects far beyond the particular regions of the countries in question—they influenced a country's overall economic, financial, and, at least indirectly, political situation. Against this background, politicians and experts began to call for interventions in the economic, health, educational, and, in part, cultural structures in the rural regions they identified as problematic.[46]

The most important tasks seemed to be an increase in agricultural production and the improvement of the conditions of rural life. Whereas in later decades most policy-makers would highlight the need to industrialize and move away from agriculture, in the early twentieth century many believed that agriculture had the potential to become the motor of overall economic modernization. For example, Russian agrarian scientists and economists challenged the idea that rural life was outdated and less valuable than urban and industrial life. Representing the so-called doctrine of agrarianism, they advocated an approach that granted agriculture a central role in the process of economic development.[47] Agrarianism was part of a larger trend in thinking about the importance of agriculture and rural life in a country's economy and culture at a time when urbanization and industrialization were gaining speed and changing social relations. Against this background, many intellectuals and politicians began to emphasize the social and cultural values of rural life and of smallholder agriculture. They argued that the social order of the nation at large depended on the conservation of existing structures in the countryside.[48] The village, as a supposedly organically functioning entity, came to be seen as the crystallization of all the values and ideals associated with a better, less complex, more harmonious past.[49]

Accordingly, many social reformers in the early twentieth century argued that if one wanted to improve the situation in the countryside one had to start in the villages.[50] Under the labels of rural uplift or rural reconstruction, existing villages were supposed to be improved and new ones built. Driven by a strong belief in the power and feasibility of social engineering, new villages were planned and set up in many parts of the world, ranging from Egypt to Greece, from India to Yugoslavia, from China to the United States. Experts like Andrija Štampar (1888–1958), a public health specialist from Croatia, carried rural reformist ideas from one country to the next, often with financial support from the American Rockefeller Foundation and in cooperation with the League of Nations. One of the first village uplift projects was implemented in India by Rabindranath Tagore (1861–1941), the influential Bengali poet and philosopher, who, with American philanthropic support, in the early 1920s established the Institute for Rural Reconstruction in the village of Sriniketan in West Bengal. In doing so, he referred directly to village improvement projects from Yugoslavia that emphasized the value of education, social surveys, and sanitation.[51]

The new or improved villages were supposed to uphold what was considered good about traditional village life while introducing new structures that were the product of modern scientific insight into the functioning of rural society.[52] Rural improvement also served an imperial purpose in the Philippines, which had come under American rule after the Spanish-American War of 1898. In the context of the war, many inhabitants had lost their homes, and many villages suffered from high levels of poverty and disease in the war's aftermath. To show the inhabitants of the Philippines and the American public that the United States was a benevolent power, the administration established schools and conducted public health campaigns in those villages.[53] The examples from Croatia, India, and the Philippines show that rural improvement was an approach that suggested itself to a number of very different political actors and interests, which is one of the reasons for its popularity at the time.

Many of the agricultural economists, agrarian sociologists, health experts, and social workers involved in the various rural improvement efforts came from rural and farming backgrounds.[54] Quite naturally, they projected many of their families' and communities' experiences with rural life onto their view of rural problems.[55] Furthermore, their suggestions on how to solve rural problems were closely connected with assumptions about how peasants functioned—for example, whether it was better to induce change by working with the peasants cooperatively or by forcing them to change their production patterns in a top-down manner.[56] The ways in which ideological positions shaped early rural development approaches become especially apparent when looking at the concept of the family farm, which was closely associated with the village ideal.[57]

According to the advocates of the family farm, the economically most efficient and politically and socially most beneficial form of organization was one in which a family worked its own land, handing it down from one generation to the next. Conceptually, the model emphasized the importance of private property, individual ambition and responsibility, and the patriarchal family as the nucleus of society. The family farm model was strongly conservative in that it rejected the idea that any other social order than the one based on the family unit could be politically and economically feasible, and in that it favored men as breadwinners and decision-makers, while relegating women to the sphere of domesticity and reproduction.[58] Socialists and Marxists criticized the smallholder family farm as a socioeconomic unit that stabilized the capitalist system. Most notably, Karl Kautsky (1854–1938) in 1899 argued that the family farm rested on the (self-)exploitation of the family members, particularly of women, who had to do the largest and hardest share of work. In his view, the smallholder farms were considered useful by the large agricultural estates because of their cheap labor resources and because their feudal-like structures prevented social change in the countryside.[59] Kautsky's interpretation seemed to be proven right when, in the years after the Russian Revolution and the collectivization of agriculture in the Soviet Union, liberal, conservative, and nationalist anti-communists promoted the family farm as a bulwark against socialist or other kinds of revolutionary tendencies.

In the postwar period the problem of low agricultural productivity began to change in the industrialized countries when newly available fertilizers and mechanized farming led to increasingly high outputs. As a result, commodity prices went down, and many smallholders fell into debt because they could not compete with the large-scale producers of foodstuffs. International speculation on commodity production increased over the course of the 1920s, and when the stock market crashed in 1929 it heavily affected agricultural and raw material producers all over the world.[60] Throughout the 1920s and 1930s several international conferences took place to coordinate and stabilize prices for foodstuffs, but these efforts could not withstand the intensity of the Great Depression or override the protectionist policies many countries introduced as a response to the crisis.[61]

Against this background, some politicians and experts called for changes in the ways in which the economies of the European colonies were administered. The colonies' task in the imperial context was to produce foodstuffs and raw materials for the colonial powers, which relied on access to cheap resources for their industrial economies to function. Connected to this material reason for the focus on rural and agricultural structures was a political one: the imperial powers understood very clearly that the colonies were weaker and thus easier to control if their economies remained agricultural.[62] Rurality meant fewer cities, fewer educational opportunities, fewer intellectual meeting points, and less political organization. Ensuring that the colonies fulfilled their role as resource providers while increasing control over rural populations was central to the interest of imperial powers. Accordingly, many of the rural improvement efforts carried out in Europe were also employed in the colonies.

The British in India used rural uplift programs primarily to prevent social unrest in the countryside.[63] In the late nineteenth century, peasants in different parts of British India rioted, protesting against high levels of taxation which produced a spiral of indebtedness and bankruptcy. The British did not consider their taxation policies to be the cause of the problem, but rather saw it in what they perceived as the low level of productivity of the Indian peasants and the existence of private moneylenders, who demanded high levels of interest and appeared to the British as the epitome of backward village society. Hence, they believed that incentives were needed for the Indian peasants to embrace a more entrepreneurial mindset. To look for inspiration, the British colonial administration sent Frederick A. Nicholson (1846–1936), who had been responsible for improving the fisheries in Madras, to Europe in the 1890s.[64] Nicholson returned to India as a strong supporter of the Raiffeisen cooperative he had come across in Germany.

The Raiffeisen cooperative was named after Protestant pastor Friedrich Wilhelm Raiffeisen (1818–1888), who was active in social reformist work to alleviate peasant poverty in particularly poor regions of Germany. In the mid-1860s, he founded a credit cooperative for peasants who otherwise would have depended on the expensive credits of private moneylenders. Membership in the Raiffeisen cooperative was open to everyone, regardless of income. By pooling the small amounts of money each peasant family could contribute, the lack of capital that characterized many rural regions would be overcome, and higher incomes, small investments, and economic growth would follow. In contrast to other cooperatives, Raiffeisen cooperatives did not pay dividends to their members. They were supposed to be a tool of self-help *of* the members *for* the members, not an opportunity for investors to make money off the peasants' poverty. In essence, the cooperatives were supposed to support small peasants in finding a way out of the vicious cycle of poverty and indebtedness, to encourage small-scale investments to increase yields and income, and to support the village community at a time when the economic pressure on smallholders was growing due to the increasing presence of capitalist market structures.[65]

With its emphasis on maintaining existing rural structures and improving agricultural production without challenging the socioeconomic order at large, the Raiffeisen model seemed ideally suited to the Indian situation. It also spoke to the British liberal belief that state intervention should be avoided at all cost and that decentralized mechanisms were much better suited to promote economic growth. From an imperial perspective, the cooperative structures and their ties to local banks and administrative units promised to provide the colonial regime with better control over the countryside. Finally, the cooperative could serve as a body through which the government introduced new agricultural technologies and convinced the peasants that cooperating with governmental extension officers was in their own interest. In that way, the likelihood of riots would be reduced and the presence of the colonial state reinforced along the ideal of indirect rule. Hence, the British in the 1900s passed laws that stipulated the establishment of agricultural credit cooperatives in India modeled on the Raiffeisen example. By 1930 British India had more than 100,000 cooperatives, several banks geared toward providing credit to those cooperatives and their members, and about four million cooperative members.[66] Cooperatives were very popular across the board: Dutch colonial administrators in Java and Sumatra set up cooperatives in the late nineteenth century, American missionaries in China in the early 1920s adapted the Raiffeisen model, and British Labour politicians in the 1930s and 1940s argued in favor of setting up rural cooperatives in the British African colonies.[67]

The colonial interest in agricultural cooperatives reflects the contemporary understanding that rural riots were not limited to spontaneous outbursts against poverty and indebtedness, and that structural interventions were necessary to improve the situation of the population.[68] High hopes were associated with cooperatives as allegedly non-political instruments of governance. They were supposed to increase efficiency and productivity, help the rural population to become familiar with modern principles of administration in a small-scale setting, transform village structures without risking dramatic change, allow the colonial administration to keep an eye on the activities of peasants and farmers, and contribute to stabilizing the countryside and preventing the break-up of traditional social structures, whose existence was in the interest of the colonial powers.[69] Seeing that cooperatives were expected to do so many things at once, it is not surprising that the results were considered disappointing in comparison. Better-off farmers secured leading positions in the newly established cooperatives, thereby benefiting from direct access to the resources and keeping old hierarchies in place. Small farmers and landless laborers had a much harder time gaining access to resources, and their interests were not as well represented. Clientelistic networks emerging around cooperatives were a common feature in many settings.[70] Furthermore, the cooperatives offered the colonial population an arena for voicing discontent with colonial policies or socioeconomic conditions, thereby creating space for dissent.[71]

The colonial strategy of promoting agricultural cooperatives shows that in the interwar period there was a growing sense that increasing productivity alone was not enough. If the peasants were supposed to embrace new, modern technologies and practices, they had to have better living conditions as well as a reason to assume that the changes were in their own interest. For that reason, basic welfare measures were added to rural improvement programs. It is here that we can detect the origins of colonial development thinking and practice—the effort of the colonial state to invest some money into the colonial economies in order to increase their value and better realize their economic potential.

Colonial development

As early as 1895, Joseph Chamberlain (1836–1914) had argued that the state should spend more money on the colonies so that "those estates which belong to the British Crown may be developed for the benefit of their population and for the benefit of the greater population which is outside."[72] This perspective inspired a policy that became known as constructive imperialism, according to which the imperial power had the duty to develop their lands abroad.[73] However, in practice these development efforts were very limited. The guiding idea of colonial economic policy until after the First World War was that of self-sufficiency: the colonies were supposed to produce what the colonial powers expected from them in terms of agricultural and mineral resources as well as labor services.[74] Bridges, roads, and railroads were built to allow for the transport of goods within the colonies and for trade with other regions. Some hospitals and schools were set up to maintain the educational and health levels necessary for the colonial administration and economy to function properly. Otherwise, the territories were not supposed to receive any funding or support from the colonial powers. In practice, this meant that many kinds of taxes were levied on the colonial subjects, and production was fully geared toward the needs of the colonial powers.[75]

The First World War and its aftermath provoked lasting changes in colonial policies. In fighting the war, the European powers had relied on their overseas possessions to support the war effort. These contributions ranged from loans to raw materials to human beings fighting the war. For example, 1.2 million individuals from India were involved in Great Britain's war effort in France, Egypt, and Mesopotamia.[76] The logical consequence of this massive commitment was that representatives of the colonial societies demanded changes in colonial policy. Political leaders of the emerging anti-colonial movements called for greater political autonomy and for more financial and economic support from the colonial powers. They argued that the living conditions of those who had helped to fight and win the war needed to improve, just as the inhabitants of the European countries expected their governments to live up to the promises they had made during the war.[77] From the point of view of the European powers, the moral aspect of these requests was less important than their political implication—the threat that if the demands of the anti-colonial leaders were not met there would be popular unrest. Against the background of the Russian Revolution, but also with regard to the stability of the imperial systems, such disorder had to be avoided, and offering some compromises seemed acceptable.

In addition to the immediate war-related demands, representatives of the colonies called for the right to self-determination—a concept Woodrow Wilson (1856–1924), the American president, had advanced in his Fourteen Points. As the former European empires dissolved and new nation states came into existence in Central and Eastern Europe, intellectuals and political leaders in the colonies asked why the colonies were denied the right to self-determination.[78] Many groups tried to use the newly founded League of Nations to make their claims heard. They lobbied government representatives and sent petitions to the League's Permanent Mandates Commission.[79] The commission had been created to oversee the situation in those colonies in Africa and in the Pacific which had belonged to Germany as well as those which had made up the Arab provinces of the former Ottoman Empire. According to Article 22 of the League of Nations Covenant, those regions were being given the status of mandates. Arguing that they were not mature enough to exist on their own, each of them was to be administered by the so-called advanced nations on behalf of the League. There were three categories of mandates: A, B, and C. Those belonging to the A category—those which emerged out of the Ottoman Empire in the Middle East—were considered most advanced. The B mandates were the colonies in Central and West Africa, while the C mandates in Southwest Africa and the Pacific islands were argued to be the least advanced. Effectively, those European powers which had occupied the regions when the war ended became the respective mandating power. Seeing that the governments which took on responsibility for a mandate (for example, Great Britain for Tanganyika, or France for Syria) were colonial powers themselves, it is not surprising that their willingness to allow the mandates to become independent was very limited. Effectively, the mandate system served to maintain European imperialism.[80]

For all its conservative elements, the system did open up new opportunities for anti-colonial actors. Perhaps most importantly, the League constituted an international arena that gave public visibility even to those who were not members of the League or who were reduced to petition-writing. Hence, the colonial governments were subject to more public attention and had to make an effort to legitimize their actions internationally. A degree of accountability that had not existed in this form before became a reality in the interwar period.[81] Furthermore, the Mandates Commission succeeded in establishing "that mandatory powers were not sovereign in the mandated territories," which meant that they could not treat them as colonial possessions.[82] As imperialism lost its seemingly self-explanatory character, colonial policy began to change, too.

Several colonial administrators in the early 1920s began to argue that development efforts had to be carried out in the colonies. In Great Britain, Lord Frederick Lugard (1858–1945), who represented his country in the Mandates Commission, propagated the concept of the dual mandate—a twist on the older idea of the civilizing mission.[83] According to Lugard, the postwar situation demanded that the colonial powers should not only guide the colonial societies toward greater political maturity but also improve their economic situation.[84] Specifically, he called for infrastructure investments, especially into schools and hospitals, and for the improvement of living conditions in the colonies. He advocated doing so through an "appropriate native policy" that responded to the particularities of tropical Africa instead of imposing European models onto the indigenous populations.[85] Together, Lugard and others hoped, these efforts would signal that the imperial power was taking its responsibility for its colony seriously. Simultaneously, development activities would help to soften public criticism in the colonies and among anti-colonial groups in Europe. Finally, and importantly, investments could have the effect of stimulating the colonial economy and increasing its productivity. Hence, the colonial power would be able to expect higher returns from its possession than if it focused exclusively on extracting resources. This was the argument the French colonial minister and former governor-general of French Indochina Albert Sarraut (1872–1962) put forward in 1923 in his program "La mise en valeur des colonies française," which called for the development of the colonial economy through investments in the colonial infrastructure in order to increase the income of France.[86]

One of the most ambitious projects that reflected Sarraut's thinking was the Office du Niger in French Soudan, today's Mali.[87] The Office du Niger had its roots in postwar efforts to promote the irrigation of the Niger. The French colonial ministry sent a civil engineer, Emile Bélime (1883–1969), to Soudan to investigate economic opportunities for France. Bélime returned as an enthusiastic advocate for the combination of large-scale irrigation and cotton production, which the British were practicing in Egypt and India. According to Bélime, France could support the French textile industry by doing the same in the Niger delta.[88] Toward that goal, African farmers would have to modernize their agricultural practices. Arguing that Africans, due to their allegedly lower civilizational status, would not be able to do so on their own, the colonial state argued that force was necessary.[89] Hence, development in the interest of *mise en valeur* would have to be organized in a top-down, hierarchical fashion.

Following intense lobbying, and under the influence of the Great Depression, the Paris government made the Niger project part of the French colonial loans program in 1931. One year later, the Office du Niger was founded as a public agency headed by Bélime. The agency was granted broad powers and possessed a direct link to the governor-general of French West Africa in Dakar; due to its relative autonomy, it quickly developed into "a virtual state within a state."[90] The land under control of the Office du Niger encompassed 8,500 square kilometers. The immense challenges of bringing the land under control become clear when compared with the original goal: by the end of the Second World War, only 50 square kilometers had been prepared for production. The key problem was the lack of labor. The land placed under the authority of the Office had to be cleared before it could be turned into cotton fields. The clearance, the building of a dam for irrigation purposes, and the preparation of the fields required immense labor resources. For that reason, the colonial authorities officially invited but practically forced peasants from other parts of the region to move to the Office territory and work for the scheme. Living and working conditions were harsh. Exploitation and physical punishment took place on an everyday basis, and the inhabitants of the Office were denied rights to the land they were working, thereby making them fully dependent on the meager salaries and the selling of produce, the price of which was controlled by the Office.[91] Under these conditions, it was not realistic to expect work to move forward quickly. At least a third of the settlers fled the scheme until the mid-1940s. Hence, there were visible signs that the Office du Niger was not producing the returns expected from it; in fact, the costs for the project were much higher than anticipated. Still, the Vichy government decided to invest 600 million additional francs into the scheme's extension, hoping that this would increase production and make France less dependent on imports.[92]

Toward the end of the war, protests against the dismal working conditions in the Office du Niger increased, and in 1946 forced labor was officially abolished. It became clear that if France wanted to gain any economic benefits from the Office it would have to change its repressive policies and practices.[93] Ending the project was simply not an option for the French because they had already invested so much money (around 50 million dollars in 1960s dollars alone until 1939). Consequently, French planners opted for more of the same—technology, investments, labor resources. Interestingly, in the late 1940s and early 1950s some of the most hierarchical aspects of the Office were revised in favor of more participatory approaches. For example, the peasants were asked about their experiences with crop rotation and the growing of vegetables and crops like rice and millet, and the forced cotton production was reduced. Thus, the most extreme exploitation made room for an approach that took the livelihoods of the peasants into consideration for utilitarian reasons.[94] Although most of the French colonial managers were convinced that European-style plow farming was superior to African-style hoe farming, they depended not only on the cooperation of the local farmers but also on their help in finding solutions to particular problems with crop rotation and soil conditions.[95]

As the case of the Office du Niger shows, implementing the concept of *mise en valeur* was much more difficult than expected by colonial authorities. Something similar was true of almost all schemes in which peasants were forced to grow a particular crop, whether it was under Soviet control in Central Asia or under German rule in East Africa.[96] Yet in the eyes of contemporaries in the imperial metropoles, the problems appeared distant and secondary at best. What mattered to them was the benefit the imperial power could expect from its colonies. For example, in Great Britain several politicians and administrators argued that colonial development would create jobs for British citizens, which was an urgent concern in the interwar period.[97] Investing money and resources into colonial development came to be seen as a way of promoting domestic interests. In terms of economic thinking, this perspective was supported by what became known as Keynesianism—the idea made prominent by British economist John Maynard Keynes (1883–1946) that the market does not always fully regulate itself, and that the government should step in in times of crisis by using public money to stimulate the economy.[98]

At least indirectly the Colonial Development Act passed by the British parliament in June 1929 was informed by this approach. According to the act, one million pounds could be spent annually to provide grants to the British colonies in order to develop their agricultural and economic structures, "with the express purpose of promoting trade with or industry with the United Kingdom."[99] However, when the Great Depression set in a few months later, British politicians shifted their attention from the colonies toward challenges at home. Until 1940, when a revised act, the Colonial Development and Welfare Act, was passed, less than seven million pounds were spent under the Colonial Development Act. Still, the 1929 act signaled that a majority of politicians considered the old policy of *laissez-faire* no longer sustainable at a time when economic and financial crises challenged the increasingly fragile imperial system.[100] Similarly, in France between 1936 and 1938, the Popular Front government, a coalition of left-wing parties, discussed possibilities for improving the labor situation of African workers in the colonies and called for more funds to be directed toward colonial development. Mirroring a concern with workers' rights in France, the wages for workers in the colonies were raised slightly and working laws were revised. However, the coalition fell apart in 1938 and was eventually replaced by the Vichy government, which took a much harsher stand on labor issues in the colonies.[101]

Whether one was against granting colonial workers more protection or whether one was an active advocate for workers' rights, in the 1930s it was impossible to ignore the labor question in the colonies, as conflicts in the colonies in the form of strikes and unrest multiplied. In part, the increasing visibility of labor issues was an effect of the work of the League of Nations and the International Labor Organization, which conducted studies on the living and working conditions of the colonial populations. The experts working for the League and for ILO concerned themselves with topics like health, nutrition, literacy rates, child labor, housing and education, and many other socioeconomic issues.[102] Their publications were read by colonial officials and sometimes taken up by domestic critics of colonialism, who called on their governments to improve the situation abroad.[103] In this way, welfare and social issues gained a place on the colonial development agenda, thereby challenging the near-exclusive focus on economic affairs. As Malcolm MacDonald (1901–1981), a British colonial official, put it in a statement in the House of Commons in 1935: "Economic development is not an end in itself. It is only a means to an end. ... We want them [the inhabitants of the colonies] to become steadily more prosperous so that more revenue can go to the Governments in those countries, so that money may be spent on improved medical, educational, social and political services."[104] While initially a minority view, over the course of the 1930s and early 1940s the new understanding of development as a socioeconomic process came to characterize the late colonial development policies of several—although not all—imperial powers.[105]

Another factor which added to the growing concern with colonial development was ecological in nature. Many world regions experienced recurring episodes of soil erosion and soil degradation in the 1920s and 1930s. At least some of the ecological problems in the African colonies at the time were the result of colonial interventions geared toward the intensification and commodification of agriculture and rural production. As the colonial powers tried to increase the economic yields of their territories by introducing monocultures like cotton, tobacco, and maize and by promoting livestock breeding, the environmental consequences were immediate.[106] In trying to explain the reasons for these problems, colonial officials often emphasized the alleged inferiority of agricultural practices like slash-and-burn farming, arguing that the African farmers lacked a deeper understanding of the ecological effects of their work. Modern science seemed essential to overcome the crisis and to prevent further ecological damage in the future. Colonial administrations set up numerous research institutes and established experimental farms in the colonies to develop better methods of farming, breeding, and bush control.[107]

Many of the findings made their way into large-scale programs of afforestation, terrace building, and river damming.[108] The conservationist efforts of the interwar period became entangled with demographic changes, or perceptions thereof. In the early twentieth century, some colonial officials were concerned that the fertility rate of African women was decreasing as a result of labor migration, as many African men were living apart from their families for months at a time. European demographers and economists warned that this trend might lead to de-population.[109] Decreasing fertility rates were a source of concern to colonial administrators, as were high mortality rates, epidemics, and malnutrition, because they affected the economic capacity of the colony and could have potentially disruptive social and political effects. For that reason, many experts called for better access to health care and basic education so that the living conditions of the African populations would be improved and birth rates stabilized.[110]

These discussions about demographic and medical problems reflected a larger concern on the part of the colonial administrations with the changes taking place in African societies. In the European colonial imagination, African societies were based on the concept of the tribe. Many administrators shared the conviction that the tribal structure needed to be preserved because it provided the only source of stability in otherwise unorganized societies.[111] As labor migration accelerated the process of urbanization in the African colonies and wage labor replaced other forms of income, European anthropologists warned that this might lead to de-tribalization, resulting in a dangerous lack of social stability.[112] To be better able to respond to those challenges, the colonial administrations commissioned a large number of ethnographic and anthropological studies. The most ambitious project in this regard was the African Research Survey, which British scholars conducted in the 1930s and early 1940s with financial support from the Rockefeller Foundation. Initially part of the effort to improve control over the colonies and to make better use of their resources, the African Survey contributed to a paradigm shift in European understandings of African societies. Instead of continuing the older line of thought about African societies as homogenous and primitive, the scholars involved stressed the heterogeneity of social life and culture in the African colonies. The survey reflected and contributed to a turn away from a racial explanation of difference to a cultural one, based on the understanding that African societies, too, were able to cope with change and adapt to it, and that Africans could embrace ideas like progress and improvement.[113]

It was in this intellectual climate that late colonial policies aimed at "a more efficient reorganization of peasant agriculture in the hope of creating stable, prosperous, healthy, self-subsisting rural communities in the face of increasing strain due to land degradation, rapid population growth, and rural-urban migration."[114] Such complex problems seemed to require extensive responses. Some colonial experts wanted to intensify the use of land so as to overcome the problem of land scarcity, while others called for reserves to be created in the colonies in order to protect wildlife and forests. For the individuals in the colonies confronted with these programs, the improvement they were promised was difficult to see. Conservationist measures implied unpaid and often forced labor like terrace-building or tie-ridging, which meant that the peasants could not tend to their own fields or animals. Also, they were forbidden to practice their established agricultural methods because the colonial administrators considered them harmful or inefficient. In many cases, planted fields were ploughed by force or seedlings ripped out or burned.[115] In addition, the affected communities were supposed to pay for the improvement programs themselves, which increased the already high levels of taxation.[116] For these reasons, it does not seem surprising that many of these colonial development projects produced political problems rather than serving the economic and ecological interests of the imperial powers.[117]

Conflicts over access to land and land tenure played a particularly important role in this context, especially when the perception of rapid

African population growth began to replace the older idea of de-population. Censuses conducted in the African colonies in the 1930s and 1940s seemed to suggest that population density was increasing significantly and that access to land was becoming scarce, resulting in tensions among white settlers and the African population.[118] For example, in Kenya members of the ethnic group of the Kikuyu had moved to parts of the highlands that were owned by white settlers. The Kikuyu performed casual labor for the settlers and were allowed to let their animals graze on the land in return. However, the colonial administration considered this grazing a danger to the ecological balance of the region and in the 1940s introduced conservationist measures. In effect this meant that many Kikuyu "were forced into demeaning contracts as wage-labourers, or expelled from their land, whence they drifted either to the crowded Kikuyu reserves, to Nairobi, or to a marginal existence between the two."[119] The conflict over land and the eviction of the Kikuyu from the land contributed at least indirectly to what emerged as the Mau Mau uprising in the early 1950s. The background was a "profound crisis in Kikuyu society, as various groups within that society … found that they were excluded from the carefully bounded religious and moral order which determined land ownership, marriage and hence personal self-determination."[120] To prevent their situation from deteriorating further, some Kikuyu leaders established the Land and Freedom Army and sought support from the population. The British saw their control under attack and reacted with military violence. They declared a state of emergency and between 1952 and 1957 fought a war against the Mau Mau movement, whose members withdrew into the forest.[121]

Problems related to land and the so-called improvement schemes reacting to these problems were at the heart of late colonial development efforts. Because they were so central to the livelihoods of the inhabitants, they quickly translated into conflicts which often involved the use of force. This was especially true of cases of resettlement. The perceived scarcity and fragmentation of land heightened existing tensions between the demands of the European settlers and the colonial population, who were criticized for not using the land efficiently enough, thereby halting the colony's development. Although rhetorically the colonial powers in the post-1945 years emphasized their respect for indigenous interests and stated that there would be no discrimination on racial grounds, in practice the African inhabitants of the contested regions were not granted equal rights in land conflicts.[122] For example, the British in Tanganyika in 1951 drew up plans to give land in the northern part of the colony to European settlers, who would supposedly use it more efficiently and wisely than the Meru people, who had been living there for a long time.[123] In November 1951, the British, in the context of what was tellingly called Operation Exodus, burned nearly 500 houses and stores of the Meru, destroyed food and property, and imprisoned those who protested. About 330 families lost their homes. While the British were apparently satisfied with the effective manner in which the operation had been conducted, they had not expected that their decision to ignore the concerns of the Meru and to use force would backfire politically as it did. Effectively, the Meru case accelerated the establishment of the Tanganyika African National Union (TANU), the nationalist movement which, under the leadership of Julius Nyerere (1922–1999), would promote and finally achieve Tanganyika's independence.[124]

In some cases, the colonial powers set up new villages for the population that was to be resettled. This was the case, for example, in Portuguese Angola in the interwar period, where demographers and medical experts had lobbied for measures to improve the living conditions of the local population in order to maintain a high fertility rate. New villages were supposed to give the population access to health care and basic education and to introduce the peasants to new agricultural methods.[125] The new villages would serve to improve the lives of rural inhabitants without giving up control over them, which seemed important as anti-colonial activities increased throughout the 1930s and 1940s.[126] As progressive as the new villages sounded in theory, in practice they were part of a colonial strategy to counter socioeconomic changes and to guard the rural population.

The coercive nature of villagization efforts became most visible in those cases in which villages were used as part of military campaigns. The Italians in Libya in the early 1930s established several camps into which they forced the population to keep them from supporting rebel groups.[127] In the context of the Mau Mau uprising, British forces ran a program that interned more than a million Kikuyu in camps (so-called villages) to prevent them from supporting the Land and Freedom Army. The idea of using village-like structures to concentrate the enemy population and to cut off its ties to the fighters was used in many cases. The British relied on it when fighting against communist anti-colonialists in Malaya in the late 1940s and early 1950s. In the late 1950s and early 1960s, the United States would replicate the practice by establishing so-called strategic hamlets in South Vietnam, and the Portuguese would use similar techniques in their attempt to defeat the anti-colonial freedom fighters in Angola and Mozambique in the 1960s and early 1970s.[128]

Internment through villagization in many cases went hand in hand with efforts to modernize the individuals living in the camps. For example, as part of the French Plan de Constantine, which President Charles de Gaulle (1890–1970) announced in 1958 to counter the activities of the Algerian liberation movement (the Front de Libération Nationale, FLN), one million inhabitants were supposed to be settled in new villages which previously had served as resettlement camps created as part of the French counterinsurgency efforts in the Algerian war. The plan also aimed at improving the socioeconomic situation in Algeria so as to pacify the population, to reduce its support for the FLN, and thereby to maintain French influence in the country and region.[129]

The individuals at whom the villagization strategies were aimed resisted them in multiple ways. Colonial improvement schemes turned into "a key issue for nationalists struggling to end colonial rule," thereby undermining the colonial powers' intent to use development as a way of maintaining colonial rule.[130] For example, Indian anti-colonial activists in the 1930s advocated the same instrument the British had tried to use to stabilize colonial rule: the agricultural cooperative. In the eyes of Indian nationalists, cooperatives could be useful in organizing peasants, educating them in the interest of nationalist anti-colonialism, and gaining their support. Additionally, the cooperative mechanisms would strengthen self-reliance and self-administration on the local level, which would challenge the British argument that colonial rule was necessary because the Indians were not able to rule themselves.[131] Similarly, anti-colonial activists in Kenya saw cooperatives as "a potential political resource of great value to any organization which promised African control over government's decisions."[132] The tension between colonial and anti-colonial understandings and uses of ideas about progress, improvement, and reconstruction came to be characteristic of late colonial development.

Modernization projects

Meanwhile, several nations which did not belong to the established imperial powers experimented with modernization and development approaches at home. In the 1920s and 1930s, authoritarian and fascist parties and regimes came into existence in many European countries. The newly established nation states in Central Eastern and South Eastern Europe were under immense pressure. Building the state involved complex negotiations and compromises, often between different ethnic groups and social classes, and economic and financial crises lasted for many years. Under these circumstances, frustration with the alleged inability of democratic systems to react quickly and efficiently increased dramatically, and many voters opted for rightwing parties that promised a return to order and stability. Authoritarian regimes took over in Hungary, Poland, Yugoslavia, Bulgaria, Greece, Portugal, Spain, and finally also in Austria.[133] Against this background the question arose as to whether a democratic government was capable of finding solutions to the impending problems, or whether a non-democratic government was in a better position to do so. This question gained urgency when fascist governments came to power in Italy and Germany.

In Italy the fascist movement under the leadership of Benito Mussolini (1883–1945) emerged out of the frustrations over the First World War and the fear of a Bolshevik revolution. Responding to popular dissatisfaction with the country's economic situation and its standing among the European powers, Mussolini promised to make Italy powerful and to give it the international respect it deserved. To demonstrate Italy's strength, Mussolini's government initiated large infrastructure projects, most famously the draining of the Pontine Marshes, which had been infested with malaria-carrying mosquitoes, and the establishment of the New Towns on the new land, which was to be settled through internal migration.[134] The German National Socialists were in part inspired by the Italian example. When Adolf Hitler (1889–1945) came to power in 1933, he, too, opted for showcase projects to signal to the German population and to international observers that under his leadership the country would rise from its humiliating defeat in 1918. Most famously, Hitler's government realized the *Autobahn* (highway) system, an infrastructure project planned long before 1933, thereby demonstrating Germany's technological advancement.[135] Investments in the country's traffic infrastructure (canals, harbors, railways, airports) were closely connected to the preparations for war. Domestically, housing projects were carried out to improve the living conditions of the "Aryan" population and secure political support for the regime, not least from those who had been unemployed and found jobs in public works programs run by the Nazi administration.[136] Additionally, both fascist regimes advocated the development of rural regions. Italy and Germany in the mid-1930s passed laws that aimed at preserving family-owned landholdings, and they invested resources into agricultural research and training in order to increase the efficiency of small-scale agriculture. The goal was to make the countries independent from food imports as part of the autarky policy; at the same time the policies were supposed to help anchor the fascist regime in every part of the country.[137]

The fascist efforts to improve, extend, and modernize their countries' infrastructure, housing, and agriculture were an expression of development policies of a particular kind. Few contemporaries would have considered Italy or Germany underdeveloped countries. However, both countries possessed regions which were very poor in terms of economic production, income, and access to basic services. Overcoming this regional inequality and the national imbalance resulting from it was a welcome opportunity for the fascist regimes to demonstrate that they were truly people's movements. In addition, the development projects and approaches tried out in Italy and Germany played an important role with regard to the imperial aspirations of the two countries. Upon its invasion of Ethiopia in 1935, Italy conducted urban and rural development projects in its new colony which were very similar to those carried out at home, yet based on a racial understanding of Italian superiority vis-à-vis Africans. Also in the 1930s, model agricultural settlements were set up in Libya and Somalia for Italian peasants to conduct progressive agriculture on African soil and thereby uplift the civilizational level of the colony.[138] Similarly, yet with much more deadly intentions and consequences, the Germans took some of their experiences with rural settlements, housing, and infrastructure development to Central Eastern Europe once they had invaded Poland in 1939 and moved further east in the following years in their quest for *Lebensraum* (living space). The *Generalplan Ost* (General Plan East) projected the "Germanization" of an enormous territory covering the Baltic countries, Poland, and Ukraine. The individuals living in the respective regions would be forced off their land, deported, or killed to make room for German settlers, who would set up new villages and economies and thereby reclaim the territory.[139]

The transfer of settlement and infrastructure concepts from a domestic to an imperial setting was not a German or an Italian singularity. Many European governments tried out new approaches first at home and then applied them to their colonies, or the other way around. Development knowledge circulated constantly, not only between colony and metropole but also across national and regional boundaries. What is particular about the German and Italian cases is the decisive role racist ideology played in deciding who would benefit from improvement projects and who would be excluded from them. Exclusion happened by force. The readiness and willingness to use violence to pursue what was otherwise portrayed as beneficial and progressive were part of the racist logic that characterized the projects of the fascist regimes at home and abroad.

The fascination with large-scale modernization projects and the willingness to apply force to realize them was something authoritarian regimes shared across extreme ideological divides. The Soviet Union's grand infrastructure projects of the 1920s and 1930s are a testament to the belief in the power of technology. Vladimir Ilyich Lenin (1870–1924) had famously argued in 1920 that "Communism is Soviet power plus the electrification of the whole country."[140] To industrialize, the people had to change, too, he argued: They would have to transform from backward peasants into modern industrial workers who constituted the fundament of the USSR. In Lenin's view, electricity was at the heart of this socioeconomic transformation, as it would imply a rapid change in lifestyles and behavior.[141] Accordingly, the first Five-Year Plan projected the construction of massive hydroelectric dams to generate the energy necessary for industrialization as well as other kinds of large-scale infrastructure projects.

The Dneprostroy Dam on the Dnieper River was the most famous of its kind. Work on the dam started in 1927; it was opened in 1932 and extended in the following years. By 1939, nine generators produced 560,000 kilowatts of energy, which were used to run a steel mill set up in the vicinity.[142] Because the engineering skills needed for such a large dam were not available in the Soviet Union at the time, Moscow officials invited American and German companies to help with the construction. The building of the dam was accompanied by intensive propaganda efforts aimed both at the domestic and the international audience to show that the Soviet Union was an advanced nation.[143] Thousands of workers from many different parts of the USSR—many of them as forced laborers—participated in the building of the dams and other large-scale infrastructures.[144] By having individuals from entirely different backgrounds living and working together, the Soviet leadership hoped to accelerate the establishment of a new kind of society that was entirely based on Soviet norms and principles. Hence, the construction sites and cities that emerged around them were considered central to the project of building socialism.[145]

Agricultural collectivization was another element of this project. Joseph Stalin (1878–1953), who became General Secretary of the Central Committee of the Communist Party in 1924, initiated the collectivization of agriculture in 1929, partly in response to acute food shortages in the winter of 1927/1928. Peasants were forced to give up their land and work on collective farms. Machine-Tractor Stations were established to promote the mechanization of agriculture. Yields were expected to increase by at least 50 percent. Collectivization also served the political goal of expanding state control over the countryside and the peasantry, especially the so-called kulaks, wealthier farmers who were portrayed as enemies of socialism. Large-scale violence surrounded the collectivization process. Soviet authorities punished alleged kulaks, sent them to gulags (labor camps), or killed them.[146] Opposition to collectivization was intense. Peasants slaughtered their animals and destroyed their crops so that they would not have to deliver them to the authorities, and they staged protests and attacked collective farms and Soviet officials.[147] The economic results of the collectivization campaigns by and large did not meet official expectations, although agricultural and industrial production did increase in some parts of the USSR. Collectivization's overall costs were immense. The situation was most dramatic in Ukraine, where the Soviets imposed unreachable grain quotas on the population, thereby creating a famine that resulted in the death of several million individuals from starvation.[148]

At the time, the Soviet authorities strictly repressed reporting about the destructive effects of the collectivization, and many admirers of the USSR and its rapid industrialization process did not want to know about the scale of violence and suffering inflicted on the population. Yet some diplomats and journalists were aware of what was happening, and they reported about it to their governments and publics.[149] Some of those who were skeptical of the authoritarian regimes in the USSR, Germany, and Italy argued that "the rhetoric of raising living standards had been used and abused to considerable effect by fascists and communists, and it was time for liberal internationalists to fight back."[150] This is what American supporters of the New Deal and, more specifically, of the Tennessee Valley Authority (TVA) tried to do.

The TVA was part of the effort to modernize the southern part of the United States, especially the region of the Mississippi Valley and along the Tennessee River. These large rivers flooded regularly, carrying away soil and infrastructure, and the land was difficult to farm. Malaria and other waterborne diseases were frequent. Poverty, lack of resources, and very few medical, educational, and social support structures characterized the region, which accordingly was classified as backward. The fact that a large part of the region's population was African American added to this perception on the part of white Americans. Plans for building a hydroelectric dam at Muscle Shoals on the Tennessee River had already been drawn up in the early twentieth century but had not been realized. It was in the context of the Great Depression and its disastrous effects that Franklin D. Roosevelt

(1882–1945), upon becoming US President in 1933, decided to make the dam part of his reform agenda, the New Deal.[151]

The TVA was conceived as a regional development agency. Similar to the Office du Niger and many other development authorities, the TVA received its own budget and a large degree of independence, which was considered necessary for it to carry out its tasks successfully and quickly. Its key task was to plan, manage, and supervise the construction of hydroelectric dams in order to develop the region economically, and to set up schools, to promote literacy, and to train peasants in new and improved agricultural techniques. The TVA officials and engineers shared with their Soviet counterparts the belief that electric energy was the key to economic and social modernization. Dams would allow for the regulation of rivers and avoid flooding, which in turn would allow farmers to use their land more efficiently. As had been the case with the Dneprostroy Dam, industrial plants would be established close to the dams, which in turn would lead to an expansion of infrastructure and accelerate the process of urbanization. Peasants would migrate to the new towns and cities and find work as factory workers. Educational and health levels would rise. Finally, the individuals who participated in building the dam and the surrounding structures would become modernized themselves, and they would understand the power of democratic planning and governance.[152]

Under its director David Lilienthal (1899–1981), an expert on public utility law and a strong supporter of the New Deal, the TVA established a reputation as being a motor of grassroots participation and democracy. Lilienthal's 1944 publication *TVA: Democracy on the March* presented the TVA as a genuinely American model of development that offered economic advancement and individual freedom.[153] In the context of the ongoing war and the fight against fascism, the TVA seemed to offer a promising alternative to authoritarian development models.[154] Even if Soviet, Italian, German, and American ideas about the need for socioeconomic modernization and the tools constituting modernity were very similar, *how* to achieve it was an intensely political question, and one to which the United States seemed to have found a genuinely liberal solution. When the war ended with Allied victory, many Americans believed that the development approach the TVA represented could be beneficial to other parts of the world, too.[155] It was, in part, this trust in the power of planning and technological modernization rooted in the TVA myth that encouraged the United States in the postwar period to become an active promoter of development abroad.

Conclusion

This chapter has provided an overview of different strands of ideas and practices that presented origins or forerunners of what later came to be understood as development. Such a perspective carries a risk of being teleological. Looking for traces of development-related thinking before 1945 with a relatively clear idea of what development would be after 1945 increases the likelihood of finding proof that development has always been in the air, even if the terms and arguments used at earlier times were different. This might lead to the perception that early welfare policies, the idea of the civilizing mission and the perceived need for interventions in the colonial context, humanitarian activities, concerns about rural life, and ambitious modernization projects sooner or later *had* to result in the emergence of development as we think of it today.

This is, of course, not the case. What became understood as development in the postwar period had its roots in the fields described above but was not just the sum of pre-1945 ideas and practices. The Second World War had a massive impact on the ways in which individuals and governments thought about problems of poverty and inequality; the technological and scientific advancements propelled by the war played an important role in this regard. Furthermore, development-related thinking would soon change in nature as it became entangled with Cold War strategies and ideologies, while the first wave of decolonization in Asia and the anti-colonial movements in Africa suggested that imperial strategies would have to change rapidly. These were issues which by and large had been unthinkable for most contemporaries before the war. The new realities of the post-1945 years demanded new responses to new problems and offered room for new ideas.

At the same time, it would be naive to assume that suddenly in 1945 an entirely new diplomatic, political, and academic field called development emerged from nowhere. As we have seen, the late nineteenth and early twentieth centuries were rich in thinking about productivity and economic divergence, about the social and political consequences of the agrarian transition and industrialization, about the role of the state in providing welfare services to its citizens, and about relations between different parts of the world, many of them unequal in political and economic standing. Some of those ideas were translated into arguments about justice and responsibility while others were presented as scientific facts that spoke for themselves or had no political implications at all. Together, this variety of perceptions, arguments, and interpretations produced an understanding that inequality was an issue that had to be approached in a systematic way, regardless of whether the goal was to prevent a second Bolshevik revolution, to improve the health situation in a colony, or to increase the national income of a European country. What characterized development thinking even in its early form was the plurality of aspects it entailed. For that reason, too, development after 1945 was never a monolith but a continuously emerging conglomerate of different types of knowledge, experiences, and interests.

CHAPTER FOUR

The Emergence of Development in the Mid-Twentieth Century

When the Second World War ended, development was probably not the most important issue on the minds of many people who had experienced the war. Those who had survived the war on one of its many fronts focused on their own lives—finding family members they had lost in the chaos of war, rebuilding houses and villages, and securing food and income. Similarly, governments were primarily concerned with re-establishing basic political, social, and economic structures and stabilizing the political situation in their countries. Reconstruction is therefore the more appropriate term to characterize the immediate postwar efforts in those regions where war had been fought. At the same time, however, questions about development came to the fore rapidly and prominently. Broadly speaking, we can identify two reasons why development began to emerge as a policy field of its own in the immediate postwar years: the efforts of the European imperial powers to maintain their colonies, and the emergence of the United States as a superpower with ambitions to remake the global setting.

Late colonial development

The Second World War strongly affected the ways in which the colonial powers thought about their colonies. During the war, European countries had drawn heavily on their territories abroad to secure the resources and foodstuffs they needed to fight and win the war. The demand for resources had resulted in high food prices and, in some cases, led to food shortages in the colonies.[1] The worst case was the Bengal famine of 1943, which was linked to British requisitions of grain and resulted in the death of two million people from starvation.[2] Wartime efforts to increase agricultural production were geared toward the needs of the colonial powers, while the living conditions of the populations in the colonies suffered.[3] Furthermore, an even larger number of individuals from the colonies served in the armies of the colonial powers than during the First World War, and the impact of the war on colonial life and politics was much more extensive and direct. Labor unrest and political agitation increased markedly during the war.[4] In India, for example, the Indian nationalist movement under the leadership of Mohandas Gandhi initiated the Quit India movement in August 1942, demanding that the British give up control over India immediately. The British, who depended on India strategically, reacted with harsh measures, imprisoning the political leadership of the movement as well as thousands of its supporters.[5]

Although political protests against the colonial powers were effectively suppressed, they made clear that European imperial rule was under increasing pressure. In this situation, several colonial powers promised the colonies "an improved, less autocratic form of colonial authority after the war had been won."[6] Investing in the colonies was seen as one way of keeping that promise without giving up the will to maintain power over them. At the Brazzaville Conference in January 1944, in French Equatorial Africa, French politicians representing Free France (the opposition to the Vichy regime) led by Charles de Gaulle and colonial administrators met to discuss the future of colonialism after the end of the war. They agreed that colonialism was not supposed to end but rather had to be reformed.[7] To do so, new forms of colonial rule would have to replace the old, extractionist practices. The French did not suddenly give up their established beliefs about the alleged civilizational inferiority of Africans, yet against the background of the war they pragmatically accepted that political and symbolic changes were required to adapt imperialism to the situation in the colonies.[8] Specifically, colonial funds for agricultural improvement, education, and social provisions were supposed to increase in order to reduce the dissatisfaction of colonial subjects and to enable them to participate in development projects.[9]

One social group which received particular attention consisted of those individuals from the colonies who had served in the colonial armies during the war, both on the so-called home front and on the battlefields. For example, African troops had made up nearly 9 percent of the French army, and until 1945 about 200,000 served France as laborers and as soldiers.[10] Since they had risked their lives and had made large sacrifices, they and their families had to be given at least some kind of elementary welfare provisions in return. Also, through the war they had come into contact with different realities, had received training and education, and were considered to be more easily politicized. Hence, the colonial powers thought about how to integrate returning soldiers into the colonial societies, making sure that they did not become a nucleus of anti-colonial activism and stayed within the racial boundaries considered crucial to maintaining imperial rule. The

British opted for the establishment of community centers and educational structures for soldiers returning to their home countries, hoping that thereby they could control their political and social behavior.[11]

The term second colonial occupation has been used to describe how the European imperial powers after 1945 made intensified claims on their colonies and tried to exert control over them.[12] Interestingly, they did so in part through intra-imperial cooperation.[13] Although theoretically competitors for power abroad, imperial governments realized that they might benefit from working together in trying to maintain their overseas empires. Development was one of the fields in which cooperation seemed feasible.[14] For example, in 1946 and 1947 representatives of the British, French, and Belgian colonial governments met in Dakar and Accra to discuss shared problems and solutions in the fields of veterinary science and public health. Apparently convinced of the usefulness of such cooperation, they decided to continue with this approach and to organize eight more conferences in Africa until 1950.[15] The overarching goal of these and similar efforts was to revise imperialism in such a way that it would be both more efficient in terms of economic resources gained from the colonies and more modern in the sense that it relied on social technologies and expertise rather than on outward violence and coercion.[16] What came to be understood as development in the postwar period was at the heart of this thinking, ranging from investments in infrastructure and economic modernization to the transfer of knowledge and technology. The history of the Colonial Development and Welfare Act passed by Great Britain is a direct expression of this logic.

In the late 1930s, strikes and violence erupted in the West Indies as a response to the poor living and working conditions that existed in Jamaica, Trinidad, and Barbados.[17] In response, the British government established a committee to study the reasons for the unrest. Its members recommended the set-up of a welfare fund aimed at improving the social situation in the West Indies. They also called for changes in agricultural production, away from the sugar cane production that served the British economy toward a more diversified production that would cater to the population's food needs and the economic stability of the islands.[18] While some committee members were undoubtedly shocked about the conditions they encountered in the West Indies, their predominant goal was to reduce the likelihood that the unrest on the islands increased and the British Empire lost control over them. Late colonial development in this situation was a tool of stabilizing empire, even if it cost money. Consequently, colonial governments turned away from loans and provided more grants to the colonies.

What distinguished *colonial* from *late colonial* development was the latter's "heightened scale and intensity," as the following numbers show.[19] The Colonial Development and Welfare Act of 1940 provided 5 million pounds annually for education and research in the colonies. The act was renewed in 1945, providing 120 million pounds over a period of ten years, and revised for a second time in 1950, when 140 million pounds were granted.[20] Additionally, the British government, through the Overseas Resources Development Bill of 1947, established the Colonial Development Corporation and the Overseas Food Corporation. Both entities were publicly run and expected to increase both the economic productivity and the living standards of the colonial populations as well as Great Britain's income from the colonies.[21] Similar to British legislation, France in 1946 instituted the Fonds d'Investissement pour le Développement Économique et Social des Territoires d'Outre-Mer (FIDES). Between 1946 and 1959, FIDES spent more than six billion francs on social and economic projects in sub-Saharan Africa.[22] Apart from the political interests tied to colonial development, the increase in development funds was also due to the fact that some of the colonies were indebted to the colonial powers and therefore unable to pay back at least some of the money if they did not receive some support to begin with.[23]

Connected to the increase in development funds was the belief that large-scale development projects had to be planned.[24] Planning came to characterize late colonial development work. Seeing that the sums available for development increased significantly, it seemed necessary to replace the ad hoc use of small sums with a long-term perspective on the direction into which the colonies should develop. Whereas in earlier times many politicians had rejected planning because they associated it with socialism or considered it harmful to the liberal economic principles they cherished, the experience of the Great Depression had weakened this position. Many contemporaries believed that the crisis could not be solved by waiting for the economy to recover. Rather, they argued that planning could help to alleviate the most dramatic effects of the economic crisis and thereby prevent future crises from happening. In part this thinking was influenced by the example of the Soviet Union's rapid industrialization effort. Even to those who kept their distance from the ideological program of the USSR, its policy of planned economic growth was impressive. Finally, the total nature of the Second World War (even more so than during the First World War) made it necessary to coordinate the use of resources and capacities of all kinds, from clothing to ammunition, from manpower to national economies. Planning became part of the strategy that was supposed to win the war.[25] Since colonial development was increasingly seen as part of a larger strategy to secure the empires, development planning gained supporters, too. Development economist W. Arthur Lewis (1915–1991) in 1949 coined the famous phrase "We are all planners now," suggesting that it was no longer a question of ideological preference what one thought about planning but a necessary paradigm.[26]

The interest in planning was characteristic of late colonial development in the early postwar years. One of the most famous expressions of this new developmental thinking was the groundnut scheme in British Tanganyika. The project was one of many organized by the European colonial powers to increase the production of oils and fats after the war; the French organized a large scheme in Senegal, for example.[27] The United Kingdom had been hit hard by the war and had amassed huge debts to the United States, to repay which it needed to be able to sell commodities.[28] Yet resources were so scarce that food rationing in Britain continued well into the 1950s. For that reason, some contemporaries considered it logical to turn to Britain's colonies in Africa. As Minister of Food, John Strachey (1901–1963) put it, this move was crucial to ensure that "the harassed housewives of Great Britain get more margarine, cooking fats and soap in the reasonably near future."[29] The British Colonial Office at the time was staffed by many supporters of Fabian ideas who believed in the power of planning to achieve progress, and who, while critical of the excesses of colonialism, considered the overseas territories a source of food and raw materials that could be used more effectively through development projects.[30]

Politically, there was an awareness that turning to the colonies for resources so shortly after the war held a political risk. British Foreign Secretary Ernest Bevin (1881–1951) warned in 1947: "We must be careful that our plans for the development of our Colonial Dependencies cannot in any way be represented as springing solely from our own selfish interests. It is above all important that in their presentation there is no possible suggestion of exploitation of the colonial populations."[31] Perhaps this sensitivity toward the colonial population's perception explains why it was not the British government or a ministry that initially came up with the idea of setting up groundnut plantations in Tanganyika, but Frank Samuel (1889–1954), the managing director of the United Africa Company, a subsidiary of Unilever, who was looking for new economic opportunities for his company.[32] With a private company taking the lead, the Colonial Office agreed to invest a total of 24 million pounds (plus 1.25 million pounds for a new railway and a new port) into the establishment of groundnut plantations in Tanganyika in order to reduce the amount it had to invest into domestic food imports by 10 million pounds. To do so, 3,210,000 acres of land were supposed to be cleared and brought under cultivation in order to produce between 600,000 and 800,000 tons of groundnuts per year. The Overseas Food Corporation was given the task of carrying out the project.[33]

In many ways, the cooperation between Unilever and the Colonial Office presented a continuation of established imperial practices, with private entrepreneurs initiating business abroad and receiving support from their domestic governments. What was characteristic of the post-1945 period was that a new type of actor joined the project: the United Nations Organization (UNO) had been founded in San Francisco in 1945, and the United Nations Educational, Scientific, and Cultural Organization (UNESCO) came into existence alongside it.[34] Under the directorship of the British biologist Julian Huxley (1887–1975), who had been involved in the African Survey in the 1930s and 1940s, UNESCO decided to contribute to the groundnut project by offering to train thirty thousand Africans in the production and harvesting of groundnuts.[35] Arguing that African societies lacked the knowledge and technology required to build up efficient economies, UNESCO promoted the idea of fundamental education, which included not only literacy but also improvements in health and the labor situation in order to raise the general standard of living. The fact that UNESCO, as a UN organization, collaborated with a colonial regime was not seen as a problem by the organization's staff, many of whom had grown up in imperial contexts or at least shared the basic assumptions of the civilizing mission. The British government in turn was interested in cooperation with UNESCO because it was an opportunity to benefit from the positive reputation of an international organization and thereby to gain legitimacy for the continuation of imperialism.[36]

The fact that the British converted tanks left over from the war into tractors to clear the bush to make room for the plantations in Tanganyika mirrored the particular, late colonial approach to development that the groundnut scheme came to symbolize.[37] Yet even military technology could not make up for the many problems the planners in London and the managers on the ground encountered. The machinery was unsuitable for the tropical conditions, the region selected for the scheme was too dry, the soil contained too much clay, and a disease destroyed many plants.[38] In short, many of the problems critics of development have since identified in development projects crystallized in the scheme. Those in favor of it shared an understanding of the superiority of European or Western technology and production methods as well as a belief in the universal applicability of expert knowledge. Furthermore, those responsible for it in London trusted that the colonial administration in Tanganyika was able to translate their ideas into realities, which was much more difficult than expected.[39] When the project ended prematurely in 1951, more than 36 million pounds "had been spent on a scheme that imported more groundnuts as seed than it actually harvested."[40]

Perhaps even more dramatic than London's financial losses were the loss of international prestige and the political and socioeconomic consequences the scheme had in Tanganyika. After all, the project, while a failure in the eyes of the British, changed the lives of the African workers involved: it "funded a dramatic rise in the number of people in wage employment, the improvement of roads, and the building of better health and educational facilities. It also stimulated rampant inflation of both goods and wages, and social unrest, of which the spread of alcoholism, prostitution and theft were the most obvious symptoms."[41] Higher income meant more spending power and the ability of the local population to behave more independently. In that sense, the implicit goal of late colonial development schemes to maintain and increase control over the colonial populations produced the exact opposite.[42]

The expectation of colonial governments that development measures would be an effective tool to rein in the forces freed and strengthened by the Second World War and thereby to stabilize their rule by and large proved to be illusory. Yet what late colonial development helped to do was to establish development measures as progressive and forward-looking activities, especially against the background of war and destruction. Late colonial policies and practices shaped the ways in which development was perceived and conducted, not only by European imperial powers but also by the United States, which rose to global power during the Second World War.

American views on global problems

The war sharpened the perception that situations of scarcity and competition over access to resources were likely to result in conflicts and lead to violence. To many observers in the United States, the global dimension of the war and American participation in it was eye-opening, pointing toward the need for and possibility of more active engagement of the United States in the world.[43] The case of the Rockefeller Foundation is telling in this regard. In November 1943 the foundation identified "Food as a possible field of interest for the Rockefeller Foundation."[44] In previous decades, the foundation had initiated plant research to breed more resistant and productive varieties and promoted new agricultural technologies to raise yields.[45] It had also funded research on the links between nutrition and health and contributed to preventive measures carried out, among others, by the League of Nation's Health Organization.[46] Malnutrition was a serious problem in many parts of the world, as were high rates of disease and rising death rates among children and pregnant women. The foundation's experience with health issues suggested making food supplies and nutritional issues more prominent against the background of the war, when scarcity, rationing, and ersatz products became an everyday reality even in comparatively wealthy industrial countries. In this situation, the political and strategic relevance of access to resources to produce food rapidly gained in importance, which made it attractive for the foundation to contribute to solving some of these problems.

By the early 1950s, as the concern about the effects of the war was being replaced by a concern about the effects of decolonization and the Cold War, the possibility of the foundation engaging in the field of food had become a clear-cut agenda. The foundation's Warren Weaver (1894–1978) stated in 1951: "Hunger, the incapacity of the hungry, the resulting general want, the pressures of expanding and demanding population, and the reckless instability of people who have nothing to lose and perhaps something to gain by embracing new political ideologies designed not to create individual freedom but to destroy it—these seem to be basic dangers of our present world." Therefore, Americans should "do everything within their power to raise the living standard of their neighbors."[47] Many policy-makers and experts shared his belief that Americans had the responsibility to do so, and that they could counter authoritarian approaches to overcoming poverty with a democratic and liberal one.[48]

The most famous expression of this idea was the Inaugural Address of President Harry S. Truman (1884–1972) on January 20, 1949. In the fourth point of his speech, Truman called on the United States to "embark on a bold new program for making the benefits of our scientific advances and industrial progress available for the improvement and growth of underdeveloped areas."[49] What became known as the Point Four speech marked the rhetorical beginning of American development aid as a tool of foreign policy and diplomacy. The belief that the United States could and should take on a key role in international development matters had emerged from contemporary interpretations of the causes of the Second World War and discussions over how to avoid similar conflicts in the future. It was closely tied to the understanding that the United States had won the war because of its superior economic and technological abilities, and that economic stability and liberal democracy were interdependent.

This view on the relation between prosperity and liberalism was not entirely new in 1949. Under Franklin D. Roosevelt, the United States had embraced an economic approach to shaping its relations with Latin American countries, which had suffered heavily from the decline in prices for raw materials in the wake of the Great Depression. Consequently, many Latin American economists and politicians called for state interventions to stabilize the economy in ways similar to the New Deal programs carried out in the United States. American observers, meanwhile, were concerned that the dire economic situation might increase Latin American support for fascist approaches and that Latin American countries might enter into alliances with Nazi Germany.[50] The Good Neighbor policy promoted by the Roosevelt administration in the late 1930s and early 1940s was an attempt to improve the financial and economic situation of Latin America through business partnerships. Specifically, the goal was to accelerate industrialization and the emergence of a consumer culture in order to achieve socioeconomic stability, reduce the attraction of radical political approaches, ensure US access to Latin American raw materials, and prevent strategic cooperation between Nazi Germany and Latin America. Toward that aim, the Office of Inter-American Affairs was established in 1939, headed by philanthropist Nelson Rockefeller (1908–1979), whose family was deeply invested in Latin American business.[51] Additionally, the late 1930s saw plans to set up an Inter-American Bank. Building on the example of the Export-Import Bank, which had been founded in 1934 by the Roosevelt administration to support US business activities in Latin America, the Inter-American Bank was supposed to provide loans to Latin American countries in order to improve their economies' productivity.[52] Although the Inter-American Bank would come into existence only in 1959, the plans for it directly reflected the Good Neighbor policy's key idea that regional stability and peace relied on economic prosperity, and that socioeconomic inequality between neighboring regions was a potential source of conflict. As Secretary of State Cordell Hull (1871–1955) put it in 1940:

> If the standards of the American peoples are to be maintained at levels already achieved, and particularly if they are to be raised in accordance with the legitimate aspirations of these peoples, production and distribution must expand, not only in this hemisphere but throughout the world. This same condition is essential to the well-being of all other areas. For no nation or group of nations can hope to become or to remain prosperous when growing poverty stalks the rest of the earth.[53]

It was this kind of global thinking that informed Roosevelt's 1941 promise of freedom from want as a precondition for peace and stability—not only in the Americas but in the world at large.[54]

The war's global reach raised American awareness about the fact that levels of poverty in many parts of the world were much more dramatic than ever imagined, and that this poverty directly affected the situation of the United States.[55] As a consequence, many observers began to argue that large-scale economic inequality presented more than a moral or economic problem: it was a strategic risk. Particularly those who worked on problems of resource allocation and planning during the war were outspoken about the need to consider the material aspect of preventing wars based on need or want.[56] They focused on macro-economic issues, talking about a global economic "unbalance"[57] and the need "to achieve an expanding world economy so that standards of living can rise, and peace and prosperity can exist."[58] The argument about a causal relation between economic growth and peace, or lack of economic growth and war, became crucial to the American and Western view on the postwar international order, especially against the background of the onset of decolonization.

George Hakim, a Lebanese economics professor and United Nations representative, in 1950 described the scenario in the following words: "The poverty-stricken, disease-ridden masses of the underdeveloped countries are slowly awakening to the misery of their condition." The "darkness and stagnation" which, according to Hakim, had characterized the lives of the inhabitants of the non-Western world for centuries was now being challenged by their "realization that their miserable condition is not immutable—that there is hope for improvement." Seeing that those expecting improvement constituted the majority of the world's population, "peace and prosperity" depended on whether the Western world succeeded in providing the right type of support in transforming "their economy into a modern industrial economy," Hakim believed.[59] Notwithstanding the fact that Asian, African, and Latin American societies had been far from stagnant, Hakim's observations suggest that perceptions of poverty gained a new quality after 1945. It was characterized by an awareness of the increasing interconnection of different world regions and of the strategic relevance of what became known as the Third World, especially in the context of the intensifying conflict between the United States and the Soviet Union.[60]

The accelerating Cold War very quickly began to change American understandings of inequality and poverty. In contrast to President Truman's Point Four speech, which emphasized humanitarian responsibility, the Cold War was very prominent in Truman's message to the US Congress a few months after his inauguration. In his speech in June 1949, Truman called on the legislators to set up a program by which the United States would provide support to so-called underdeveloped countries. To underline the urgency, he pointed out that if the inhabitants of the poor regions did not experience any meaningful improvement in their situation soon, they might become "frustrated and disappointed" and "turn to false doctrines which hold that the way of progress lies through tyranny."[61] The use of the term tyranny was an undisguised reference to the Soviet Union's communism, much like the emphasis on the need to use development as a way of promoting "the democratic way of life" and "human freedom."[62] Congress responded to Truman's words by appropriating 27 million dollars to the program (though notably less than the 45 million dollars Truman had asked for).[63]

The Point Four program was to be carried out by the newly established Technical Cooperation Administration. As the name suggests, the emphasis of the program was on technical assistance, by which the proponents meant the transfer of American knowledge and technology to improve living standards abroad. Instead of conducting large-scale projects, the program was supposed to provide small sums for self-help projects, in which an American expert or organization would support a local community. This structure would provide an incentive to those in need and circumvent the imperial type of development, which was driven by the interests of the donor. Furthermore, Point Four, instead of drawing on public capital funds, advocated private investments, which would help to build trade relations and contribute to strengthening liberal political structures.[64]

In the early and mid-1950s, the Point Four program served as a reference point for many American and Western international observers to discuss problems of global importance. Many of these commentators were particularly concerned with population growth, specifically with the high population growth rates in Asia and the Middle East, which they believed presented a possible handicap to economic growth in those regions.[65] While the connection between the two factors remained largely undefined in 1950, not least because the demographic data available was rather sketchy, by the mid-1950s population growth had become established as a crucial development variable. In 1956, sociologist and demographer Kingsley Davis (1908–1997) published a piece in which he argued that economic development was "rendered improbable" if demographic growth continued or increased. Davis warned about "the political situation which the combination of rapid population growth and widespread poverty provokes in the underdeveloped countries." More specifically, he considered it dangerous that many of the countries in question ("India, Egypt, China, Pakistan, Indonesia, Greece, and Nigeria") shared a "superabundance [of] manpower" and a proximity to nationalism. If external or internal pressure on the countries increased, their governments might turn to these two "resources" to fight a war, which would likely turn into a global war.[66] The picture Davis painted was based on a revised version of Malthusian thinking. Instead of fighting for food or land, the new nations were competing for recognition and power, and as long as their economic development was slow or stagnant because of their high demographic growth rates, they would not be satisfied and peaceful. Hence, population growth had to be kept in check to maintain global stability, contemporaries like Davis believed. It was only in the 1960s that birth control, or family planning, became an integral part of international development assistance programs, but the belief that population was one of the resources that co-determined the process of development and thus was relevant with regard to prosperity and security was present much earlier in the debate.[67]

A second aspect which played a prominent role in the discussion about the future global order as seen through the Point Four lens was European imperialism. Those in favor of Point Four agreed that the support the United States could provide had to be very different from European colonial projects. President Truman had made this point in his speech when he stated: "The old imperialism—exploitation for foreign profit—has no place in our plans."[68] Yet the European colonial powers were not willing to allow the Americans to interfere with what they considered their possessions and privileges. Great Britain especially had to be treated carefully because it was the closest ally of the United States in postwar Europe, and Washington could not afford to attack British imperialism without risking friction.[69] Although many Americans felt that European colonialism was outdated and should end, the alternative seemed problematic, too: if the European powers left their territories too quickly, this might result in a political vacuum the Soviet Union would surely exploit. Hence, although rhetorically the United States presented itself as a former colony in solidarity with present-day colonies, American foreign policy until the late 1950s and early 1960s tolerated and supported European imperialism for geopolitical reasons.[70]

As a compromise, the United States called for the establishment of the UN Trusteeship Council within the United Nations Organization.[71] The role of the council was to administer those colonies which had become mandates after the First World War; they now became UN Trust Territories. In many ways, the UN Trusteeship Council, which came into existence in 1946 and was headed by Ralph Bunche (1903–1971), an African American political scientist and diplomat known for his radical critique of colonialism, continued the work of the League of Nations Mandate Commission. The Trusteeship Council was given much more direct responsibility than its predecessor. It was supposed to actively promote the trust territories' development and to prepare them for self-government or independence.

Furthermore, the new system did not categorize the colonies based on their alleged level of development but treated all of them as equals (although they were ranked according to their military relevance).[72] Also, the Council included countries which did not possess colonies, which meant their representatives could voice criticism of colonialism vis-à-vis the colonial powers. In addition, the agreements on which the mandates were based included the obligation to provide information on the colonies to the Special Committee, which was established by the UN General Assembly, particularly by those countries critical of colonialism. Hence, the mandate powers were under greater pressure to adhere to public expectations and to justify their decisions and actions than they had been under the League of Nations' system.[73]

For the colonial powers the new structure meant that they were not autonomous in their dealings with the colony but had to accept that UN representatives would request information on the colony's situation, conduct regular visits, and request changes in colonial policy. For the colonial societies the UN trusteeship status meant that there was an official channel through which it was possible to criticize colonial rule, point out injustices, the use of violence, and human rights violations, and gain international attention and support. Petitions and letters served this goal.[74] Petitioning had been used widely under the mandate system, too, of course. Yet the formal conditions for letters and petitions to be accepted had been very high, and many of them had never entered the official circuits.[75] The UN trusteeship system was less rigid in this regard and had lower barriers for criticism to be voiced.

Unsurprisingly, the colonial powers in charge of the trust territories tried to prevent the Trusteeship Council from gaining too much insight into the situation in the colonies. Specifically, they tried to contain knowledge about the UN system and to limit UN activities in the trust territories. For example, the British in Tanganyika "resisted the requirement of flying the UN flag next to their own," and they tried to prevent the opening of a UN office in Dar es Salaam.[76] They also went to great lengths in preparing the visits of UN delegations in order to keep problematic aspects out of sight.[77] However, African activists in the trust territories, in close cooperation with international NGOs, found ways of publicly critiquing the colonial policies and practices of racial discrimination and suppression of political dissent. While the colonial powers argued that what they were doing in the trust territories was a domestic affair and should not concern the United Nations, the anti-colonial activists "began to use the United Nations as a forum through which to penetrate the barriers of national sovereignty ... and to speak directly to an international audience."[78] By documenting human rights abuses in the form of reports, letters, witness accounts, and photographs to supporters in New York, the African activists made themselves heard and put pressure on the colonial powers.

The United States tried not to become entangled in these kinds of disputes, but they also did not intend to stay out of European spheres of influence in Africa or Asia. Technical assistance and other forms of development aid provided a unique opportunity to try to influence the situation in countries and regions considered relevant to American security interests and those of the so-called free world more generally. The Cold War, security-driven rationale of US aid became predominant in the 1950s and replaced the older, internationalist view of development as expressed in the late 1930s and early 1940s.[79] For example, a policy draft by the US Bureau of Near Eastern, South Asian and African Affairs from 1954 contained the recommendation to the US government to "make the most practical use of economic, technical and where applicable military assistance so as to influence the process of political change to effect the best compromise of Western interests and to offer the maximum promise of stable non-Communist regimes."[80] It was with this strategy in mind that the United States began to promote the Point Four logic within the newly established organizations that were designed to build a new, secure global order: the Bretton Woods organizations—the International Bank for Reconstruction and Development (IBRD, or World Bank) and the International Monetary Fund (IMF)—and the United Nations organizations.

New international organizations

The Bretton Woods structure created under British-American aegis reflected the attempt to establish international structures that would prevent financial and economic crises like the Great Depression, which were believed to create situations in which anti-democratic forces could come to power more easily. In the eyes of American politicians, the protectionist economic practices of Germany and Japan, but also of the European empires were economically and politically harmful in that they undermined the principles of a liberal world order in which free trade helped to build connections across borders and kept conflicts at a minimum. In planning for the postwar future, the United States pushed against imperial preferences and secret agreements and for free trade and international negotiations. Roosevelt's Atlantic Charter of 1941 was, in part, an attempt to secure Great Britain's commitment to a postwar order based on free trade.[81] The idea of free trade as the key to peace and stability also informed the discussions prior to and at the Bretton Woods deliberations in New Hampshire in July 1944.

The Bretton Woods system was supposed to provide what the Versailles system had not been able to secure: effective mechanisms to achieve financial, economic, political, and social stability on an international scale. However, Great Britain, France, and many of the other countries involved in the negotiations were hesitant about the American push for free trade. Preferential trade agreements and currency unions involving their imperial zones of influence had clear economic advantages for those who were part of them. Since many national economies had been greatly weakened due to the war, using protectionist measures to rebuild the economies seemed like an obvious choice. Hence, the outcome of the Bretton Woods discussions was a compromise between American pressure for free trade and European demands for protections and regulations.[82] Yet the conference was much more than a transatlantic effort to find a solution to international trade problems. For one, many Latin American, Asian, and, to a lesser degree, African countries were represented at the conference, and they made their particular concerns and demands heard. Specifically, many countries called for better access to international capital and for support with their economic development.[83] For example, the Indian delegation lobbied that the International Monetary Fund should be tasked "to assist in the fuller utilisation of the resources of economically underdeveloped countries."[84] This sentence was not included in the final version of the Fund's mandate, yet the Indian suggestion shows that the issue of international development was present at the Bretton Woods conference. Already in early drafts for the set-up of postwar structures had the theme of development featured prominently. The mechanisms and practices tried out vis-à-vis Latin America as part of the Good Neighbor policy were an important source of inspiration for US policy-makers involved in drafting the future international structure and its organizations. The 1930s discussions about the Inter-American Bank directly fed into the thinking that informed the establishment of the World Bank and the International Monetary Fund.[85]

Early on, critics argued that the Bretton Woods organizations and the system as a whole were predominantly geared toward securing American access to markets and resources abroad. Some saw the Bretton Woods system as a tool of American imperialist aspirations. To be sure, economic and financial interests did play an important role in American thinking about the postwar order. As shown above, the belief that the prosperity and well-being of the United States was tied to the situation in other parts of the world was an essential element of American efforts to re-think international relations. Also, US politicians understood very clearly that they needed the support of the American business community to realize their plans, and therefore underlined the potential economic benefits of stronger international commitment. For example, Harry Dexter White (1892–1948), a senior American official at the US Treasury who represented the United States at the Bretton Woods negotiations, argued in a 1943 memorandum that making capital available to "underdeveloped" countries meant "not only that those countries will be able to supply at lower costs more of the goods the world needs but that they will at the same time become better markets for the world's goods."[86] White and others did not try to cover up the economic interests of the United States but acknowledged them openly. For that reason, it would be difficult to interpret the Bretton Woods system as a Trojan horse supposed to secretly carry real American interests into the world. The Bretton Woods organizations were clearly defined by economic interests, yet they were supposed to coordinate those interests in a transparent manner.

The International Bank for Reconstruction and Development and the International Monetary Fund were meant to complement each other. The World Bank would provide loans and credits to countries to promote their economic development, whereas the IMF would stabilize the international currencies. The World Bank, which started operating in 1946, had originally been geared toward the reconstruction of Europe.[87] However, this function was soon taken over by the European Recovery Program, and the World Bank had to look for alternative fields of activity. Lending money to the so-called developing countries was the natural choice. The bank's staff was initially dominated by bankers and financial experts recruited from Wall Street.[88] To them it was logical that a bank's focus had to be on projects which promised to increase a country's productivity, as Eugene R. Black (1898–1992), its second president, emphasized in 1952.[89] Consequently, most of the funds went to industrialization and infrastructure projects, especially hydroelectric dams.[90] In line with contemporary development economic thinking, rural and agricultural issues played only a minor role in the Bank's early perception of how to accelerate economic growth.[91] Similarly, problems like unequal access to land or resources were not at the forefront of the World Bank's concerns in the first two decades of its existence.

The majority of the first generation of World Bankers strongly rejected any notion of political interests tied to credits. Bank leadership put an emphasis on professionalism and expertise regardless of nationality, as Eugene Black's statement demonstrates: "We do not think of a man as a Dane, a Cuban or an Indian, but as an economist, a lawyer, or an accountant."[92] This professional approach to development banking was supposed to ensure an objective strategy in which political or ideological interests did not play any role. Yet of course the World Bank was not free from political influences, and the objectivity its leadership claimed was as fictional as any kind of objectivity. Elite backgrounds, a largely unquestioning belief in the superiority of the liberal-capitalist system, a strong male bias, and a belief in the neutrality of science and technology together produced a picture of the world that was in fact far from neutral but very much in line with the position of the United States in the Cold War. The dominant position of the United States within the Bank was also ensured by the voting system of the executive board, which allocated votes according to shareholdership.[93]

Compared to the World Bank, which emphasized economic expertise, the United Nations Organization was more actively concerned with political problems, most importantly with maintaining peace and promoting international cooperation. As the successor to the League of Nations, the UN was expected to learn from past mistakes and to do better in the future. In August 1939, the Bruce Report had identified the shortcomings of the League of Nations and outlined future fields of action for the League, particularly in the field of technical cooperation. The war prevented this agenda from being realized, yet the report served as an inspiration to the

United Nations and its developmental mission. Development was not an original element of the UN's mandate, but the organization and its sub-organizations turned to the development field very quickly and made it part of their efforts toward global governance.[94] Talking of the United Nations as a single actor is misleading because the organization was constituted by its members, whose number increased steadily over time. The UN's agenda was shaped by the ability of its members to gain majorities in the UN assemblies and the various committees founded over the years. For example, Chinese and Brazilian representatives to the San Francisco conference strongly supported the establishment of the United Nations Economic and Social Council (ECOSOC), for which the original idea had been introduced by the United States in previous years.[95] ECOSOC served as an overseer of the specialized agencies that were founded in the mid-1940s: the Food and Agriculture Organization (FAO); UNESCO; the United Nations Children's Fund (UNICEF); and the World Health Organization (WHO).[96]

In 1949 India's representatives to the United Nations made an effort to establish a Special United Nations Fund for Economic Development (SUNFED).[97] The idea for this fund came from Indian economist and politician V. K. R. V. Rao (1908–1991), a student of Keynes, who believed that more resources were needed to allow countries like India to grow economically.[98] Like Rao, many representatives of the so-called underdeveloped countries considered the United Nations more likely to listen to their concerns than organizations like the World Bank and the IMF, which were dominated by the Western industrialized countries and, in the eyes of their critics, pursued goals different from those of the so-called Third World. And, indeed, American politicians considered the SUNFED proposal politically dangerous. They feared that SUNFED could give the non-industrialized countries too strong a voice in debates about world market structures, and they "flatly rejected" the proposal.[99] As an alternative that was closer to their own priorities, the United States pushed their Western allies to support the establishment of the International Development Association (IDA) within the World Bank. Founded in 1960, IDA was tasked with providing soft loans to particularly poor countries at more favorable conditions, and it did so by drawing on multilateral funds.[100] At least indirectly, then, the critique by the so-called developing countries and their demand for more aid did result in organizational and procedural changes. More generally, the establishment of IDA showed that the United Nations served as a forum for the less powerful countries not only to make their voices heard but to challenge international governance structures. Apart from the fact that more money became available, the multilateral character was important to many politicians from the Global South who believed (often correctly) that industrialized countries used bilateral assistance as a tool to further their own interest—an approach that was more difficult to realize in a multilateral context.[101]

Whereas the World Bank and the IMF were clearly dominated by the United States, the Colombo Plan for Cooperative Economic Development in South and Southeast Asia was a development organization that mainly reflected Great Britain's geopolitical interests in Asia. The Colombo Plan was established as a regional intergovernmental organization in 1950 by the Commonwealth Conference of Foreign Ministers at a meeting in Colombo, Sri Lanka. The original members were India, Pakistan, Sri Lanka, Malaysia, Canada, Australia, and the United Kingdom.[102] Visibly, the emphasis was on former British colonies in Asia, which had become independent soon after the Second World War. The interest of the United Kingdom in providing aid to these countries was to maintain British influence in Asia beyond the end of colonial rule. Connectedly, there was a distinct anti-communist interest in Great Britain's support of the Colombo Plan members. The British feared that the Asian regions might turn to communism, especially after the communist victory in China in 1949. As Frederic Benham (1900–1962), a British economist and former adviser on colonial development issues, put it in 1956:

> It is often argued that they [the Asian countries] are so poor that it is difficult for them to save more without resorting to compulsory saving under a dictatorship similar to those of the Communist countries. ... external aid must be greatly increased if they are to make sufficient economic progress within their present framework, which they wish to retain, of a free and democratic society.[103]

Hence, the economic and political interests of the former imperial power now engaged in the Cold War merged in the Colombo Plan. However, the Asian countries were in a very different position from where they had been before 1945. Their governments actively and confidently asked for economic and financial support from Great Britain, and they were aware that they had bargaining power because of the British geostrategic interest in the region. Some of the Asian representatives shared the perception that the rise of communism was a serious threat, while others used the argument to press for more funding.

The economic function of the Colombo Plan was to foster growth in South and Southeast Asia and to encourage cooperation among the members toward this goal. Initially, the organization's work was supposed to last for six years, but it was renewed continuously and still exists today. In contrast to the Point Four program, the Colombo Plan did not establish its own fund to finance projects. Instead, the members met on a regular basis to discuss development priorities and to coordinate projects on a regional basis; the industrialized countries then decided which projects to fund. In the 1950s and 1960s, Colombo Plan projects focused on multi-purpose infrastructure development, generation of electric energy, irrigation and extension of cultivated land, and training of skilled workers needed for industrialization projects.[104]

Not all of the new international organizations that came into existence in the postwar years were directly concerned with fostering economic growth.

Other forms of development-related activities grew out of the experiences of war and were primarily concerned with alleviating the effects of war in their many forms. Humanitarian efforts were required all over the globe to remedy the worst effects of war, hunger, flight, and expulsion. The United Nations Relief and Rehabilitation Administration (UNRRA) was established in November 1943 to coordinate international wartime relief efforts. Until 1947, UNRRA spent about 3.7 billion dollars to help civilians, prisoners of war, displaced persons (the inmates of concentration and labor camps), and many others who had suffered due to the war.[105] UNRRA closely cooperated with private and non-governmental humanitarian organizations which emerged during the Second World War. One of them was the organization CARE (Cooperative for American Remittances to Europe). Due to its widened scope of activities, it changed its name in 1953 to Cooperative for Assistance and Relief Everywhere. Originally founded during the Second World War to send food parcels to civilians suffering from hunger, the organization's managers in the 1950s and 1960s turned CARE into an internationally active not-for-profit enterprise that cooperated closely with governmental and non-governmental bodies active in the field of relief and development work.[106]

Apart from the need for humanitarian interventions in the context of the war, the massive problems of hunger and disease that existed in many parts of the world greatly concerned contemporaries. Many of the ideas and suggestions on how to secure sufficient food supplies went back to the interwar period and to the League of Nations' activities. Because international coordination had largely failed due to protectionist interests and the economic crisis of the 1930s, it seemed necessary to ensure that efforts to increase agricultural productivity and to formulate coherent food and nutrition policies were finally and effectively aligned on an international level.[107] Consequently, the Food and Agriculture Organization was founded in 1943 at an international conference in Hot Springs, Virginia. Drawing on the organizational basis of the International Institute of Agriculture in Rome, which the Italian fascists had taken over in the 1930s, and on the work of the League of Nations, FAO was tasked with improving agricultural practices, rural living standards, and the distribution of food.[108] The first two items were closely linked to development issues: increasing agricultural productivity was considered crucial to achieving economic growth and industrialization. Yet higher yields required higher living standards. Rural populations needed better and more resources to be able to conduct the kind of agriculture that would allow them to produce more—to save, to sell, and to invest, and thus to leave behind the subsistence economy in favor of a surplus economy.

Meanwhile, the World Health Organization, which was founded in 1946, was to ensure that diseases that could be cured did not have lethal consequences, that nutritional deficiencies did not increase the likelihood of epidemics, that the lack of sanitation and education did not prevent infants from reaching adulthood, and that the spreading of infectious diseases was contained through international control and coordination. The standardization of sanitation procedures and the coordination of information had been at the center of the work of the League of Nations Health Organization, too.[109] WHO was supposed to continue and expand this work.[110] On a more political level, concerns with productivity and political stability at least indirectly influenced WHO's perspective on the so-called developing countries. If individuals suffered from chronic diseases and hunger, their ability to contribute to the national income was clearly reduced; at the same time, hungry and sick people might be more willing to embrace radical political ideas and revolt.

What did the new organizations do similarly to or differently from their forerunners, and how did their activities shape development thinking and development approaches in the postwar period? Historians have emphasized the strong continuities between the pre-1945 organizations and those created after. This was especially true of the League of Nations and the United Nations, both in terms of personnel and structures. Many experts and administrators who had been involved in the League of Nations' activities continued their work after the war, either in one of the newly established organizations or as independent advisers. Individuals who had worked on rural reconstruction, on public health, on financial reforms, or on educational efforts drew on their experiences in the new framework of the United Nations and its specialized agencies.[111] While the political, economic, and academic factors that influenced development thinking changed over time, many of the basic beliefs about the problems of so-called underdeveloped regions and the measures that were best suited to solve them were carried across the political caesura of 1945.

One of the reasons for this conceptual continuity was that the number of individuals with first-hand knowledge of different regions and cultures was limited in the postwar years. Consequently, those who could claim some kind of expertise had relatively easy access to policy-makers and were much sought after by many of the new organizations. The value of expert knowledge presented a particular advantage to colonial advisers and officers, especially when decolonization seemed to become more likely over the course of the 1950s and 1960s and positions in colonial administrations were no longer as attractive as they had been in earlier decades. The new international organizations realized the chance the changing political and career prospects implied. They needed personnel with experience in development-related fields and therefore looked for individuals who had been or were still working for colonial bodies. For example, the Food and Agriculture Organization in the 1950s actively approached British forestry experts working for the colonial service in African countries and offered them jobs with FAO. The British Colonial Office was not amused by FAO's recruiting activities, which it considered an intrusion into its sovereignty, and it feared that the better salaries and career opportunities at FAO would encourage too many of its staff to leave the colonial service.[112] At the same time, cooperating with an international organization provided the Colonial Office with a "convenient way of boosting public support and ameliorating humanitarian criticism" against imperialism.[113] As this example suggests, the new organizations did not so much replace older structures as complement them, especially in the years before decolonization.

The transfer of individuals from colonial administrations to international organizations meant that some of their assumptions and their knowledge, which had been produced and consolidated in the colonial context, lived on in the new international setting.[114] This is not to say that organizations like FAO followed colonial agendas or simply continued what the colonial powers had been doing earlier. Each organizational structure shapes existing knowledge in different ways, and knowledge does not remain static but changes over time, too. Yet, at least in the early years of international postwar development work, many of the ideas that had been discussed in the interwar period received new attention because of the new organizations' interest in expertise. The Million-Acre Settlement Scheme in Kenya is a good example.

In the early 1960s, the World Bank, the Commonwealth Development Corporation, and the British government funded a program that was geared toward making land available to peasants in Kenya. In the context of the Million-Acre Settlement Scheme, African peasants were supposed to receive credits so that they could buy and farm land that had belonged to European settlers. The scheme was a reaction to the process of decolonization that culminated in Kenya's independence in late 1963. Yet its conceptual roots were older: already in the early 1950s British colonial officers had made plans for a program that aimed at introducing crops like tea and coffee, which sold for high prices and promised to increase the United Kingdom's income from the colony. Additionally, the program, which became known as the Swynnerton Plan, after its initiator Roger Swynnerton (1911–2000), had a political goal. Swynnerton and his colleagues considered the increasing fragmentation of land a grave challenge to Kenya's political stability. They understood the Mau Mau rebellion as an expression of conflicts over access to land and land tenure between Africans and Europeans, and they hoped that by making land available to African farmers these conflicts would be ameliorated.[115] Conceptually, the Swynnerton Plan was driven by an understanding that the landed elite and the smallholders constituted the backbone of the economy and provided a counterweight to radical political tendencies, while the landless peasants would serve as laborers on the farms, where they could be controlled by their employers.[116]

The Million-Acre Settlement Scheme contained many of the assumptions that had been inherent in the Swynnerton Plan, too. Like the latter, it relied on an understanding that individual land tenure was essential to political stability, and that private property based on land titles and organized around smallholder farms provided the best incentive for economic efficiency.[117]

Since the scheme was begun at a time when Kenya was still a colony, the British had a large influence on its design and implementation. Furthermore, those officers who had been part of the Swynnerton Plan continued their careers in those development agencies that underwrote the Million-Acre Settlement Scheme. Most prominently, Roger Swynnerton served as Permanent Secretary of the Ministry of Agriculture in Kenya and later became Agricultural Adviser for the Colonial Development Corporation. Several other experts who had worked on the Swynnerton Plan joined the World Bank's Agricultural Development Service in the 1960s, which was based in Nairobi. Well into the 1970s, several British agricultural experts who had worked in colonial Kenya joined the World Bank as advisers.[118]

The transfer of personnel from the colonial service to the World Bank was one reason for the high degree of conceptual continuity between the two schemes. Another reason was that many of the World Bank representatives shared the colonial administrators' assumptions about the connection between land, economic growth, and political stability. The World Bank, too, was interested in promoting more intensive and thus more productive agriculture, arguing that economic development in general and industrialization in particular demanded an efficient agricultural sector.[119] Hence, in the eyes of World Bank staff, the ideas inherent in the Million-Acre Settlement Scheme made perfect sense and deserved support. This kind of continuity was not an exception. Many of the large rural development projects continued beyond decolonization. For example, when Mali became independent in 1960, the new Malian government continued the Office du Niger project along the lines instigated by the French colonial administration. The Office still exists, several regime changes later and, since the 1970s, has received numerous grants from international development organizations, most importantly from the World Bank, but also from the Netherlands, France, the Soviet Union, the People's Republic of China, and the European Community.[120]

Highlighting the continuities between the new international organizations dealing with development should not keep us from acknowledging the changes in development theories and practices that took place after 1945. The World Health Organization's work offers an example. In the interwar period, health-related programs conducted by the League of Nations Health Organization and other groups had been largely characterized by preventive approaches that stressed the interconnection between rural improvement and medical prevention. WHO, in contrast, in the 1950s and 1960s emphasized the potential of new technologies in eradicating diseases. The trust in technology was closely related to the experiences of the Second World War, in which the technological superiority of the United States had been decisive in winning the war. The availability of drugs like penicillin and of chemicals like DDT, which had been used to clear military zones of mosquitoes carrying malaria, added to the perception that many of the problems that had required complicated and time-consuming approaches in earlier years could now be solved with much quicker and more effective means. This seemed especially promising in the eyes of the newly independent nations, whose governments struggled to provide the financial and organizational funds necessary to improve health levels. If WHO could step in and apply the new kinds of technologies available to eradicate smallpox or malaria, the pressure on the governments and on the economies would be relieved significantly, and they could focus on other aspects of their developmental agendas.[121] Arguably, then, technological changes did have an impact on the way in which the representatives of development agencies after 1945 thought about how to achieve the kinds of development they envisioned.

Another new feature of postwar development assistance conducted by international organizations was the prominence granted to technical assistance.[122] Many of those in favor of technical assistance valued social-democratic ideas about the state providing services and regulatory mechanisms, and many felt that their trust in planning and coordination had been proven right due to "the success of the wartime collaboration against fascism." Against this background, "solutions based upon international cooperation and upon the promotion of prosperity and alleviation of poverty by government policy seemed plausible, natural ways of approaching problems."[123] In many ways, technical assistance mirrored the Western internationalist idealism that surrounded the establishment of the United Nations.[124] In June 1950, the UN Expanded Program for Technical Assistance (EPTA) was established, which by 1959 was spending 30 million dollars on a variety of projects. In 1965, EPTA was transformed into the United Nations Development Program (UNDP), which became the official framework for the different kinds of technical assistance that existed within the UN universe.[125]

The UN was the largest player in the field of technical assistance but not the only one. Another influential actor was the International Labor Organization. Founded in 1919 as part of the Versailles accords, ILO had been active in the field of standard-setting in labor relations. In the context of the Second World War its leadership shifted the organization's focus toward "the economic and social advancement of the less developed regions of the world," as ILO's Declaration of Philadelphia of May 10, 1944, put it.[126] On this basis, ILO members passed a recommendation on minimum standards of social policy in the colonies, arguing that the colonial governments had to invest more into the economic development of their territories, and that forced labor, suppression of basic rights, and discrimination were no longer acceptable. The Philadelphia Declaration marked a crucial shift in development thinking and increased expectations toward the colonial powers. The fact that representatives of the colonies were present in Philadelphia and made the concerns of their countries heard added to the public pressure.[127]

ILO's work did not translate into immediate changes in practice. The British Colonial Office, for example, paid lip service to the importance of minimum standards but internally argued that for financial and political reasons it was not realistic to introduce social security measures in the African colonies.[128] However, in the early postwar years, when decolonization began to gain momentum in Asia, newly independent countries like India as well as the Latin American countries, which had gained independence long ago but remained economically weak, called on ILO to realize its promise to promote socioeconomic development.[129] Under its director David Morse (1907–1990), ILO responded to these demands—and to the opportunity to secure the organization's position in the international arena—by offering technical assistance, vocational training, and expertise to the so-called developing countries.[130] Morse, who had been a prominent representative of the New Deal in the 1930s and early 1940s, in the context of the Cold War embraced a liberal anti-communist position, arguing that socioeconomic development and democracy went hand in hand, and that therefore the inhabitants of the poor countries needed to receive material and technical support from the Western world. In his view, it was not sufficient to rebuild Europe; structural poverty in the so-called Third World was just as dangerous as the destruction in Europe, he believed.[131]

The amount of money ILO invested in technical assistance increased rapidly: from 20 percent of its budget in 1948 to 80 percent in 1958. In spending the money, the organization followed a particular strand of modernization thinking, the industrialism approach. American representatives of this concept like economist Clark Kerr (1911–2003) and sociologist Wilbert Moore (1914–1987) "saw industrialization as not merely the implementation of an organizational economic principle, but rather as an initiative that covered all areas of life."[132] In their view, it was not sufficient to build factories and wait for industrialization to set in. Rather, social structures, individual and collective behavior, and cultural values had to change, too, so that the factories would not be alien bodies in an otherwise traditional setting.[133] Hence, development and modernization efforts had to integrate the technical and the social, the economic and the cultural levels.

What made technical assistance so attractive was the underlying idea that support in the form of technology, physical infrastructure, but also administrative knowledge was less prone to political and ideological entanglements than other forms of development aid, especially those with colonial and imperial legacies. The understanding of technical assistance as being apolitical was particularly useful to donors because it allowed them to focus on the specific needs of a country or region without having to engage in political arguments about development priorities or global hierarchies. Several organizations used the argument of technical assistance being apolitical in order to stay out of Cold War conflicts and to avoid becoming a victim of the conflict between the Soviet Union and the United States. For example, ILO's leadership argued that the universal nature of industrial modernization did not require a particular political or ideological position but was applicable in any context.[134]

However, many of those engaged in technical assistance were quite aware that the field was far from being neutral. John H. E. Fried (1911–1990), the legal adviser of the United Nations Technical Assistance Administration (TAA), in 1952 stated explicitly that technical assistance was "a new form of diplomacy."[135] The TAA focused on public administration, economic development, and social welfare—fields which were by nature highly political and strongly contested. From a historical point of view, it does not seem surprising that, when the TAA contributed to Indonesia's economic planning efforts, it soon became entangled in the country's political affairs. Indonesia had declared its independence from the Netherlands immediately after the war, in 1945. The Dutch went to war to regain their former colony but did not succeed. This was a political situation that clearly called for the UN's engagement as an international authority dedicated to self-determination and security, and the TAA seemed to be able to offer exactly the kind of support Indonesia needed. Under the leadership of Sumitro Djojohadikusumo (1917–2001), an influential economist who followed Keynesian ideas, the Indonesian government in the late 1940s and early 1950s embraced a development approach that "reserved a strong role for the government but left small and medium enterprises to the private sector and welcomed foreign investors in those large industries defined as non-strategic."[136] Economic planning was at the heart of this strategy, yet Indonesia lacked economists with the skills needed for this kind of work. Hence, the TAA provided expertise to the Indonesian Planning Bureau by sending international advisers on financial, administrative, and labor issues. There were continuous discussions and conflicts about the status and reporting of the TAA experts. The Indonesian government emphasized its sovereignty and tried to limit the amount of information that left Indonesia, whereas the TAA considered it important to be fully informed about the developments to which its experts contributed.[137]

Thus, even for an organization that actively tried to distinguish itself from colonial bodies, it was difficult to overcome the distrust toward external interventions that seemed quite natural for a former colony and a newly independent nation. Similarly, those administrative experts involved in the United Nations' work to set up new administrative structures in Bolivia had to realize that their expertise was relevant to several political projects, namely those of the different Bolivian governments as well as those of the main contributors to the United Nations, especially the United States. Notably, UN officials took on positions within the Bolivian civil service, thereby not only providing expertise from the outside but participating actively in the shaping of the Bolivian administration. This rather liberal interpretation of technical assistance led to criticism from many sides, especially from those who believed that the UN was abusing its international position to realize its own institutional interests as well as those of its member states.[138]

By the mid-1950s the political support for technical assistance as the best way of helping allegedly underdeveloped countries to overcome their deficiencies began to wane among Western development proponents. One of the reasons for their growing skepticism was that the recipient countries "generally preferred money to advice and that technical assistance was much more difficult than had initially been realised."[139] Technical assistance was not free from cultural and political assumptions, and more often than not it became caught in a complicated net of conflicting interests. For example, American anthropologist Gordon T. Bowles (1904–1990), who had lived and worked in the Pacific region, in a 1950 article emphasized the challenges inherent in engineering socioeconomic change with technical means: "Not infrequently it happens that the very people who try to alleviate distress succeed only in increasing it." He offered the example of a project in the Philippines, where the United States Bureau of Science had tried to introduce a Chinese variety of carp to overcome the scarcity of fish. Ecologically this proved to be a disaster because the other fish fell prey to the carp, and culturally and economically it turned out to be a failure because the Filipinos "did not like carp. The only fish they really liked were gone, and many people lost their livelihood."[140] The technical fix, with its underlying trust in the power of universal knowledge and technology, had failed to achieve its goal.

Similar problems abounded. Over the course of the 1950s, as the number of technical assistance projects as well as the unexpected problems with them increased rapidly, it became clear that the transfer and application of particular development solutions was more complicated than had been assumed in the optimistic 1940s. To apply the new technologies specific kinds of knowledge were necessary; if they did not exist in the locality to where the technology was imported, it was useless. As a result, many development experts in the late 1950s began to call for more training and education for the so-called developing countries.[141] The term human capital that became established in this context was coined by American economist Theodore W. Schultz (1902–1998) in 1961.[142] Schultz, who had been studying problems of economic productivity in terms of capital and labor, argued that an important factor was left out of the development equation: the ways in which education and training affected how labor and capital were employed. In his book *The Economic Value of Education* (1963) he provided a systematic account of this interrelation.[143]

In the following years, international organizations began to devote more resources to training programs for individuals from the so-called developing countries as well as to research on the types of education and knowledge needed to allow development to happen. Connectedly, the role of different types of technologies related to development projects began to receive more systematic attention. As a result, the previously rather narrow focus on economic factors slowly made room for a more integrative perspective on development in the 1960s. International organizations were at the forefront of promoting educational initiatives. UNESCO made universal education a central element of its agenda, especially after the passing of the International Covenant on Economic, Social and Cultural Rights in 1966.[144]

The establishment of development studies

The new organizations working on development or in development-related areas required a large number of personnel, and experiences with the challenges of development projects suggested that more specialized training was needed. In response, the organizations established their own research and training centers to train staff and to produce the expertise required to conduct their projects. The Graduate Institute of International Studies in Geneva was the oldest of these centers. It had been founded in 1927 as part of the League of Nations to provide research on international relations and to train experts working for the League and for ILO. At the time it received its major funding from the Rockefeller Foundation. It continued its work after the war and became a center of education and training for UN officials. Later it merged with the African Institute of Geneva, which had been founded in 1961, and worked on development-related topics.[145]

The World Bank in 1946 established a Research Department chaired by French investment banker Leonard Rist (1905–1982), who envisioned the new unit as a center of policy-making based on the results of academic research. Yet the organization until the mid-1960s was not as influential in shaping development economics as a discipline as one might assume. There was competition within the bank, and its top management was more interested in financing specific projects than in developing a long-term strategy toward economic development. The suggestion to establish an Institute of Advanced Studies in the Economic Development of Underdeveloped Countries was not taken up, and the Economic Development Institute that was founded instead in 1955 was primarily concerned with training. It was only under the presidencies of George Woods (1901–1982) and Robert McNamara (1916–2009) that macro-economic research on overcoming poverty began to gain a more prominent position in shaping the IBRD's activities.[146]

Apart from the international organizations that created their own research and training centers, a large number of university centers and departments working on development issues came into existence in the 1950s and 1960s. One of them was the Center for International Studies (Cenis) at the Massachusetts Institute of Technology, which was founded in 1950 and had close relations with US intelligence services. Cenis was not a development studies center in the strict sense but rather a social science research institute whose members were very much inspired by American strategic interests. It was here that modernization theories were tested and policy recommendations drafted.[147] In comparison, the Research Center in Economic Growth at Stanford University (1960) and the Yale Economic Growth Center at Yale University (1961) were more focused on development economics. In Western Europe, the International Institute of Social Studies in The Hague, founded in 1952, the Institute for Development Studies at the University of Sussex in Brighton, and the School of Development Studies at the University of East Anglia were among the most prominent institutes.[148] Interestingly, these research and training centers were not housed at famous British universities like Oxford or Cambridge but at more recently founded universities that had to establish themselves and make up for their relative lack of tradition and reputation by offering new and innovative programs.

In the late 1950s, the Soviet Union started to fund research on development issues abroad. Under Stalin, the USSR's relations with countries outside the Soviet sphere of influence had been extremely limited.[149] It was only after Stalin's death in 1953 and the Twentieth Party Congress in February 1956 that the Soviet leadership began to consider a more active role for the USSR in the world. In doing so, Nikita Khrushchev (1894–1971), Stalin's successor, replaced the concept of the world being divided into two antagonistic camps with the concept of peaceful coexistence.[150] For the Soviet Union and the countries in its sphere of influence, this implied the need to become acquainted with other regions of the world and their problems. The Institute of Oriental Studies of the Soviet Academy of Sciences and the Institute of World Economy and International Relations became hubs of research on the situation in Asia and the Middle East. Institutes dedicated to Africa followed soon and became very active in carrying out research and providing policy advice.[151]

The political relevance of socialist research into the socioeconomic challenges of the so-called developing countries was made clear by the Armenian economist Anushavan A. Arzumanyan (1904–1965), chairman of the Soviet Committee for Solidarity with Afro-Asian Countries, who, in 1959, wrote to the Secretary of the Communist Party: "If Soviet scholars do not participate in the elaboration of a theory of industrialization for underdeveloped countries, the topic will pass completely into the hands of bourgeois scholars of the West."[152] Competition between East and West was not solely an academic issue but had grave political implications. In the eyes of Khrushchev, the Soviet Union had to be able to offer a model of development that appealed to the leaders of the former colonies and that could compete with the Western model.[153] Similarly, scholars working for the research organizations established in the Western sphere of influence all had to position themselves toward the Cold War conflict in one way or another. For example, the International Institute for Labour Studies founded by ILO in 1960 was strongly inspired by the Western position in the Cold War and reflected the assumption that labor conflicts arising out of socioeconomic transformation processes had to be mediated before they could translate into political radicalism.[154]

Importantly, development studies centers were not only set up by potential providers of development assistance but also in so-called developing countries.[155] For example, the Centre for the Study of Developing Societies came into being in New Delhi in 1963. Originally "steeped" in modernization theory, the center in the late 1960s and early 1970s became a hotspot for critical discussions of Western understandings of tradition and modernity.[156] In 1973, the University of Dar es Salaam in Tanzania founded the Institute of Development Studies, which focused on African development issues. It is telling that these centers, which were in many ways closest to empirical development problems and solutions, did not become as famous internationally as did the institutes in the United States and the United Kingdom. The inequalities between the so-called First and the so-called Third World were reproduced on the academic landscape, too, and the limited resources many of the former colonies were able to commit to new universities and research centers played their part. The history of development has not yet been able to overcome this inequality; it is no coincidence that the non-Western institutes are mentioned last and very briefly in this account, too.

Next to the set-up of new centers and departments, the Western development field witnessed the emergence of a growing number of academic journals—another sign of the professionalization process the field was going through. Journals like *Economic Development and Cultural Change* (founded in 1952), *The Journal of Development Studies* (1964), *World Development* (1970), *Development and Change* (1971), *Third World Quarterly* (1979), *Journal of International Development* (1989), and many others testify to the growing and continuous interest in development studies throughout the second half of the twentieth century.[157] The first textbooks on development economics were published in the late 1950s and early 1960s. Additionally, the United Nations produced relevant materials, among them the *World Economics Reports* published by the UN Secretariat, which were directed by the Polish economist Michał Kalecki (1899–1970), who initiated "comparative cross-country studies of major economic variables such as output, employment, and income distribution." Furthermore, the UN invited economists like Jan Tinbergen (1903–1994), Hans W. Singer (1910–2006), Simon Kuznets, W. Arthur Lewis, Theodore W. Schultz, and Gunnar Myrdal (1898–1987) to conduct research on economic development issues.[158]

With the amount of empirical research on development processes and variables continuously growing, the basis for academic criticism and revisionism increased, too. Although it is safe to say that in the 1950s and 1960s growth-centered, modernization-inspired development models were predominant in the Western part of the world, there were always alternative and critical voices challenging established assumptions. This was true both for the theoretical level of development economics and for the practical level of development projects. In terms of theoretical discussions, many scholars criticized the narrow focus on the Gross Domestic Product, for example, arguing that work conducted in the informal economy did not find its way into the official calculations, and that thereby the contribution of groups like peasants and women, who in many countries did not have access to formal markets, was overlooked.[159]

With regard to the practical experiences with development, a 1965 sociological study on the construction of the Rourkela steel mill in India was one of the earliest critiques.[160] In the book, Jan Bodo Sperling, who had lived and worked on the construction site for several years, argued that the "engineering mentality" of the West German companies that had built the steel mill was a key reason for the massive problems the construction process had been characterized by. The book challenged the top-down nature of development planning and emphasized the importance of cultural and social factors in carrying out technical assistance projects.[161] In 1967, Albert Hirschman in his *Development Projects Observed*, presented similar findings from an international study tour conducted in 1964 and 1965 at the request of the World Bank. The countries Hirschman visited were El Salvador, Ecuador, Peru, Uruguay, India, Pakistan, Thailand, Italy, Uganda, Ethiopia, and Nigeria. The projects, all of which were funded by the World Bank, included a hydroelectric power station, the construction of highways and irrigation systems, livestock and pasture management, river development, paper production, telecommunication, and the modernization and extension of railways.[162] Hirschman emphasized the relevance of psychological factors in the planning and execution of development projects, the plurality of interests involved in each project, and the unexpected effects many of the interventions had. In line with his earlier argument that development could not be planned in an entirely rational way, his 1967 book suggested that the practice of development assistance was much more complicated than commonly assumed.[163] Studies like these challenged the optimism of the postwar years and prepared the ground for the revision of development thinking that would take place in the late 1960s and 1970s.

Conclusion

In the introduction, this book has argued that the pre-1945 forerunners of development need to be taken seriously, and that the history of development has roots that reach back much further. So what was particular about the development thinking which came to be associated with the postwar order? Was it just a continuation of older ideas, or is there something particular we can identify as postwar development thinking?

The analysis of late colonial development policies, of the emergence of the United States as a development actor, and of the internationalization of development shows that the year 1945 itself does not play a central role in this regard; neither does 1949. The crucial changes that shaped what came to be understood as development took place over a period of time that stretched from the early 1930s to the early 1950s. During this time, the notion of development gained a new quality insofar as it was no longer primarily a tool to maintain imperial rule but became part of an ambitious strategy to reduce global inequalities. Accelerated and intensified by the Cold War, competition emerged between different ideas of what development aid was supposed to achieve and how it should be carried out. The competition was duplicated in the coexistence of colonial services and new international organizations dealing with development-related problems. Together, these factors created a dynamic that made it necessary for older, imperial ideas about development to adapt to new realities, especially to the growing critique of colonialism and the demise of the European empires.

For American proponents of development assistance, the fact that there existed a large body of developmental knowledge that was tied to colonialism meant that there were resources to be drawn on, both in terms of personnel and in terms of expertise and policies. Contrastingly, the political legacy of colonialism meant that US representatives tried to distance themselves from older forms of development thinking, and to promote a new interpretation of what development should achieve and how it should be conducted. The inherently emancipatory spirit this new version entailed rarely found its way into existence, yet we should not judge the optimism of the immediate postwar period as naive or simplistic. The effects the experience of two world wars, the Great Depression, and technological advances had on several generations strongly shaped the vision of policy-makers and experts on the future.

However, the promise of development represented by Western-dominated international organizations and by the United States could not be realized in isolation from other factors. From its emergence in the 1930s, the new notion of development was tied to international relations in many ways, ranging from trade to imperialism, from ecological concerns to ideological conflicts. After the war, the process of decolonization and the Cold War became the two most influential phenomena that imprinted themselves on development thinking and practice, and development aid in turn influenced the ways in which these two phenomena played out.

CHAPTER FIVE

Development in the Context of Decolonization and the Cold War

The process of decolonization gained traction during and after the Second World War, and it was in this context that new ideas about the possible benefits and uses of development assistance emerged. The leaders of anti-colonial movements formulated development plans for their countries once they became independent, and the former colonies in South and Southeast Asia began to experiment with different approaches to realize their visions. In many of the African colonies, which gained independence from the late 1950s onward, late colonial development schemes were supposed to limit anti-colonial protests. At the same time, the Cold War began to influence the way in which the two superpowers and their allies looked at Africa, Asia, and Latin America. Soviet and American interests in those regions soon translated into military interventions but also into massive developmental efforts. Against this backdrop, the process of decolonization became closely entwined with Cold War agendas.

This is not the place to provide a full account of the history of decolonization and its connections to the Cold War.[1] What this chapter provides instead is an overview of the development concerns of the newly independent nations, their interests in international development assistance, the use of aid as a foreign policy tool, and the efforts of some governments to find a third way between the two models of development represented by the superpowers.

Postcolonial states and their development goals

When former colonies became independent, they turned into sovereign nation states—at least, this is the general understanding. In recent years, historians have begun to challenge the assumption that the nation state was the only type of political organization available or imaginable to the former colonies. Historians of Africa in particular have pointed out that in the period leading up to independence many African intellectuals and politicians considered imperial and federal models as an alternative to the nation state.[2] Effectively, however, the alternatives discussed did not become a reality, and the nation-state model—a highly normative concept that did not exist as an ideal type but came in many forms and shades—dominated. One of the reasons for the reliance on the nation state was that the colonial powers had established political and administrative units in the colonies which reflected their own nation-state structures. For the new governments it was easier to draw on existing structures than to develop entirely new ones, especially when considering the economic and political constraints under which they had to maneuver.[3] Connectedly, the political leaders of the former colonies were aware that to be acknowledged internationally their countries had to be on a par, at least formally, with the established nations, and this seemed more likely if they were structurally similar, too.

Thus, the new states that emerged in Africa and Asia adapted many elements of nation states existing in other parts of the world. What contributed to the adaptation process was the fact that many of their political leaders had been educated in Western Europe, and that they had embraced many of the assumptions about modern nation states and modes of governance anchored there.[4] Many also shared an understanding of constituting the new nation's elite and having to guide the population through the nation-building process. There was a distinct paternalistic sense of responsibility and power inherent in the making of the postcolonial state.[5] Gaining and establishing control over what were often highly fragmented societies was crucial to the political project of developing a strong, modern nation.[6]

And yet the continuity between colonial and postcolonial states should not be overemphasized. Institutional structures may have remained in place for a long time, yet the political circumstances changed significantly and affected the ways in which political power was produced and fought over, how citizens related to the state, and which socioeconomic ideas the new governments followed and promoted.[7] Also, while many postcolonial leaders looked for inspiration on how to shape their societies in different parts of the world, they did not embrace foreign examples uncritically. The notion of African socialism is telling in this regard. While many African politicians were interested in socialist ideas, they felt that Western European or Soviet-style socialism did not match their countries' particular needs and interests, and they formulated alternative versions of socialism they believed were better suited. For example, in Tanzania, under the leadership of Julius Nyerere, the ruling TANU party embraced the concept of *Ujamaa* as an expression of a specifically African sense of community, communal ownership, and the obligation to work. Nyerere and his supporters emphasized the fact that African socialism was something distinct. "We, in Africa, have no more need of being 'converted' to socialism than we have of being 'taught' democracy," Nyerere argued.[8] The *Ujamaa* concept served as a tool to promote the nation-building process by offering an overarching framework that abstracted from Tanzania's tribal and ethnic plurality and focused on commonalities instead.

Development more generally served as one of the central pillars on which many new nation states and their governments based their legitimacy. Long before the end of colonialism, representatives of the colonies had criticized the piecemeal approach to development of "a bridge here, a wharf there" and demanded a more active development policy from the European governments.[9] For example, Hezekiah Habanyama, the chief councilor of the Gwembe Tonga Native Authority in Northern Rhodesia, who served as a liaison between the local population and the colonial government, stated in 1960: "The Northern Rhodesia Government has a duty to develop us. It has an obligation to spend money on our benefit."[10] When the former colonies became independent, the role of the anti-colonial leaders and parties turned from being the opposition that criticized the colonial power for its lack of development efforts to that of being the provider of developmental resources for the new nation. This also meant that the success of a postcolonial government would be assessed based on whether the promised development goals were reached and whether the new regime realized its claim to be morally and politically superior to its colonial predecessor.[11] Development thus served as a tool of nation-building.[12]

To live up to their self-set expectations in terms of economic, social, and moral improvement, many postcolonial leaders opted for a strong state.[13] In the case of India, for example, the state assumed responsibility for "jobs, ration cards, educational places, security, cultural recognition," but also for economic growth, access to health care, and democratic participation.[14] Taking on such broad tasks was a way to gain legitimacy and to promote the nation-building process of territories which were often comprised of a large number of different ethnicities as well as language and religious groups. Under these circumstances, many postcolonial governments considered it too risky to allow for political liberties and opposition politics. The trend toward one-party regimes was strong, and in many cases the political opposition was closely reined in or suppressed.[15]

Political leaders argued that in a situation in which a new nation was being established and had to prove its ability to sustain itself, the only way in which development could be achieved was to use state power to control economic and financial resources as well as political decision-making processes. Consequently, the state sector expanded rapidly in many of the former colonies, with massive increases in the number of civil servants employed and of public agencies responsible for development-related projects. In Tanzania, for example, the number of parastatals—organizations like the aforementioned Office du Niger, which had their own budgets and broad executive powers—increased from 64 in 1967 to 139 in 1974 to 360 in 1983.[16] To pay for all of the new positions, agencies, and projects, the state needed larger budgets and incomes. In the eyes of state officials, increasing taxation to do so was problematic because of the colonial legacy: a large part of the everyday opposition toward the colonial powers had been caused by their excessive taxation regimes. If the new governments drew on taxation to finance their development projects, they risked losing their claim of truly representing the interests of the population. Therefore, many postcolonial states resorted to using unpaid labor to conduct some of the development schemes considered to be most urgent.

Under the heading of community development, villagers, youths, and students were asked or forced to participate in the construction of new streets, wells, schools, and clinics, and to conduct agricultural work.[17] In Tanzania, the *Ujamaa* concept was reformulated when the government's legitimacy was rapidly decreasing in the face of general dissatisfaction with the country's development since independence, especially with the difficult economic situation the peasants found themselves in. In catering to their interests, TANU in February 1967 approved the Arusha Declaration, according to which Tanzania was to become a socialist state that would pay particular attention to the rural population. Apart from the nationalization of the economy, this agenda included the establishment of *Ujamaa* villages, which were supposed to serve as the basis on which the socialist developmental order would emerge. Arguing that the peasantry and its values constituted the nucleus of African society, peasants were supposed to practice communal farming and together develop the Tanzanian economy.[18] However, instead of relying on volunteers as originally promised, the government soon began to coerce individuals and families to move to the newly established villages and practice improved forms of agriculture under the guidance of government officials in the name of development.[19]

The International Labor Organization strongly criticized the use of unpaid labor, arguing that it was incompatible with international standards, specifically with the Abolition of Forced Labour Convention of 1957. Yet many postcolonial governments believed that the use of unpaid labor was the only way for them to provide the most basic structures for their new nations. This argument was tied to a larger one about whether international norms as represented by ILO, UN, and other organizations were appropriate and feasible for newly independent countries. For example, Tom Mboya (1930–1969), Kenyan Minister of Economic Planning and Development, in 1963 stated that the new African countries had the choice of either following international norms and risking the slow-down of their economic progress, or of not following the norms and thereby advancing their progress. Hence, he questioned the implicit idea of universal norms by pointing toward developmental differences. This position signaled a turn away from the anti-colonial argument used before independence, when "international standards had been a point of reference outside the existing power structure which could be used to challenge the status quo."[20] Whereas from a Western international point of view development served to reduce differences, from the perspective of the former colonies it was important to allow for variety and difference instead of being dictated as to how to develop or being forced to remain underdeveloped.

Not least to challenge the power asymmetry, the governments of many of the new nations considered industrialization to be their central goal. Their countries' economies had suffered from colonial exploitation and the one-sided focus on resource extraction, which had made them vulnerable to changing commodity prices. Industrial products promised much higher returns, and industrial structures like hydroelectric dams, factories, and steel mills signaled that a country was culturally, socially, and politically comparable with others, especially in terms of its urban culture.[21] Jawaharlal Nehru (1889–1964), independent India's first prime minister, who was one of the most outspoken supporters of hydroelectric dams and other development-related infrastructure projects, according to legend argued that dams were the "new temples of India." The quote is not confirmed, yet there can be no doubt that Nehru was convinced that a developing country like India should not miss the opportunities provided by modern science and technology, and that remaining rural was not an option.[22]

For one, industrialization meant that the newly independent countries needed vast amounts of electric energy. Hydroelectric dams were the most frequent option, but nuclear energy, which became available in the post-1945 years, seemed even more attractive to some. At the International Conference on the Peaceful Uses of Atomic Energy in August 1955, the Secretary to the Indian Department of Atomic Energy, Homi J. Bhabha (1909–1966), stated: "For the full industrialization of the under-developed areas, for the continuation of our civilization and its further development, atomic energy is not merely an aid; it is an absolute necessity."[23] Many shared Bhabha's enthusiasm for nuclear energy because it promised to end the energy shortages once and for all and, at least as importantly, it would demonstrate to the world how modern the newly independent nations had become.

Secondly, more capital was required to be able to pay for these investments in infrastructure and industrialization. For that reason, some governments accepted deals with multinational companies, even though they were very costly because the companies demanded many tax and marketing privileges to make up for the risks of investing in what was perceived as an unstable political climate.[24] Thirdly, the newly independent countries called for the continuation of the preferential trade agreements of colonial times and for financial and technical support from the industrial countries. It was this concern with the financial and economic effects of the abrupt end of established trade relations (even if they had been to the disadvantage of the colonial economies in the long term) that led the majority of French African colonies to decide to remain associated with France in the form of the

French Community instead of opting for immediate independence in 1958. Only Guinea chose the other path, but had to accept that France "cut all its assistance and left the country—taking even the light bulbs, according to some reports."[25] As the example indicates, many former colonies were caught in a situation in which they wanted independence but depended on foreign aid and private investments, which limited not only their independence but also their freedom to decide how and in which direction to develop.

Development models

It was against this background that many representatives of the so-called developing countries looked for ideas and models of development tried out elsewhere, hoping that this would help them save time and resources and allow their countries to benefit from the practical experiences of others. In doing so, they received much attention (and some pressure) from political actors and experts who advertised particular development approaches. For example, the US government invited study groups from all over the world to visit the Tennessee Valley Authority to showcase its concept of integrated development and liberal modernization.[26] The Soviet Union organized tours for delegations from Asian and African countries to the Central Asian republics of the USSR, where new cities, irrigation projects, state farms, and industrial sites were being set up, promising equal access to resources and opportunities to all citizens regardless of race and class background.[27] On a more abstract level, the two dominant development models available in the postwar period can be summarized as follows:

> One, symbolized by the United States, promised intensive urban-based growth in both the private and the public sectors, the import of advanced consumer products and the latest technology through joining the global capitalist market, and an alliance with the world's most powerful state. The other, that of the Soviet world, offered politically induced growth through a centralized plan and mass mobilization, with an emphasis on heavy industry, massive infrastructural projects, and the collectivization of agriculture, independent of international markets. The US model was tainted by the association of US capitalism with the capitalism of the colonial oppressors. The Soviet model suffered from the image of the Soviet Union as the "secondary" superpower and from what was often seen as second-rate Soviet products and technology. Both, however, offered a road to high modernity through education, science, and technological progress.[28]

The two superpowers argued that their own experiences with development provided a valuable resource for the so-called developing countries in that they could benefit from their expertise and resources. The competition over models of social and economic organization neatly reflected the intense ideological component of the Cold War, and the field of development was one of the arenas in which this competition played out most actively.

Yet one should not follow the self-representation of the superpowers too closely and assume that the two models were strictly limited to the domestic development experiences of the Soviet Union and the United States. The American model was heavily inspired by perceptions of Europe's socioeconomic development since the industrial revolution and by US participation in the continent's postwar reconstruction. Specifically, the work of the European Recovery Program (ERP) became seen as a promising example of economic development in structurally weak regions of the world. The program was more widely known as the Marshall Plan, for US Secretary of State George C. Marshall (1880–1959), who, in a speech in 1947, suggested that the United States should provide money and capital goods to help the European countries recover from the destruction of war—a strategy aimed at stabilizing Western Europe in order to prevent it from drifting into the Soviet zone of influence. From 1948 onward, the United States gave 13 billion dollars in grants and loans to eighteen European countries. Although in theory all countries in Europe were invited to participate in the ERP, only those in Western Europe did, with Great Britain, France, and West Germany being the recipients of the largest sums.[29] The Soviet Union did not allow the countries in its sphere of influence to participate (although Yugoslavia challenged Moscow's dictate and approached the United States for support, which, in 1949, it began to receive). Instead, the Moscow government created the Council for Mutual Economic Assistance (COMECON) to promote the economic reconstruction of Central and Eastern Europe by coordinating the production and trade of goods within the Eastern orbit.[30]

In practice, the Marshall Plan helped to rapidly rebuild the European economies belonging to the Western sphere of influence. Its funds were also employed in those regions which, for a long time, had remained less developed. This seemed true especially of Southern Europe, with the south of Italy, the so-called Mezzogiorno, standing out as a particularly problematic region in the eyes of contemporaries.[31] The Mezzogiorno was predominantly rural and agricultural, with a small number of very large estates (*latifundi*) and an extremely high number of poor peasants and landless laborers. Many Italian and international observers advocated the region's industrialization, arguing that only factories and production sites would be able to create the number of jobs needed to absorb the underemployed laborers and to increase the region's productivity.[32] Not least because the United States feared a communist take-over in Italy, they argued that it was important to support the Mezzogiorno's industrialization with funds from the European Recovery Program.[33] In addition, the region attracted support from the World Bank, whose staff described the region's situation in the late 1940s as one of underdevelopment but of high potential because of the availability of labor and other resources.[34]

Over the course of the 1950s, the World Bank granted seven loans to the Italian government, providing a total of 300 million dollars. To oversee and implement the investment of the money, the Cassa per il Mezzogiorno was established, in part inspired by the Tennessee Valley Authority.[35] Despite the large sums involved and the political relevance granted to development efforts, the Italian South remained far behind the economic performance and the level of industrialization of the North. Many large plants for chemical and steel production were set up in the Mezzogiorno, but only a very few of them had the diffusionist effect expected of them. The number of local entrepreneurs who clustered around the large production centers was small, the large plants remained largely isolated, and the industrialization of the South stalled.[36] However, this disappointing outcome was not foreseeable to those contemporaries who, in the early 1950s, believed in the big-push model underwritten by development economists. Furthermore, their observation that many regions in the world exhibited structural problems similar to those of the Italian South was quite accurate. Among the commonalities they identified were a large gap between different regions of a country, often in the form of a North–South slope, with the South depending on the North for investment, emigration, and economic resources; the longevity of established social structures and economic patterns, which were perceived as expressions of backwardness and, at the same time, as the reason for the difficulty to develop the region; and the centrality of the land question and its connection with labor struggles and class conflicts. Of course, the Mezzogiorno was characterized by many cultural, political, economic, and geographic particularities that would not be found in the same combination in Asian, African, and Latin American countries. Yet in the eyes of many observers at the time the parallels outweighed the specificities. They considered the idea of investing large amounts of money and technology into underdeveloped regions as a way of modernizing them in a very short period of time, and they believed that what seemed to be working in a European setting could be transferred to other regions.[37] For this reason, it is important to include both Europe as an image and European actors in the history of international development efforts in the postwar period.

The many faces of international development assistance

The understanding that underdevelopment was caused by a lack of capital and that development could be achieved by investing foreign capital and technology was predominant among economists and politicians in the postwar period.[38] Quite naturally the question arose as to why those who had huge surpluses should not share their wealth, especially since some of it had been amassed as a result of colonial exploitation, as many postcolonial leaders argued. Hence, there seemed to be a moral obligation on the part of the industrialized countries to help the newly independent nations. Although moral arguments alone were not sufficient, new organizations like the United Nations provided opportunities for the former colonies to make their grievances heard, thereby turning moral into political power. Furthermore, in the context of decolonization, the range of potential providers of resources increased rapidly: the European colonial powers no longer had exclusive, or near-exclusive, access to their former colonies. The United States and the Soviet Union as well as many other countries began to cooperate with the new nations, and in many cases they pushed the former colonial powers to the margins.[39] International assistance by industrialized countries to so-called developing countries became an extremely popular tool of foreign and economic policy in the postwar period.

Postwar international assistance consisted of several elements. The most common form was economic and technical assistance, with the transfer of money, technology, and expertise geared toward increasing productivity and thereby encouraging economic growth and social modernization of one or the other kind. Another field was food aid, which was closer to humanitarian support in that it delivered food to regions suffering from food shortages but did not necessarily include structural, lasting interventions. A third category of foreign assistance that became very prominent in the Cold War period was military aid, ranging from financial assistance to buy weapons to direct deliveries of military technology and expert advice. Donor countries provided military aid to the governments of countries they considered strategically relevant. Military assistance could affect the development process of a country or region "by supporting the suppression of insurgents who call[ed] for a different kind of development, by altering the intraelite balance of power, and by sometimes enabling the military to become a major force in the economy itself."[40] Furthermore, military aid was often connected with counterinsurgency efforts; the previously mentioned villagization and resettlement campaigns are prominent examples. While in terms of budgets military aid constituted a very large share of international assistance, economic and technical assistance were most directly related to development thinking and practices as they are discussed in this book.

The main reference point in the field of Western international assistance became Official Development Assistance (ODA), which represented the amounts of aid given by the members of the Organization for European Economic Cooperation (OEEC), the forerunner of the Organization for Economic Cooperation and Development (OECD).[41] On the initiative of the United States, the OEEC in 1960/1961 set up the Development Assistance Committee (DAC, earlier known as Development Assistance Group), which brought together the largest Western foreign aid providers.[42] The DAC served "as a forum to co-ordinate bilateral aid policies, to formulate criteria for the level and terms of aid and to review the performance of the member states according to the agreed aid policy."[43] The amounts of assistance the DAC members provided increased steadily over the years, from 36.6 billion dollars in 1960 to 127.5 billion dollars in 2010 (in 2010 dollars).[44] Within COMECON, the Commission for Technical Assistance (CTA) served to coordinate the provision of development assistance among the socialist countries.[45]

In the 1950s and well into the 1960s, foreign aid consisted mostly of bilateral assistance. It included foreign private investments and public aid, which was channeled from one government to another in the form of loans, grants, and materials.[46] The European colonial powers directed the largest share of their foreign aid to their overseas territories. France and Great Britain, between 1960 and 1966, spent 92 percent and 90 percent, respectively, of their aid on their (former) colonies.[47] Italy's foreign assistance budget of 1962 included large payments to Somalia and Libya, its former colonies.[48] Similarly, in 1961, the Netherlands gave 6.9 million dollars to Surinam and the Dutch Antilles and 26.7 million dollars to Dutch New Guinea, compared to 4.4 million dollars transferred to the United Nations and its development agencies. For a relatively small country like the Netherlands, technical assistance offered several advantages, among them the chance to "advertise Dutch science and Dutch business in the world," new job opportunities for Dutch expatriates returning from the colonies, the opening up of new export markets as imperial ones were lost or became harder to access, and an improved international standing.[49] Interestingly, while the Dutch budget for development assistance fell after decolonization, in France and Great Britain the level of financial aid transferred to the colonies remained the same or increased, pointing to different approaches to a country's relationship with its former colonies.[50] In 1957, the British government had wanted to phase out payments once the colonies gained independence, arguing that the "special responsibility" the United Kingdom had for the colonies would end in that moment.[51] In the following years, however, as a growing number of African colonies became independent, politicians in London realized that it might be better to continue providing development assistance to maintain their interests beyond decolonization.

Among the Western countries, the United States was by far the largest provider of bilateral foreign aid (both military and economic) in the 1950s. This was logical insofar as the United States was initially the only country after the war that had the resources available to deliver large-scale spending on development. Several US organizations were established over the course of the 1950s and 1960s to carry out foreign assistance programs. In 1951, the nexus between security interests and development policy became most visible when the Mutual Security Agency was set up to provide development aid. In 1953 it was replaced by the Foreign Operations Administration, not least because the recipients of US aid felt that the security interests of the United States should not be as prominent as the organization's original name suggested. However, in practice they continued to be highly influential in shaping American development aid policy.[52] One of the most prominent programs was the Food for Peace initiative, which was based on the Agricultural Trade Development and Assistance Act passed in 1954, also known as Public Law (PL) 480. According to the act, the United States could ship surplus commodities to strategically important countries, and non-governmental organizations could receive American agricultural stocks from the federal government and hand them out as part of their humanitarian efforts.[53] One of the goals driving PL 480 was to reduce American agricultural surpluses; another was to support geopolitically relevant countries in order to consolidate them in the Western sphere of influence.[54]

As the economic situation of the other industrial countries improved over the course of the 1950s, there was no reason from the American point of view why the United States should shoulder the largest part of the bill for international assistance. More generally, many American politicians challenged the provision of development aid, particularly to countries they suspected of having socialist leanings, and called for trade not aid, or at least for trade and aid.[55] The mood changed toward the end of the 1950s, when a majority came to argue that it was better to integrate countries into the capitalist world economy by providing them with loans, which could also be beneficial to American business interests. Consequently, American diplomats in the late 1950s began to push their Western counterparts to make more money available both for multilateral funds and on a bilateral level.[56]

Apart from Great Britain, the United States expected Japan, Italy, and the Federal Republic of Germany (FRG) to become more active in the field of development assistance. While these countries were not pleased about the pressure from Washington, they clearly had to follow suit, or at least show their willingness to do so. Italy increased aid contributions in the late 1950s, not least to overcome its reputation as a poor recipient of aid, to gain a better standing in the Western alliance, and to open the door to business opportunities in the Mediterranean and the Middle East. In 1960, Italy spent 303 million dollars on aid to Greece, Yugoslavia, Turkey, Egypt, Brazil, and Argentina. However, due to a grave economic crisis in the early 1960s the Italian payments did not reach the levels envisaged.[57] Japan's provision of development assistance was rooted in the reparations the country had to pay to thirteen Asian countries after the Second World War, which amounted to two billion dollars until 1977. The transfer of money was replicated in the field of aid, with so-called developing countries requesting support from Japan for specific projects. Japanese companies recognized the business opportunities inherent in the provision of loans and actively suggested projects to be funded by Tokyo. For that reason, Japan's official assistance in the 1950s and 1960s was predominantly bilateral in nature, and mostly focused on industrial and infrastructure projects.[58] Meanwhile, West Germany, which had built up a high trade surplus and large currency reserves over the course of the 1950s, increased official development aid contributions from 3.7 billion DM between 1950 and 1960 to 20.2 billion

DM between 1960 and 1970.[59] Apart from the political pressure from the United States, the decision to make development assistance a more prominent field of foreign policy was also in the interest of the three countries. It gave them a chance to present themselves as benevolent powers—a great advantage with regard to the fascist legacy they shared—and to try to influence political and economic developments in their respective regions of interest.

More generally, a growing number of countries in the Western realm began to realize the advantages of development assistance in the 1950s and 1960s. The Scandinavian countries, Switzerland, Canada, and Kuwait, among others, started to look for opportunities to become active in the field of development assistance.[60] They conducted bilateral aid projects but also paid into multilateral funds, especially those of the World Bank and the UN organizations, and contributed to international development consortia.[61] For example, Switzerland, following a request by the United Nations to commit resources to its technical assistance program, in 1949/1950 established a committee at the Swiss Federal Institute of Technology to consider possibilities of becoming active in development assistance. The choice fell on Nepal, not least because the Swiss experts involved felt that they had the skills needed in this mountainous setting.[62] Similar cases of donor countries searching for a feasible region or project abounded in the 1950s, when the development field was still in the making. In some instances, the rhetoric surrounding the search for a project was similar to older discussions about the alleged need to claim and secure a colonial territory before everything was controlled by other imperial powers.[63] Development assistance even in its early stages contained a distinct competitive element.

Domestic and strategic concerns played an important role in the decision of many countries to become active in development aid. For example, Norway started to provide development assistance in 1952, at a time when the population was still suffering from the effects of war and German occupation. Oslo's decision to finance a fisheries project in India was based on a number of factors: Norway's self-understanding as a social democratic country which prized egalitarian and humanitarian principles; the legacy of Norwegian missionary work in Africa and South Asia since the mid-nineteenth century; strategic concerns relating to the Cold War; and the raging debate about Norway's rearmament, from which the governing Labour Party tried to divert attention by engaging in foreign assistance. By contrast, economic interests did not play a decisive role in Norway's decision to engage in development aid. Although the country had long-standing trade relations with Latin America, the Middle East, and West Africa, its development focus was on entirely different regions.[64]

Many development actors argued that their work represented a particular national style that reflected the alleged characteristics of their home countries. For example, the Swedish International Development Authority

(SIDA) in the 1960s and 1970s argued that the Swedish approach to rural development was particularly successful. What SIDA's representatives described as the Swedish style was characterized by an emphasis "on the need to adapt agricultural knowledge to local settings" and a preference for technical solutions—a description that would have been equally applicable to many other approaches of different national background.[65] Furthermore, there were very few projects which did not share some aspects with projects conducted elsewhere and by other actors because development had been a genuinely transnational field of activity since its emergence in the early twentieth century. In fact, the approach SIDA practiced in a project in Ethiopia "built on strategies developed in Pakistan, on education provided in the United States, on experiences from Nigeria, on plant material from Kenya and Mexico, on European cattle, and so on."[66] Whether in practice the perceived national particularities translated into approaches that were notably different from others is difficult to determine. It seems that in many cases the emphasis on national styles was most important to the experts who planned a project and saw it as an opportunity to try out a new approach, or who tried to advertise their ideas to receive funding or political support from development organizations.

In planning and carrying out their development policies, the European colonial powers mostly drew on existing bodies. Only in the 1960s, when development assistance was becoming more established and more multilateral in composition did they set up new organizations dedicated to aid. For example, the Netherlands in 1964 established the National Advisory Council for Development Aid, whose first chair was economist Jan Tinbergen, a social democrat who advocated higher assistance levels and gave support to demands from the so-called developing countries for a new international economic order in later years. Meanwhile, the Dutch Ministry of Foreign Affairs in 1964 established a department of development aid and made Theo H. Bot (1911–1984), a former colonial official, its first minister.[67] Hence, two approaches to development aid co-existed in the Dutch national setting.

A similar tension can be observed among many of the newcomers to the field of development. For example, the West German Foreign Office started foreign aid activities in 1953. It tried to use development assistance to prevent countries in Asia and Africa from recognizing the German Democratic Republic (GDR), which it considered an illegitimate state.[68] In 1961, the Federal Ministry of Economic Cooperation (BMZ) was established, yet the Foreign Office was not willing to share its responsibilities and tried to marginalize the new ministry.[69] Against this backdrop, the BMZ had to work hard to establish itself as a relevant actor. Civil servants actively sought out projects and connections which were not controlled by the Foreign Office.[70] Similar institutional strategies could be observed in many other countries which discovered development assistance as a policy field in the postwar period. Development aid was not only about international relations but also about institutional competition, careers, and jobs.

Politically, the provision of development aid offered opportunities for cooperation between Western European countries. For example, in the early and mid-1950s French politicians and entrepreneurs worked together with their West German counterparts to lobby for public-private partnerships to develop Africa.[71] In doing so, they referred to the idea of Eurafrica, which reached back to the interwar period and was conceptualized as a historical connection between Europe and Africa. In practice, it served to legitimize economic interests in what were still colonial possessions or UN trusteeships of Belgium, France, the Netherlands, and Italy.[72] Apart from the strategic and business interests tied to it, the Eurafrica project, by promoting the establishment of joint institutional structures, served as a platform that contributed to the process of European economic integration.[73]

The European Economic Community (EEC) in the late 1950s and 1960s became a development actor in its own right. When the EEC was created through the Treaties of Rome in 1957, many advocates of colonial interests hoped that the new organization's contribution to development assistance could also serve economic and strategic goals abroad at a time when imperial and colonial ties were becoming looser or less reliable as a result of decolonization. European imperial powers in particular considered the Europeanization of development assistance useful to secure access to economic resources and, politically speaking, to keep a foot in the door of their (former) colonies.[74] France was the most outspoken in this regard. In the late 1950s, Paris lobbied the other European governments to support the Association of the Overseas Countries and Territories to the EEC. The Association was supposed to provide a framework for the former French colonies in Africa and to keep them aligned with France beyond their independence. Toward that goal, the Association would provide financial support and technical assistance to the former colonies, and Paris called on the members of the EEC to pay for these development activities. The Netherlands and West Germany strongly opposed the idea of using multilateral funds for what were in essence national interests, and they also feared that France would benefit unduly from this kind of financial support. To find a compromise, the EEC members in 1958 agreed to establish the European Development Fund (EDF), to which all the member states would contribute. The fund, which was modeled on FIDES, was renewed several times in the following decades.[75]

At the same time, the former African colonies and the EEC negotiated trade agreements that were supposed to replace the former colonial trade relations, which had guaranteed stable prices for the colonies' raw materials. After the end of colonialism, the new nations urgently needed to secure export markets and achieve good prices so that they could build up their economies. The Western European countries, despite their inclusive rhetoric, were not willing to give up their trade privileges, and there was much discussion among the EEC members about the particular terms of trade with the African countries. The first Yaoundé Convention was signed in 1963, a second one in 1969. In 1975 it was replaced by the Lomé Convention, which established the Atlantic-Caribbean-Pacific Partnership.[76] Furthermore, the European Investment Bank, which had come into existence as part of the Treaties of Rome, provided loans to the associated countries in Africa, much of it in the context of the European Development Fund.[77]

Within the EEC, Directorate General (DG) VIII was responsible for development assistance. In the first years of its existence, the majority of DG VIII officials were former French colonial administrators, and they shaped the work of the European Development Fund very much along their established practices.[78] DG VIII's funding included projects to improve the agricultural production of African countries, arguing that a more efficient agricultural sector was the precondition for industrialization. Generally, the majority of the DG VIII staff believed that it would be too time-consuming to wait for African governments to request assistance with industrialization projects, and therefore made direct suggestions for projects geared toward industrialization.[79] One of the reasons why the EEC members were so keen on promoting industrialization in African countries was their hope that European companies and economies would benefit from this process. For example, the French company Berliet established two construction plants for trucks and buses in Senegal in the early 1960s. Until then these kinds of vehicles had been imported from France and West Germany; producing them in Senegal was part of the import substitution industrialization strategy the country followed at the time. Berliet's contract with the Senegalese government specified that the company was entitled to a guaranteed share of 90 percent of the domestic demand and that comparable products from other countries would not be allowed into the country. This meant in essence that Berliet had a monopoly on public transportation vehicles and trucks in Senegal, which it probably would not have been able to secure under different political conditions.[80]

The case of Berliet was no exception. Many Western companies received highly valuable contracts from the industrializing countries and thus benefited from their economic and development needs.[81] Governments realized that the interest in industrialization could be beneficial to their own economies, and they tried to introduce technology that would put the emerging industrial powers on a path that would establish lasting business connections with companies. For example, Italy in 1963 granted Greece (which at the time was seen as a developing country) a six million dollar loan on the condition that the Greek government bought a television system from Italy.[82] The West German government decided to give financial support to India to train Indian students in mechanical and engineering skills. At the time Japan was becoming more active in development assistance to India, and Bonn feared that the Japanese might surpass the West Germans in terms of visibility. Among the projects financed by the FRG was a training center where Indian students were supposed to learn how to handle industrial machinery by working with tools imported from West Germany. The Bonn administration hoped that the use of German products would provide an entry point into the Indian market.[83]

Apart from the business opportunities they saw in aid, Western governments also considered it important to spur on the industrialization process of the so-called developing countries for strategic reasons related to the Cold War and decolonization. They believed that industrialization would help to ensure that postcolonial societies developed in a way that was closer to the capitalist than to the socialist model. If more and more people came into contact with what characterized industrial societies—factories, schools, cities, wage labor, technology, mass consumption—they would be better able to understand the advantages of the liberal model, many believed.[84] The idea of the factory as a school for modern political life was very prominent among social scientists at the time. Alex Inkeles (1920–2010), an American sociologist who conducted comparative studies on the effects of factory work on the self-understanding of individuals, argued: "The factory evidently is a school for citizenship. It may work less efficiently, or more slowly, than does education, but it is effective in transforming attitudes, values, and behavior so as to make men more participant citizens."[85] The idea that individuals would have to become active citizens was closely tied to assumptions about what constituted a modern nation, and was clearly based on Western norms of political organization.

On the other end of the ideological spectrum were Soviet experts and politicians who had understood the value of factory work to overcome social differences early on and had made the factory central to their efforts at building a socialist society.[86] In the context of development aid they tried to translate their experiences into approaches that could be of value to African, Asian, and Latin American societies. The Soviet Union began to engage in development assistance in the mid-1950s. Following de-Stalinization, development aid became a key tool in the struggle to "undermine the positions of Imperialism, to stimulate the national liberation movement, and to use all resources and possibilities for the formation of the most advantageous conditions for the maturation of the socialist revolution," as a report at the Soviet Communist Party's plenum in 1960 put it.[87] Those countries which already had socialist leanings were supported to strengthen their socialist parties or movements. In countries where there was no socialist foundation yet, economic and other types of assistance were supposed to create goodwill.[88]

Egypt under President Gamal Abdel Nasser (1918–1970) received Soviet economic assistance to build the Aswan Dam in 1954, and Syria and Iraq accepted support from the USSR in the second half of the 1950s. At the same time, Afghanistan, although not socialist at the time, was promised technical and economic support by the Soviet Union as early as 1954.[89] When the pace of decolonization grew quicker in the late 1950s and over the course of the 1960s, socialist aid went to many countries in the Middle

East, Asia, and Africa, either to support those countries' so-called national liberation movements or to help the newly independent countries to overcome their dependence on the former colonial powers.[90] For example, Ghana and Guinea, the first African colonies to become independent, received massive financial and economic assistance from the Soviet Union in the late 1950s and early 1960s. Both countries, due to their small size and their need for economic support from abroad, were seen as promising cases to advertise the non-capitalist development path.[91]

Some countries asked for Soviet aid directly, not necessarily waiting for an offer from Moscow. This was the case with Egypt, which requested assistance from the USSR in the context of the struggle over the Suez Canal. The Soviet Union recognized the chance to win Egypt over as an ally when Great Britain and France reacted with force to the nationalization of the canal, and was eager to follow Egypt's call for support.[92] Next to Egypt, Indonesia received the largest share of Soviet support until the mid-1960s. Indonesia and the USSR set up diplomatic relations in 1954, and soon afterward trade and political exchanges between the two countries began to expand. Indonesia received one-third of all Soviet development assistance until 1965. For the USSR, providing aid was a way to improve the quality of Soviet relations with Indonesia, which the United States, too, considered crucial in geostrategic terms. Moscow had an early Cold War success when the United States under President Dwight D. Eisenhower (1890–1969) in 1956 refused to grant Indonesia a loan President Sukarno (1901–1970) had asked for. Khrushchev then offered to loan 100 million dollars to Indonesia at a very low rate of interest. A second, even larger loan was granted in 1960, when Khrushchev visited Indonesia.[93]

In providing economic support, the Soviet Union drew on its own development experience and favored large-scale industrialization and infrastructure projects. Hydroelectric dams, the mechanization of agriculture, steel mills, and heavy industry figured most prominently in Soviet development aid in the 1950s and 1960s. The provision of money, material, and expertise was linked to the expectation that the recipient countries would set up a centralized type of economy, with the state as the decisive force in economic planning.[94] In contrast to Western governments and international organizations like the World Bank, the USSR and the Eastern European countries did not tie their support to "explicit performance conditions" but provided aid based on the principle of political proximity and loyalty.[95] Also, the socialist countries were in favor of loans instead of grants. Loans differed from grants in that they had to be repaid, and the use of loans seemed to prove that the socialist countries considered the recipients as equals, not as less-developed inferiors who depended on the goodwill of donors. The emphasis on equality and mutual advantage was important to the USSR, whose leaders wanted to avoid the image of the exploitative imperialist power and stressed the value of cooperation as a genuinely socialist and internationalist project.[96]

It needs to be stressed that, for the Soviet Union, whose economy had in large part been destroyed during the war by the Germans, for a long time it was more difficult to provide the kind of assistance the Western countries could offer relatively easily. This does not mean, however, that Soviet assistance was in any way morally superior to Western aid. The USSR, like all donors, had its very particular reasons for giving financial and other support to so-called developing countries, and it was neither more nor less strategic in doing so. The fact that the USSR did not dictate to the recipients what to do with its loans meant that in practice many of the governments and groups used Soviet money to establish their armies and to buy weapons. For example, nearly 90 percent of Soviet aid to Indonesia was invested in the build-up of the military.[97] Secondly, and relatedly, Czechoslovakia and the Soviet Union gave military aid to anti-colonial and anti-Western groups and movements and intervened in situations that seemed promising from a Cold War point of view.[98] The Congo Crisis of 1960 was one of the most dramatic expressions of this kind of intervention in the name of supporting an anti-imperialist movement.[99]

The crisis began in the summer of 1960 when democratically elected President Patrice Lumumba (1925–1961) declared Congo's independence from its former colonial power, Belgium. A civil war-like situation broke out when the Katanga region, which was rich in strategic minerals, under the leadership of Moïse Tshombe (1919–1969) tried to secede from the Republic of Congo. Tshombe and his supporters disapproved of the centralized nation state Lumumba wanted to create and argued in favor of a regional federation of states organized on the basis of language, religion, and culture.[100] Belgium sent paramilitary troops to protect the Belgian population and the economic interests of Belgian enterprises in Congo. This was a clear violation of international law, and the United Nations sent a peacekeeping mission to Congo. The mission had the task to restore law and order, to prevent other nations from being drawn into the conflict, to build up the country's economy, and to prevent a breaking-apart of the Congolese nation state. However, the mission carried only a defensive mandate and struggled to stabilize the situation. Lumumba became increasingly suspicious vis-à-vis the United Nations and feared that the organization was not on his side. Disillusioned with the UN, he asked Moscow to support his cause, to which the USSR responded by sending military advisers and material to Congo. The reason for the Soviet leadership to intervene in this way was tied to its effort to challenge the United Nations' set-up, which, they argued, unduly privileged Western interests. In the end, the Soviet attempt to use the crisis to achieve an organizational reform of the UN did not come to fruition.[101] More generally, the case of the Congo crisis shows that it was difficult for the Soviet Union to control the effects of its military support and to ensure that the groups and individuals receiving aid stayed loyal and followed Moscow's expectations.[102]

Another characteristic of socialist assistance in the 1950s and 1960s were bilateral trade agreements under which the USSR and Eastern European countries delivered goods to so-called developing countries in exchange for industrial raw materials, fuels, and crops, and paid them a guaranteed price for their products.[103] The advantage for the African and Asian countries was that the agreements were long-term ones based on non-convertible currencies, with prices above world-market levels, and that they were able to reduce their dependence on the companies of the former colonial powers and on the United States. The advantage for the Eastern European countries was that they received goods otherwise difficult or very expensive to procure.[104]

The training of skilled workers, engineers, and executive personnel was a field into which the Soviet Union began to invest in the early 1960s. Soviet politicians were acutely aware of the value of education as a tool to promote among the elites of the new nations a political perspective in line with socialist and Soviet interests, and, more generally, goodwill toward the USSR. Hence, they offered education and training to students and professionals from Asian, Arab, Latin American, and African countries. They also set up research institutes and colleges in so-called developing countries, providing infrastructure as well as teachers to run courses and train students. In the early years of Soviet development activities, finding qualified personnel to be sent to the newly established institutes abroad was a challenge. For example, the Indian Institute of Technology (IIT) in Bombay received only five instead of the promised fifteen Soviet professors, which resulted in a Western majority among the IIT's faculty.[105] The 1960 establishment of the Peoples' Friendship University in Moscow (which was named "Patrice Lumumba" following Lumumba's assassination one year later) was the most visible sign of the Soviet interest in providing technical assistance and know-how to students from countries considered strategically and politically relevant to the socialist bloc. Between 1960 and 1991, about 43,500 students from sub-Saharan African went to study in the Soviet Union alone; many more studied in other socialist countries.[106] The fact that research and training were accompanied by political indoctrination sometimes led to conflicts between students and universities as well as between the national governments of the countries sending their students to study abroad.[107] However, the quality of the training was high, and many participants in these Soviet-sponsored courses appreciated their newly gained knowledge and effectively used it in their home countries—though not necessarily solely in the interest of national development or building socialism but also to advance their individual careers.[108]

Relations between recipients and providers of aid

The overview of the different providers of foreign assistance and their agendas tied to development suggests that there were very few, if any, instances in which aid was not connected to larger political, economic, ideological, or strategic positions. Cold War concerns figured prominently, as did business interests and, in the case of the European countries, the effort to use development assistance to maintain influence in their former overseas territories. However, looking at development aid policies from the point of view of the providers can result in a rather one-sided perspective that sheds much more light on strategies and intentions than on the behavior of the recipients and the ways in which it supported or challenged the assumptions of the providers of aid.

For example, India, which claimed a neutral status in the Cold War, in the 1950s received food aid both from the Soviet Union and from the United States. Initially the Indian government and press praised Soviet food aid for being generous and philanthropic, while it criticized American food aid for being imperialistic and capitalistic. Yet in the mid-1950s the tide turned. A growing number of Indians began to grow weary of Moscow's attempts to use food aid to spread fake news about food crises created by capitalist greed to gain the support of the Indian population. Of course, Americans, too, used food aid for propagandistic purposes and to undermine Soviet promises, but the amounts of assistance the United States offered were larger and more steadily available, and Indian public support for socialism decreased over the years. More and more Indians questioned whether the Soviet and Chinese efforts to increase agricultural productivity with the help of collectivization, mechanization, and large-scale irrigation projects were suited to their country. By the early 1960s, under the pressure of continuous food shortages and a growing concern about population growth, Indian politicians with a less favorable attitude toward socialism than Nehru began to call for closer cooperation with the United States in order to benefit from its technological possibilities and development assistance, thereby turning toward the capitalist model of agricultural development.[109]

Where Moscow did have an advantage, though, was in its experience with large-scale industrialization projects, especially with the construction of steel works. Again, India was at the forefront of the Cold War competition for the prestige associated with shiny industrial complexes. Upon Nehru's visit to Moscow in 1955, the USSR promised to support India's industrialization effort by building a steel and iron works in Bhilai in central India. Construction began soon afterward, and the first blast furnace was opened in February 1959—just a few days after the steel works in Rourkela, in the state of Orissa, not far from Bhilai, had started running, which had been built by a consortium of West German companies. In contrast to the steel mill in Bhilai, which was financed and staffed by the Soviet Union, the Indian government had to pay the West German companies in full, with the FRG granting a series of credits to New Delhi. Hence, while Rourkela mirrored the capitalist approach to industrialization, the Indian communist press presented Bhilai as an act of Soviet solidarity with India and lauded the willingness of Soviet engineers and technicians to work side by side with Indian workers—in contrast to Rourkela, where the arrogant attitude of many of the West German engineers involved seemed to confirm stereotypes about Western neo-colonialists.[110] The image of Soviet generosity was further strengthened when, in the late 1950s, India asked the United States for support to build a third steel works, Bokaro. Congress debated the issue for so long that finally New Delhi withdrew the request, a situation the Soviet leadership used by offering to cover the costs of Bokaro. Even if the Indians might have preferred to receive US technical aid, the American hesitation had given the USSR a chance to score a goal in the Cold War game of development aid, and India's politicians believed that they could not afford to wait for another outcome if they wanted to realize their Five-Year Plan.[111]

Not all development assistance projects carried out by one of the superpowers or their allies in the context of the Cold War were complemented by a project from the other side. For example, the Alliance for Progress, which was initiated by the United States in 1961, did not have a socialist equivalent. This program was an attempt on the part of the Kennedy administration to fight communist tendencies in Latin America after the Cuban revolution of 1959 by investing twenty billion dollars into the Latin American economies over a period of ten years, with the United States Agency for International Development (USAID) responsible for coordinating the activities of the different organizations involved. The Alliance for Progress was strongly inspired by modernization theory with its assumption that capital was the most important element in propelling economic growth.[112] Educational initiatives, housing and infrastructure projects, land reforms, and the liberalization of markets were expected to create the basis on which capitalist, democratic structures would take root.[113]

Initially, the growth rates of some of the Latin American countries receiving Alliance funds did rise, yet the tendency did not continue as expected. Furthermore, many of the governments accepted the financial support from the United States but did not follow the American demands to redistribute land and liberalize their markets.[114] Their own political goals did not match those of the United States, and they used the resources in ways very different from those envisioned by the Americans. For example, in Brazil the leftist government headed by João Goulart (1918–1976) aimed at improving the situation of workers and peasants through measures deemed socialist by the United States. For that reason, the Americans placed restrictions on the funds they provided to Brazil, hoping that they would be able to steer its political development in a more moderate direction. Later on they stopped the payments entirely because they believed that Goulart was becoming too radical. This American interference strengthened the Brazilian conservative opposition, and in 1964 the military conducted a coup against Goulart which was backed by the US government.[115] The goal of transforming seemingly traditional societies into liberal democracies with the help of development projects proved difficult to realize. In practice, US representatives often found it easier to work with authoritarian and military regimes, which "were considered to possess qualities no other institution in newly independent countries had. They seemed better organized, commanded technical know-how, and supplied a variety of specialists. And they were seen as the best available bulwarks against communism."[116] The strong social engineering component inherent in modernization thinking lent itself readily to top-down practices controlled by social elites.

Cases like the Alliance for Progress show that, although there was stark inequality in terms of economic and political power between the North and the South, the so-called developing countries were not entirely helpless and dependent on their donors but had at least some leverage in demanding, accepting, or rejecting aid. The precise degree of leverage varied, depending on a variety of factors particular to each country. For that reason it was difficult for the providers of aid to know how their offers would be treated and which kinds of effects they might have. Consequently, using development assistance as a political tool created room for maneuver to third parties rather than binding the recipient and the provider closer together.[117]

Conclusion

In December 1961, the United Nations Organization declared the 1960s retroactively as the Development Decade, with the goal of securing 5 percent growth per annum over the course of the decade.[118] The declaration was the rhetorical high point of the use of foreign aid as an instrument to achieve economic growth in the context of decolonization and the Cold War. Those years were also the moment in which the danger of the Cold War escalating was highest, with the Cuba Crisis of 1962 as the most dramatic moment. Against this background, politicians were eager to use all instruments at their disposal to maintain at least some control over the increasingly complicated international situation. It was in this context that foreign assistance gained immense popularity as a highly flexible tool to influence the development process of so-called Third World countries.

Yet as much as the use of aid was associated with the political opportunities and crises of the time, we should not forget that foreign assistance was more than a political tool employed by former imperial powers, new superpowers, or small nations. Foreign aid had evolved as an approach to address global and regional inequalities out of the global situation produced by the Second World War and the new international structures emerging from it. What representatives from the industrial countries understood as the complexities of decolonization and the Cold War in the early 1960s had not existed as such in the late 1940s. Similarly, Western European governments looked at development assistance much more as a tool to maintain influence in former colonial regions or to promote business interests than as a Cold War tool the way the Soviet Union and the United States did. Development aid effectively contributed to the internationalization of politics. As multilateral assistance gained in scope, international organizations claimed an increasingly influential position in global governance issues, and the foreign policy interests of different nation states became increasingly entangled and institutionalized in new bodies like the Development Assistance Committee and the multilateral development consortia.

From the point of view of the so-called developing countries, the growing popularity of development aid in the international arena presented opportunities as well as dangers. The opportunities were obvious: immense technical and financial resources were becoming available through international assistance, allowing the countries suffering from low levels of productivity and income to envision ambitious development projects. Due to the Cold War, the ratio between demand and supply was in favor of the potential recipients of aid, and many of them proved to be skilled at playing the two sides against each other in securing access to the resources they needed. Yet the aid game carried risks because the geopolitical constellations that characterized the Cold War could change rapidly. Also, the strategic use of assistance could create new dependencies, which the former colonies had wanted to discard urgently but often found themselves caught in again.

CHAPTER SIX

Development Approaches and Practices in the Postwar Period

As mentioned before, many of the so-called developing countries aspired to industrialize as quickly as possible, and many development grants and loans were dedicated to supporting this process. However, because most of their economies were predominantly rural in character and would remain so until the end of the twentieth century, projects concerned with rural and agricultural development, health and education affected a much larger number of individuals and probably had more direct effect on the majority of the population. For that reason, this chapter focuses on those areas which, in the postwar decades, were considered decisive for laying the basis for future development: community development, education, agricultural development, and public health and birth control.

Community development

The label most commonly used for a variety of development projects from the interwar period to the mid-1960s was community development. This term was applied so broadly and by so many actors that it is difficult to define. Generally speaking, community development was concerned less with macroeconomic development interventions than with improving the immediate living conditions of the population, especially of the very poor living in rural regions and, to a lesser degree, in cities. Community development most often included primary education, especially literacy training, sanitation, health and hygiene measures, support for handicrafts and small-scale industries, road-building, and agricultural improvement efforts. In many cases the concept of self-help was central to community development projects: the idea that instead of installing state-run apparatuses to conduct development the people on the ground should take care of their own interests, supported by a few extension officers or experts working with them.[1] In democratic settings, the emphasis on self-help went hand in hand with an attempt to strengthen participatory and grassroots mechanisms in societies that were considered traditional and therefore allegedly skeptical toward change. Grassroots practices were supposed to activate individuals and allow them to embrace new technologies and practices. Hence, community development projects were also geared toward creating a populace that took matters into its own hands. In democratic and non-democratic settings alike, the fact that small-scale, grassroots programs cost much less than centrally organized projects with high capital demands was another reason for the popularity of the community development approach.[2]

The vagueness of the term community development was one of the reasons why it was attractive to many different political actors. European colonial powers drew on community development approaches in the interwar and postwar periods to provide the basis for more efficient agricultural production and to improve their relations with the colonial populations. In their eyes, literacy training, primary schools, and hygiene campaigns offered a bridge to social groups that were suspicious of contacts with colonial officials but considered crucial to the success of colonial policies. For example, the British in the early 1950s conducted a literacy campaign in North Pare, Tanganyika, which initially met with a lot of resistance from the local population. After a while, however, women and girls began to attend literacy classes, and the British officer in charge argued that having gained their trust gave the colonial administration access to the community to conduct an anti-erosion campaign in the region. In other words, while literacy was something the population wanted, the educational project served as an opportunity for the colonial power to promote its own economic and ecological interests.[3]

Community development was also the method of choice of many of the former colonies' political leaders and development advocates. In a context characterized by a scarcity of economic resources, the need for rapid socioeconomic improvement, the rejection of colonial categories, and the attempt to build a nation, community development appeared to be the natural choice. It promised to integrate different parts of the population by helping them to gain an understanding of what it meant to belong to a nation and to enjoy the possibility of shaping one's own life and environment instead of being ruled by force. It offered a major labor resource by engaging the population in basic infrastructure works in their own localities. Furthermore, it gave the new governments the chance to prove that they took their responsibilities seriously and that they deserved the trust and support of their country's inhabitants. But community development was not a purely political or social instrument—it was primarily supposed to improve the economic situation of the new nations.

The Comilla Project in Pakistan became one of the most famous and most widely studied community development projects of this kind. Akhtar Hameed Khan (1914–1999), a Pakistani social scientist, was its initiator. A civil servant by training, Khan became interested in rural problems and turned to grassroots approaches to improve the living conditions of the rural population. In the late 1950s he spent time in the United States to study American rural development approaches. In 1959, with support from the government of Pakistan, he founded the Pakistan Academy for Rural Development in Comilla, East Pakistan (today's Bangladesh). The Academy was supposed to train the personnel needed to promote the kind of bottom-up development approaches Khan favored, with an emphasis on cooperatives as instruments of self-help and participation, and based on an understanding of the region as the central unit of action.[4] The regional dimension was particularly important to the Comilla project because of its location in East Pakistan, which was heavily affected by the consequences of the division of former British India in 1947. In the context of the violent partition, most of the Hindus living in the region had fled to what became India, while the Muslim population largely stayed in newly established Pakistan and was joined by Muslim refugees from India. The partition also had grave economic effects on East Pakistan. Calcutta had been the most important trading center for the rural region, yet as the city became part of India the opportunities for farmers from East Pakistan to sell their produce diminished. Under these circumstances, the socioeconomic situation was deteriorating rapidly, and the Pakistani government was under intense pressure to improve the condition of the population in the border region.[5]

Whereas the establishment of agricultural and other types of cooperatives were the focus of attention in the early years of the Comilla project, other development-related elements were introduced later on. For one, the establishment of schools was considered important to increase the population's educational levels, which would allow peasants and laborers to find better jobs in the countryside instead of migrating to the cities. A "ruralistic bias" was deeply ingrained in Khan's thinking and mirrored in the design of the Comilla project.[6] Secondly, the project advocated sanitation and public health measures as well as family planning, based on the understanding that the large number of children many of the couples in the region had presented an economic challenge for the families and a health burden for the mothers. Notably, Khan, instead of inviting external experts to tell the villagers about the advantages of sanitation and birth control, decided to engage local musicians and singers who "would compose songs in the local style and sing them publicly before audiences in the bazaars."[7] The advantage of this approach was that it was relatively cheap and easy to organize, and that many individuals were more willing to engage in this kind of communication than to listen to an expert from outside their community.

The US government, several American universities, and the American Ford Foundation supported the Comilla project with money and advice. The reason why Americans were so eager to promote community development measures like the ones practiced in Comilla had to do with domestic experiences. Many US advocates of community development approaches in the so-called Third World before 1945 had been active in efforts to improve the socioeconomic conditions in remote regions like the Appalachians and the American South. The New Deal programs of the 1930s had provided them with the opportunity to try out their ideas as part of publicly funded programs.[8] Their work received academic backing from new approaches in the behavioral sciences, which gained prominence in the 1930s and 1940s. In part driven by the emergence of authoritarian regimes, many sociologists, psychologists, political scientists, and educational scientists at the time conducted research into the possibilities of affecting individual and collective behavior patterns and planting democratic practices in social groups. Community development reflected this perspective on engineering society through expert intervention and training.[9] After the Second World War many development advocates drew on these concepts in turning toward apparently underdeveloped regions outside the United States, which they "imagined as a vast sea of peasant villages" in need of reform and improvement.[10] Based on the assumption that the problems of village life and the rural world were more or less the same everywhere, most community development programs of the postwar years conducted by American organizations or with US participation shared many traits and approaches, regardless of the specific location they were conducted in.

While community development before 1945 had been a field dominated by non-governmental and individual actors, in the postwar period it became a key element of official development programs. By the early 1960s, the United States government spent about fifty million dollars on projects in thirty countries across the globe.[11] President John F. Kennedy (1917–1963), in his inaugural address in 1961, had made a strong case for the ability to overcome poverty: "Man holds in his mortal hands the power to abolish all forms of human poverty."[12] The creation of the Peace Corps, which was supposed to mobilize young Americans to help poor communities in so-called developing countries, was one expression of this belief. Yet why focus on poverty abroad when poverty levels at home were very high, too? Against this background, Kennedy's successor, Lyndon B. Johnson, tried to connect community development programs abroad with the War on Poverty in the United States.[13] In 1964, the Peace Corps was replicated on the domestic level in the form of Volunteers in Service to America (VISTA).[14] The volunteers were sent to rural regions in the United States and to particularly poor parts of American cities.[15] Community development was the strategy of choice both of the Peace Corps and of VISTA. As Sargent Shriver (1915–2011), the director of the two programs, put it: "Community development in Ecuador is, philosophically and substantially, no different than doing the same thing in some West Virginia hollow."[16] Shriver did not mean to suggest that Ecuador and West Virginia were entirely the same, but he did recognize so many mental and behavioral similarities among their inhabitants that he considered them structurally of the same kind.[17] It was this understanding of the universality of poverty that explains, in part, the immense popularity of community development approaches in the United States at the time, and the enthusiasm for conducting and supporting similar programs across the globe.

Another factor responsible for the American investment in community approaches as part of development initiatives was that they fit very well into a specific Cold War understanding of the geopolitical risks and potential of rural regions.[18] In the eyes of Western anti-communists, the lesson from the Russian Revolution was that the concerns and interests of peasants needed to be taken much more seriously if one wanted to prevent them from turning to the proponents of socialism. Notably, liberal and anti-communist commentators implicitly accepted the Marxist notion that exploitation was a key feature of feudal society that produced political conflict. To solve this problem in a non-socialist way, they advocated development measures that would improve the situation of the peasants and rural inhabitants. Land reforms were considered urgent in this regard.

One of the most outspoken proponents of land reform initiatives was Wolf Ladejinsky (1899–1975), who had grown up in Russia and whose family had fled the Bolsheviks.[19] In the United States Ladejinsky studied agrarian economics and joined the US Department of Agriculture. After the war he served as an adviser to the American occupation regime in Japan, where he was responsible for planning a land reform—a project the United States considered essential to democratizing Japanese society and creating an economic system that was in line with American ideas about individualism, entrepreneurship, and economic growth. Ladejinsky's thinking about land reform was clearly informed by the Russian experience. In 1950, he wrote: "The Communists would never have obtained power in Russia had they not successfully exploited the peasants longing for the landlords' acres." From this he concluded: "The only way to thwart Communist designs on Asia is to preclude such revolutionary outbursts through timely reforms, peacefully, before the peasants take the law into their own hands and set the countryside ablaze."[20] While decidedly anti-communist, Ladejinsky did not consider the peasants as the source of the problem per se. He embraced a distinctly pro-peasant view, arguing that peasants needed state support to improve their living conditions and to produce higher yields, and that this was in the interest of the overall socioeconomic and political situation.

While in Japan and South Korea the US occupation regimes enforced redistributive land reforms, in other countries and different political contexts it was much more difficult to overcome the vested interests of the upper classes whose property and privileges were under attack. For example, in Italy's Mezzogiorno, which, as has been mentioned, served as a reference point for many international development advocates, the Italian Communists under the leadership of Fausto Gullo (1887–1974) in 1944 called for an extensive land reform. They wanted to improve the situation of the peasants by giving them better contracts, allowing them to cultivate unused or underused land belonging to estate owners, and forbidding middlemen.[21] The peasants made their demands heard at the local and regional levels, and they succeeded in establishing more than a thousand cooperatives that took over estate land. Yet the majority of their requests were rejected by the local authorities, who were staffed by representatives of the landed elites. In 1946 Gullo was replaced by a conservative politician who opted for a much less radical approach to tackling the agrarian question.[22] The Christian Democratic government under Alcide de Gasperi (1881–1954) in 1950 passed a set of laws that aimed at modernizing social structures and production patterns in the countryside while maintaining existing property relations. The plan was to give land to landless laborers and peasants, to provide them with credits, training, irrigation, and housing, and to set up cooperatives to increase efficiency and income. The state would compensate landowners for the land they gave up.[23] Yet the amount of land that changed hands was much smaller than anticipated, its quality was very low, and land prices increased significantly. In the long term, the local elites benefited more than the peasants and laborers, and the number of rural landless laborers increased dramatically. Migration to the industrial centers in the northern parts of Italy did not provide a solution to this problem.[24]

In independent India, too, the government initially called for land reform but failed because the large-scale landowners, unwilling to share their wealth and privileges across caste differences, refused to cooperate. Under pressure to maintain electoral support, the Nehru government accepted that a redistributive land reform was difficult to realize in a democratic setting and gave up on its plan. As an ersatz, Nehru promoted the establishment of the country-wide Community Development Programme, which drew on Indian and international experiences from the interwar period and connected rhetorically to the Gandhian legacy.[25] Although community development received official political support from the central government of India and was granted ministerial status during the 1950s, it did not solve the core problem of lack of access to land and the unequal distribution of resources. Dire inequality remained at the heart of the rural development challenge in India as well as in many other countries and regions.[26] Community development promised to reduce this inequality at least on a basic level by giving the inhabitants of rural regions the skills and knowledge needed to improve their living situation.

Community development approaches experienced their highest popularity during the 1950s and into the early 1960s, not only in the newly independent countries but also among international organizations. The United Nations Organizations and many of their sub-organizations and non-governmental partners financed and carried out community development projects.[27] Yet as food shortages and famines multiplied in many regions over the course of the 1960s, and as international concern with population growth intensified, the critical voices grew louder.[28] Many began to argue that community development was not addressing the pressing problem of the food-population nexus effectively, and that the only solution was the systematic use of newly available kinds of technology to increase agricultural production. Hence, in the 1960s, agricultural intensification measures began to receive more attention from the Western international development community.

Agricultural development

The idea that agricultural practices had to be improved was not new in the 1960s, of course; the situation of agriculture and food production had concerned experts and politicians for a long time. Yet the call to modernize agriculture as part of an international development effort was relatively new. Development economist and Nobel Prize winner W. Arthur Lewis, who would later serve as economic adviser to newly independent Ghana, was one of the most prominent scholars to advocate the modernization of agriculture.[29] Lewis had grown up on the island of St. Lucia, which at the time was part of the British West Indies, and possessed intimate insight into the nature of everyday colonialism. The first black professor to be hired at a British university, he served as an economic expert on the Colonial Economic Advisory Committee for several years during the war. Already in 1944 he argued that the colonies should not be limited to agricultural production, and that the colonial administration should help them to industrialize. To do so, it was necessary to increase the productivity of agriculture. Only if the practice of dividing land into ever smaller plots, the ineffective agricultural practices, the lack of credits, and the inefficient marketing structures were overcome could the colonies produce the amount of food needed to feed an industrial workforce.[30] Lewis also advocated the introduction of development services in the fields of health, education, hygiene, and education, arguing that they were required to allow for economic growth.[31]

The Colonial Office in London did not agree with these positions and argued that industrialization was neither in the interest of the colonies nor of the empire.[32] Lewis resigned from his position on the committee in protest. In the following years he elaborated his argument for the need to modernize agriculture and to use its yields to accelerate the industrialization process. In his view, the colonies' advantage was that they had a large pool of laborers who were either unemployed or underemployed, and those labor resources should be channeled into industrialization. This was the key message of his 1954 article "Economic Development with Unlimited Supply of Labour," in which he argued that so-called developing countries had two economic sectors, with the agricultural one being the larger but less efficient one that could be used as a "feeder" for the industrial sector.[33] Lewis called for state-directed interventions to encourage the rural population to migrate to the urban centers, where they would become employed in industry, while agriculture would be mechanized and therefore need a much smaller workforce.[34]

The underlying assumption that agriculture was a less developed and less important part of the economy was challenged in the 1960s. Several scholars made a case for taking agriculture seriously instead of dismissing it as traditional.[35] In 1961 Bruce E. Johnston and John W. Mellor published an article on "The Role of Agriculture in Economic Development" in which they emphasized the economic and development potential of agriculture.[36] Three years later, William H. Nicholls followed with a chapter on the place of agriculture in economic development which highlighted the relevance of agriculture to overall economic development.[37] In 1964, too, the book *Transforming Traditional Agriculture* by Theodore W. Schultz appeared. The economist challenged the widespread assumption that peasants were passive, irrational, and generally opposed to change. In his view, the reason for low productivity rates was that peasants lacked access to technology and capital, which was the precondition for successful entrepreneurship.[38] Therefore, peasants needed more systematic support, Schultz demanded, and argued that education played a crucial role in this context.[39]

Generally, more intensive agricultural practices were seen as decisive to increasing yields in such a way that they resulted in a meaningful surplus. Some agricultural experts believed that partial or full mechanization was the best way of achieving this goal. For example, French colonial planners and agricultural engineers in the postwar years called for the systematic introduction of tractors to increase the efficiency of African agriculture and to open up new land to cultivation.[40] Others, however, warned of the socioeconomic consequences of mechanization, arguing that it would take away employment opportunities and result in large-scale migration to the cities because manual labor would no longer be a source of sufficient income. However, in the long term at least a degree of mechanization was considered inevitable if the subsistence economy of rural regions was to be overcome. For example, Norway in the 1950s and 1960s initiated and financed a project to modernize the fishing industry of southern India, including efforts to introduce mechanized boats that would allow for larger catches and the industrial processing of fish. The difficulties faced by Norwegian fisheries experts in Kerala were numerous, not least because the "recipient fishermen had not asked to participate in this experiment" and were reluctant to risk their small but steady income by investing in new technologies. Their reluctance proved to be well-founded as the introduction of the mechanized boats created all kinds of logistical problems, from an oversupply of fish that the local market could not absorb to navigational difficulties with larger crew sizes and landing beaches.[41]

A different type of technology many agricultural economists and politicians had high hopes for was chemical fertilizer. Chemical fertilizers, which had been in use in the industrialized countries since the early twentieth century, promised to multiply yields in a very short time but were very expensive, especially for countries that had to import them from abroad. For that reason, the provision of fertilizers became part of international development efforts. In 1959 the Food and Agriculture Organization, under its General Secretary Binay Ranjan Sen (1898–1993), sent a team to Asia and the Middle East to collect information on the potential and needs of agriculture in those regions. The results of the survey informed the meetings of FAO with representatives of international fertilizer companies in 1959 and 1960. The members of the newly established Fertilizer Industry Advisory Board were asked to provide expertise and to donate some of their fertilizer directly to the countries in question. In 1961, Sen incorporated the fertilizer project into FAO's Freedom from Hunger campaign, thereby granting fertilizer (and the fertilizer industry) a key position in the organization's strategic efforts to overcome food shortages.[42]

Sen had been a relief commissioner during the Bengal famine, and it seems likely that his concern with food stability was influenced by that experience. In the context of the Freedom from Hunger campaign, which aimed at conducting rural and agricultural development programs in order to increase production, he worked to intensify FAO's cooperation with non-governmental organizations and to improve the organization's public image so as to gather support for the campaign. However, the United States strictly opposed the campaign because American producers were eager to continue selling their agricultural surplus to so-called developing countries as part of food aid programs. Under the Kennedy administration, resistance to FAO's approach decreased, and the World Food Programme was established by FAO and the UN with US support in 1961. Yet national economic and strategic interests tied to food aid continued to be influential, and FAO's institutional position remained relatively weak.[43] Against this background, cooperating with private companies was one possibility for circumventing those actors whose interests were detrimental to FAO's.

In 1966, Sen advocated the establishment of the Food Production Resources Program, which was to provide the so-called developing countries with chemical fertilizers, pesticides, and insecticides annually worth 500 million dollars. FAO, which suffered from a continuously small budget, was supposed to pay fifty million dollars of that amount, and the Western governments would contribute the rest. When the program was set up, its name differed from Sen's original proposal: it was called Industry Cooperative Program, signaling the demand of the companies involved to have a larger say in how the program was run.[44] What this meant for FAO is difficult to determine. Certainly, the companies did not limit their activities to projects conducted by the organization but went to look for business opportunities independently. For example, the Swiss chemical company CIBA in the late 1960s was involved in a large-scale spraying program in Indonesia to eradicate a type of insect that harmed rice. The program, which also involved the distribution of chemical fertilizers, was conducted in direct cooperation with the Suharto government, which at the time was interested in rapidly increasing yields to overcome an acute food shortage. CIBA regarded this situation as an opportunity to showcase its technological products and to open up new markets. FAO seems not have been involved in this undertaking.[45]

From the point of view of governments and organizations, identifying the need for intensive agriculture was not sufficient. The next step was to create demand for chemical fertilizers among peasants and farmers who had not used this input before. Consequently, money was made available to advertise chemical fertilizers by handing it out to peasants for free or for prices below market-price, hoping that they would recognize its benefits and then start buying it on their own. Agricultural policy-makers were aware that in many cases peasants lacked the money to purchase expensive technological inputs like chemical fertilizers, so they advocated making cheap credit available to peasants on a local and regional basis. Several development banks contributed funds for credit facilities to be set up to lend money to rural populations.[46]

Furthermore, the so-called developing countries were eager to build fertilizer plants in order to substitute expensive imports from abroad. This was a step which in many cases involved granting contracts to European, American, Canadian, or other companies that sold the technology and machinery necessary to construct the plants in the first place. For example, the American company Amoco India, a subsidiary of the American International Oil Company, in 1965 went to great lengths to secure a contract from the government of India to build a chemical fertilizer factory in Madras. The total cost including credit and spare parts was estimated at 67 million dollars. To pay for the costs, USAID was willing to provide a loan to the government of India. However, the agency demanded that a private company, not the Indian government, carry out the distribution of the fertilizer produced in Madras. Also, the American negotiators insisted that no additional fertilizer plants be built in the region, and that imports of fertilizer would be stopped at times when the plant in Madras was not producing at full speed. In sum, the American investment depended on conditions that were supposed to guarantee a profit, while the Indian side tried to limit foreign intervention as much as possible.[47]

The trust in agricultural and chemical technologies to solve problems of production increased over the course of the 1960s. Instead of waiting for long-term approaches to yield the necessary increases in food production, the systematic application of modern technology was supposed to overcome food shortages and allow countries to export grain. This conceptual shift was reflected in FAO leadership: when Addeke Hendrik Boerma (1912–1992), an agronomist by training, replaced Sen in 1968 as Secretary General, the effort to support small-scale farmers was replaced by a focus on the Green Revolution.[48] This was the attempt to use a package of scientifically designed technologies to allow for more intensive agricultural production.

Specifically, it involved high-yielding varieties bred to resist plant diseases and to respond to chemical fertilizers, pesticides, and insecticides, and it was based on the assumption that modern agriculture would have to be fully mechanized.

Most of the research on which the Green Revolution technology rested was funded by private companies and by non-governmental organizations, particularly by the Rockefeller Foundation. The most famous scientist working for the foundation was agronomist and plant pathologist Norman Borlaug (1914–2009), who would later be awarded the Nobel Peace Prize for his research on high-yielding varieties of grain.[49] In the 1940s and early 1950s, the Rockefeller Foundation had been active in efforts to mechanize Mexican agriculture and introduce new, more resistant wheat and maize varieties to Mexico, Chile, and Colombia. Rice entered the discussion in the mid-1950s, when foundation representatives concerned themselves with the food and agricultural situation in Asia. They found that rice was "the major food for those parts of the world which are underprivileged, and where the race between food and population is so grim that starvation is a constant threat and a not infrequent reality." Consequently, they argued that systematic research was necessary to better understand the possibilities and risks involved in rice growing—an undertaking that would be "*of direct benefit to millions of persons.*"[50] In their view, the best way to approach the problem was to establish an international institute where all of the relevant knowledge would be centralized, and to disseminate the findings and solutions from there to different parts of Asia.

In 1960, the International Rice Research Institute (IRRI) was founded in Los Baños in the Philippines in cooperation with the Ford Foundation and the government of the Philippines.[51] The IRRI was supposed to develop rice varieties suitable for different Asian soil and climate conditions and to train scientists from the countries involved to make them independent from foreign expertise. The Rockefeller Foundation alone invested five million dollars to achieve "a rapid scientific breakthrough" in rice breeding.[52] Apart from IRRI, three more agricultural research institutes were founded in the following years: the International Maize and Wheat Improvement Center in Mexico, the International Institute of Tropical Agriculture in Nigeria, and the International Center for Tropical Agriculture in Colombia. Each of them was conceptualized as a center of knowledge from which the newly developed technology would spread to the regional and local levels.

The first years of IRRI's existence were characterized by great optimism. The Ford Foundation stated in 1967 that the institute was:

> a resounding success, having turned out new varieties that are now being sown on hundreds of thousands—shortly to be millions—of acres and producing yields that are double or more than double those of the varieties they are replacing. Of potentially even greater importance, perhaps, the results of IRRI's work ... have demonstrated to political

and scientific leaders throughout Asia the enormous potential gains from scientific work in agriculture. In consequence, the governmental leaders of several Asian countries are for the first time giving appropriate status and priority to scientific research in agriculture in their own countries.[53]

As this statement suggests, IRRI was considered a tool to persuade the governments of the Asian countries to trust in modern science and to acknowledge the relevance of agriculture vis-à-vis industrialization. And the work of IRRI did have lasting consequences for agricultural practices in Asia.[54] Most famous was IR 8, a rice variant dubbed Miracle Rice, which produced much higher yields and became a symbol of the Green Revolution. Some believed that IR 8 "would win the Cold War."[55] The most direct expression of that belief was the effort on the part of the governments of the United States and of South Vietnam to use this variety as a strategic device in the Vietnam War, based on the idea that if peasants obtained higher yields and incomes they would not support the communists.[56]

The political role granted to IR 8 and other high-yielding varieties was not everywhere as strong as in the Vietnamese case, but the effects it had on regional and local agricultural techniques and socioeconomic structures in Asia were extensive. In India, for example, rice varieties bred at IRRI were introduced as part of the Intensive Agricultural District Programme (IADP), an initiative carried out by the Indian government in response to domestic and American pressure to invest in the intensification of agriculture in order to solve the country's ongoing food problem. Yields in those IADP districts where new varieties, chemical fertilizers, pesticides, and insecticides were used doubled and tripled within a short time.[57] In 1969, a consultant to the Rockefeller Foundation stated: "India's farmers are breaking out of centuries-old patterns of subsistence agriculture into a new day of commercial food production. Given demonstrably superior seed and a price incentive to produce, they are impressing the world with their enterprise. The result is that India approaches self-sufficiency."[58] Furthermore, some Indian farmers' lives began to change: They no longer had to rely on their children as a workforce and could send them to school instead, and due to surplus income they could afford to pay for new housing and for small luxuries, from which merchants and craftsmen in the villages benefited. In short, the new agrotechnology seemed to be affecting the kind of socioeconomic transition the proponents of Western modernization had advocated for a long time.[59]

Yet the numerical success did not come easily or without side effects. Many of the administrators charged with popularizing the new technologies among the peasants felt overburdened by the number of villages and individuals they were responsible for. The methods and inputs produced in laboratories and on model farms had to be made compatible with the agronomic practices of the peasants.[60] The extension officers often did not receive adequate training to guide this translation of different types of knowledge into practice, and many found it frustrating to deal with peasants who were illiterate and seemed stubborn. For that reason, many extension workers focused their attention on better-off farmers who seemed to be more interested in the new techniques because they could afford to be from an economic point of view. Consequently, the intensification approach tended to deepen social inequalities by privileging the better-off farmers, in addition to which the use of market-driven incentives led to an increase in food prices, from which the poor parts of the population suffered the most. Finally, the massive application of pesticides, insecticides, and herbicides without adequate protection caused diseases among peasants as well as ecological damage.[61]

By the early and mid-1970s, as the critique of the unintended consequences of the Green Revolution intensified, the trust in the power of cutting-edge technology began to be disputed. For one, even the most elaborate technological approach was useless in the face of environmental disasters like droughts and floods, which caused massive famines in Bangladesh and Ethiopia in 1974.[62] Secondly, voices grew louder calling for appropriate technology, a concept made popular by Ernst F. Schumacher (1911–1977), the author of the 1973 bestseller *Small is Beautiful*.[63] Schumacher and his collaborators in the Intermediate Technology Development Group in London argued that technologies had to be adapted to the particular social and cultural conditions in which they were to be employed, and that small-scale approaches were more useful in this regard because they were more flexible.[64] Similarly, in 1974, the Rockefeller Foundation stated with regard to its involvement in the Green Revolution in Asia: "Technology developed on research farms, even if it produces high yields under experimental conditions, is not necessarily transferable to farmers' fields."[65] To overcome or prevent their resistance it was essential to take into consideration indigenous forms of agronomic knowledge instead of disqualifying them as traditional or primitive. Therefore, more and more development practitioners called for approaches which focused on the needs and experiences of peasants, and demanded to provide them with better access to training so as to enable them to make efficient use of the new agricultural practices and to improve their own living conditions.

Education for development

The lack of specialized knowledge was considered one of the most serious problems the so-called developing countries were facing in the postwar period. This was especially true of many former colonies, seeing that an independent country required a much larger number of well-educated individuals than colonial rule had allowed for. In many ways, this lack of knowledge was a legacy of the colonial period, when the imperial powers had closely monitored their colonial subjects' access to education and training.

Well into the twentieth century, formal schooling in most of the colonies had largely been limited to missionary schools, which taught basic reading, writing, and arithmetic skills to boys and domestic skills to girls, mirroring the gender norms of imperial societies. In the interwar period, the colonial powers began to acknowledge the need for more skilled and educated workers in the interest of higher economic and financial gains, but also as a response to growing dissatisfaction with colonial rule.[66] Consequently, the number of male colonial subjects who were able to study either in newly founded colleges in the colonies or at universities in European countries increased slowly during the 1920s and 1930s. For example, the first secondary school and teacher training college in British West Africa (today's Ghana) was established in 1924/1925.[67]

However, a large part of the colonial populations did not have any access to formal education, and illiteracy rates remained high on purpose. In the eyes of colonial administrators, colonial education served as a means of promoting a certain standard of civilization without risking the alleged need for foreign rule becoming obsolete because the colonial subjects had become too developed and thus able to rule themselves.[68] In the African colonies in particular, the focus of colonial education was on agricultural and technical skills, based on the argument that Africans were not developed enough yet for more intellectual work, and that their natural place was in the countryside. This kind of thinking was also promoted by African American leaders in the United States. Most prominently, Booker T. Washington (1856–1915), W. E. B. DuBois (1868–1963), and Thomas Jesse Jones (1873–1950) in the late 1890s and early 1900s argued that the black population in the United States should follow a path of assimilation by embracing white norms and patterns of living. By doing so, they would eventually form a black middle class, which would allow them to become part of mainstream society and overcome their marginalization and discrimination.[69] The Tuskegee Institute in Alabama, which provided African Americans with agricultural and industrial training, became the center of these ideas. The Tuskegee philosophy was based on the idea of the dignity of labor as a means of promoting emancipation and social mobility, and as such was similar to colonial arguments about teaching the African populations an appropriate approach toward manual labor in a capitalist setting.[70] Jones and other educational reformers participated in trips to Africa in the early 1920s to study the educational situation in the African colonies, and the European powers cooperated with the Americans in formulating educational programs for the colonial populations.[71]

Apart from the educational efforts related to late colonialism, there were some initiatives by individual activists to promote education. For instance, Chinese nationalist Y. C. James Yen (1890–1990) and American missionary Frank Laubach (1884–1970) conducted large-scale literacy campaigns in China and the Philippines in the 1920s and 1930s. Yen organized rural reconstruction programs that included literacy training.[72] Laubach developed a teaching method according to which each literate person could teach an illiterate one, thus creating a snowball effect.[73] Yet these kinds of initiatives remained the exception to the rule. It was only in the 1940s, against the backdrop of growing anti-colonial dissent, that discussions about popular education gained in intensity.[74] For example, the British in 1941 installed a committee to study education problems in the colonies. Three years later, the committee published a report in which its members stressed the need for so-called mass education. The report made direct reference to the Colonial Development and Welfare Act of 1940, arguing that Great Britain had claimed a responsibility to prepare the colonies for their future independence, and one of the preconditions for independence was the elimination of illiteracy. Hence, more schools for children and adults had to be established and funded by the colonial government, and teaching materials had to be made available in sufficient numbers.[75]

The domestic British debate at the time strongly influenced the committee's considerations. The 1942 Report on the Social Insurance and Allied Service, or Beveridge Report, laid the basis for what would become the postwar British welfare system with its inclusive insurance system (social security, unemployment, and family allowances) and the National Health Service. The state took on the role of the provider of public goods and resources to guarantee a minimum level of security and welfare for everyone.[76] In this climate, it became increasingly difficult to argue why colonial populations should be excluded from these new provisions. As early as 1940 Ernest Bevin, Britain's Minister of Labor and National Service, had spoken of the need to provide people everywhere—not only in Great Britain or Europe—with "security against poverty, care in sickness and trouble, protection against injury, provision for old age."[77] Apart from welfare measures, educational opportunities seemed crucial to improve overall living standards and to equip colonial societies with the skills needed to master socioeconomic changes. For example, Margaret Read (1889–1991), a social anthropologist who conducted research on Indian peasants who became factory workers, argued that so-called traditional societies were very well able to adapt to industrialization and urbanization, or modernization, if they received the necessary support. Education played a crucial role in this process, she believed, and advised the British Colonial Office to carry out education programs in the colonies.[78]

It was against this background that mass education campaigns were conducted in several of the colonies in the postwar years. Such programs were in line with the demands of anti-colonial leaders like Ghana's future President, Kwame Nkrumah (1909–1972), who had called for the eradication of illiteracy in 1951.[79] It is difficult, however, to assess the effects these campaigns had on the participants and whether they considered them an improvement or an intrusion.[80] Furthermore, many European officials in the colonies were not willing to follow the directives to promote education among the African population. In their eyes, this would have meant losing influence and giving up established ideas about the danger of de-tribalization.[81] Hence, there was considerable resistance within the colonial service to systematic educational campaigns in the colonies. Additionally, the emphasis on European languages as languages of instruction made it difficult for many students in the colonies to qualify for the existing schools and colleges. Access to academic training remained scarce in most colonies until the end of colonialism.[82]

Consequently, many of the newly independent countries awarded education a key position in their development plans. All forms of education, from primary schools to technical training to university education, were needed to staff the new nations' administrations, their economies' public and private sectors, as well as fields like health, transport, agriculture, education, and construction, which were required for the physical and material development of the new nations, their economic growth, and the well-being of their inhabitants.[83] On the political level, education, like community development, was seen as crucial to the nation-building process. Public schooling in particular provided a means of bringing together members of different regions and social, ethnic, religious, and language groups of the country and introducing them to ideas, languages, and concepts that, in the eyes of their political leaders, constituted the new nation. The symbolism that surrounded this practice ranged from national flags and anthems to public holidays and commemorations. In this way, the alleged characteristics of the new nation states were supposed to grow roots in the population and bring forth citizens who identified with the nation's ideals. Posters, movies, and documentary films were used to reach the illiterate parts of the population.[84]

Educational campaigns also served to transport the political positions of the postcolonial parties. For example, in Ghana mass education was closely tied to the goal of socialist reconstruction that Nkrumah and his Convention People's Party lobbied for. In 1962, the party passed the Programme for Work and Happiness, which emphasized the role of the entire population in increasing economic productivity, which was required to pay for the social benefits promised to the Ghanaians. Literacy training played an important role in the context of mass education, as it lent itself to conveying the party's stand on the role of the individual in a Ghanaian socialist society. By emphasizing the centrality of the villages and their inhabitants, who were supposed to help themselves and each other in learning to read and write, the literacy programs also allowed the party to gain access to the rural population and to exercise a degree of control over them.[85]

While postcolonial governments considered education very much a national responsibility, many welcomed or pragmatically accepted support from international actors. In many cases the former colonial powers continued their educational work, though officially in a different function. Additionally, various governments provided education and training as part of development assistance programs. As mentioned before, the Soviet Union was particularly active in this field, and there was much competition with offers from Western governments. Among the international organizations, UNESCO was the most active in providing financial and technical support for building education systems across the world.[86] Importantly, the field of higher education in the 1950s and 1960s also attracted many smaller, non-governmental organizations.[87] Many political leaders of the newly independent countries were skeptical of bilateral development assistance in as sensitive a field as education, and they welcomed private providers of aid because their work was seen as primarily focused on development issues.

For example, the Carnegie Corporation in the 1950s and 1960s became a strong presence in higher education in African countries. In cooperation with the British Colonial Office, the foundation in the 1920s and 1930s had financed educational projects in British African colonies. When, after the Second World War, the demand for development experts and development-related knowledge grew, the Carnegie Corporation was at an advantage because of its experience and connections. In 1958, the foundation organized a conference that brought together representatives of British and American universities, aid organizations, and private companies to discuss Western interests in Africa and African educational needs. The goal was to define potential fields of activity for Western development actors, and the foundation began to coordinate these activities as decolonization progressed.[88] In addition, the Carnegie Corporation increased its own contributions to educational projects in African countries. In the early 1960s, it oversaw investments of 1.7 million dollars for university programs in teacher training, educational research, and adult education, and for library training and library development.[89] Furthermore, with support from the US government, it funded scholarship programs for African students to study in the United States.[90] The reason for the foundation to intensify its activities so rapidly is best expressed in the words of one of its representatives, who in 1963 stated that "the political commitment to education in Africa and the sense of urgency on the part of individuals and governments alike make it the best buy, dollar for dollar, anywhere."[91] In other words, the foundation was looking for fields in which its commitment would have a visible and lasting effect. The type and content of education available to the elites of the newly independent nations was seen as decisive for their future, and thus also for their relations with other parts of the world.

The image on the cover of this book is another expression of the contemporary understanding that education was central to the development path a country would take. Taken by a UN photographer in 1961, the image is titled "Agricultural Students Learn New Techniques in Congo." It shows students from different parts of Congo participating in a three-month agricultural course sponsored by the United Nations Operation in the Congo (ONUC) and the Agricultural Production Development Bureau of Paris (APDB). The three men in front of the classroom were, from left to right, a French agricultural engineer from the APDB, ONUC's agricultural economist from Haiti, and a professor from the APDB. The United Nations presence in Congo involved large-scale development programs, ranging from health to infrastructure to education, which aimed at stabilizing the country that had been so badly shaken by the crisis of 1960. Against this backdrop, it seemed crucial to provide a constructive perspective to the young generation in Congo, which, it was feared, might otherwise be lost to violence and despair. Hence, UN agencies, national governments, and non-governmental organizations from the Western bloc invested in the training of a Congolese elite which, they hoped, would be sympathetic toward Western ideals. For example, the Ford Foundation spent large amounts of money on establishing the National Institute of Political Studies and the National School of Law and Administration in Congo and sent Americans there to provide expertise.[92] The training course documented on the cover was another effort in this direction. Its goal was to make the participants familiar with concepts of modern, capitalist agriculture, specifically with cooperatives and credits, as the terms written on the blackboard suggest.

The combination of actors captured in the photo is particularly interesting because it symbolizes the synchronicity of the colonial legacy in the form of French experts and the postcolonial influence, with a Haitian teacher working for the United Nations. Another notable feature contained in the image is the fact that all of the individuals are men. Development-related education, whether it was carried out by international organizations or by national governments, in the 1950s and 1960s was predominantly geared toward men, with women being seen as responsible for private, household-related matters or not being considered at all. Only in the 1970s would women begin to receive more attention as actors in the development process.

Public health and birth control

The high levels of poverty, malnutrition, and disease many societies in the so-called Third World suffered from contributed to the perception that development was an urgent task. National governments were often overwhelmed by their responsibilities; others were not willing to invest the resources needed to help the very poor and instead diverted resources to seemingly more prestigious projects. For this reason, international organizations and non-governmental groups became active in the field of public health.

As mentioned above, the World Health Organization, the Food and Agriculture Organization, and many other organizations carried out preventive measures and tried to introduce standardized procedures aimed at treating recurring diseases. Their initiatives generally met with much support from governments in Latin America and Asia, which were eager to overcome what they perceived as obstacles to socioeconomic development.[93] For example FAO, UNICEF, and WHO in cooperation with the Central American Institute of Nutrition (INCAP) in Guatemala tried to improve the health levels of infants in the 1950s. INCAP had been founded in 1949 as part of an ongoing cooperation between the Pan American Sanitary Bureau and the Massachusetts Institute of Technology. Situated in Guatemala, INCAP attracted American and international attention when the left-leaning government was overthrown with US support in 1954 and replaced by a pro-Western government. In the following years, the American government and Western international organizations provided large sums of development assistance to Guatemala to ensure that the country stayed on the supposedly right path. Development projects in the field of health were part of this effort, and INCAP was considered an important local actor.[94]

INCAP researchers worked toward identifying local foods which could be used in new ways to ensure that infants received all the nutrients they needed. FAO supported the idea of a country's food autonomy, which promised to be cheaper than the introduction and import of foreign foods. However, UNICEF at the time was eager to change local diets by using powdered skim milk to feed infants. The milk powder was a surplus from American agriculture, but it was also considered to be superior to local Guatemalan foodstuffs in terms of nutritional value. At least implicitly this assumption was informed by the belief that modern societies were milk-drinking societies, and that physical strength as it was required for industrialization was impossible to obtain without milk and meat. A sense of civilizational superiority was attached to a particular Western food culture, similar to the belief that only scientifically tested dietary formulas could be part of modern health care efforts. Challenging this hegemonic claim, INCAP and WHO representatives argued that it was counterproductive to introduce milk to a country where storage and supply was a problem and where local food habits were entirely different. Although UNICEF carried out its plans to distribute powdered milk in Guatemala, INCAP researchers in the second half of the 1950s experimented with a milk substitute that could be produced with locally available ingredients. The result was Incaparina, a drink which provided as much protein to children as milk and was very cheap to make, thus catering to the goal of INCAP's director, Moisés Béhar (1922–2015), of reducing Latin America's dependence on the North.[95]

Despite the fact that powdered milk imported from Western countries became a constant presence in many Latin American countries parallel to Incaparina, the activities of INCAP show that "local conditions often mattered more than abstract ideas" about development and modernization.[96] Regional and local actors did have a voice in shaping development strategies and accepting or rejecting particular approaches from international organizations and national governments. Furthermore, the case demonstrates that health, like any other development field, was contested politically and charged ideologically. The Cold War interests of international actors brought resources to INCAP, yet at the same time they shaped the selection of development approaches considered feasible or unacceptable. Latin American concerns about a continuing or growing dependence on the industrial countries had an impact on the developmental outlook of INCAP's work and its position vis-à-vis international organizations. The latter cooperated but also competed with each other for institutional power and promoted their respective preferences even if the medical and social value of a specific approach was debated.

A similar complexity of motives and interests characterized the field of birth control, which was closely related to public health. Since the interwar period, many individuals had been concerned with population growth in what later came to be seen as the Third World. The quality of the demographic data available for most of these countries was relatively low at the time, yet the trend and its implications seemed clear to most observers: larger populations meant larger demands on education, housing, employment, health, and other resources. While eugenic measures lost much of their appeal in the postwar period, birth control as a socioeconomic device gained in relevance. India was the first of the so-called developing countries to establish a nationwide family planning program in 1952.[97] Swedish and Norwegian non-governmental organizations supported Indian birth control efforts in the 1950s. In doing so, they drew on experiences with social reformist and eugenic approaches practiced at home in earlier years, and they transferred some of their ideas to the newly independent countries and made them heard in international development organizations.[98]

Over the course of the 1950s, as more and more development scholars and practitioners visited and studied Asian, African, and Latin American countries, the impression that these countries suffered from unsustainable population growth increased. Even if economic productivity and income levels were to rise, the growing populations would prevent lasting growth from happening by consuming the available resources. On a cultural level, the perception of overpopulation was closely tied to normative assumptions about what a modern family and society looked like. From a Western bourgeois (and, in part, a eugenic) point of view, for a family to have more than three or four children was an expression of the lack of control over sexuality and a sign of backwardness or asocial behavior.[99] This understanding was driven by a fear that the absolute number of poor people in specific regions and in the world more generally would increase rapidly and challenge the security and the privileges of the few. Family planning measures tied to development assistance were supposed to serve as a strategic intervention to keep this scenario from happening.

Demographic transition theory provided the academic framework for these impressions. In its postwar version, it was closely connected with Frank Notestein (1902–1983) and Kingsley Davis, American demographers working at Princeton University. Their model of demographic change was very similar to modernization thinking. According to demographic transition theory, "all societies—regardless of race—pass through three stages: a traditional stage of high fertility and high mortality, a transitional phase of high fertility and low mortality, and a final 'advanced' phase of both low fertility and low mortality."[100] From this perspective, the industrial countries had already reached the final phase, whereas the majority of the so-called Third World countries were just arriving in or going through the transitional phase. In the eyes of Western demographers and politicians, it was crucial to ensure that the transition took place sooner rather than later; waiting for it to set in was believed to be irresponsible and dangerous with regard to the demographic, economic, and political balance of the different world regions.[101]

In the late 1950s and 1960s, Malthusian fears gained in prominence as newly available demographic statistics seemed to suggest that population growth rates were increasing rapidly. Many observers on the national and international levels believed that population growth would outpace food production, and that this would lead to conflict and, possibly, war. The United Nations World Population Conference in Belgrade in 1965 established this fear as an accepted fact.[102] As a consequence, calls for more extensive birth control programs multiplied, and development organizations increasingly added family planning measures to their range of activities. For example, the organizers of the aforementioned Comilla project in East Pakistan, in cooperation with the Pakistani government, in the early 1960s experimented with family planning approaches to lower the birthrate of villagers in the region. Drawing on American social scientific methods, they tried to convince the rural dwellers that it was in their own interest to have fewer children because their economic situation would improve. However, as a 1964 report on the preliminary results of the birth control campaign pointed out, the peasants in the Comilla region did not embrace this logic fully. When asked about family sizes, many stated that a smaller family was better, but in fact the number of children they had was larger than the ideal number they had identified. For them, family planning was a socioeconomic tool: as long as their economic situation was stable they did not see the need to limit their family size; only when they experienced economic crises did they practice birth control.[103]

Such selective behavior toward family planning seemed irresponsible to experts and administrators concerned with population growth in the 1960s. In their view it was absolutely crucial to reduce population growth within a relatively short period of time, and to maintain the lower level of fertility in the future, not as a matter of individual preference but an issue of national importance. For example, the Kenyan government in 1965, barely two years after Kenya's independence, asked the American Population Council for support in its effort "to pursue vigorously policies designed to reduce the rate of population growth."[104] The request implied the assumption that Kenya's population growth rate was too high. The roots of this assumption were manifold: Tom Mboya, Kenya's Minister of Economic Planning and Development, was in touch with many international experts and administrators who shared this perception. Secondly, many British officials remained active in Kenya beyond independence, among them the former colonial government demographer. The fact that a former colonial officer was heard in Kenya beyond independence was far from exceptional. Many colonial administrators continued their work as advisers to the newly established governments, and their expertise was much sought-after.[105] Another adviser present in Kenya was American economist Edgar O. Edwards (1919–2010), who, on behalf of the Ford Foundation, conveyed the assumption that Kenya, like any allegedly underdeveloped country, had a population problem.[106]

With such a broad consensus about Kenya's demographic challenge, the Kenyan government in the second half of the 1960s began to make birth control and information about reproduction available to Kenyan families. Family planning was expected to have two development-related effects. First, it was supposed to lower the national population growth rate and thereby provide the basis for economic growth and progress. Secondly, birth control was expected to result in the modernization of Kenyan families by turning away from clan-like structures and toward nuclear families in which each child received an education, thereby uplifting Kenyan society at large. However, the results of these birth control efforts were disappointing to its promoters: in the 1980s Kenya's demographic growth was considered to be the highest globally.[107] Many of the countries which carried out family planning programs in the 1960s had similar experiences.

Against this background, the United States began to tie the provision of money and food aid to demands that the recipient countries granted birth control a more prominent role in their development plans. In 1967, President Lyndon B. Johnson argued: "Developing nations with food deficits must put more of their resources into voluntary family planning programs."[108] India was at the center of attention in this regard because of its strategic and symbolic relevance in the Cold War struggle. As the largest democracy in Asia and as a neighbor to communist China, from a Western point of view it was decisive that India remained politically stable, and its stability seemed to crumble in the mid-1960s amid several food crises. Therefore, Johnson threatened to cut aid to India if the government did not intensify birth control measures.[109] This political pressure translated into an increasingly interventionist approach to family planning. Whereas in the 1950s and early 1960s the emphasis had been on educating individuals about the possibilities of limiting family size, in the second half of the 1960s there was a growing tendency to work with financial threats and incentives and, later on, to use coercive measures to increase the number of sterilizations carried out and of intra-uterine devices inserted.[110] International organizations as well as national governments supported these measures and provided the resources needed to realize them. For example, Norway and Sweden both financed birth control programs in India involving sterilization schemes. When, during the state of emergency (1975–1977), hundreds of thousands of individuals were sterilized by force, the funding from Scandinavia initially continued. Only in 1979, when criticism from the Indian and Swedish public increased, did the Swedish agency decide to end its support for the birth control program. Norway financed population control activities in India until 1995.[111] Generally, the international development community turned away from birth control programs in the second half of the 1970s as concerns over human rights violations intensified and as it became clear that even the most interventionist approaches did not result in lasting reductions of birth rates.

Conclusion

The overview of different development approaches and practice provided in this chapter is far from complete. Many other cases, actors, and regions would have to be included to allow for a systematic comparison. However, even a selective account shows that the field of development, however narrowly it might have been defined at the time, encompassed a very broad and interconnected variety of activities and approaches. In some cases Cold War concerns were the reason why a project was initiated and carried out; in other cases the Cold War was not relevant at all. Universalist assumptions about the right development path influenced development strategies to a large degree, yet they rarely translated into practice as expected and more often than not became entangled in particular local configurations.[112]

Technology-centered approaches turned out to be very effective but also very unreliable because to function they depended on a stable environment, on regular maintenance, and on continuous management. This was not feasible in many regions and under varying political, social, and geographical conditions. Furthermore, the cases described show that development was not exclusively an international initiative but grew out of and was advocated by politicians and administrators from the so-called developing countries. International development actors reacted to these demands and provided resources because they considered them an opportunity to promote their own interests. However, the degree of control they were able to exercise over development projects was limited.

What all of this meant with regard to the experiences of individuals who were given the choice to participate in or made part of development projects is difficult to assess. Ethnological and sociological studies have shown that individuals and social groups understood very well that the various development programs they experienced were not exclusively geared toward improving their situation but were strongly influenced by the expectations of the donors to achieve their own goals. The recipients of aid reacted to the plurality of interests involved and, for very rational reasons, tried to benefit from those aspects they considered useful while avoiding those they believed to be harmful.[113] It was, in part, this selective appropriation that led to the growing disillusionment among development practitioners and experts that characterized the debates of the 1970s.

CHAPTER SEVEN

Challenges to Development

The 1970s are generally regarded as the decade when the development order established in the postwar years became the object of growing criticism, and when older assumptions about development became increasingly challenged. Yet it would be misleading to speak of a concerted attack on mainstream development ideas; it was rather a multiplicity of very different, if sometimes overlapping, types of critique with very different suggestions for changes and alternatives. This complexity makes the 1970s a highly dynamic but also somewhat confusing period in the history of development. The following chapter tries to identify the key phenomena and the ways in which they were connected with each other. It begins with the international policy dimension and moves on to the internal debates in the field of development.

Toward a new international economic order

In the 1970s, the range of actors active in the development assistance field increased significantly, and relations within the field changed. For one, several countries which previously had not been considered very influential in international development became much more visible. The People's Republic of China had already begun, in the early 1960s, to engage in development assistance in Asian and African countries. Chinese aid levels and activities increased notably after the Sino-Soviet split.[1] By the early 1970s Beijing spent about 5 percent of its budget on foreign assistance, particularly in Africa.[2] One of the biggest Chinese projects of the 1970s was the railroad connection between Zambia and Tanzania, which covered a length of 1,300 miles and figured as the third-largest infrastructure project in sub-Saharan Africa at the time.[3] Secondly, the members of the Organization of Petroleum Exporting Countries (OPEC) were emerging as influential providers of bilateral aid. As petroleum prices increased in the mid-1970s, the money available and the political flexibility on the part of OPEC members—Algeria, Ecuador, Iran, Iraq, Kuwait, Libya, Nigeria, Qatar, Saudi Arabia, the United Arab Emirates, and Venezuela—grew, and they began to use development assistance as part of their foreign policy efforts.[4] By the mid-1970s, OPEC aid constituted at least a quarter, at times nearly a third, of all official development aid, which meant that the hegemony of the Cold War powers in international development was undermined.[5]

Parallel to those countries' increasing activism, the Soviet Union began to reassess its role as the largest provider of development aid among the socialist countries and decided to reduce its commitments. The high hopes of the early 1960s that the newly independent African countries could be won over for the socialist path of development had quickly given way to frustration with the perceived unreliability of African leaders and their interest in prestige projects as well as with the high political and financial costs associated with development projects.[6] On the ground, the Soviet development model did not function as smoothly as expected, and many of the so-called Third World countries preferred assistance from the Western countries because of the higher quality of technology.[7] Additionally, Moscow's goal of defining and controlling what socialist development was supposed to be became increasingly difficult to uphold against the expectations of the other socialist countries. Within COMECON, many representatives from Central Eastern European countries advocated a different, less centralized model of development than the Soviet Union.[8] Also, countries like Cuba and Algeria promoted their revolutionary agendas in the former colonies. So-called South-South cooperation in the form of military, technical, and educational assistance added to the plurality of the development arena in the 1970s.[9]

As the socialist countries in Eastern Europe began to experience growing economic and financial problems, the generosity of earlier years was replaced by an emphasis on mutually beneficial trade relations. Raw materials that were difficult to procure for the Soviet Union and its allies became the center of attention in the 1970s. In negotiating trade agreements with African and Asian countries, the Soviet Union in those years abolished the fixed prices of earlier times and conducted trade based on convertible currencies because it needed foreign currencies to pay for Western imports of industrial goods. Simultaneously, the USSR began to delegate responsibility for development assistance to its allies.[10] Specifically, the German Democratic Republic, Poland, Czechoslovakia, Hungary, and Yugoslavia were expected to provide increasing amounts of support to African and Asian countries in the 1970s.[11] Vietnam, Cuba, and Mongolia received the biggest share of socialist aid in those years, with the GDR being the largest donor, followed by Czechoslovakia. Hungary and Bulgaria provided smaller amounts of aid to countries like Nicaragua, Tanzania, Ethiopia and Angola.[12] Yugoslav economists used the opportunity to promote the concept of worker self-management, which spoke to the self-understanding of socialism but allowed for more flexibility than a rigid system of centralized state planning. Yugoslav participation in international organizations, particularly in the World Bank, helped to spread their ideas internationally.[13] The practice of burden-sharing meant that the Soviet Union gave up its control over the field of development aid, implicitly suggesting that its political relevance was no longer decisive in the Cold War struggle.[14]

Already in the late 1960s advocates of détente had suggested that the use of aid as a Cold War tool was outdated, and that development assistance could serve as a field of cooperation between governments and companies in Western and Eastern Europe.[15] The German case is telling in this regard: by the early 1970s, as the German Democratic Republic joined the United Nations Organization and the two Germanies signed a treaty, it no longer made sense for the Federal Republic of Germany to negate the existence of the GDR as a legitimate state; it seemed much more useful to cooperate in selected fields.[16] From the mid-1970s onward, tripartite cooperation in the field of industrial development became prominent, bringing together Western firms, Eastern experts and machinery, and the so-called Third World countries, which contributed labor and raw materials.[17] Whether for pragmatic or for idealistic reasons, foreign assistance in the 1970s was no longer used in such a direct way to achieve specific goals in the Cold War struggle as it had been in the 1950s and 1960s.

Another, related phenomenon which contributed to the redefinition and reconfiguration of development was the steadily growing number of non-governmental organizations active in the field. As governments questioned the use of development aid as an instrument to influence bilateral relations, and as multilateral assistance gained in importance (the percentage of bilateral aid by the DAC members decreased from 54.2 percent in 1960 to 37.9 percent in 1970, while the amount spent on multilateral aid increased continuously),[18] the possibility for non-governmental actors to participate in development activities increased. Of course, many Western countries had long cooperated with civil organizations and churches in carrying out development projects. Yet in the 1970s the situation changed in character as public interest in political activities increased rapidly, ranging from environmental to human rights to development groups.[19] The extensive media coverage of the famines in the context of the Biafra war and the Sahel crisis drew public attention to Africa and triggered a rush of activism on the part of individuals and private groups.[20] The United Nations provided a platform for the non-governmental organizations involved and offered them an opportunity to contribute to international discussions and activities.[21] Consequently, the field of development actors diversified, adding many more, and often more critical, voices to it.

However, the most influential challenge to the international development system came from the so-called developing countries, which voiced their dissatisfaction with the status quo. In the early 1960s India and Yugoslavia, as leading members of the Non-Aligned Movement, had advocated the establishment of a World Trade and Development Conference at the United Nations. Their goal was to change existing global trade and economic structures in such a way that the newly independent countries and the poor nations would have easier access to world markets and to financial and technical support from the industrial powers. In 1964, they reached their first goal: the United Nations Conference on Trade and Development (UNCTAD) came into existence with the votes of many of the so-called developing countries and the Non-Aligned Movement. Through UNCTAD and the Group of 77, which was founded in parallel, they joined forces "to put pressure on the Western countries which they were unable to exert bilaterally."[22] In doing so, they challenged the primacy of the industrial powers and made their demands heard on an international level, especially by using the media in very effective ways.[23]

Initially, the Soviet Union and China, too, supported UNCTAD, hoping that its existence would weaken the Western countries cooperating in the General Agreement on Tariffs and Trade (GATT), the predecessor of the World Trade Organization (WTO, founded in 1995).[24] GATT members argued that liberal trade and international competition would allow the so-called developing countries to industrialize and to catch up with the industrial nations. From this point of view, it was the responsibility of the so-called Third World countries to engage more competitively in international trade in order to lay the foundations for future development. In turn, UNCTAD members argued that global economic structures had to change first in order to allow the newly independent countries to develop.[25] As Doudou Thiam (1926–1999), the foreign minister of Senegal, put it in a speech in 1966:

> We must lay the foundations for a new world society; we must bring about a new revolution; we must tear down all the practices, institutions and rules on which international relations are based, in so far as these practices, institutions and rules sanction injustice and exploitation and maintain the unjustified domination of a minority over the majority of men. Not only must we reaffirm our right to development, but we must also take the steps which will enable this right to become a reality.[26]

The idea of a right to development was new at the time but quickly gained popularity—not so much in the sense of human rights but rather as a right for a country to realize its economic potential to the fullest by having complete control over its resources.

UNCTAD's work was driven by the argument that the terms of trade had created structural inequalities between different regions, and that the privileges of the so-called First World depended on the so-called Third World remaining the producer of raw materials instead of manufacturing and selling refined goods itself. What became known as dependency theory was based on the work of Raúl Prebisch (1901–1986) and Hans W. Singer who, in the late 1940s and 1950s, had argued that the terms of trade under which the Latin American economies had to sell their raw materials had continuously declined. Singer, who had studied economics with John Maynard Keynes and was influenced by Joseph Schumpeter (1883–1950), was among the first scholars to be hired by the United Nations' department of economic affairs in 1947. Previously, he had analyzed unemployment figures and land rights in Great Britain—issues which were also relevant to countries with agrarian economies.[27] Singer's findings on the declining terms of trade were taken up by Prebisch, an economist from Argentina.[28] In the context of the Great Depression, he had attended meetings on monetary issues in London and Geneva, which increased his interest in and support of state-led economic and financial regulation. In the mid-1930s, he participated in the establishment of Argentina's central bank and became its first manager. As a visiting expert to Mexico in the mid-1940s, Prebisch started to look at Latin America as a regional unit held together by shared cultural traits and economic structures. It was in this context that he began to think about the relations between center and periphery, with the center being the politically and economically dominant power on which the periphery depended. Prebisch argued that to overcome their dependence on the United States the Latin American countries had to industrialize, but they needed to do so in a protected setting because otherwise the external pressure would be too strong.[29] German economist Friedrich List (1789–1846) had argued similarly in the mid-nineteenth century, stating that what became called infant economies needed to protect themselves from international competition for a while until they were ready to compete.[30]

Prebisch developed his thinking further in a report on Latin America's economic situation he wrote for the United Nation's Economic Commission for Latin America (ECLA) in 1948/1949. In the report, he argued that the economic power of the Latin American countries had deteriorated because the industrialized countries paid less and less for their products. This also meant that the costs of capital imports were increasing dramatically. Hence, the economic situation of Latin America could not be understood in isolation but had to be placed in the global economic context. Furthermore, Prebisch recommended import substitution industrialization, which meant that the capital goods needed for industrialization should be produced in the country itself instead of buying them from abroad. In later years, especially as Secretary General of UNCTAD, Prebisch began to challenge the concept of import substitution industrialization and emphasized the need for so-called developing countries to engage in international trade— yet a type of trade that was free of tariffs and provided stable commodity prices so that the producing countries would be less vulnerable to price fluctuations.[31]

Dependency theory became strongly politicized in the late 1960s and 1970s, when many scholars in the Western world engaged with Marxist ideas. Most famously, Andre Gunder Frank (1929–2005) stated in 1969 that the so-called Third World's underdevelopment was not an accident of history but "in large part the historical product of past and continuing economic and other relations between the satellite underdeveloped and the now developed metropolitan countries."[32] Based on his research on Latin American economies, Frank argued that it had been part of the capitalist strategy of the colonial powers to keep their satellites abroad dependent on them so that they could benefit from cheap raw materials and export markets for refined goods.[33]

It was in this political and intellectual context that many governments in the so-called developing countries radicalized their positions vis-à-vis the industrial countries. Algeria was the most outspoken in this regard. Having achieved independence from France in 1962 after a protracted and violent war, the country's leadership embraced a socialist order, became a leading force in the Non-Aligned Movement, and supported anti-colonial movements in other parts of the world.[34] Under President Houari Boumediene (1932–1978), the Algerian oil and gas industry was nationalized in 1971, thereby ending the French monopoly on the sector. It was Boumediene, too, who demanded the establishment of the Conference for International Economic Cooperation (CIEC), the North–South dialogue which took place between 1975 and 1977 in Paris, to discuss ways of giving former colonies and so-called developing countries better chances of realizing their economic potential and becoming truly independent.[35]

Together with Algeria, many countries represented in UNCTAD demanded a more equal global economic order. Importantly, they did not advocate the overthrow of the capitalist economy but rather called for it to be adapted to their needs. Their goals were expressed in the Declaration on the Establishment of a New International Economic Order (NIEO), which was passed in 1974 by the UN General Assembly with support from the Group of 77 and the Non-Aligned Movement.[36] Most importantly, the declaration emphasized the sovereign equality of all states and the right to self-determination of all peoples. All countries were to be given the right to choose their own socioeconomic system, and each of them was supposed to have "full permanent sovereignty" over its natural resources and economic activities, if necessary through the nationalization of resources. Furthermore, the declaration demanded a moratorium on the debts many countries had amassed over the years, and it called for international cooperation in solving global economic problems with a view toward the need "to ensure the accelerated development of all the developing countries." To do so, it advocated stable commodity prices on the world market, improved terms of trade, and higher levels of development assistance, which should be "free of any political or military conditions."[37]

The reactions of those countries to whom the declaration was addressed varied. The social democratic governments of Canada, Norway, Sweden, Denmark, Ireland, and the Netherlands were generally open to the demands and formed a "like-minded" group to discuss the central problems underlying the demands.[38] Many other members of the Development Assistance Committee rejected the call for a new economic order outright, fearing that their trade privileges would suffer, even if they were contradicting their own position on the importance of free trade. Yet for all their opposition the DAC members could not entirely ignore the growing pressure from UNCTAD and an increasingly empathetic public, and they finally promised to give 1 percent of their respective gross domestic product to foreign assistance—a promise some countries kept for some years while many others did not.[39]

UNCTAD's critique that First World interests dominated the international order was mirrored in demands for structural reforms in the international organizations. As the number of African countries gaining independence increased throughout the 1960s, the original set-up of organizations like the International Labor Organization and their development practices came under scrutiny. In the early 1960s countries like Ghana, Guinea, and Egypt criticized ILO for supposedly representing capitalist and imperialist interests and called for changes in its representative mechanisms to ensure that ILO would not serve as a tool of neo-colonialism.[40] The portrayal of international organizations as Trojan horses which pretended to represent universal ideals but really were trying to realize the interests of Western governments and companies gained support over the course of the decade and beyond. In the field of development practice, meanwhile, the idea that Western knowledge was the key to development came under scrutiny, and the call for alternative approaches grew louder. This brings us to the political and intellectual debates within the development field in the 1970s.

Intellectual and political challenges to development

The late 1960s and early 1970s saw a rapidly intensifying critique of established development beliefs and a growing "donor fatigue."[41] As the new nations gained in self-confidence but also experienced growing economic and political problems, the idea of relying on international aid seemed increasingly questionable. Many of the attempts to transfer development concepts to other parts of the world had not brought about the expected results. Frustration and disillusionment spread among many of those who had initially believed in the universal quality of development and who came to realize that the models were not functioning as expected. The idea that the state could serve as the driver of development came under attack, too, and some economists began to argue that after all the market was the better tool to achieve growth.[42]

Arguments that served to explain the apparent failures of development policies and practices were manifold. One crucial factor seemed to be the neglect of women in development. For a long time, there had been very little or no awareness of the role of women in the development process. Development scholars had been predominantly male, and very few of them had paid attention to gender differences in the societies they studied. Modernization theory in particular relied on a heavily gendered understanding of the actors involved. Men in so-called traditional societies were believed to be decisive in affecting change, just as men in industrial societies were seen as responsible for political issues. Meanwhile, women were given the role of the keepers of tradition and as mothers of the nation.[43] In the late 1960s and 1970s, when women in industrial countries intensified their demands for equal rights and opportunities, the insensitivity of mainstream development thinking toward women and gender came under pressure, too.

Danish economist Ester Boserup (1910–1999) was one of the most influential individuals in directing attention to the role of women in the development process. She criticized Western development theories for neglecting the position of women in so-called underdeveloped societies and argued that it was problematic to dismiss cultural particularities affecting women's lives in non-Western societies just because they did not conform to the beliefs of Western feminists or social reformers more generally. In a text on polygamy published in 1970, Boserup emphasized that for women in rural communities in African countries being married and having many children meant a higher social status, especially if they could not gain status through work. Against this background, she saw "a danger in such a community that the propaganda for birth control, if successful, may further lower the status of women both in the eyes of men and in their own eyes."[44] In other words, the specific position of women in society needed to be acknowledged and respected instead of either ignoring or dismissing it as irrelevant. Boserup's name soon came to be associated with the concept of Women in Development, which stressed the positive impact women could have on the development process if they were granted attention and support. The overarching goal of this approach was to overcome the seemingly gender-neutral discrimination of women in development planning and to acknowledge that they did a very large share of the work that made development possible in the first place, even if they were not included in official labor statistics.[45]

Boserup was in great demand in the early 1970s. She drafted the key documents for the 1972 Interregional Meeting of Experts on the Integration of Women in Development, emphasizing that the effects of "women's exclusion from economic development programs had been a significant factor in the rapid growth of population, illiteracy, malnutrition, poor health, and poverty—all key obstacles to development." From this the experts drew the conclusion that women needed to be given a more central role in development programs.[46] Symbolic and political measures followed. The year 1975 was declared International Women's Year by the United Nations.

The same year saw the First World Conference on the Status of Women in Mexico City, with a United Nations Decade for Women being declared for the years 1976 to 1985. Additionally, the United Nations Development Fund for Women (UNIFEM) was established.[47] A women's conference in 1980 in Copenhagen emphasized the need to give women "equal access to education, employment opportunities and adequate health services."[48]

On the practical level, international organizations and development agencies made an effort to integrate women more actively into their programs. For example, in the late 1970s, the Dutch government agreed to provide financial and technical aid to the Office du Niger in Mali on the condition that special projects were set up to improve the situation of women. In the early 1980s, the Dutch, in cooperation with the Office and as part of a larger scheme to repair irrigation canals, carried out several projects aimed at giving women access to the market and at helping them to secure a small but steady income. The goal was to allow women to reduce their dependence on male family members and to strengthen their position in the village community at large. To do so, they were encouraged to set up cooperative structures through which they could apply for small-scale credits and rent or buy machinery for hulling rice, which they could then sell independently.[49] Involving women more actively in development schemes carried some risks, contemporaries pointed out. For example, in her 1985 book *Male Bias in the Development Process*, development scholar Diane Elson argued that focusing on women in development placed too much responsibility on those who were already doing the largest share of work.[50] Yet, when looking back, many of the women credited the Dutch project with allowing them to gain more confidence in their own abilities and thereby improving their social positions.[51] Thus, a theoretical debate on the neglect of women translated into a reconsideration of development concepts and into new practical approaches to development.

Another strand of criticism of established development thinking was inspired by the growing concern with the problematic effects of technology and planning. In the late 1960s and early 1970s, more and more people felt uncomfortable with large-scale economic systems and technologies which, in their eyes, neglected human needs and cultural particularities.[52] Concern with the ecological and health effects of intensive agriculture turned from an expert discourse into a mass phenomenon in the years following the publication of Rachel Carson's (1907–1964) famous book *Silent Spring* (1962).[53] When the United States began to use herbicides to defoliate entire forests during the Vietnam War, a growing number of scientists began to speak out about the ecological implications of such measures, causing public outrage about chemical warfare.[54] In the American context in particular, but also far beyond the US setting, the Vietnam War played a crucial role in challenging many of the established assumptions about development. Especially to the younger generation, the war seemed to symbolize everything that they believed to be problematic about the American rise to power since the Second World War. Instead of using its wealth and potential in a peaceful, constructive way, the United States, under the banner of containing communism, was using bombs and chemical weapons to kill peasants who had earlier been promised the benefits of modern life.

The outrage over the brutality of the war helped to trigger a romanticized image of peaceful and sustainable peasant life in harmony with nature which seemed to be superior to Western technology and consumption. On the academic level, the debates surrounding the war fostered a growing interest in peasant cultures and rural livelihoods, of which the emergence of the field of Peasant Studies was one expression.[55] A prominent example of this field of studies was James C. Scott's 1976 book *The Moral Economy of the Peasant*.[56] In his book Scott argued that peasants in Vietnam and Burma had been behaving entirely rationally in practicing a subsistence economy instead of aiming for higher yields, and that it was colonial interference with their established patterns of life that had caused conflict and violence.[57] Meanwhile, in India the Subaltern Studies Group was trying to give a voice to those groups and individuals who, for lack of political power and literacy skills, had been overlooked (or dismissed) by historians: peasants, rural laborers, forest dwellers, and many others.[58]

These academic debates contributed to and mirrored the questions many people in the 1970s expressed about the moral and cultural assumptions based on which development aid was carried out. What made Westerners believe that their lifestyles were superior to those of others? Why follow the growth paradigm if other societies seemed to fare well on a lower level of income? Why intervene in what seemed to be well-functioning socioeconomic systems if the results were conflict and destruction? As the Western way of life came under attack, so did the assumption that it had anything to offer to other parts of the world, and the civilizing mission of development assistance as it had become enshrined in postwar organizations and practices lost legitimacy. Of course, not everyone who was critical of mainstream development assistance was driven primarily by moral concerns regarding self and other or hoped for a revolution. Many people were more interested in promoting fair trade than in overthrowing global capitalist structures. Some had Christian motives while others argued from a strictly Marxist perspective. Many self-declared tiermondists (Third worlders) shared an enthusiasm for liberation movements and rejected development assistance as an imperial tool, while others supported the idea of solidarity in terms of sharing and redistributing resources through peaceful means.[59]

Yet again others called for an end to the provision of aid as a response to the so-called debt crisis, a phenomenon that was closely tied to the temporary rise in world market prices for raw materials in the early 1970s. As their income increased rapidly, many of the governments in the so-called Third World believed that finally they would be able to attract international investors and finance their development goals based on income from the export of raw materials, and they began to take out credits in large volumes. The socialist countries had long warned that the provision of credits was a problem because it tended to prolong the recipients' dependence on the allegedly imperialistic powers, but Western international organizations as well as national governments were eager to provide funding for projects they considered useful or strategically relevant.[60] However, world market prices for raw materials fell soon after and private lending rates went up, and many Latin American, Asian, and African governments found themselves incapable of repaying the credits they had taken out. Against this backdrop, providers of development assistance became increasingly reluctant to give out more funds.[61]

New development approaches

The protectionist measures many industrial countries installed in reaction to the economic recession resulting from the 1973 oil shock and the general cutbacks related to the recession directly affected the levels of international development assistance available.[62] Consequently, many groups and organizations working in the field of development had to rethink their mission and approaches in order to attract new funding.[63] What accelerated this internal revision was a generational change. As the individuals who had built up the field in the postwar years began to retire, their successors argued that more scientific methods were available to plan and carry out development work, and that the field needed to be professionalized.[64] For example, when Robert McNamara, previously US Secretary of Defense, became World Bank President in 1968, he reorganized the bank along the lines of a multinational company. Specifically, he installed new management and accounting systems, and recruited many economists with a specialization in development issues, thereby ending the predominance of bankers and lawyers in the organization.[65]

Among the problems McNamara and others identified in the field of development in the late 1960s and early 1970s were high population growth rates, high degrees of unemployment or underemployment, stagnating or slow economic growth, growing indebtedness, and heavy demands on urban infrastructures.[66] Against this background, it seemed urgent to find new ways to stimulate economic growth. One of the most popular approaches formulated in this context was the creation of employment, based on the understanding that if more people had better jobs, they would be able to invest more into health and education, migration from the countryside to the cities would slow down, and productivity levels would rise. Hence, in contrast to older approaches, employment was supposed to generate development, not the other way around. The International Labor Organization established its World Employment Program in 1969, and many organizations joined the effort to make planning for job opportunities a more central issue.[67]

Meanwhile, the World Bank discovered urban development as a new field of activity, following up on US initiatives which had promoted the idea of universal homeownership since the early 1950s.[68] The IBRD's turn to urban development was triggered by the growing awareness of the massive problems of rapidly growing cities in so-called Third World countries and of the increasing number of slums. Books like Gunnar Myrdal's *Asian Drama* and Paul Ehrlich's *The Population Bomb*, both of which appeared in 1968, strengthened the Western belief that population growth, or overpopulation, in Asian cities was a particularly serious problem, and that a crisis was looming.[69] The growing concern with the environmental challenges related to development added to this perception. In a contribution to a discussion on "Economic Growth and its Discontents," sociologist Alex Inkeles argued in 1973 that environmental pollution was a direct result of poverty, caused by the lack of sanitation and hygiene that characterized living conditions in many parts of the so-called Third World:

> Anyone who has seen the villages of tenant farmers in India and Pakistan, or the urban shanty towns that exist all over the world, will recognize the serious and immediate danger to human life which is posed when two to three hundred thousand people are forced to deposit human wastes in the same water that is also used for drinking and bathing.[70]

What seemed called for were approaches to fighting poverty to reduce the environmental and social costs of so-called underdevelopment.

Consequently, the World Bank in the 1970s began to invest in urban development projects, ranging from reducing air pollution in Mexico City to securing clean water in São Paolo to modernizing Calcutta's infrastructure.[71] The Calcutta Urban Development Project started in 1973 and ran until the late 1980s. In close cooperation with the Indian government and the state of West Bengal, the World Bank invested 269 million dollars into the construction of highways, bridges, sewage and drainage systems, and housing. The overarching goal was to make up for decades of infrastructural neglect, to increase Calcutta's capacity as an economic and trade center, and to provide stability after years of political conflict that had shaken the city and brought communist governments to power. The inhabitants of Calcutta's slums were considered to be particularly prone to radical views, and the Indian government agreed with the World Bank that this tendency had to be countered. For that reason, the Calcutta project included so-called slum improvement efforts. The approach was informed by the ideas that slums, as problematic as they were from a social and sanitary point of view, could not just be demolished because they housed too many people. Instead they had to be modernized so as to ensure a basic standard of hygiene, well-being, and security. Specifically, the World Bank, in cooperation with UNICEF, WHO, and many Indian organizations, supported the installation of public washrooms, toilet systems, and lighting in the slums of Calcutta. Additionally, the Bank provided funds to small-scale entrepreneurs in the slums to set up or expand their own businesses, hoping that this would help them to earn higher incomes, which in turn would enable them to invest in the education of their children, which, ideally, would interrupt the spiral of poverty.[72] It was in projects like these that new anti-poverty measures like the microcredit concept were tested and refined. The Self Employed Women's Association (SEWA), an Indian union, was one of the first to promote the concept on a broad scale in the 1970s, with support from the Ford Foundation.[73] In 1983, the Grameen Bank was established by economist Muhammad Yunus in Bangladesh, making the concept internationally popular as a way of overcoming poverty on a small-scale level.[74]

Closely connected to the prominence of urban development was the (re)discovery of rural development, which was driven by a concern about migration from the countryside to cities like Calcutta and the need to ensure food security for a growing population.[75] The interdependence between urban and rural development was problematized in Michael Lipton's book *Why Poor People Stay Poor* (1977).[76] Lipton argued that development policies were shaped by urban middle-class interests and privileged urban populations. As a consequence, access to health services and education was much more difficult to obtain in rural regions, which encouraged migration from the countryside to the cities. Lipton called for a more balanced allocation of resources to make sure that the rural regions received the shares they needed, arguing that investments in agriculture resulted in higher return rates than investments in industrialization.[77] Proponents of rural development took up his arguments eagerly. The World Bank's funding for rural development increased nearly fourfold between 1969 and 1974.[78]

Rural development as an approach responded to the public interest in peasants and rural livelihoods as well as to the demand for development models that were different from the technology-centric, top-down ones of earlier years. Since modernization schemes were perceived as overly compartmentalizing—creating artificial divisions between society and economy, between the agricultural and the industrial sector, between national income and individual living conditions—many experts and activists now called for more organic strategies. For example, medical experts in the 1970s realized that the high mortality rates in the so-called developing countries were linked to the "'pneumonia-diarrhoea complex', which could be caused by a number of pathogens and which depended on the nutritional status of the individual."[79] Hence, instead of targeting individual diseases, it seemed crucial to improve the quality and availability of nutrition, sanitation, and basic health care so that individuals would be less likely to fall ill in the first place.

It was in this context that integrated development strategies became popular. The term reflected the belief that the interdependence of different elements of development needed to be taken seriously. Many integrated development projects of the 1970s focused on rural regions and were geared toward "simultaneously increasing agricultural production and improving health, education, sanitation, and a variety of other social services."[80] The overarching goal of integrated rural development was to advance living standards in the countryside and thereby to promote the nations' overall economic development.[81] There was a notable similarity between this goal and rural development approaches of the first half of the twentieth century. Interwar projects had focused on agricultural efficiency and on conservationist measures; their aim had been to increase yields and to stabilize the socioeconomic situation in rural regions at a time when migration to urban centers was increasing and conflicts over access to land were intensifying. In the 1970s, too, many experts were concerned with mass migration from the countryside to the cities, and as in earlier times, they advocated better access to credit, health, and educational services as well as the introduction of new agricultural technologies.[82]

What was new at the time was the emphasis on *individual* needs as it was embodied in the basic human needs approach, which gained in popularity in the late 1970s and 1980s and received philosophical backing from scholars like Amartya Sen and Martha Nussbaum. Nussbaum argued that a dignified life was one in which individuals enjoyed a minimum standard of basic principles which translated into capabilities, which all human beings shared regardless of their gender, religion, geographical background, or social status.[83] Amartya Sen proposed the concept of development as freedom—the idea that development should be measured in terms of the freedom it endowed individuals with to live the lives they aspired to, to have political, social, and economic opportunities, to be protected from arbitrary decisions affecting their lives, and to be guaranteed a degree of transparency concerning the structures defining their freedom of action. Only if individuals enjoyed these freedoms would they be able to use their abilities fully, thereby allowing for development at large.[84] In many ways the basic human needs concept reflected the general dissatisfaction with economy-focused development approaches and their emphasis on industrial projects that left out a large part of the population. Why focus on urban prestige projects when so many people were living in dire poverty, infant mortality rates were so high, and education and sanitation a luxury? With these questions in mind, many development strategists advocated doing "first things first."[85]

An early example of this effort was India's Integrated Rural Development Programme (IRDP), which was initiated in 1978 and made the basic needs approach part of a larger rural development policy. India had been experimenting with different ways of solving the food problem, and the Green Revolution was finally resulting in significantly higher yields. Yet many Indian and international observers argued that the agricultural intensification approach had increased poverty in the countryside instead of reducing it, and that it was necessary to help those who, for structural reasons, were not able to benefit from the modernization process. At the same time, the domestic situation in India grew increasingly conflictual in the 1970s, as popular dissatisfaction with continuous socioeconomic problems and Indira Gandhi's (1917–1984) leadership intensified. The state of emergency installed by Gandhi marked the dramatic highpoint of this crisis. When a coalition government won the elections in 1978, its priority was to win back the trust of the population who had been promised an end of poverty but whose living situation had not improved in any notable way. In this situation, an integrated development program focused on India's rural poor seemed very promising.

IRDP, which received support from many international development groups and organizations, was geared toward individuals and families who lived below the poverty line, and it paid particular attention to women. Its goal was to provide education, health services, and credits to very poor rural dwellers, and to support them in setting up grassroots structures so that they would have a say in how development was to take place instead of receiving technical and financial support from above.[86] The very high ambitions of IRDP were difficult to realize for a variety of reasons, and the program did not achieve its goal of eradicating rural poverty once and for all. However, because of its size, the resources invested, and the public attention it received, IRDP did contribute to establishing the basic needs approach in the development field, and similar programs were carried out in the following years in many of the so-called developing countries. Also, from an institutional point of view, the approach was attractive to development organizations and representatives because it seemed to provide a way of regaining some of the legitimacy they had lost in the debates about the fallacies of development.[87]

Conclusion

The late 1960s and 1970s witnessed a highly dynamic and very productive discussion of mainstream development thinking and practice. Many of the critical voices which had been marginal in earlier years now came to the fore, and new positions and demands were formulated by an increasingly diverse set of actors. In part, this shift can be explained by the effects of generational and academic changes taking place and, more generally, by the process of professionalization the field experienced. More important than these intrinsic factors was the critique of mainstream development approaches by representatives from the so-called developing countries who stated their interests and demands with a previously unknown intensity. That they were so determined reflected, in part, their understanding that they had to ask for a maximum to secure a minimum because vested interests were unlikely to be given up easily. In fact most of the calls for structural changes in the global economy met with much resistance and remained theory.[88]

From the point of view of the DAC members, it was easier to provide more development assistance than to give in to more consequential demands. At the same time, the practice of using foreign aid as it had been employed in the previous decade lost some of its diplomatic appeal as the formal decolonization process was slowly coming to an end and the former Cold War dichotomy was replaced by an increasingly polycentric and complex constellation.

In terms of development theories and practices, the late 1960s and 1970s constituted a phase of substantial reconsideration and experimentation. The turn from centralized, state-organized models to grassroots approaches carried out by non-state actors, from the preference for industrial projects to the privileging of rural development, from male-centered to female-centered development was defining for the following decades. However, all of these changes did not challenge the underlying productivist rationale of development policy. Providing incentives for economic growth and higher efficiency remained the key goal. Yet the amounts of money and goodwill available for development assistance were no longer as generous, and when the global economic situation worsened, the discussion turned again, this time in the direction of questioning the usefulness of aid in general.

CHAPTER EIGHT

The Disintegration of Development

After the tumultuous 1970s, it was unclear how to continue with development. For all the constructive potential the critique of mainstream development entailed, it turned out to be difficult to translate it into lasting structures. In the 1980s, political and ideological positions on development diverged and hardened, with some commentators attacking the idea of aid as such and others demanding more and better aid. In the 1990s, when the Cold War order had dissolved, the understanding of what development was or should be became increasingly vague, as many development organizations tried to redefine their missions.

Rights, markets, and sustainability

Seeing that the demands for a New International Economic Order by and large did not result in significant structural changes, the debate about the need to address global inequalities continued in the early 1980s. For example, the Independent Commission on International Development Issues headed by Willy Brandt (1913–1992), the former West German chancellor, in 1980 published its report "North-South: A Programme for Survival."[1] The report highlighted the problem of a growing gap between income levels of the Global North and the Global South (the so-called Brandt Line) and called for measures to work toward a more just global order, in particular with regard to human rights.[2]

Whereas the call for a national right to development had been central in the 1960s, the debate turned toward individual development rights in the following decades. In 1986, the UN General Assembly adopted the

Declaration on the Right to Development, stating that development was "an inalienable human right by virtue of which every human person and all persons are entitled to participate in, contribute to, and enjoy economic, social, cultural and political development, in which all human rights and fundamental freedoms can be fully realized."[3] This position responded to and was reinforced by the concept of the basic human needs approach.

Yet instead of charging governments with the task of guaranteeing development rights to every citizen, many people in the Western development community in the late 1970s and 1980s advocated a move away from the emphasis on the nation state as the provider of development and toward individual responsibility. In their eyes, the debt crisis and the food crises of the 1970s together reflected the lack of efficiency, responsibility, and reliability on the part of the so-called developing countries. The most famous articulation of this position was the Berg Report of 1979, the result of a World Bank study initiated after a request by African finance ministers. The report titled "Accelerated Development in Sub-Saharan Africa: An Agenda for Action" argued that the most influential factors responsible for the increasingly difficult situation of many African countries were their "'domestic policy inadequacies,' such as overvalued exchange rates, protectionist trade policies, and bloated public sectors."[4] A few years later, the famine in Ethiopia strengthened the Western perception that many African governments were incapable of adequately dealing with economic problems, and the notion of failed states became associated with countries in sub-Saharan Africa.[5]

As a consequence, many critics of established development practices called for measures to adapt the political, financial, and administrative structures of recipient countries in such a way that they would encourage economic growth rather than inhibiting it: Structural Adjustment Policies (SAPs) were one result of this debate.[6] The policy of structural adjustment meant that so-called developing countries received loans only on the condition that they reduce public spending, liberalize their markets, devalue their currencies, and end the policy of guaranteed incomes and prices so as to encourage entrepreneurship and competition.[7]

The move to structural adjustment mirrored a debate in American economics which was closely associated with the Chicago School. Scholars like Milton Friedman (1912–2006) and Friedrich August von Hayek (1899–1992) argued that the Keynesian method of using public funds to promote economic growth in times of crisis was misguided. More generally, they believed that the state was interfering too much in the economic sector and was inhibiting market forces through regulations and interventions. Some, like writer Ayn Rand (1905–1982), popularized the idea that the state was dangerous because it infringed upon individual freedom. In the eyes of those who came to be called or called themselves neoliberals, it was crucial to cut back state spending and to create more room for individual entrepreneurship and private enterprise, which, through its competitive nature, would bring the greatest wealth to the greatest number of people rather than expecting the state to take care of them.[8] Several Western countries, especially Great Britain under Margaret Thatcher (1925–2013) and the United States under Ronald Reagan (1911–2004), began to implement domestic privatization and liberalization measures in the 1980s. These approaches informed many of the programs carried out by international organizations to restructure and revive the formerly socialist economies of the Central and Eastern European countries after 1989.[9] The structural adjustment programs the World Bank and the International Monetary Fund conducted vis-à-vis African, Asian, and Latin American countries in the 1980s and 1990s were part of this trend, which became associated with the term Washington Consensus.[10] Whereas the New International Economic Order had advocated more regulation, the Washington Consensus opted for liberal trade as the key to economic growth. In that sense, the concerns of the so-called developing countries were overruled by the interests of the industrial world.

However, it would be one-sided to consider neoliberal development policies solely as a Western invention pressed onto the so-called Third World. Many governments in Asia and Latin America in the 1970s and 1980s actively embraced market-centered development strategies—not primarily as a reaction to American or World Bank pressure but because it fit their own needs and interests.[11] For example, Chile's dictator, General Augusto Pinochet (1915–2006), after the coup against socialist Salvador Allende (1908–1973) in 1973 asked a group of Chilean economists, many of whom had studied in Chicago, to advise him on restructuring the country's economy. Their recommendations emphasized the potential of the market and the importance of competition, similar to the teachings of Friedman and others. Yet Pinochet accepted the economists' advice not because they were associated with the Chicago School but because "neoliberalism *as a development strategy*" offered him an opportunity "to get legitimacy back by economic growth, satisfy his backers in the Chilean propertied class, and keep the diplomatic support of the United States, without giving an opening to his opponents in the political parties and labor movement."[12] Specifically, Pinochet oriented the Chilean economy toward mining and commercial agriculture, which favored private entrepreneurs over industrial workers, and he opened Chile to international investment, which was in line with the interests of the Chilean upper class. More generally, governments in so-called developing countries used liberal economic strategies to build national and transnational alliances, which helped them to stay in power despite broad public dissent.[13] The case of the Asian Tigers (Hong Kong, Singapore, South Korea, and Taiwan), which managed to industrialize rapidly between the 1970s and 1980s, was often presented as proof of the feasibility of a neoliberal approach to development, while critics argued that their economic success rested on the acceptance of authoritarian regimes.[14]

Meanwhile, some countries in the socialist bloc began to give a more active role to private enterprise in otherwise state-controlled economies. This tendency, which could be observed in Yugoslavia, Hungary, Czechoslovakia, and the Central Asian republics, was a reaction to the problems encountered with the state-directed industrialization and welfare model that had dominated the socialist agenda since the 1950s. Under increasing economic pressures, and due to growing frustration with the political and cultural problems of transforming rural and agricultural into urban and industrial societies, many experts, managers, and politicians (in part based on exchanges with colleagues from the Western bloc) in the 1980s advocated a new approach to socioeconomic organization, one in which the task of the state as the body responsible for all aspects of society was reduced and individual activity was granted more importance.[15]

What these cases show is that the trend to redefine the role of the state in the development process was a global one, shared by elites across the geographical spectrum. Moreover, the history of market-centered development agendas suggests that many of the governments of the so-called developing countries were skilled in selectively drawing on international offers and adopting those aspects they considered useful while rejecting others. Structurally, this was a phenomenon very similar to the competition for development assistance in the Cold War setting.

Interestingly, the neoliberal critique of social-democratic development thinking overlapped in part with the aforementioned critique of top-down development approaches. Many development practitioners called for alternatives to state-centric development policies, which they regarded as paternalistic and overly bureaucratic, and demanded that non-governmental organizations should take on a more prominent role in the field of development assistance. Private foundations and companies functioning on a local or regional level seemed much closer to the everyday problems of individuals and social groups than governmental apparatuses, and were therefore in a better position to react flexibly and efficiently.[16] From the point of view of governments and international organizations suffering from budget constraints, granting non-governmental organizations a larger stake in the development field on a subsidiary basis made sense because it promised to cut costs and to make assistance more effective. It was this perspective which encouraged international organizations and national governments to cooperate more closely with and to delegate development tasks to locally active NGOs. For example, the European Community (EC) in 1976 established the EC-NGO Liaison Committee. The committee was supposed to intensify and coordinate cooperation between the EC and non-governmental organizations, which were considered to be in a better position to encourage grassroots participation. The EC also began to invest in projects run by NGOs.[17] Public-private partnerships in development projects increased rapidly in the late 1970s and over the course of the 1980s.[18]

Partly connected with the effort to make development not only more efficient but also more responsive to local problems was the growing concern with sustainability that became prominent in the 1980s. As early as 1972 the participants of the United Nations Conference on the Human Environment in Stockholm had discussed the possibilities of solving the most urgent environmental problems on an international basis.[19] The Club of Rome's report *The Limits to Growth*, which appeared in the same year, became the most famous expression of the concern over the consumption of natural resources in the interest of industrialization and economic growth.[20] Representatives from so-called Third World countries criticized the industrialized countries for what they considered an effort to keep them in a state of underdevelopment by trying to restrict their consumption of natural resources. For example, in 1970 the Brazilian delegation to the Stockholm conference argued in a preparatory paper that "environmental regulations ... must be 'planned as a means to promote development and not as an obstacle and a barrier to the rising expectations of the underdeveloped world.'"[21] Many of the Group of 77 members shared this position. A bridge between the two positions was the emphasis on the potential of technology to overcome scarcity and reduce the dangerous effects of industrial development on the environment.[22] Yet the issue as such—the question of how to align economic growth and development with the problem of finite resources and the protection of the environment—continued to be a point of contention between the so-called developing and the industrialized countries.

It was only in 1987 that a sort of compromise emerged, when the United Nations World Commission on Environment and Development, headed by Norwegian prime minister Gro Harlem Brundtland, published its report "Our Common Future." The report helped to plant the concept of sustainability in the development arena, defining sustainable development as "the need 'to ensure that [development] meets the needs of the present without compromising the ability of future generations to meet their own needs.'"[23] This broad understanding of sustainable development was a response not only to the concern of the industrial countries about the environmental costs of development but also to the demand by the so-called developing countries for social and economic justice in development more generally. From the point of view of many of the so-called Third World countries, however, the concept of sustainable development lacked real meaning, seeing that global economic structures had not changed significantly since the 1970s, and that massive inequalities between the industrial and the so-called developing countries in terms of income and gross national product continued to exist.[24]

Despite all national and international efforts since the postwar period, poverty as such had not been overcome, and the optimism of earlier times dissolved under political criticism and economic pressures. The decline of the Soviet Union in the 1980s mirrored the demise of the state-led development model more generally. As the USSR's financial and economic situation grew worse, Mikhail Gorbachev decided to drastically limit the provision of development assistance, signaling not only the end of the Cold War competition but also the disillusionment with the idea of planned development more generally.[25]

Poverty eradication, dead aid, and degrowth

In the view of many Western observers, the end of real-existing socialism after 1989 implied that Marxist interpretations had lost their legitimacy. Research institutes concerned with studying inequality and development from a structuralist perspective were dismantled, and economic approaches rooted in capitalist logic became hegemonic. As has been noted, socialist development approaches, too, had advocated increases in economic productivity, yet the notion that the state should play the central role in planning and overseeing these activities lost its credence after the end of the Cold War. Those who favored, broadly speaking, social democratic models of development faced harsh criticism from those who prioritized market competition and individual entrepreneurship as the drivers of growth. For example, US economist Jeffrey Sachs, in his 2005 book *The End of Poverty*, argued that the problematic political situation in many African countries was a result of poverty, and that poverty could be overcome with the help of intensified development assistance efforts. Once poverty was eradicated the political situation would improve, too, he trusted.[26]

At the other end of the spectrum were those who considered aid as the source of all problems. Two of the most famous accounts of this kind were William Easterly's *The White Man's Burden: Why the West's Efforts to Aid the Rest Have Done So Much Ill and So Little Good* (2006) and Dambisa Moyo's *Dead Aid: Why Aid Is Not Working and How There Is Another Way for Africa* (2009). Easterly, a World Bank economist at the time he was writing his book, argued that international development aid was similar to colonial practices of trying to remake societies according to European ideals—a project doomed to fail because it did not respond to the needs and dispositions of the individuals involved. Instead of relying on development planning conducted by experts, Easterly argued that people on the ground should define their own goals and carry them out independently.[27] Similarly, Moyo, a Zambian economist, argued that the provision of development assistance was preventing African individuals and societies from taking matters into their own hands, and that corruption was flourishing because of international aid. She demanded that African entrepreneurs receive more support in trying to set up businesses and in attracting investment instead of relying on foreign assistance.[28]

The attack on public development aid was closely connected to the concern about good governance. This concept, which became prominent in the 1990s, was rooted in the perception that many of the problems observed in so-called developing countries were connected to a lack of democratic norms and structures. Democracy promotion entered the development arena after the end of the Cold War, when Western liberalism seemed to have won over Eastern communism. At a time when some considered the end of history to have arrived, the continuing existence of authoritarian systems and dictatorships particularly in African countries was disturbing. Large international organizations, but also small NGOs, understood that to gain public support for their development work they were well advised to promote not only economic growth and public health but also improved political conditions. The precise meaning of good governance was difficult to define, yet it was closely tied to some of the key principles that informed structural adjustment policies, ranging from political liberalization and accountability to financial transparency.[29] The strong normative character of the good governance concept—the idea that Western democracy was the best possible form of government, and that Western institutional structures were most effective in encouraging economic growth—was rarely reflected on in the early 1990s but came under heavy criticism in later years, especially when opponents of globalization gained in strength around the world.

Generally, the post-Cold War period saw a continuous broadening of the understanding of development. In 1990, the United Nations Development Program established the Human Development Index, based on the work of Pakistani economist Mahbub ul Haq (1934–1998) and Amartya Sen. Integrating life expectancy at birth, knowledge, and national gross income, the index aimed to replace the narrow focus of development thinking on economic growth.[30] Ten years later, the Millennium Development Goals, which were adopted at the United Nation's Millennium Summit in September 2000, reflected the increasing concern of development policy-makers with problems beyond economic indicators. They included seven fields of action: "peace, security, and disarmament; development and eradicating poverty; protecting our common environment; human rights, democracy, and good governance; protecting the vulnerable; meeting the special needs of Africa; and strengthening the United Nations."[31] Kofi Annan, General Secretary of the UN, called for a reduction in the number of people living in extreme poverty by half by 2015.[32] The goal has not been reached yet but the UN continues its efforts to realize it.

Today, most scholars agree that poverty cannot be measured in purely economic terms. For example, the Oxford Poverty and Human Development Initiative states: "Money alone is an incomplete measure of 'poverty'. Human development is about giving people the opportunities to live lives they value, and focuses on what people are able to be and to do."[33] The initiative lists five dimensions that should be integrated into our understanding of poverty: quality of work, empowerment, physical safety, social connectedness, and psychological well-being. These categories, which are close to those contained in the basic human needs approach, reflect the perception that subjective and individual aspects of life, even if they are difficult to standardize, need to be taken seriously. The most explicit variant of thinking about development in terms of quality of life is the concept of *buen vivir*, which originated in the 2000s in Latin American countries and was closely related to concerns over the deteriorating livelihoods of indigenous groups in the process of development.[34] In 2008 and 2009, respectively, Ecuador and Bolivia integrated the concept into their constitutions, making a holistic understanding of development and the right to access to natural resources part of their efforts to establish socialist systems.[35]

Meanwhile, in North America and Western Europe, the concept of degrowth has appeared.[36] Its proponents worry about the ecological and social effects of unlimited consumption seen as characteristic of capitalist societies. Consequently, they challenge the idea that economic growth should be the goal of economic policies, and argue in favor of "a lower and sustainable level of production and consumption, a shrinking of the economic system to leave more space for human cooperation and ecosystems."[37] Concepts like the sharing economy and redistributive measures are closely related to this thinking, which in many ways is similar to the debates about the tension between development and environmental conservation of the 1970s mentioned earlier. At the same time, inspired by the financial crisis of 2008, economists have again become interested in the structural reasons for uneven development and inequality.[38]

Perhaps the most prominent political angle from which development assistance is being discussed today is its use as an instrument to fight extremism and terrorism. Following the 9/11 attacks, the European Union started to pay much more attention to security concerns in its provision of development support and made development part of its strategy in the "war on terror."[39] Similarly, American strategists in the mid-2000s formulated the so-called 3D approach, which posits development next to diplomacy and defense as national security tools. In his 2015 introduction to the US National Security Strategy, President Barack Obama emphasized the importance of reducing poverty and inequality as part of the effort to prevent radicalization.[40] These steps suggest that the idea of the 1990s that development assistance could and should be freed from its political superstructure has been a short-lived intermezzo.

Conclusion

The history of development after the 1970s was characterized by strongly diverging yet in part connected tendencies. On the one hand, there were efforts to respond to the critiques of the 1970s by gearing international development more actively toward the needs of the so-called developing countries, which were linked to a concern with the importance of making development more responsive to individual livelihoods. On the other hand, the willingness to experiment with development approaches was challenged by those who argued that the interventionist impetus of development assistance as such was a problem, and that it was much better to rely on trade and structural adjustment to address poverty. There was a curious proximity between those voices that called for increased funding for grassroots projects and those who advocated reducing the role of the state in favor of granting more developmental agency to individuals. The debate about the potential and the risks of development assistance reflected the disintegration of the development discourse, which was no longer about the best approach to development but about whether development assistance should be considered an option at all. While some called for ambitious, global development plans, others suggested that the vision of development as it had become so prominent in the postwar years was no longer relevant, and that development should be discarded along with socialism.

What the changing understanding of development meant in practice remains to be studied in much more depth. Comparative historical studies of the effects of neoliberal development approaches are scarce. Similarly, while there is much literature on the growing number and importance of non-governmental organizations, the historical understanding of the ways in which the activities of NGOs have shaped development practices remains limited.[41] Importantly, more research on the changes in development approaches from a non-Western perspective is needed, seeing that toward the late twentieth century former recipients of aid had turned into providers of aid and were establishing their own organizations to provide support to each other on a regional basis. The founding of the New Development Bank (NDB) by Brazil, China, India, Russia, and South Africa in 2015, whose goal it is to provide a non-Western alternative to the World Bank and the International Monetary Fund, is only one of the latest signs that new international networks and alliances will shape the meaning of development in the future.

CHAPTER NINE

Conclusion and Outlook

The history of development in the postwar period and in the twentieth century more generally is difficult to summarize because of the many different actors, regions, and problems involved, and the term development does not necessarily become less opaque when taking all of the different phases and interpretations into account. However, the advantage of looking at the history of development from a *longue durée* perspective is that it allows us to identify several phases and turning points that can offer some orientation on how the understanding of development changed over time and how it was related to international economic and political structures.

It is notable that several of those development ideas which were very prominent in the early and mid-twentieth century momentarily lost their popularity in the 1950s and 1960s, when modernization theory was predominant in Western international development thinking. In the 1970s and 1980s, they were rediscovered and revived. This is particularly evident with regard to the emphasis on rural life as well as on grassroots approaches. Of course, integrated rural development approaches practiced in the 1970s were not the same as rural reconstruction projects carried out in the 1930s. In the interwar period the concern with agricultural practices and rural living conditions had been quite logical because of the large number of people who lived in rural regions and the much higher importance of agriculture to the overall economy compared to the industrial sector. Contrastingly, the interest in rural relations and rural development in the 1970s was due to the perception that the previous emphasis on industrialization had not brought about the overall development results envisioned by the planners, and that one had to address rural concerns to solve development problems more generally. For a few decades, rural life had been overshadowed by the concern with urban and industrial structures, yet issues of land ownership, labor resources, and food production had never lost their relevance, even if shiny new factories and cities had attracted more visual and symbolic attention. In that sense, the time when rural and agricultural problems were considered secondary constitutes an exceptional period in the twentieth-century history of development.

Similarly, the *longue durée* view provides insight into the changing understanding of the role of the state in development. Interestingly, for most of the twentieth century the state was *not* the most important actor in this regard; it was one of many political entities involved, next to and often in cooperation with private networks, international organizations, companies, and non-governmental organizations. Only in the postwar decades did the state take on the planning, financing, and carrying out of development programs. Broadly speaking, the reason for the unusual prominence of the state in the development field at this time was rooted in a combination of three factors: first, the experience of the Second World War and its drive toward centralized planning together with imperial efforts to maintain control over the colonies; second, the governmental promise of socioeconomic improvement in the form of welfare and modernization, both domestically in the newly independent nations and on the imperial level; and third, the changing academic understanding of the principles of economic growth and the nature of development as they came to be associated with Keynesian thinking and industrialization theories.

For a period of about three decades, the state-centered formula functioned relatively well. Yet when the experience of the war lost its relevance in terms of self-understanding and behavior, when welfare provisions were no longer able to provide sufficient political legitimacy, and when the economic theories of the postwar era were challenged, the belief in the power of the state as the driver of development vanished rapidly. In many ways, the rise of non-governmental organizations and companies as initiators and executors of development projects in the 1970s and 1980s was similar to the situation in the early twentieth century, when most development-related work had been carried out by non-state actors. In that sense, the 1950s and 1960s were more atypical than one might assume based on the political and public attention the development field was receiving. This particular periodization, in which the postwar decades appear to have been an exception rather than the rule, concerns the type of development thinking and practice much more than the general importance development was granted in international politics. The 1950s and the first half of the 1960s was the moment in time when public excitement about the needs for and the possibilities of development was at its highest compared to other periods in the twentieth century, and when the field experienced a rapid professionalization process. Even if many of the theories and models formulated in the postwar period later lost their appeal or were revised, the amount of specialized, yet interdisciplinary knowledge produced in this period seems difficult to match.

Development, with its future-directed quality and its implicit promise of progress, attracted idealists and pragmatists, specialists and universalists alike. It was a field in which an unusual number of highly talented individuals thought of entirely new ways of conceptualizing economic life and social relations. There seemed to be room for (nearly) everyone, and the work appeared to be open-ended. As much as the advocates of development planning insisted that their respective plans would make a country or region modern within five, twenty, or fifty years, development planning as such was never meant to end. It was a field of continuous refinement, in which existing knowledge could be used to formulate even better solutions and more efficient approaches. Yet in practice the continuous existence of poverty and inequality presented harsh realities that had little to do with the intellectual pleasantries of refining development theories. For all the scholarly creativity and productivity the development field was characterized by, and for all the temporal, regional, cultural, and social particularities of different development cases, political interest in development was at most times narrowly defined. Whether the imperial powers tried to use development to make their colonies more profitable, the League of Nations carried out development projects to improve socioeconomic conditions, the United States invested in development to prevent radical political ideas from taking hold in the so-called Third World, or the Soviet Union provided development assistance to prove the superiority of the socialist model—the overarching political goal of development was to promote economic growth and to gain control over social structures and behavior.

At the heart of the political use of development lay the very basic yet very powerful understanding shared by individuals across the political and geographical spectrum that economic structures in the broadest sense, from local property relations to the availability of capital to access to international markets, to a large degree defined the political possibilities individuals and social groups had. Depending on one's political and ideological position, interventions into existing economic structures could be used to promote specific forms of behavior and to prevent others. In that sense, development served as an instrument of rule. Yet pointing out the relationship between development and rule does not necessarily discredit development as an idea or goal. After decades of discussions about governmentalist practices and the power-knowledge nexus, historians have become very sensitive about invisible power relations and intricate ways of steering social relations in specific directions. Against this background, developmental interventions may appear as yet another attempt by an elite to encourage or pressure individuals with lesser social status to behave in ways alien to their own needs and concerns. And of course it is true that many development projects were informed by hierarchical notions of difference and inferiority as well as by power and class interests. However, the history of development in the twentieth century provides a more differentiated perspective on the ways in which development as an instrument of rule played out in practice. Many development projects did not miss their original targets because they were badly planned. They did so, too, because individuals and groups opposed and fought them, adapted them to their own interests, or diverted the resources involved in ways which seemed more rational from their point of view. It is precisely the complexity of these social dynamics which makes development projects so interesting and relevant from a historical point of view.

In historiographical terms, development is a particularly rich field. Historians of global intellectual history can find as much food for thought as historians of rural life and agriculture. To those interested in international history the field is attractive because it allows them to study how abstract phenomena like decolonization and the Cold War played out in practice, or to analyze the relations between international organizations and individuals on the local level. Gender historians can use the history of development as productively to study changing perceptions of gender norms as economic historians draw on it to analyze global economic structures. Yet what do we make of the history of development beyond the academic and intellectual interest, and how does it relate to current and future concerns with development?

Today, the potential benefits and challenges of development assistance are discussed heatedly. Against the backdrop of continuing large-scale migration and the increasing danger felt by international terrorism, many politicians have identified development aid as a promising tool to reduce socioeconomic imbalances, to increase social stability, and to prevent radical political positions from gaining supporters. Calls for a Marshall Plan for Africa can be heard every day. The German Ministry of Economic Cooperation initiated such a program in 2017, though it has met with strong criticism on the part of international development experts who fear that development assistance is being used in the interest of the political goals of the donors (primarily preventing migration from Africa to Europe) instead of providing the kind of help the people in the respective countries are asking for.[1] The European Commission is considering using development funds to support military efforts to improve the quality of military systems, armies, and coordination in Africa, arguing that development depends on security.[2] At the same time, the US government aims to cut American development assistance by around a third and wants to make the granting of aid dependent on the recipient countries' political relations with the United States.[3] Thus, while the topic of development assistance is very present in the media, the question of what it should be and how it should be carried out is far from answered and rarely agreed upon in conversations between practitioners, politicians, and experts.

From a historical point of view, it is important not to overemphasize the continuity between the international interest in development aid after the Second World War and today's emphasis on the international potential of development assistance. For one, decades of often frustrating, but sometimes also exhilarating experiences with development have left their imprint on expectations toward and perceptions of development assistance. There is a certain awareness that more of the same is not an option, although how new approaches are supposed to be different is not entirely clear either. Secondly, there are new concerns and dogmas that present themselves to anyone thinking about development. The issue of sustainability is perhaps the most prominent among them. Whether it concerns the environmental consequences of large-scale development projects or the growing criticism of the role of financial capitalism in increasing socioeconomic inequality, public observers are much more outspoken in demanding a greater sense of responsibility and transparency from development actors, and this demand is being heard. For example, investment bankers in Frankfurt, in cooperation with development organizations and environmental NGOs, in 2017 signed an agreement on aligning their activities with the Sustainable Development Goals of the United Nations.[4]

With these symbolic and conceptual changes in mind, what lessons can we draw from the history of development that might be useful with regard to current and future development efforts? As development economist Irma Adelman emphasized, development theory in the second half of the twentieth century was characterized by a tendency to look for a single causal factor responsible for the lack of development. Such a perspective is understandable for functional reasons, but it overlooks the fact that "economic development is a highly multifaceted, nonlinear, path-dependent, dynamic process that involves systematically shifting interaction patterns among different aspects of development and therefore requires predictable changes in policies and institutions over time."[5] This change over time is rarely reflected on in the development field although it constitutes an important aspect of development itself.

Many development practitioners have not had a chance to hear much about their profession's history. In their training, they learn about different development approaches and their respective advantages and benefits, but this happens very rarely with an eye toward the reasons why certain approaches have become prominent and others have been forgotten, or why some models have been discarded whereas others have been hyped. Hence, many development workers start out from the assumption that they are the first ones to be confronted with a particular situation or problem, and that they have to come up with a unique solution. Similarly, many development projects do not reflect on the fact that the situation of a social group or a village that seems to demand a development intervention is not purely a result of local conditions but to a large degree the effect of regional and global socioeconomic structures and discourse about what constitutes development or underdevelopment.

Development practitioners are not solely responsible for the lack of historical context in planning development approaches. Historians share the responsibility. Many historians believe that we are unlikely to learn anything from historical experiences because of the historical particularity of each case, which makes it difficult to deduce any lessons and apply them to different contexts. Social scientists, contrastingly, tend to be more willing to identify factors that appear to be decisive for a project's fate. Some even speak of the success and failure of different development approaches.[6] This is a vocabulary most historians abhor because it implies a contemporary normative standard against which historical events should not be measured. Yet what do we make of a project that wastes money and ecological resources, fails expectations, and does not promote progress of any sort for anyone but increases the likelihood of conflicts which, if worst comes to worst, escalate and produce violence? It certainly cannot be called a success, but what is gained from analyzing it and stating that it happened in a very particular historical constellation that cannot be generalized? In other words, is there anything historians can contribute to improving development policies and practices beyond a critique of the shortcomings of particular projects?

Many scholars think that they can.[7] Historical perspectives can offer insight into the complexities of past development projects, and they can help us to better understand which factors have contributed to making a project likely to fulfill its goals or have made it unlikely to do so. Using history to better understand present and future development challenges requires historians to overcome their reluctance to comment on present problems and to become better at translating their expertise into policy advice. If we believe that the history of development is important because development is important, we need to be willing to engage in conversations not only with fellow historians but with everyone involved in the development field. In 1973, in a discussion about the concept of zero growth, Alex Inkeles stated: "We may not grow, but we must develop."[8] Something similar seems true today. We will never find the perfect development formula because the challenges will always be different, but we should continue to look for ways of using the knowledge we have about development in history to improve development practices and approaches in the future.

NOTES

Chapter 1

1 Cf. James Vincent, "Bolivia Rejects 'Offensive' Chicken Donation from Bill Gates," *The Verge*, June 16, 2016, http://www.theverge.com/2016/6/16/11952200/bill-gates-bolivia-chickens-refused (accessed July 18, 2016).

2 Bill Gates, "Why I Would Raise Chickens," *Gates Notes*, June 7, 2016, https://www.gatesnotes.com/Development/Why-I-Would-Raise-Chickens (accessed July 18, 2016).

3 Cf. Melinda Gates, "The Small Animal That's Making a Big Difference for Women in the Developing World," https://medium.com/bill-melinda-gates-foundation/the-small-animal-thats-making-a-big-difference-for-women-in-the-developing-world-15d31dca2cc2#.3h3q5313j (accessed July 18, 2016).

4 Ibid.

5 Vincent, "Bolivia."

6 For an overview of these discussions, see Finn Tarp, "Aid, Growth, and Development," in George Mavrotas, ed., *Foreign Aid for Development: Issues, Challenges, and the New Agenda* (New York: Oxford University Press, 2010), 20–53, 20–21.

7 Cf. Guy Fiti Sinclair, "International Social Reform and the Invention of Development," *SSRN*, September 1, 2016, http://dx.doi.org/10.2139/ssrn.2842441 (accessed July 31, 2017); Joseph Morgan Hodge, *Triumph of the Expert: Agrarian Doctrines of Development and the Legacies of British Colonialism* (Athens, OH: Ohio University Press, 2007), 2–3; Marc Frey, "Entwicklungspolitik," in Jost Dülffer and Wilfried Loth, eds., *Dimensionen internationaler Geschichte* (München: Oldenbourg, 2012), 293–312, 295–298.

8 Cf. Hodge, *Triumph*, 25; Andro Linklater, *Owning the Earth: The Transforming History of Land Ownership* (New York: Bloomsbury, 2013), 79–85.

9 Cf. Heinz W. Arndt, *Economic Development: The History of an Idea* (Chicago: University of Chicago Press, 1987), 1–2, 14–15, 36–37.

10 Cf. Frey, "Entwicklungspolitik," 307; Eric Helleiner, *Forgotten Foundations of Bretton Woods: International Development and the Making of the Postwar Order* (Ithaca, NY: Cornell University Press, 2014), 187–190.

11 Cf. Hodge, *Triumph*, 40–44.

12 See, most famously, Frederick W. Taylor, *The Principles of Scientific Management* (New York: Harper & Brothers, 1911).

13 Cf. David L. Hoffmann, *Stalinist Values: The Cultural Norms of Soviet Modernity, 1917–1941* (Ithaca, NY: Cornell University Press, 2003), 45–56.

14 Daniel T. Rodgers, *Atlantic Crossings: Social Politics in a Progressive Age* (Cambridge, MA: Belknap Press of Harvard University Press, 1998); David Ekbladh, *The Great American Mission: Modernization and the Construction of an American World Order* (Princeton, NJ: Princeton University Press, 2010); Daniel Immerwahr, *Thinking Small: The United States and the Lure of Community Development* (Cambridge, MA: Harvard University Press, 2015); Kiran Klaus Patel, *New Deal: A Global History* (Princeton, NJ: Princeton University Press, 2016).

15 See Stefan Couperus, Vincent Lagendijk, and Liesbeth van de Grift, eds., "Experimental Spaces—Planning in High Modernity," *Journal of Modern European History* 13.4 (special issue) (2015).

16 See Jennifer E. Sessions, *By Sword and Plow: France and the Conquest of Algeria* (Ithaca, NY: Cornell University Press, 2011); Paul A. Kramer, *The Blood of Government: Race, Empire, the United States, and the Philippines* (Chapel Hill: University of North Carolina Press, 2006); Christian Teichmann, "Cultivating the Periphery: Bolshevik Civilizing Missions and Colonialism in Soviet Central Asia," *Comparativ* 19.1 (2009): 34–52.

17 Cf. Suzanne Moon, *Technology and Ethical Idealism: A History of Development in the Netherlands East Indies* (Leiden: CNWS, 2007), 19–21; Hodge, *Triumph*, 43.

18 Cf. Monica M. Van Beusekom and Dorothy L. Hodgson, "Lessons Learned? Development Experiences in the Late Colonial Period," *Journal of African History* 41 (2000): 29–33, 29.

19 See Julian Go, *American Empire and the Politics of Meaning: Elite Political Cultures in the Philippines and Puerto Rico during U.S. Colonialism* (Durham: Duke University Press, 2008); Preeti Chopra, *A Joint Enterprise: Indian Elites and the Making of Bombay* (Minneapolis: University of Minnesota Press, 2011).

20 Cf. Patricia Clavin, *Securing the World Economy: The Reinvention of the League of Nations, 1920–1946* (Oxford: Oxford University Press, 2013), 172–178.

21 Cf. Helleiner, *Forgotten Foundations*, 19–20.

22 Cf. Frey, "Entwicklungspolitik," 299.

23 See the recommendations by Max F. Millikan and Walt W. Rostow for the Central Intelligence Agency, "Notes on Foreign Economic Policy" [1954]. Re-printed in Christopher Simpson, ed., *Universities and Empire: Money and Politics in the Social Sciences during the Cold War* (New York: The New Press, 1998), 39–55. Also see Mark H. Haefele, "Walt Rostow's Stages of Economic Growth: Ideas and Action," in David C. Engerman et al., eds., *Staging Growth: Modernization, Development, and the Global Cold War* (Amherst: University of Massachusetts Press, 2003), 81–103; Odd Arne Westad, *The Global Cold War: Third World Interventions and the Making of Our Times* (New York: Cambridge University Press, 2005), 32–37.

24 Cf. Michael E. Latham, "Ideology, Social Science, and Destiny: Modernization and the Kennedy-Era Alliance for Progress," *Diplomatic History* 22.2 (1998): 199–229.

25 See Michael E. Latham, *Modernization as Ideology: American Social Science and "Nation Building" in the Kennedy Era* (Chapel Hill: University of North Carolina Press, 2000); Ron Robin, *The Making of the Cold War Enemy: Culture and Politics in the Military-Intellectual Complex* (Princeton, NJ:

Princeton University Press, 2001); Engerman et al., eds., *Staging Growth*; Nils Gilman, *Mandarins of the Future: Modernization Theory in Cold War America* (Baltimore: Johns Hopkins University Press, 2003); David Milne, *America's Rasputin: Walt Rostow and the Vietnam War* (New York: Hill and Wang, 2008).

26 Michael E. Latham, "Modernization," in Theodore M. Porter and Dorothy Ross, eds., *The Modern Social Sciences* (Cambridge: Cambridge University Press, 2003), 721–734, 727–728.

27 Frederick Cooper, "Development, Modernization, and the Social Sciences in the Era of Decolonization: The Examples of British and French Africa," [2004] in Miguel Bandeira Jerónimo and António Costa Pinto, eds., *The Ends of Colonial Empires: Cases and Comparisons* (Basingstoke: Palgrave Macmillan, 2015), 15–50, 32. Also see Frederick Cooper, *Decolonization and African Society: The Labor Question in French and British Africa* (Cambridge: Cambridge University Press, 1996), 376.

28 David Halloran Lumsdaine, *Moral Vision in International Politics: The Foreign Aid Regime, 1949–1989* (Princeton, NJ: Princeton University Press, 1993), 184. Italics mine.

29 Cf. Frederick Cooper, "Writing the History of Development," *Journal of Modern European History* 8.1 (2010): 5–23, 6–7; Barbara Weinstein, "Developing Inequality," *American Historical Review* 113.1 (2008): 1–18, 17–18.

30 Cooper, "Writing," 7.

31 For overviews, see Sara Lorenzini, *Una strana guerra fredda: Lo sviluppo e le relazioni Nord-Sud* (Bologna: Il Mulino, 2017); Joseph Morgan Hodge, "On the Historiography of Development (Part 1: The First Wave)," *Humanity* 6.3 (2015): 429–463; idem, "Writing the History of Development (Part 2: Wider, Longer, Deeper)," *Humanity* 7.1 (2016): 125–174; Frey, "Entwicklungspolitik"; Marc Frey and Sönke Kunkel, "Writing the History of Development: A Review of Recent Literature," *Contemporary European History* 20.2 (2011): 215–232; Corinna R. Unger, "Histories of Development and Modernization: Findings, Reflections, Future Research," *H-Soz-u-Kult*, September 12, 2010, http://hsozkult.geschichte.hu-berlin.de/forum/2010-12-001 (accessed July 22, 2016).

32 See, for example, Tirthankar Roy, "Geography or Politics? Regional Inequality in Colonial India," 2013, http://economics.yale.edu/sites/default/files/roy_paper_09_13.pdf (accessed July 21, 2016). For different interpretations on the inequality in terms of power and economic wealth, see David S. Landes, *The Wealth and Poverty of Nations: Why Some Are So Rich and Some Are So Poor* (New York: W. W. Norton, 1998); Jared M. Diamond, *Guns, Germs, and Steel: The Fates of Human Societies* (New York: W. W. Norton, 1997); Daron Acemoglu and James A. Robinson, *Why Nations Fail: The Origins of Power, Prosperity, and Poverty* (New York: Crown Publishers, 2012); Wolfgang Reinhard, *Die Unterwerfung der Welt: Globalgeschichte der europäischen Expansion, 1415–2015* (München: Beck, 2016).

33 Cf. Weinstein, "Developing Inequality."

34 Kenneth Lipartito, "Reassembling the Economic: New Departures in Historical Materialism," *American Historical Review* 121.1 (2016): 101–139, 101. Also see ibid., 135.

Chapter 2

1   Arndt, *Economic Development*, 1.
2   Hla Myint and Anne O. Krueger, "Economic Development," *Encyclopedia Britannica*, https://www.britannica.com/topic/economic-development (accessed July 4, 2017).
3   Cf. Robert E. Wood, *From Marshall Plan to Debt Crisis: Foreign Aid and Development Choices in the World Economy* (Berkeley: University of California Press, 1986), 11–12.
4   Most famously Amartya Sen, *Development as Freedom* (Oxford: Clarendon Press, 1999). For a synthesis of the book's argument, see Amartya Sen, "What Is Development About?" in Gerald M. Meier and Joseph E. Stiglitz, eds., *Frontiers of Development Economics: The Future in Perspective* (Oxford: World Bank and Oxford University Press, 2000), 506–513.
5   Richard Peet with Elaine Hartwick, *Theories of Development: Contentions, Arguments, Alternatives* (New York: The Guilford Press, 2009), 1. Also see the definition in Richard Jolly et al., *UN Contributions to Development Thinking and Practice* (Bloomington: Indiana University Press, 2004), 13.
6   One of the most influential books in this regard has been Arturo Escobar, *Encountering Development: The Making and Unmaking of the Third World* (Princeton, NJ: Princeton University Press, 1995).
7   See, among others, Wolfgang Sachs, ed., *The Development Dictionary* (London: Zen Books, 1992); James Ferguson, *The Anti-Politics Machine: "Development," Depoliticization, and Bureaucratic Power in Lesotho* (Minneapolis: University of Minnesota Press, 1994); James C. Scott, *Seeing Like a State: How Certain Schemes to Improve the Human Condition Have Failed* (New Haven, CT: Yale University Press, 1998).
8   See Niels P. Petersson, "'Großer Sprung nach vorn' oder 'natürliche Entwicklung'? Zeitkonzepte der Entwicklungspolitik im 20. Jahrhundert," in Hubertus Büschel and Daniel Speich, eds., *Entwicklungswelten: Globalgeschichte der Entwicklungszusammenarbeit* (Frankfurt am Main: Campus, 2009), 89–111.
9   Vincent, "Bolivia."
10 Cf. Michael Cowen and Robert Shenton, "The Invention of Development," in Jonathan Crush, ed., *Power of Development* (London: Routledge, 1996), 27–43, 28. Also see Joseph M. Hodge and Gerald Hödl, "Introduction," in Joseph M. Hodge, Gerald Hödl, and Martina Kopf, eds., *Developing Africa: Concepts and Practices in Twentieth-Century Colonialism* (Manchester: Manchester University Press, 2014), 1–34, 3.
11 Cf. Petersson, "Großer Sprung nach vorn"; Frey, "Entwicklungspolitik," 302.
12 Cf. Latham, *Modernization as Ideology*, 151. On the debate about the quote, see Nick Cullather, "Bomb Them Back to the Stone Age: An Etymology," *History News Network*, October 6, 2006, http://historynewsnetwork.org/article/30347 (accessed April 24, 2017).
13 See Nadine Vivier, ed., *The Golden Age of State Enquiries: Rural Enquiries in the Nineteenth Century. From Fact Gathering to Political Instrument* (Turnhout: Brepols, 2014).
14 Cf. Clavin, *Securing the World Economy*; Amy L. Sayward, *The United Nations in International History* (London: Bloomsbury, 2017), 85.

15 Cf. Arndt, *Economic Development*, 34–36; Juan Pan-Montojo, "International institutions and European agriculture: From the IIA to the FAO," in Carin Martiin, Juan Pan-Montojo and Paul Brassley, eds., *Agriculture in Capitalist Europe, 1945-1960: From food shortages to food surpluses* (Abingdon: Routledge, 2016), 23-43. Amy L. S. Staples, *The Birth of Development: How the World Bank, Food and Agriculture Organization, and World Health Organization Changed the World, 1945–1965* (Kent, OH: Kent State University Press, 2006), 69–71; Amalia Ribi Forclaz, "Agriculture, American Expertise, and the Quest for Global Data: Leon Estabrook and the First World Agricultural Census of 1930," *Journal of Global History* 11.1 (2016): 44–65, 47; idem, "A New Target for International Social Reform: The International Labour Organisation and Working and Living Conditions in Agriculture in the Interwar Years," *Journal of Contemporary European History* 20.3 (2011): 307–329; Ruth Jachertz and Alexander Nützenadel, "Coping with Hunger? Visions of a Global Food System, 1930–1960," *Journal of Global History* 6 (2011): 99–119, 103; Silvia Salvatici, *Nel nome degli altri: Storia dell'umanitarismo internazionale* (Bologna: Il Mulino, 2015), 257.

16 See Daniel Maul, *Human Rights, Development and Decolonization: The International Labour Organization, 1940–70* (Basingstoke: Palgrave Macmillan, 2012); Sandrine Kott and Joëlle Droux, eds., *Globalizing Social Rights: The International Labor Organization and Beyond* (Basingstoke: Palgrave Macmillan, 2013).

17 Matthias Schmelzer, *The Hegemony of Growth: The OECD and the Making of the Economic Growth Paradigm* (Cambridge: Cambridge University Press, 2016), 86.

18 Cf. Arndt, *Economic Development*, 35, 50–51; Schmelzer, *The Hegemony of Growth*, 88–92; Daniel Speich Chassé, *Die Erfindung des Bruttosozialprodukts: Globale Ungleichheit in der Wissensgeschichte der Ökonomie* (Göttingen: Vandenhoeck & Ruprecht, 2013), chapter 1.

19 For example, Landes, *The Wealth and Poverty of Nations*; Joel Mokyr, *A Culture of Growth: The Origins of the Modern Economy* (Princeton, NJ: Princeton University Press, 2017).

20 Cf. Kenneth Pomeranz, *The Great Divergence: China, Europe, and the Making of the Modern World* (Princeton, NJ: Princeton University Press, 2000); Bin Wong, *China Transformed: Historical Change and the Limits of the European Experience* (Ithaca, NY: Cornell University Press, 1997). Also see Patrick O'Brien, "Ten Years of Debate on the Origins of the Great Divergence," *Reviews in History* 1008 (2010), http://www.history.ac.uk/reviews/review/1008 (accessed January 19, 2017); Gareth Austin, "Reciprocal Comparison and African History: Tackling Conceptual Eurocentrism in the Study of Africa's Economic Past," *African Studies Review* 50.3 (2007): 1–28.

21 On Gerschenkron, see Robert Gwynne, "Alexander Gerschenkron," in David Simon, ed., *Fifty Key Thinkers on Development* (Abingdon: Routledge, 2006), 116–121.

22 Cf. Alexander Gerschenkron, "Economic Backwardness in Historical Perspective," in B. F. Hoselitz, ed., *The Progress of Underdeveloped Areas* (Chicago: University of Chicago Press, 1962), 3–29. Also see Michele Alacevich, *The Political Economy of the World Bank: The Early Years* (Stanford, CA: Stanford Economics and Finance and the World Bank, 2009), 74.

23 Clavin, *Securing the World Economy*, 196.

24 Cf. Arndt, *Economic Development*, 29–31.

25 See R. W. Davies, *Soviet Economic Development from Lenin to Khrushchev* (Cambridge: Cambridge University Press, 1998), 43–55; Robert C. Allen, *Farm to Factory: A Reinterpretation of the Soviet Industrial Revolution* (Princeton, NJ: Princeton University Press, 2003), 102–106.

26 See Paul N. Rosenstein-Rodan, "Problems of Industrialisation of Eastern and South-Eastern Europe," *Economic Journal* 53 (1943): 202–211. Also see Arndt, *Economic Development*, 58; Helleiner, *Forgotten Foundations*, 237–239.

27 Cf. Alacevich, *The Political Economy*, 71–72.

28 Ibid., 72. Also see Arndt, *Economic Development*, 54–55.

29 On Hirschman, see John Brohman, "Albert O. Hirschman," in Simon, ed., *Fifty Key Thinkers*, 126–132; Jeremy Adelman, *Worldly Philosopher: The Odyssey of Albert O. Hirschman* (Princeton, NJ: Princeton University Press, 2013); Anna Barbara Sum, "Widerspruch als Prinzip: Nachruf auf Albert O. Hirschman (7 April 1915—10 Dezember 2012)," *Geschichte und Gesellschaft* 39.1 (2013): 125–138.

30 Albert O. Hirschman, *The Strategy of Economic Development* (New Haven, CT: Yale University Press, 1958), 5.

31 Cf. Adelman, *Worldly Philosopher*, 346–347; Alacevich, *The Political Economy*, 74–75; Arndt, *Economic Development*, 59–60.

32 Walt W. Rostow, *The Stages of Economic Growth: A Non-Communist Manifesto* (Cambridge: Cambridge University Press, 1960).

33 Ibid., 1.

Chapter 3

1 Cf. Lumsdaine, *Moral Vision*, 184.

2 Friedrich Engels, *The Condition of the Working Class in England in 1844. With a Preface Written in 1892* (London: George Allen & Unwin, 1892). On early socialist thinkers, see Keith Taylor, *The Political Ideas of the Utopian Socialists* (Abingdon: Routledge, 1982).

3 See Anthony Brundage, *The English Poor Laws, 1700–1930* (Basingstoke: Palgrave Macmillan, 2002).

4 Cf. Lynn Hollen Lees, *The Solidarities of Strangers: The English Poor Laws and the People, 1700–1948* (Cambridge: Cambridge University Press, 1998), 14, 60.

5 Ibid., 150.

6 Cf. ibid., 147, 144.

7 Cf. Jürgen Osterhammel, "'The Great Work of Uplifting Mankind': Zivilisierungsmission und Moderne," in Boris Barth and Jürgen Osterhammel, eds., *Zivilisierungsmissionen: Imperiale Weltverbesserung seit dem 18. Jahrhundert* (Konstanz: UVK Verlag, 2005), 363–425.

8 Cf. Sebastian Conrad, "'Eingeborenenpolitik' in Kolonie und Metropole: 'Erziehung zur Arbeit' in Ostafrika und Ostwestfalen," in Sebastian Conrad and Jürgen Osterhammel, eds., *Das Kaiserreich transnational: Deutschland in der Welt 1871–1944* (Göttingen: Vandenhoeck & Ruprecht, 2004), 107–128. For similar discourses on labor and discipline, see Eric Worby, "'Discipline without Oppression': Sequence, Timing and Marginality in Southern Rhodesia's Post-War Development Regime," *The Journal of African History*

41.1 (2000): 101–125, 104–107. On the notion of the protestant work ethic and its translation into practice, see Andrew Zimmerman, *Alabama in Africa: Booker T. Washington, the German Empire, and the Globalization of the New South* (Princeton, NJ: Princeton University Press, 2012), 212–217.

9 Cf. Conrad, "'Eingeborenenpolitik'"; Hubertus Büschel, *Hilfe zur Selbsthilfe: Deutsche Entwicklungsarbeit in Afrika, 1960–1975* (Frankfurt am Main: Campus, 2014), 137–140. Also see Zimmerman, *Alabama in Africa*, 138–139.

10 Cf. Osterhammel, "The Great Work," 420–421.

11 Cf. Cláudia Castelo, "Developing 'Portuguese Africa' in Late Colonialism: Confronting Discourses," in Hodge, Hödl, and Kopf, eds., *Developing Africa*, 63–86, 64–65. Also see Miguel Bandeira Jéronimo, *The "Civilizing Mission" of Portuguese Colonialism (c. 1830–1970)* (London: Palgrave Macmillan, 2015).

12 Cf. Osterhammel, "The Great Work," 382.

13 Michael Mann, "'Torchbearers Upon the Path of Progress': Britain's Ideology of a 'Moral and Material Progress' in India," in Harald Fischer-Tiné and Michael Mann, eds., *Colonialism as Civilizing Mission: Cultural Ideology in British India* (London: Anthem Press, 2004), 1–26, 5.

14 See Salvatici, *Nel nome degli altri*, 35–50; Amalia Ribi Forclaz, *Humanitarian Imperialism: The Politics of Anti-Slavery Activism, 1880–1940* (Oxford: Oxford University Press, 2015); Osterhammel, "The Great Work," 401–403, 406–408.

15 See Adam Hochschild, *King Leopold's Ghost: A Story of Greed, Terror, and Heroism in Colonial Africa* (New York: Houghton Mifflin, 1999); Osterhammel, "The Great Work," 404–406; Matthew G. Stanard, *Selling the Congo: A History of European Pro-Empire Propaganda and the Making of Belgian Imperialism* (Lincoln: University of Nebraska Press, 2011).

16 Cf. Osterhammel, "The Great Work," 364.

17 Cf. Stefan Hübner, "Muscular Christianity and the Western Civilizing Mission: Elwood S. Brown, the YMCA, and the Idea of the Far Eastern Championship Games," *Diplomatic History* 39.3 (2015): 532–557.

18 Cf. Osterhammel, "The Great Work," 371.

19 See Daniel Laqua, "Inside the Humanitarian Cloud: Causes and Motivations to Help Friends and Strangers," *Journal of Modern European History* 12.2 (2014): 175–185.

20 See Davide Rodogno, *Against Massacre: Humanitarian Interventions in the Ottoman Empire, 1815–1914: The Emergence of a European Concept and International Practice* (Princeton, NJ: Princeton University Press, 2012).

21 See W. Boyd Rayward, ed., *Information Beyond Borders: International Cultural and Intellectual Exchange in the Belle Èpoque* (Farnham: Ashgate, 2014); Michaela M. Hampf and Simone Müller-Pohl, eds., *Global Communication Electric: Business, News and Politics in the World of Telegraphy* (Frankfurt am Main: Campus, 2013).

22 See Salvatici, *Nel nome degli altri*, 83–100.

23 See the contributions on famines and humanitarian relief in *European Review of History* 22.6 (2015): 855–970. Also see Salvatici, *Nel nome degli altri*, 141.

24 Cf. Lumsdaine, *Moral Vision*, 188–191.

25 Cf. Daniel Roger Maul, "The Rise of a Humanitarian Superpower: American NGOs and International Relief, 1917–1945," in Miguel Bandeira Jerónimo and José Pedro Monteiro, eds., *Internationalism, Imperialism, and the Formation of the Contemporary World: The Pasts of the Present* (Basingstoke: Palgrave Macmillan, 2017), 127–146, 136–137.

26 Cf. Olav Stokke, *The UN and Development: From Aid to Cooperation* (Bloomington: University of Indiana Press, 2009), 37.

27 Semih Çelik, "Between History of Humanitarianism and Humanitarianization of History: A Discussion on Ottoman Help for the Victims of the Great Irish Famine, 1845–1852," *WerkstattGeschichte* 68 (2015): 13–28.

28 Esther Möller, "Between Globalisation and Contestation: Humanity as a Polemical Concept within the Red Cross and Red Crescent Movement," in Fabian Klose and Mirjam Thulin, eds., *Humanity: A History of European Concepts in Practice from the 16th Century to the Present* (Göttingen: Vandenhoeck & Ruprecht, 2016), 209–227; Yannan Li, "Red Cross Society in Imperial China, 1904–1912: A Historical Analysis," *Voluntas* 27.5 (2016): 2274–2291.

29 Cf. Salvatici, *Nel nome degli altri*, 119.

30 See, for example, Stefan Dyroff, "Minority Rights and Humanitarianism: The International Campaign for the Ukrainians in Poland, 1930–1931," *Journal of Modern European History* 12.2 (2014): 216–230; Staples, *The Birth of Development*, 129–130.

31 See Salvatici, *Nel nome degli altri*, 146–152.

32 Cf. Lumsdaine, *Moral Vision*, 192.

33 See Salvatici, *Nel nome degli altri*, 123–176.

34 Cf. Maul, "The Rise of a Humanitarian Superpower," 132–133; Salvatici, *Nel nome degli altri*, 163–174; David C. Engerman, *Modernization from the Other Shore: American Intellectuals and the Romance of Russian Development* (Cambridge, MA: Harvard University Press, 2003), chapter 6. Also see Nick Cullather, "The Foreign Policy of the Calorie," *American Historical Review* 112.2 (2007): 337–364, 348–352.

35 Cf. Rodgers, *Atlantic Crossings*, chapter 6.

36 See Roger Chickering and Stig Förster, eds., *Great War, Total War: Combat and Mobilization on the Western Front, 1914–1918* (Washington, DC: German Historical Institute; New York: Cambridge University Press, 2000); Hodge, *Triumph*, 92–93.

37 Cf. Michael Geyer, "Ein Vorbote des Wohlfahrtsstaates: Die Kriegsopferversorgung in Frankreich, Deutschland und Großbritannien nach dem Ersten Weltkrieg," *Geschichte und Gesellschaft* 9.2 (1983): 230–277.

38 See Adam Tooze, *The Deluge: The Great War and the Remaking of Global Order, 1916–1931* (London: Allen Lane, 2014), chapter 12; Pierluigi Pironti, "Post-war Welfare Policies (Version 1.1)," *1914–1918 Online: International Encyclopedia of the First World War* (2017), doi: 10.15463/ie1418.10358/1.1 (accessed April 12, 2017).

39 Cf. Hodge, *Triumph*, 187–188.

40 See Helga Schultz and Angela Harre, eds., *Bauerngesellschaften auf dem Weg in die Moderne: Agrarismus in Ostmitteleuropa 1880 bis 1960* (Wiesbaden: Harrassowitz, 2010); Wim Van Meurs, "Demokratie oder Sozialismus? Bauernparteien in Südosteuropa um die Jahrhundertwende als Träger der Demokratisierung. Eine Skizze," *Archiv für Sozialgeschichte* 53 (2013): 93–112.

41 Cf. Nicole Sackley, "The Village as Cold War Site: Experts, Development, and the History of Rural Reconstruction," *Journal of Global History* 6 (2011): 481–504, 487.

42 Cf. Benjamin Zachariah, *Developing India: An Intellectual and Social History* (New Delhi: Oxford University Press, 2005), chapter 4; Rana P. B. Singh, "Mohandas (Mahatma) Gandhi," in Simon, ed., *Fifty Key Thinkers*, 106–111.

43 Cf. Helen Tilley, *Africa as a Living Laboratory: Empire, Development, and the Problem of Scientific Knowledge, 1870–1950* (Chicago: University of Chicago Press, 2011), 132–133; Patel, *The New Deal*, 31–32; Hodge, *Triumph*, 181.

44 Cf. Jachertz and Nützenadel, "Coping with Hunger?" 102.

45 See Thomas Robertson, *The Malthusian Moment: Global Population Growth and the Birth of American Environmentalism* (New Brunswick, NJ: Rutgers University Press, 2012), 13–22.

46 Cf. Clavin, *Securing the World Economy*, 179–180, 195; Sunil S. Amrith, "Internationalising Health in the Twentieth Century," in Glenda Sluga and Patricia Clavin, eds., *Internationalisms: A Twentieth-Century History* (Cambridge: Cambridge University Press, 2017), 245–264, 249.

47 Cf. Katja Bruisch, *Als das Dorf noch Zukunft war: Agrarismus und Expertise zwischen Zarenreich und Sowjetunion* (Köln: Böhlau, 2014), 17.

48 Cf. Zimmerman, *Alabama in Africa*, chapter 2; Lorraine Bluche and Kiran Klaus Patel, "Der Europäer als Bauer: Das Motiv des bäuerlichen Familienbetriebs in Westeuropa nach 1945," in Lorraine Bluche, Veronika Lipphardt and Kiran Klaus Patel, eds., *Der Europäer—ein Konstrukt: Wissensbestände, Diskurse, Praktiken* (Göttingen: Wallstein, 2009), 135–157, 137; Fritz Georg von Graevenitz, *Argument Europa: Internationalismus in der globalen Agrarkrise der Zwischenkriegszeit (1927–1937)* (Frankfurt am Main: Campus, 2017), 132–133; Patel, *The New Deal*, 57; Gunther Mai, "Die Agrarische Transition: Agrarische Gesellschaften in Europa und die Herausforderungen der industriellen Moderne im 19. und 20. Jahrhundert," *Geschichte und Gesellschaft* 33.4 (2007): 471–514, 485–490.

49 Cf. Mai, "Die Agrarische Transition," 490–498; Sackley, "The Village," 484–485.

50 Cf. Subir Sinha, "Lineages of the Developmentalist State: Transnationality and Village India, 1900–1965," *Comparative Studies in Society and History* 50.1 (2008): 57–90.

51 Cf. Amrith, "Internationalising Health," 249–252.

52 Cf. Sackley, "The Village," 485–487; Liesbeth van de Grift, "'On New Land a New Society': Internal Colonisation in the Netherlands, 1918–1940," *Contemporary European History* 22.4 (2013): 609–626.

53 Cf. Sackley, "The Village," 486; Ekbladh, *The Great American Mission*, 21–25.

54 Cf. Joseph M. Hodge, "British Colonial Expertise: Post-Colonial Careering and the Early History of International Development," *Journal of Modern European History* 8.1 (2010): 24–46, 29; Corinna R. Unger, *Entwicklungspfade in Indien: Eine internationale Geschichte, 1947–1980* (Göttingen: Wallstein, 2015), 109.

55 See the overview by Mai, "Die Agrarische Transition."

56 See, among others, Margherita Zanasi, "Exporting Development: The League of Nations and Republican China," *Comparative Studies in Society and History* 49.1 (2007): 143–169.

57 Cf. Clavin, *Securing the World Economy*, 197; Zimmerman, *Alabama in Africa*, 80–81; Ann-Christina L. Knudsen, "Ideas, Welfare, and Values: The Framing of the Common Agricultural Policy in the 1960s," in Kiran Klaus

Patel, ed., *Fertile Ground for Europe? The History of European Integration and the Common Agricultural Policy since 1945* (Baden-Baden: Nomos, 2009), 61–78, 73–74.

58 Cf. Bluche and Patel, "Der Europäer," 139, 146–147; Graevenitz, *Argument Europa*, 136–138.

59 Cf. Zimmerman, *Alabama in Africa*, 98.

60 Cf. Patel, *The New Deal*, 32–33.

61 See Graevenitz, *Argument Europa*.

62 Cf. Helleiner, *Forgotten Foundations*, 16.

63 Cf. Zachariah, *Developing India*, 115–117. The following is based on Corinna R. Unger, "The Decolonization of Development: Rural Development in India Before and After 1947," in Bandeira Jéronimo and Monteiro, eds., *Internationalism*, 253–278.

64 Cf. Ajantha Subramanian, *Shorelines: Space and Rights in South Asia* (Stanford, CA: Stanford University Press, 2009), 106–109, 117; Unger, *Entwicklungspfade*, 25–26.

65 Cf. Unger, *Entwicklungspfade*, 27–29. Also see Sackley, "The Village," 486.

66 Cf. Unger, *Entwicklungspfade*, 30; Sinha, "Lineages," 67, footnote 22.

67 Cf. Paul Kelemen, "Planning for Africa: The British Labour Party's Colonial Development Policy, 1920–1964," *Journal of Agrarian Change* 7.1 (2007): 76–98, 80; Ekbladh, *The Great American Mission*, 29; Marc Frey, "Control, Legitimacy, and the Securing of Interests: European Development Policy in South-east Asia from the Late Colonial Period to the Early 1960s," *Contemporary European History* 12.4 (2003): 395–412, 397.

68 Cf. Rohland Schuknecht, *British Colonial Development Policy after the Second World War: The Case of Sukumaland, Tanganyika* (Berlin: Lit, 2010), 267.

69 Cf. Kelemen, "Planning for Africa," 85–86; Schuknecht, *British Colonial Development Policy*, 268–269; Unger, *Entwicklungspfade*, 29.

70 Cf. Schuknecht, *British Colonial Development Policy*, 280–281; Unger, "The Decolonization of Development," 268–269.

71 Cf. Schuknecht, *British Colonial Development Policy*, 285.

72 Cited in Hodge, *Triumph*, 8; Frey, "Entwicklungspolitik," 295.

73 Cf. Tilley, *Africa*, 64.

74 Cf. Frey, "Entwicklungspolitik," 296; Stokke, *The UN*, 34; Tilley, *Africa*, 124.

75 Cf. Herward Sieberg, *Colonial Development: Die Grundlegung moderner Entwicklungspolitik durch Großbritannien, 1919–1949* (Stuttgart: Steiner, 1985), 1–8.

76 Cf. Erez Manela, *The Wilsonian Moment: Self-Determination and the International Origins of Anticolonial Nationalism* (Oxford: Oxford University Press, 2007), 81.

77 Cf. Tooze, *The Deluge*, 180–189, 382–390. Also see Sanjoy Bhattacharya and Benjamin Zachariah, "'A Great Destiny': The British Colonial State and the Advertisement of Post-War Reconstruction in India, 1942–1945," *South Asia Research* 19.1 (1999): 71–100.

78 See Manela, *The Wilsonian Moment*.

79 Cf. Susan Pedersen, *The Guardians: The League of Nations and the Crisis of Empire* (Oxford: Oxford University Press, 2015), 78–95. Also see Tracey Banivanua Mar, *Decolonisation and the Pacific: Indigenous Globalisation*

and the Ends of Empire (Cambridge: Cambridge University Press, 2016), chapter 3.

80 See Pedersen, *The Guardians*, 1–3, 61.

81 Cf. ibid., 4; Mar, *Decolonisation and the Pacific*, 95, 98–99, 102.

82 Pedersen, *The Guardians*, 231.

83 On Lugard's role in the Permanent Mandates Commission, see ibid., 107–111.

84 Frederick J. D. Lugard, *The Dual Mandate in British Tropical Africa* (Edinburgh: W. Blackwood and Sons, 1922).

85 Cited in Hodge, *Triumph*, 118.

86 Cf. Cooper, *Decolonization and African Society*, 32; Pedersen, *The Guardians*, 110; Alice L. Conklin, *A Mission to Civilize: The Republican Idea of Empire in France and West Africa, 1895–1930* (Berkeley: University of California Press, 1997), 217–218; Hodge, *Triumph*, 119.

87 See Marc Frey, "Doctrines and Practices of Agrarian Development: The Case of the Office du Niger in Mali," *Comparativ* 27.2 (2017): 15–34; Monica M. Van Beusekom, "Disjunctures in Theory and Practice: Making Sense of Change in Agricultural Development at the Office du Niger, 1920–60," *Journal of African History* 41.1 (2000): 79–99; Hodge and Hödl, "Introduction," 11–12.

88 Cf. Frey, "Doctrines and Practices," 18.

89 Cf. Cooper, *Decolonization*, 34. Also see Conklin, *A Mission to Civilize*, 223–235.

90 Van Beusekom, "Disjunctures," 82.

91 Cf. Frey, "Doctrines and Practices," 19–20.

92 Cf. Van Beseukom, "Disjunctures," 83–84.

93 Cf. ibid., 85.

94 Cf. Frey, "Doctrines and Practices," 22.

95 Cf. Van Beusekom, "Disjunctures," 98.

96 On Soviet cotton growing efforts in Uzbekistan, see Christian Teichmann, "Canals, Cotton, and the Limits of De-colonization in Soviet Uzbekistan, 1924–1941," *Central Asian Survey* 26.4 (2007): 499–519. On German efforts to establish a commercial cotton industry in Togo in the early twentieth century, see Zimmerman, *Alabama in Africa*, chapter 3. Zimmerman argues that the effect of the project, which had promised progress, resulted in the regression "from literate office work to agricultural labor, from domesticity to social disintegration, from prosperity to poverty, from skilled work to forced labor, and from freedom to domination." Ibid., 171.

97 Cf. Sieberg, *Colonial Development*, 22–24, 61–64; Hodge, *Triumph*, 106.

98 On Keynes, see Robert Skidelsky, *John Maynard Keynes (1883–1946): Economist, Philosopher, Statesmen* (New York: Penguin, 2005); Richard Davenport-Hines, *Universal Man: The Seven Lives of John Maynard Keynes* (London: Basic Books, 2015).

99 Hodge, *Triumph*, 106. Also see Sieberg, *Colonial Development*, 56–57; Lumsdaine, *Moral Vision*, 209.

100 Cf. Sieberg, *Colonial Development*, 69, 77–78.

101 Cf. Cooper, *Decolonization*, 73–107.

102 Cf. Staples, *The Birth of Development*, 72–74.

103 Cf. Sieberg, *Colonial Development*, 132–142.

104 Cited in ibid., 143.

105 Cf. Cooper, *Decolonization*, 111.

106 Cf. William Beinart, "Soil Erosion, Conservationism, and Ideas about Development: A Southern African Exploration, 1900–1960," *Journal of Southern African Studies* 11.1 (1984): 52–83, 66; Schuknecht, *British Colonial Development Policy*, 51–55.

107 Cf. Beinart, "Soil Erosion," 68–70; Schuknecht, *British Colonial Development Policy*, 63–67; Hodge, *Triumph*, chapter 3; Tilley, *Africa*, 154–159; Sven Speek, "Ecological Concepts of Development? The Case of Colonial Zambia," in Hodge, Hödl, and Kopf, eds., *Developing Africa*, 133–154, 138–145.

108 See James Fairhead and Melissa Leach, "Desiccation and Domination: Science and Struggles over Environment and Development in Colonial Guinea," *The Journal of African History* 41.1 (2000): 34–54; Hodge, *Triumph*, 164–166; Robertson, *The Malthusian Moment*, 26.

109 Cf. Maria Dörnemann, "Seeing Population as a Problem: Influences of the Construction of Population Knowledge on Kenyan Politics (1940s to 1980s)," in Heinrich Hartmann and Corinna R. Unger, eds., *A World of Populations: Transnational Perspectives on Demography in the Twentieth Century* (New York: Berghahn Books, 2014), 201–221, 203–204. Also see Hodge, *Triumph*, 123–124; Samuël Coghe and Alexandra Widmer, "Colonial Demography: Discourses, Rationalities, Methods," in The Population Knowledge Network, ed., *Twentieth Century Population Thinking: A Critical Reader in Primary Sources* (Abingdon: Routledge, 2016), 37–64, 40.

110 Cf. Hodge, *Triumph*, 171–175.

111 Cf. Dorothy L. Hodgson, "Taking Stock: State Control, Ethnic Identity and Pastoralist Development in Tanganyika, 1948–1958," *Journal of African History* 41 (2000): 58–78, 65; Hodge, *Triumph*, 134, 137–141, 168–170. Also see D. A. Low and J. M. Lonsdale, "Introduction: Towards the New Order, 1945–1963," in D. A. Low and Alison Smith, eds., *History of East Africa*, 3 vols. (Oxford: Oxford University Press, 1976), vol. 3, 1–63, 22–32.

112 Cf. Cooper, "Development," 19–21; Schuknecht, *British Colonial Development Policy*, 14–15, 17–18; Kelemen, "Planning for Africa," 77.

113 Cf. Tilley, *Africa*, 4–5; Cooper, "Development," 29–30.

114 Hodge, *Triumph*, 231.

115 Cf. Schuknecht, *British Colonial Development Policy*, 130, 136; Beinart, "Soil Erosion," 80–81; Stephanie Lämmert, *Finding the Right Words: Languages of Litigation in Shambaa Native Courts in Tanganyika, c. 1925–1960*. PhD dissertation, European University Institute, 2017, chapter 2.

116 Cf. Hodgson, "Taking Stock," 58–59.

117 Cf. Sackley, "The Village," 503–504; Cooper, *Decolonization*, 212; Schuknecht, *British Colonial Development Policy*, 30; Hodge, *Triumph*, 217–223; Hodge, "British Colonial Expertise," 30, footnote 10.

118 Cf. Dörnemann, "Seeing Population," 204–205; Hodge, *Triumph*, 157, 166–167, 183. On demographic data on Tanganyika produced in the 1930s, which suggested high population growth rates, see Schuknecht, *British Colonial Development Policy*, 60–61.

119 Martin Shipway, *Decolonization and its Impact: A Comparative Approach to the End of the Colonial Empires* (Malden, MA: Blackwell Publishing, 2008), 147.

120 Ibid., 148–149.

121 Cf. ibid., 149, 168.

122 Cf. Ullrich Lohrmann, *Voices from Tanganyika: Great Britain, the United Nations and the Decolonization of a Trust Territory, 1946–1961* (Berlin: Lit, 2007), 298; Castelo, "Developing 'Portuguese Africa' in Late Colonialism," 72–74.

123 See Michael McWilliam, "The Managed Economy: Agricultural Change, Development, and Finance in Kenya," in Low and Smith, eds., *History of East Africa*, vol. 3, 251–289.

124 See Lohrmann, *Voices*, 316–348.

125 Cf. Samuël Coghe, "Reordering Colonial Society: Model Villages and Social Planning in Rural Angola, 1920–45," *Journal of Contemporary History* 52.1 (2017): 16–44.

126 Cf. Cooper, *Decolonization*, 226–227.

127 See Nicola Labanca, "Italian Colonial Internment," in Ruth Ben-Ghiat and Mia Fuller, eds., *Italian Colonialism* (Basingstoke: Palgrave Macmillan, 2005), 27–36.

128 Cf. Sackley, "The Village," 497–503; Miguel Bandeira Jéronimo, "Rural (In)Securities: Resettlement, Control, and 'Development' in Angola (1960s–1970s)," *Comparativ* 27.2 (2017): 75–97; Stephan Malinowski, "Modernisierungskriege: Militärische Gewalt und koloniale Modernisierung im Algerienkrieg (1954–1962)," *Archiv für Sozialgeschichte* 48 (2008): 213–248.

129 Cf. Muriam Haleh Davis, "Restaging *Mise en Valeur*: 'Postwar Imperialism' and the Plan de Constantine," *Review of Middle East Studies* 44.2 (2010): 176–186, 176–177; Moritz Feichtinger, "'A Great Reformatory': Social Planning and Strategic Resettlement in Late Colonial Kenya and Algeria, 1952–63," *Journal of Contemporary History* 52.1 (2017): 45–72; Gérard Bossuat, "French Development Aid and Co-operation under de Gaulle," *Contemporary European History* 12.4 (2003): 431–456, 445.

130 Beusekom and Hodgson, "Lessons Learned?" 33.

131 Cf. Kris Manjapra, *Age of Entanglement: German and Indian Intellectuals across Empire* (Cambridge, MA: Harvard University Press, 2014), 155–158; Unger, *Entwicklungspfade*, 31–33.

132 Low and Lonsdale, "Introduction," 46.

133 See Eric Hobsbawm, *The Age of Extremes: A History of the World, 1914–1991* (New York: Pantheon Books, 1994), chapter 4.

134 See Federico Caprotti, *Mussolini's Cities: Internal Colonialism in Italy, 1930–1939* (Amherst: Cambria Press, 2007).

135 See Thomas Zeller, *Driving Germany: The Landscape of the German Autobahn, 1930–1970* (New York: Berghahn Books, 2007), chapter 4.

136 See, among others, Dan P. Silverman, *Hitler's Economy: Nazi Work Creation Programs, 1933–1936* (Cambridge, MA: Harvard University Press, 1998).

137 See Stefano Grando and Gianluca Volpi, "Backwardness, Modernization, Propaganda: Agrarian Policies and Rural Representations in the Italian Fascist Regime," in Lourenzo Fernández Pietros, Juan Pan-Montojo, and Miguel

Cabo, eds., *Agriculture in the Age of Fascism: Authoritarian Technocracy and Rural Modernization, 1922–1945* (Turnhout: Brepols, 2014), 43–83; Gesine Gerhard, "The Modernization Dilemma: Agrarian Policies in Nazi Germany," in ibid., 139–155; Willi Oberkrome, "National Socialist Blueprints for Rural Communities and their Resonance in Agrarian Society," in Martina Steber and Bernhard Gotto, eds., *Visions of Community in Nazi Germany: Social Engineering and Private Lives* (Oxford: Oxford University Press, 2014), 270–280; Adam Tooze, *The Wages of Destruction: The Making and Breaking of the Nazi Economy* (London: Allen Lane, 2006), chapter 6.

138 See Mia Fuller, *Moderns Abroad: Architecture, Cities and Italian Imperialism* (Abingdon: Routledge, 2007), chapter 8.

139 See Isabel Heinemann and Patrick Wagner, eds., *Wissenschaft, Planung, Vertreibung: Der Generalplan Ost der Nationalsozialisten* (Stuttgart: Steiner, 2006); Michael Burleigh, *Germany Turns Eastwards: A Study of Ostforschung in the Third Reich* (New York: Macmillan, 2002). On the debates about connections between German colonialism, the Nazi occupation and exploitation of Central Eastern and Eastern Europe during the Second World War, and the Holocaust, see Birthe Kundrus, "Colonialism, Imperialism, National Socialism: How Imperial Was the Third Reich," in Bradley Naranch and Geoff Eley, eds., *German Colonialism in a Global Age* (Durham: Duke University Press, 2014), 330–346; Jürgen Zimmerer, *From Windhoek to Auschwitz: On the Relationship between Colonialism and the Holocaust* (Abingdon: Routledge, 2018).

140 Cited in Anne D. Rassweiler, *The Generation of Power: The History of Dneprostroi* (New York: Oxford University Press, 1988), 13.

141 Cf. ibid., 13–19.

142 Cf. ibid., 8–11.

143 See Michael David-Fox, *Showcasing the Great Experiment: Cultural Diplomacy and Western Visitors to the Soviet Union, 1921–1941* (Oxford: Oxford University Press, 2012); Engerman, *Modernization*, chapter 8; Patel, *The New Deal*, 37–38, 91–92; Westad, *The Global Cold War*, 80–81.

144 Cf. Rassweiler, *The Generation of Power*, 92–98.

145 Cf. Stephen Kotkin, *Magnetic Mountain: Stalinism as a Civilization* (Berkeley: University of California Press, 1995).

146 See R. W. Davies and Stephen G. Wheatcroft, *The Years of Hunger: Soviet Agriculture, 1931–1933* (Basingstoke: Palgrave Macmillan, 2004); Constantin Iordachi and Arnd Bauernkämper, eds., *The Collectivization of Agriculture in Communist Eastern Europe: Comparison and Entanglements* (Budapest: Central European University Press, 2014); Allen, *Farm to Factory*, 97–102.

147 See Lynn Viola, *Peasant Rebels under Stalin: Collectivization and the Culture of Peasant Resistance* (Oxford: Oxford University Press, 1996); Sheila Fitzpatrick, *Stalin's Peasants: Resistance and Survival in the Russian Village after Collectivization* (Oxford: Oxford University Press, 1994); Adrienne Lynn Edgar, *Tribal Nation: The Making of Soviet Turkmenistan* (Princeton, NJ: Princeton University Press, 2004), 205–210; Christian Teichmann, *Macht der Unordnung: Stalins Herrschaft in Zentralasien, 1920–1950* (Hamburg: Hamburger Edition, 2016), 133–135.

148 See Teichmann, *Macht der Unordnung*, 119–121; Robert Conquest, *The Harvest of Sorrow: Soviet Collectivization and the Terror-Famine* (New York:

Oxford University Press, 1986); Ann Applebaum, *Red Famine: Stalin's War on Ukraine* (New York: Doubleday, 2017).

149 See Engerman, *Modernization*, chapter 9.

150 Cf. Clavin, *Securing the World Economy*, 176, 196.

151 Cf. Ekbladh, *The Great American Mission*, 42–49.

152 Cf. ibid., 53–56.

153 Cf. David Ekbladh, "'Mr. TVA': Grass-Roots Development, David Lilienthal, and the Rise and Fall of the Tennessee Valley Authority as a Symbol for U.S. Overseas Development, 1933–1973," *Diplomatic History* 26.3 (2002): 335–374, 340–344.

154 For a comparison of three regimes and their respective modernization policies, see Wolfgang Schivelbusch, *Three New Deals: Reflections on Roosevelt's America, Mussolini's Italy, and Hitler's Germany, 1933–1939* (New York: Metropolitan Books, 2006).

155 Cf. Stephen Macekura, "The Point Four Program and U.S. International Development Policy," *Political Science Quarterly* 128.1 (2013): 127–160, 132–133; Frey, "The Limits of Modernization," 48. Not everyone shared this perception: Agrarian economist Karl Brandt (1899–1975) argued in 1953 that the TVA had received more attention than it deserved, both with regard to its role in modernizing the American South and with regard to its potential usefulness for other world regions. Cf. Karl Brandt, "The Economic Objectives of F.A.O., Point IV, and the Colombo Plan," in *Proceedings of the Eight International Conference of Agricultural Economists* (London: Oxford University Press, 1953), 117–133, 128–129.

Chapter 4

1 Cf. Ruth Ginio, "Vichy Rule in French West Africa: Prelude to Decolonization?" *French Colonial History* 4 (2003): 205–226, 218. Also see Elizabeth Thompson, *Colonial Citizens: Republican Rights, Paternal Privilege, and Gender in French* Syria *and Lebanon* (New York: Columbia University Press, 2000), chapter 14.

2 See Janam Mukherjee, *Hungry Bengal: War, Famine, and the End of Empire* (New York: Oxford University Press, 2015); Madhusree Mukerjee, *Churchill's Secret War: The British Empire and the Ravaging of India during World War II* (New York: Basic Books, 2010).

3 Cf. Taylor C. Sherman, "From 'Grow More Food' to 'Miss a Meal': Hunger, Development, and the Limits of Post-Colonial Nationalism in India, 1947–1957," *South Asia* 36.4 (2013): 571–588; Schuknecht, *British Colonial Development Policy*, 86–87.

4 See Shipway, *Decolonization*, chapters 2 and 3.

5 Cf. Yasmin Khan, *India at War: The Subcontinent and the Second World War* (New York: Oxford University Press, 2015), 51–61, 132–141; Shipway, *Decolonization*, 75–77.

6 Robert L. Tignor, W. *Arthur Lewis and the Birth of Development Economics* (Princeton, NJ: Princeton University Press, 2006), 42.

7 Cf. Maul, *Human Rights*, 56.

8 Cf. Cooper, *Decolonization*, 177–182; Frederick Cooper, *Citizenship between Empire and Nation: Remaking France and French Africa, 1945–1960* (Princeton, NJ: Princeton University Press, 2014), 27–28.

9 Cf. Hodge, *Triumph*, 8, 198–199; Schuknecht, *British Colonial Development Policy*, 89–91; Frederick Cooper, "Possibility and Constraint: African Independence in Historical Perspective," *Journal of African History* 49 (2008): 167–196, 171.

10 Cf. Shipway, *Decolonization*, 65–67.

11 Cf. Andreas Eckert, "Regulating the Social: Social Security, Social Welfare and the State in Late Colonial Tanzania," *Journal of African History* 45.3 (2004): 467–489, 476–478. Also see Charles Ambler, "Alcohol, Racial Segregation and Popular Politics in Northern Rhodesia," [1990] in James D. Le Sueur, ed., *The Decolonization Reader* (New York: Routledge, 2003), 341–357, 343–344; McWilliam, "The Managed Economy," 276–277.

12 Cf. Low and Lonsdale, "Introduction," 12–16, 43.

13 On earlier instances of intra-imperial cooperation, see Volker Barth and Roland Cvetkovski, eds., *Imperial Co-operation and Transfer, 1870–1930* (London: Bloomsbury, 2015).

14 Cf. Sieberg, *Colonial Development*, 565–570; Cooper, *Decolonization*, 221–222.

15 Cf. Vernon McKay, "Needs and Opportunities in Africa," *Annals of the American Academy of Political and Social Science* 268 (1950): 75–84, 80.

16 Cooper, "Development," 25. Also see Tilley, *Africa*, 71; Hodge, *Triumph*, 12.

17 Cf. Sieberg, *Colonial Development*, 152–166; Hodge, *Triumph*, 181–182; Cooper, *Decolonization*, 58; Schuknecht, *British Colonial Development Policy*, 13.

18 Cf. Sieberg, *Colonial Development*, 216–217.

19 Beusekom and Hodgson, "Lessons Learned?" 31.

20 Cf. Hodge, *Triumph*, 192, 208; Sieberg, *Colonial Development*, 527–539; Cooper, *Decolonization*, 67; Kelemen, "Planning for Africa," 83; Lumsdaine, *Moral Vision*, 209.

21 Cf. Kelemen, "Planning for Africa," 76; Cooper, *Decolonization*, 205.

22 Cf. Bossuat, "French Development Aid," 435; Lumsdaine, *Moral Vision*, 209; Dirk Van Laak, "Detours around Africa: The Connection between Developing Colonies and Integrating Europe," in Alexander Badenoch and Andreas Fischer, eds., *Materializing Europe: Transnational Infrastructures and the Project of Europe* (Basingstoke: Palgrave Macmillan, 2010), 27–43, 34; Cooper, *Decolonization*, 194–195; Hodge, *Triumph*, 192, 196–206.

23 Cf. Sieberg, *Colonial Development*, 220.

24 Cf. Beusekom and Hodgson, "Lessons Learned?" 31.

25 Cf. Sieberg, *Colonial Development*, 239–240.

26 Cited in Tignor, *W. Arthur Lewis*, 30. Also see Hodge, *Triumph*, 196.

27 See Marina Diallo Cô-Trung, *La Compagnie générale des oléagineux tropicaux en Casamance. Autopsie d'une opération de mise en valeur coloniale (1948–1962)* (Paris: Karthala, 1998). Also see Schuknecht, *British Colonial Development Policy*, 216–222; Hodgson, "Taking Stock"; Hodge, *Triumph*, 214–223.

28 Cf. Hodge, *Triumph*, 208; Cooper, *Decolonization*, 203–204; Schuknecht, *British Colonial Development Policy*, 196–198; William Roger Louis and

Ronald Robinson, "The Imperialism of Decolonization," [1994] in Le Sueur, ed., *The Decolonization Reader*, 49–79, 51.

29 Cited in David Fieldhouse, "Decolonization, Development, and Dependence: A Survey of Changing Attitudes," in Prosser Gifford and Wm. Roger Louis, eds., *The Transfer of Power in Africa: Decolonization 1940–1960* (New Haven, CT: Yale University Press, 1982), 483–514, 488.

30 See Kelemen, "Planning for Africa"; Schuknecht, *British Colonial Development Policy*, 19–20, 209–210; Hodge, *Triumph*, 208–209.

31 Cited in Schuknecht, *British Colonial Development Policy*, 204. Also see Kelemen, "Planning for Africa," 91.

32 Cf. Hodge, *Triumph*, 251.

33 Cf. Matteo Rizzo, "What Was Left of the Groundnut Scheme? Development Disaster and Labour Market in Southern Tanganyika, 1946–1952," *Journal of Agrarian Change* 6.2 (2006): 205–238, 207; Hodge, *Triumph*, 210; Schuknecht, *British Colonial Development Policy*, 211.

34 On the San Francisco conference and the discussion of the UN Charter, see Glenda Sluga, *Internationalism in the Age of Nationalism* (Philadelphia: University of Pennsylvania Press, 2013), chapter 3.

35 On Huxley, see Tilley, *Africa*, 87–88; Hodge, *Triumph*, 257.

36 Cf. Sluga, *Internationalism*, 108–109.

37 Cf. Schuknecht, *British Colonial Development Policy*, 213.

38 Cf. Rizzo, "What Was Left," 209–210; Hodge, *Triumph*, 211; Schuknecht, *British Colonial Development Policy*, 213–214.

39 Cf. Schuknecht, *British Colonial Development Policy*, 31; Hodge, *Triumph*, 212–213.

40 Rizzo, "What Was Left," 208.

41 Ibid., 217, 211.

42 Cf. Beusekom and Hodgson, "Lessons Learned?" 33.

43 On changing American perceptions of the world in the context of the Second World War, see Timothy Barney, *Mapping the Cold War: Cartography and the Framing of America's International Power* (Chapel Hill: University of North Carolina Press, 2015), 30–36.

44 Rockefeller Foundation, "Food as a Possible Field of Interest for the Rockefeller Foundation: Collected Memoranda," November 4, 1943 (900 PRO Food 1). Rockefeller Archive Center (RAC), Rockefeller Foundation (RF), Record Group (RG) 3.2, Series 900, Box 39, Folder 207.

45 Cf. Jonathan Harwood, "Peasant Friendly Plant Breeding and the Early Years of the Green Revolution in Mexico," *Agricultural History* 83.3 (2009): 384–410; Marcus Cueto, ed., *Missionaries of Science: The Rockefeller Foundation and Latin America* (Bloomington: Indiana University Press, 1994); W. H. Schneider, ed., *Rockefeller Philanthropy and Modern Biomedicine: International Initiatives from World War One to the Cold War* (Bloomington: Indiana University Press, 2002).

46 See Iris Borowy, *Coming to Terms with World Health: The League of Nations Health Organisation, 1921–1946* (Frankfurt am Main: Peter Lang, 2009).

47 Warren Weaver, "The World Food Problem, Agriculture, and the Rockefeller Foundation," June 21, 1951. RAC, RF, RG 3, series 915, Box 3, Folder 23.

48 See Arndt, *Economic Development*, 64; Staples, *The Birth of Development*, 8–21.

49 Harry S. Truman, "The Fourth Point in President Truman's Inaugural Address, January 20, 1949," *Annals of the American Academy of Political and Social Science* 268 (1950): 183.

50 See Uwe Lübke, *Bedrohliche Nähe: Die USA und die nationalsozialistische Herausforderung in Lateinamerika, 1937–1945* (Stuttgart: Steiner, 2004).

51 Cf. Helleiner, *Forgotten Foundations*, 31–32; Macekura, "The Point Four Program," 127–128, 133–134.

52 Cf. Helleiner, *Forgotten Foundations*, 44, 57, 64.

53 Cited in ibid., 47–48.

54 See Elizabeth Borgwardt, *A New Deal for the World: America's Vision for Human Rights* (Cambridge, MA: Belknap Press of Harvard University Press, 2005), chapter 2; Lumsdaine, *Moral Vision*, 202–207.

55 Cf. Helleiner, *Forgotten Foundations*, 120–123; Paul Orders, "'Adjusting to a New Period in World History': Franklin Roosevelt and European Colonialism," in David Ryan and Victor Pungong, eds., *The United States and Decolonization: Power and Freedom* (New York: Palgrave Macmillan, 2000), 63–84, 69; Barney, *Mapping the Cold War*, 144–158.

56 See, for example, John K. Rose, "Needs and Resources of the Brave New World," *Annals of the American Academy of Political and Social Science* 268 (1950): 9–21; Howard S. Piquet, "Point Four and World Production," *Annals of the American Academy of Political and Social Science* 268 (1950): 148–159.

57 James P. Warburg, "A New Look at the Economic Challenge," *Annals of the American Academy of Political and Social Science* 270 (1950): 22–34, 24.

58 Willard L. Thorp, "The Objectives of Point Four," *Annals of the American Academy of Political and Social Science* 268 (1950): 22–26, 24.

59 George Hakim, "Point Four—The Need and the Impact," *Annals of the American Academy of Political and Social Science* 270 (1950): 68–73, 68, 69, 73, 71.

60 On the concept of the Third World, see Escobar, *Encountering Development*; B. R. Tomlinson, "What Was the Third World?" *Journal of Contemporary History* 38.2 (2003): 307–321; Carl E. Pletsch, "The Three Worlds, or the Division of Social Scientific Labour, Circa 1950–1975," *Comparative Studies in Society and History* 23 (1981): 565–590; Barney, *Mapping the Cold War*, 141–144.

61 Harry S. Truman, "The President's Message to the Congress on 'Point Four Legislation,'" *Annals of the American Academy of Political and Social Science* 268 (1950): 184–187, 184.

62 Ibid., 187. Also see Macekura, "The Point Four Program," 146–147; Thorsten V. Kalijarvi, "Point Four in the Contemporary Setting," *Annals of the America Academy of Political and Social Science* 268 (1950): 1–8, 7–8; William Yandell Elliott, "Prospects for 'Personal Freedom and Happiness for All Mankind,'" *Annals of the America Academy of Political and Social Science* 268 (1950): 173–182, 173–176.

63 Cf. Helleiner, *Forgotten Foundations*, 265.

64 Cf. Macekura, "The Point Four Program," 140–148.

65 See Chia Lin Pan, "Demographic Aspects of Underdeveloped Countries," *Annals of the America Academy of Political and Social Science* 270 (1950): 42–50; Halford L. Hoskins, "Point Four with Reference to the Middle East," *Annals of the America Academy of Political and Social Science* 268 (1950):

85–95, 91; Francis R. Valeo, "Point Four Problems in the Far East," *Annals of the America Academy of Political and Social Science* 268 (1950): 104–111, 110. Also see Robertson, *The Malthusian Moment*, 61–64.

66 Kingsley Davis, "The Unpredicted Pattern of Population Change," *Annals of the American Academy of Political and Social Science* 305 (1956): 53–59, 59.

67 See Robertson, *The Malthusian Moment*, 66–69.

68 Truman, "The Fourth Point," 183.

69 Cf. Elliott, "Prospects," 179–180; McKay, "Needs and Opportunities," 79–81. Also see Louis and Robinson, "The Imperialism of Decolonization."

70 See Marc Frey, *Dekolonisierung in Südostasien: Die Vereinigten Staaten und die Auflösung der europäischen Kolonialreiche* (München: Oldenbourg, 2006), chapter 7; John Kent, "The United States and the Decolonization of Black Africa, 1945–63," in Ryan and Pungong, eds., *The United States*, 168–187; Orders, "Adjusting to a New Period in World History," 77–79.

71 See Victor Pungong, "The United States and the International Trusteeship System," in Ryan and Pungong, eds., *The United States*, 85–101, 95–97; Sayward, *The United Nations*, 27–28.

72 Cf. Lohrmann, *Voices*, 25–26.

73 Cf. Maul, *Human Rights*, 96.

74 Cf. Lohrmann, *Voices*, 1; Meredith Terretta, "'We Had Been Fooled into Thinking that the UN Watches over the Entire World': Human Rights, UN Trust Territories, and Africa's Decolonization," *Human Rights Quarterly* 34.2 (2012): 329–360.

75 See Giorgio Potì, *Imperial Violence, Anti-Colonial Nationalism and International Society: The Politics of Revolt across Mediterranean Empires, 1919–1927*. PhD dissertation, European University Institute, 2016.

76 Cf. Lohrmann, *Voices*, 55.

77 Cf. ibid., chapter 3.

78 Terretta, "We Had Been Fooled," 337.

79 Devesh Kapur, John P. Lewis, and Richard Webb, *The World Bank: Its First Half-Century*, 2 vols. (Washington, DC: Brookings Institution Press, 1997), vol. 1, 220. On the security aspect of American aid, see Dennis Merrill, *Bread and the Ballot: The United States and India's Economic Development, 1947–1963* (Chapel Hill: University of North Carolina Press, 1990); Robert J. McMahon, *The Cold War on the Periphery: The United States, India, and Pakistan* (New York: Columbia University Press, 1994); John H. Perkins, *Geopolitics and the Green Revolution: Wheat, Genes, and the Cold War* (New York: Oxford University Press, 1997), 119–120.

80 Cited in Kent, "The United States," 173.

81 Cf. G. John Ikenberry, *After Victory: Institutions, Strategic Restraint, and the Rebuilding of Order after Major Wars* (Princeton, NJ: Princeton University Press, 2000), 165, 173–174; David Ryan, "By Way of Introduction: the United States, Decolonization and the World System," in Ryan and Pungong, eds., *The United States*, 1–23, 12–13. Also see Borgwardt, *A New Deal for the World*, chapter 2.

82 Cf. Ikenberry, *After Victory*, 185.

83 Cf. Helleiner, *Forgotten Foundations*, 13–15.

84 Cited in ibid., 20.

85 Cf. ibid., 52, 76, 102.

86 Cited in ibid., 117.
87 For the early history of the World Bank, see Edward Mason and Robert Asher, *The World Bank since Bretton Woods* (Washington, DC: Brookings Institution, 1973); Alacevich, *The Political Economy*; Staples, *The Birth of Development*, 22–45; Kapur, Lewis, and Webb, *The World Bank*.
88 Cf. Staples, *The Birth of Development*, 24–30.
89 Cf. Eugene R. Black, "The World Bank at Work," *Foreign Affairs* 30.3 (1952): 402–411, 404.
90 See, for example, Julia Tischler, *Light and Power for a Multiracial Nation: The Kariba Dam Scheme in the Central African Federation* (Basingstoke: Palgrave Macmillan, 2013).
91 Cf. Marc Frey and Corinna R. Unger, "The World Bank and Agrarian Development, 1945 to the 1990s." Unpublished manuscript, 2013.
92 Cited in Staples, *The Birth of Development*, 24.
93 Cf. ibid., 23, 31, 40–43.
94 Cf. Frey, "Entwicklungspolitik," 296–297, 304.
95 Cf. Sayward, *The United Nations*, 55.
96 Cf. Amrith, "Internationalising Health," 254.
97 On SUNFED's history, see Jolly et al., *UN Contributions*, 73–83.
98 Cf. Helleiner, *Forgotten Foundations*, 269.
99 Heide-Irene Schmidt and Helge Pharo, "Introduction," *Contemporary European History* 12.4 (2003): 387–394, 389.
100 Cf. Woods, *From Marshall Plan to Debt Crisis*, 73; Michele Alacevich, "Not a Knowledge Bank: The Divided History of Development Economics and Development Organization," *Social Science History* 40 (2016): 627–656, 647; Helleiner, *Forgotten Foundations*, 272; Heide-Irene Schmidt, "Pushed to the Front: The Foreign Assistance Policy of the Federal Republic of Germany, 1958–1971," *Contemporary European History* 12.4 (2003): 473–507, 475–476; Patrick Sharma, *Robert McNamara's Other War: The World Bank and International Development* (Philadelphia: University of Pennsylvania Press, 2017), 15–16.
101 Cf. Tarp, "Aid," 33; Esther Helena Arens, "Multilateral Institution-Building and National Interest: Dutch Development Policy in the 1960s," *Contemporary European History* 12.4 (2003): 457–472, 463, footnote 24.
102 Cf. Frederic Benham, *The Colombo Plan and Other Essays* (London: Oxford University Press, 1956), 1–2.
103 Benham, *The Colombo Plan*, 19–20.
104 Cf. Brandt, "The Economic Objectives of F.A.O.," 128.
105 See Salvatici, *Nel nome degli altri*, 192–207; Jessica Reinisch, "Internationalism in Relief: The Birth (and Death) of UNRRA," *Past & Present* 210.6 (2011): 258–289; Sayward, *The United Nations*, 58.
106 Cf. Heike Wieters, "Of Heartfelt Charity and Billion Dollar Enterprise: From Postwar Relief to Europe to Humanitarian Relief to 'Everywhere'—CARE, Inc., in Search of a New Mission," in Marc Frey, Sönke Kunkel, and Corinna R. Unger, eds., *International Organizations and Development, 1945–1990* (Basingstoke: Palgrave Macmillan, 2014), 220–239.
107 See Staples, *The Birth of Development*, 69–76.
108 Cf. ibid., 78.
109 See Borowy, *Coming to Terms with World Health*.

110 Cf. Staples, *The Birth of Development*, 132–143.
111 Cf. Amrith, "Internationalising Health," 255; Staples, *The Birth of Development*, 137.
112 Cf. Jennifer Gold, "The Reconfiguration of Scientific Career Networks in the Late Colonial Period: The Case of the Food and Agriculture Organization and the British Colonial Forestry Service," in Brett Bennett and Joseph Hodge, eds., *Science and Empire: Knowledge and Networks of Science across the British Empire, 1800–1970* (Basingstoke: Palgrave Macmillan, 2011), 297–320.
113 Ibid., 300.
114 Cf. Hodge, *Triumph*, 256–262; also see Hodge, "British Colonial Expertise."
115 See Robert Bates, *Beyond the Miracle of the Market: The Political Economy of Agrarian Development in Kenya* (Cambridge: Cambridge University Press, 1989), chapter 1.
116 Cf. Hodge, "British Colonial Expertise," 30–32; Hodge, *Triumph*, 248–249.
117 Cf. Cooper, "Possibility and Constraint," 181.
118 Cf. Hodge, "British Colonial Expertise," 34–37.
119 Cf. ibid., 35, 38–39.
120 Cf. Frey, "Doctrines and Practices," 26; idem, "Entwicklungspolitik," 303.
121 Cf. Amrith, "Internationalising Health," 256–257.
122 Cf. Arndt, *Economic Development*, 62–66; Maul, *Human Rights*, chapter 4.
123 Lumsdaine, *Moral Vision*, 200. Also see Latham, "Modernization," 728–729.
124 Cf. David Webster, "Development Advisors in a Time of Cold War and Decolonization: The United Nations Technical Assistance Administration, 1950–59," *Journal of Global History* 6 (2011): 249–272, 250–255, 258.
125 Cf. Jolly et al., *UN Contributions*, 68–72; Frey, "Entwicklungspolitik," 304; Sayward, *The United Nations*, 92. Also see Stephen Browne, *The United Nations Development Programme and System* (Abingdon: Routledge, 2011), chapter 1.
126 Cited in Daniel Maul, "'Help Them Move the ILO Way': The International Labor Organization and the Modernization Discourse in the Era of Decolonization and the Cold War," *Diplomatic History* 33.3 (2009): 387–404, 389. Also see Maul, *Human Rights*, 75–79; Lumsdaine, *Moral Vision*, 195; Cooper, *Decolonization*, 216–224.
127 Cf. Maul, *Human Rights*, 62–69, 82–83.
128 Cf. Eckert, "Regulating the Social," 474.
129 Cf. Maul, "Help Them Move the ILO Way," 390.
130 On ILO's Technical Assistance Program, see Maul, *Human Rights*, chapter 4.
131 Cf. Maul, "Help Them Move the ILO Way," 391–394.
132 Ibid., 393.
133 Cf. Maul, *Human Rights*, 137; Cooper, "Development," 32–33.
134 Cf. Maul, "Help Them Move the ILO Way," 396, 398. Also see Erez Manela, "A Pox on Your Narrative: Writing Disease Control into Cold War History," *Diplomatic History* 34.2 (2010): 299–323; Vincent Lagendijk, "The Structure of Power: The UNECE and East-West Electricity Connections, 1947–1975," *Comparativ* 24.1 (2014): 50–65.
135 Cited in Webster, "Development Advisors," 250.
136 Ibid., 262.
137 Cf. ibid., 262–268.

138 Cf. Eva-Maria Muschik, *Building States through International Development Assistance: The United Nations between Trusteeship and Self-Determination, 1945 to 1965*. PhD dissertation, New York University, 2016, chapter 3.

139 Arndt, *Economic Development*, 65.

140 Gordon T. Bowles, "Point Four and Improved Standards of Living," *Annals of the American Academy of Political and Social Science* 268 (1950): 140–147, 143.

141 Cf. Arndt, *Economic Development*, 61–62.

142 Theodore W. Schultz, "Investment in Human Capital," *American Economic Review* 51.1 (1961): 1–17.

143 Theodore W. Schultz, *The Economic Value of Education* (New York: Columbia University Press, 1963).

144 Cf. Jolly et al., *UN Contributions*, 94–97, 203–209. Also see Valeska Huber, "Planning Education and Manpower in the Middle East, 1950s–60s," *Journal of Contemporary History* 52.1 (2017): 95–117.

145 Cf. "Graduate Institute of International and Development Studies," https://en.wikipedia.org/wiki/Graduate_Institute_of_International_and_Development_Studies (accessed May 2, 2017).

146 Cf. Alacevich, "Not a Knowledge Bank," 631–632, 637–638, 640–641, 651.

147 See Latham, "Ideology," 207; David C. Engerman, "West Meets East: The Center for International Studies and Indian Economic Development," in Engerman et al., eds., *Staging Growth*, 199–223.

148 Cf. Alacevich, "Not a Knowledge Bank," 642–643.

149 See Westad, *The Global Cold War*, 39–66.

150 Cf. Ragna Boden, "Cold War Economics: Soviet Aid to Indonesia," *Journal of Cold War Studies* 10.3 (2008): 110–128, 112–114; Roger E. Kanet, "Vier Jahrzehnte sowjetische Wirtschaftshilfe," in Bernd Greiner, Christian Th. Müller, and Claudia Weber, eds., *Ökonomie im Kalten Krieg* (Hamburg: Hamburger Edition, 2010), 45–62, 47; Alessandro Iandolo, "The Rise and Fall of the 'Soviet Model of Development' in West Africa, 1957–64," *Cold War History* 12.4 (2012): 683–704, 685–686.

151 Cf. Andreas Hilger, "Building a Socialist Elite? Khrushchev's Soviet Union and Elite Formation in India," in Jost Dülffer and Marc Frey, eds., *Elites and Decolonization in the Twentieth Century* (Basingstoke: Palgrave Macmillan, 2011), 262–286, 269; Westad, *The Global Cold War*, 68; Artemy M. Kalinovsky, "Not Some British Colony in Africa: The Politics of Decolonization and Modernization in Soviet Central Asia, 1955–1964," *Ab Imperio* 2 (2013): 191–222, 206–207; Steffi Marung, "A 'Leninian Moment'? Soviet Africanists and the Interpretation of the October Revolution, 1950s–1970s," *Journal für Entwicklungspolitik* 33.3 (2017): 21–48.

152 Cited in Hilger, "Building a Socialist Elite?" 269.

153 Cf. Iandolo, "The Rise and Fall," 685.

154 Cf. Maryse Gaudier, "The International Institute for Labour Studies: Its Research Function, Activities and Publications 1960–2001," http://www.ilo.org/wcmsp5/groups/public/—dgreports/—inst/documents/genericdocument/wcms_192540.pdf (accessed May 2, 2017), 4–5.

155 Cf. Sharad Chari and Stuart Corbridge, eds., *The Development Reader* (Abingdon: Routledge, 2008), 262.

156 Cf. Centre for the Study of Developing Societies, http://www.csds.in/history (accessed June 22, 2017).

157 Cf. Chari and Corbridge, eds., *The Development Reader*, 262.

158 Cf. Alacevich, "Not a Knowledge Bank," 645 (quote 644); Jolly et al., *UN Contributions*, 88–95.

159 Cf. Speich, "The World of GDP," 12–16.

160 On the Rourkela project, see Unger, *Entwicklungspfade*, 193–211.

161 Jan Bodo Sperling, *Die Rourkela-Deutschen* (Stuttgart: Deutsche Verlagsanstalt, 1965); Jan Bodo Sperling, *The Human Dimension of Technical Assistance: The German Experience of Rourkela* (Ithaca, NY: Cornell University Press, 1969).

162 Cf. Albert O. Hirschman, *Development Projects Observed* (Washington, DC: Brookings Institution, 1967), 2.

163 Cf. Adelman, *Worldly Philosopher*, 403–406.

Chapter 5

1   For such accounts, see Westad, *The Global Cold War*; Christopher E. Goscha and Christian Ostermann, eds., *Connecting Histories: Decolonization and the Cold War in Southeast Asia, 1945–1962* (Washington, DC: Woodrow Wilson Center Press; Stanford, CA: Stanford University Press, 2009); Leslie James and Elisabeth Leake, eds., *Decolonization and the Cold War: Negotiating Independence* (London: Bloomsbury, 2015); Jeffrey James Byrne, *Mecca of Revolution: Algeria, Decolonization, and the Third World Order* (Oxford: Oxford University Press, 2016).

2   See Meredith Terretta, "Cameroonian Nationalists Go Global: From Forest *Maquis* to a Pan-African Accra," *Journal of African History* 51.2 (2010): 189–212; Frederick Cooper, "Reconstructing Empire in British and French Africa," *Past & Present* 210, Supplement 6 (2011): 196–210, 206–210; Cooper, *Citizenship*.

3   See Andrew Burton and Michael Jennings, "Introduction: The Emperor's New Clothes? Continuities in Governance in Late Colonial and Early Postcolonial East Africa," *The International Journal of African Historical Studies* 40.1 (2007): 1–25; Taylor C. Sherman, William Gould, and Sarah Ansari, "Introduction," in Taylor C. Sherman, William Gould, and Sarah Ansari, eds., *From Subjects to Citizens: Society and the Everyday State in India and Pakistan, 1947–1970* (New Delhi: Cambridge University Press, 2014), 1–9.

4   Cf. Burton and Jennings, "Introduction," 4–9; Westad, *The Global Cold War*, 79–86; Louisa Rice, "Between Empire and Nation: Francophone West African Students and Decolonization," *Atlantic Studies* 10.1 (2013): 131–147; Michael Goebel, *Anti-Imperial Metropolis: Interwar Paris and the Seeds of Third World Nationalism* (New York: Cambridge University Press, 2015).

5   Cf. Leander Schneider, "Colonial Legacies and Postcolonial Authoritarianism in Tanzania: Connects and Disconnects," *African Studies Review* 49.1 (2006): 93–118, 107.

6   Cf. Westad, *The Global Cold War*, 90–91, 95.

7   Cf. Kate Skinner, "Who Knew the Minds of the People? Specialist Knowledge and Developmentalist Authoritarianism in Postcolonial Ghana," *Journal of Imperial and Commonwealth History* 39.2 (2011): 297–323, 298, 300; Sinha, "Lineages," 58–59.

8   Cited in Andreas Eckert, "Julius Nyerere, Tanzanian Elites, and the Project of African Socialism," in Dülffer and Frey, eds., *Elites*, 216–240, 227. Also see Daniel Speich, "The Kenyan Style of 'African Socialism': Developmental Knowledge Claims and the Explanatory Limits of the Cold War," *Diplomatic History* 33.3 (2009): 449–466, 460–461.

9   Fieldhouse, "Decolonization," 493.

10 Cited in Julia Tischler, "Resisting Modernisation? Two African Responses to the Kariba Dam Scheme in the Central African Federation," *Comparativ* 21.1 (2011): 60–75, 65.

11 Cf. Cooper, "Writing," 11; Burton and Jennings, "Introduction," 11; Frey, "Entwicklungspolitik," 308.

12 Cf. Partha Chatterjee, "The National State," in Partha Chatterjee, *The Partha Chatterjee Omnibus* (New Delhi: Oxford University Press, 1999), 200–219; Schneider, "Colonial Legacies," 106–110; Sinha, "Lineages," 73; Michael Jennings, "'A Very Real War': Popular Participation in Development in Tanzania during the 1950s & 1960s," *International Journal of African Historical Studies* 40.1 (2007): 71–95, 73.

13 Cooper, "Possibility and Constraint," 183.

14 Sunil Khilnani, *The Idea of India* (New York: Farrar Straus Giroux, 1999), 41.

15 Cf. Burton and Jennings, "Introduction," 11–12; Westad, *The Global Cold War*, 95; Terretta, "We Had Been Fooled," 357–358.

16 Cf. Burton and Jennings, "Introduction," 14.

17 See Immerwahr, *Thinking Small*; Büschel, *Hilfe*, 447–449.

18 See Leander Schneider, *Government of Development: Peasants and Politicians in Postcolonial Tanzania* (Bloomington: Indiana University Press, 2014); Jennings, "A Very Real War"; Scott, *Seeing Like a State*, chapter 7.

19 Cf. Eckert, "Julius Nyerere," 228–232.

20 Cf. Maul, *Human Rights*, 262–264 (quote 262).

21 Arndt, *Economic Development*, 57.

22 See Zachariah, *Developing India*, 238–241; Judith Brown, *Nehru: A Political Life* (New Haven, CT: Yale University Press, 2003), 200–201. On the quote, see Immerwahr, *Thinking Small*, 208, footnote 15.

23 Cited in John Krige, *Sharing Knowledge, Shaping Europe: US Technological Collaboration and Nonproliferation* (Cambridge, MA: MIT Press, 2016), 25.

24 Cf. Fieldhouse, "Decolonization," 513.

25 Carol Lancaster, *Foreign Aid: Diplomacy, Development, Domestic Politics* (Chicago: University of Chicago Press, 2008), 146.

26 See Ekbladh, *The Great American Mission*, 166.

27 Cf. Kalinovsky, "Not Some British Colony in Africa," 212; Iandolo, "The Rise and Fall," 687, 692–693.

28 Westad, *The Global Cold War*, 92.

29 See Martin Schain, ed., *The Marshall Plan: Fifty Years After* (Basingstoke: Palgrave Macmillan, 2001); Michael Holm, *The Marshall Plan: A New Deal for Europe* (Abingdon: Routledge, 2016).

30 See Jenny Brine, *Comecon: The Rise and Fall of an Internationalist Socialist Organization* (Oxford: Clio Press, 1992); Elena Dragomir, "The Creation of the Council for Mutual Economic Assistance as Seen from the Romanian Archives," *Historical Research* 88.240 (2015): 355–380; Uwe Müller, "Der RGW als Schlüssel zu einer transnationalen Wirtschaftsgeschichte des östlichen Europas in der zweiten Hälfte des 20. Jahrhunderts," *IWVWW—Berichte* (April–June 2015): 32–50.

31 See Jonathan Morris, "Challenging Meridionalismo: Constructing a New History for Southern Italy," in Robert Lumley and Jonathan Morris, eds., *The New History of the Italian South: The Mezzogiorno Revisited* (Exeter: University of Exeter Press, 1997), 1–19; Jane Schneider, ed., *Italy's "Southern Question": Orientalism in One Country* (Oxford: Berg, 1998).

32 See Sara Lorenzini, "Ace in the Hole or Hole in the Pocket? The Italian *Mezzogiorno* and the Story of a Troubled Transition from Development Model to Development Donor," *Contemporary European History* (2016), doi: 10.1017/S0960777316000576; Michele Alacevich, "Postwar Development in the Italian Mezzogiorno: Analyses and Policies," *Journal of Modern Italian Studies* 18.1 (2013): 90–112, 97–100; Christian Grabas, "Planning the Economic Miracle? Industrial Policy in Italy between Boom and Crisis, 1950–1975," in Alexander Nützenadel and Christian Grabas, eds., *Industrial Policy in Europe after 1945: Wealth, Power and Economic Development in the Cold War* (Basingstoke: Palgrave Macmillan 2014), 134–183, 142.

33 Cf. Alacevich, "Postwar Development," 101; Stokke, *The UN*, 42; Paul Ginsborg, *A History of Contemporary Italy: Society and Politics, 1943–1988* (London: Penguin, 1990), 78–79.

34 Cf. Leandra D'Antone, "L'interesse straordinario' per il Mezzogiorno (1943–1960)," *Meridiana* 24 (1995): 17–64, 18–20; Alacevich, "Postwar Development," 101–102.

35 Cf. D'Antone, "L'interesse straordinario,'" 19, 25.

36 Cf. Grabas, "Planning," 148, 154; Alacevich, "Postwar Development," 103–106.

37 Cf. Stokke, *The UN*, 41–42; Daniel Speich Chassé, "Towards a Global History of the Marshall Plan: European Post-war Reconstruction and the Rise of Development Economic Expertise," in Nützenadel and Grabas, eds., *Industrial Policy*, 187–212.

38 Cf. Irma Adelman, "Fallacies in Development Theory and Their Implications for Policy," in Meier and Stiglitz, eds., *Frontiers of Development*, 103–134, 106.

39 See, for example, Abou B. Bamba, "Triangulating a Modernization Experiment: The United States, France and the Making of the Kossou Project in Central Ivory Coast," *Journal of Modern European History* 8.1 (2010): 66–83.

40 Wood, *From Marshall Plan to Debt Crisis*, 11.

41 For case studies on ODA practices, see Thorsten Borring Olesen, Helge Ø. Pharo, and Kristian Paaskesen, eds., *Saints and Sinners: Official Development Aid and its Dynamics in a Historical and Comparative Perspective* (Oslo: Akademika, 2013).

42 Cf. Tarp, "Aid," 22.

43 Schmidt and Pharo, "Introduction," 389.

44 Cf. Frey, "Entwicklungspolitik," 299.

45 Cf. Sara Lorenzini, "Comecon and the South in the Years of *Détente*: A Study of East-South Economic Relations," *European Review of History* 21.2 (2014): 185.

46 Cf. Tarp, "Aid," 30; Schmidt and Pharo, "Introduction," 390–391.

47 Cf. Wood, *From Marshall Plan to Debt Crisis*, 70–71, 86. Also see Bossuat, "French Development Aid," 439; Jim Tomlinson, "The Commonwealth, the Balance of Payments and the Politics of International Poverty: British Aid Policy, 1958–1971," *Contemporary European History* 12.4 (2003): 413–429.

48 Cf. Elena Calandri, "Italy's Foreign Assistance Policy," *Contemporary European History* 12.4 (2003): 509–525, 517.

49 Cf. Arens, "Multilateral Institution-Building," 464, 457–459 (quote 459).

50 Cf. ibid., 460; Bossuat, "French Development Aid," 431; Lancaster, *Foreign Aid*, 29.

51 Cited in Tomlinson, "The Commonwealth," 417.

52 Cf. Frey, *Dekolonisierung*, 127–133.

53 Cf. Office of the Historian, Department of State, "USAID and PL 480, 1961–1969," https://history.state.gov/milestones/1961-1968/pl-480 (accessed August 16, 2017).

54 On PL 480, see Christopher D. Barrett and Daniel G. Maxwell, *Food Aid After Fifty Years: Recasting its Role* (Abingdon: Routledge, 2005), 18–24; Kristin L. Ahlberg, *Transplanting the Great Society: Lyndon Johnson and Food for Peace* (Columbia: University of Missouri Press, 2008); Merrill, *Bread and the Ballot*, 109; Perkins, *Geopolitics*, 156.

55 Cf. Schmidt and Pharo, "Introduction," 391.

56 Cf. Tomlinson, "The Commonwealth," 418, 420; Schmidt and Pharo, "Introduction," 391, 390; Unger, *Entwicklungspfade*, 173–174; Schmidt, "Pushed," 477–478.

57 Cf. Calandri, "Italy's Foreign Assistance Policy," 511–513, 517, 515.

58 Cf. Lancaster, *Foreign Aid*, 112–116.

59 Cf. Frey, "Entwicklungspolitik," 301; Schmidt, "Pushed," 474, 481.

60 Cf. Sayward, *The United Nations*, 95. See Patricia Purtschert and Harald Fischer-Tiné, eds., *Colonial Switzerland: Rethinking Colonialism from the Margins* (Basingstoke: Palgrave Macmillan, 2015); Helge Pharo and Monika Pohle Fraser, eds., *The Aid Rush: Aid Regimes in Northern Europe during the Cold War*, 2 vols. (Oslo: Unipub, 2008).

61 See Amit Das Gupta, "Development by Consortia: International Donors and the Development of India, Pakistan, Indonesia and Turkey in the 1960s," *Comparativ* 4.19 (2009): 96–111.

62 Cf. Sara Elmer, "Postkoloniale Erschließung ferner Länder? Die erste Schweizer Nepalmission und die Anfänge der technischen Hilfe an unterentwickelte Länder," in Patricia Purtschert, Barbara Lüthi, and Francesca Falk, eds., *Postkoloniale Schweiz: Formen und Folgen eines Kolonialismus ohne Kolonien*, 2nd ed. (Bielefeld: transcript, 2013), 245–266, 257.

63 See Helge Ø. Pharo, "Entrepreneurship and Development Aid: The Case of the Indo-Norwegian Fisheries Project," in Pharo and Pohle Fraser, eds., *The Aid Rush*, vol. 2, 53–93; Lukas Zürcher, "'So fanden wir auf der Karte diesen kleinen Staat': Globale Positionierung und lokale Entwicklungsfantasien der Schweiz in Rwanda in den 1960er Jahren," in Büschel and Speich, eds., *Entwicklungswelten*, 275–309.

64 Cf. Helge Pharo, "Altruism, Security and the Impact of Oil: Norway's Foreign Economic Assistance Policy, 1958–1971," *Contemporary European History* 12.4 (2003): 527–546, 528–532, 542–543, 535.

65 Cf. Karl Bruno, "An Experiment in Ethiopia: The Chilalo Agricultural Development Unit and Swedish Development Aid to Haile Selassie's Ethiopia, 1964–1974," *Comparativ* 27.2 (2017): 54–74, 57.

66 Ibid.

67 Cf. Arens, "Multilateral Institution-Building," 460.

68 See Schmidt, "Pushed"; Amit Das Gupta, *Handel, Hilfe, Hallstein-Doktrin: Die bundesdeutsche Südasienpolitik unter Adenauer und Erhard, 1949 bis 1966* (Husum: Matthiesen, 2004); Unger, *Entwicklungspfade*, 170–173; Hendrik Grote, "Von der Entwicklungshilfe zur Entwicklungspolitik: Voraussetzungen, Strukturen und Mentalitäten der bundesdeutschen Entwicklungshilfe, 1949–1961," *Vorgänge* 43.2 (2004): 24–35.

69 See Bastian Hein, *Die Westdeutschen und die Dritte Welt: Entwicklungspolitik und Entwicklungsdienste zwischen Reform und Revolte* (München: Oldenbourg, 2005), chapter 1; Lancaster, *Foreign Aid*, 171–175.

70 Cf. Manfred Glagow, Wilfried Gotsch, and Andreas Stucke, *Das Bundesministerium für Wirtschaftliche Zusammenarbeit (BMZ): Entstehungszusammenhang, Personalstruktur, Steuerungsfähigkeit* (Pfaffenweiler: Centaurus-Verlagsgesellschaft, 1989), 38–49.

71 Cf. Van Laak, "Detours around Africa," 34.

72 Cf. Giuliano Garavini, "The *Eurafrica Factor*: European Community Development Policy (1957–1992)," in Ulrich Krotz, Kiran Klaus Patel, and Federico Romero, eds., *The History of EC Foreign Relations, 1957–1992*. Forthcoming.

73 Cf. Peo Hansen and Stefan Jonsson, "Building Eurafrica: Reviving Colonialism through European Integration, 1920–1960," in Kalypso Nicolaïdis et al., eds., *Echoes of Empire: Memory, Identity and Colonial Legacies* (London: I. B. Tauris, 2015), 209–226; Thomas Moser, *Europäische Integration, Dekolonisation, Eurafrika: Eine historische Analyse über die Entstehungsbedingungen der eurafrikanischen Gemeinschaft von der Weltwirtschaftskrise zum Jaunde-Vertrag, 1929–1963* (Baden-Baden: Nomos, 2000).

74 Cf. Garavini, "The *Eurafrica Factor*."

75 Cf. Martin Rempe, "Entangled Industrialization: The EEC and Industrial Development in Francophone West Africa," in Nützenadel and Grabas, eds., *Industrial Policy*, 236–255, 237–238; idem, "Decolonization by Europeanization? The Early EEC and the Transformation of French-African Relations," *KFG Working Paper Series* 27 (May 2011), http://www.polsoz. fu-berlin.de/en/v/transformeurope/publications/working_paper/WP_27_ Rempe.pdf (accessed August 10, 2017); Urban Vahsen, *Eurafrikanische Entwicklungskooperation: Die Assoziierungspolitik der EWG gegenüber dem subsaharischen Afrika in den 1960er Jahren* (Stuttgart: Steiner, 2010).

76 Cf. Martin Rempe, "Airy Promises: Senegal and the EEC's Common Agricultural Policy in the Nineteen-Sixties," in Patel, ed., *Fertile Ground*, 221–240; Wood, *From Marshall Plan to Debt Crisis*, 74–75; Garavini, "The *Eurafrica Factor*."

77 See Éric Bussière et al., eds., *The Bank of the European Union: The EIB, 1958–2008* (Luxembourg: European Investment Bank, 2008), 94–98.

78 Cf. Véronique Dimier, *The Invention of a European Development Bureaucracy: Recycling Empire* (Basingstoke: Palgrave Macmillan, 2014); Véronique Dimier, "Bringing the Neo-Patrimonial State back to Europe: French Decolonization and the Making of the European Development Aid Policy," *Archiv für Sozialgeschichte* 48 (2008): 433–457.

79 Cf. Rempe, "Entangled Industrialization," 241–242.

80 Cf. ibid., 245–246.

81 See Lancaster, *Foreign Aid*, 112, 171, 174–175; Corinna R. Unger, "Export und Entwicklung: Westliche Wirtschaftsinteressen in Indien im Kontext der Dekolonisation und des Kalten Krieges," *Jahrbuch für Wirtschaftsgeschichte/ Economic History Yearbook* 1 (2012): 69–86; Antoine Acker, *Volkswagen in the Amazon: The Tragedy of Global Development in Modern Brazil* (Cambridge: Cambridge University Press, 2017).

82 Cf. Calandri, "Italy's Foreign Assistance Policy," 522.

83 Cf. Unger, "Export und Entwicklung," 74–75.

84 Cf. Unger, *Entwicklungspfade*, 201–202.

85 Alex Inkeles, "Participant Citizenship in Six Developing Countries," *American Political Science Review* 63.4 (1969): 1120–1141, 1137.

86 See Kenneth M. Straus, *Factory and Community in Stalin's Russia: The Making of an Industrial Working Class* (Pittsburgh, PA: Pittsburgh University Press, 1997).

87 Cited in Hilger, "Building a Socialist Elite?" 269. Also see Martin Rudner, "East European Aid to Asian Developing Countries: The Legacy of the Communist Era," *Modern Asian Studies* 30.1 (1996): 1–28, 3–5.

88 Cf. Iandolo, "The Rise and Fall," 686; Rudner, "East European Aid," 13–14; Kanet, "Vier Jahrzehnte," 50; Boden, "Cold War Economics," 124–125; David C. Engerman, "The Second World's Third World," *Kritika* 12.1 (2011): 183–211.

89 See Timothy Nunan, *Humanitarian Invasion: Global Development in Cold War Afghanistan* (New York: Cambridge University Press, 2016); Antonio Giustozzi and Artemy Kalinovsky, *Missionaries of Modernity: Advisory Missions and the Struggle for Hegemony in Afghanistan and Beyond* (London: Hurst & Company, 2016).

90 Cf. Kanet, "Vier Jahrzehnte," 47–48; Boden, "Cold War Economics," 114.

91 Cf. Iandolo, "The Rise and Fall."

92 Cf. Guy Laron, *Origins of the Suez Crisis: Postwar Development Diplomacy and the Struggle over Third World Industrialization, 1945–1956* (Washington, DC: Woodrow Wilson Center Press; Baltimore: Johns Hopkins University Press, 2013).

93 Cf. Boden, "Cold War Economics," 115–116.

94 Cf. Kanet, "Vier Jahrzehnte," 48; Iandolo, "The Rise and Fall," 692. Also see Massimiliano Trentin, "Modernization as State-Building: The Two Germanys in Syria, 1963–1972," *Diplomatic History* 33.3 (2009): 487–505; Bernd Schaefer, "Socialist Modernization in Vietnam: The East German Approach, 1976–89," in Quinn Slobodian, ed., *Comrades of Color: East Germany in the Cold War World* (New York: Berghahn Books, 2015), 95–116.

95 Rudner, "East European Aid," 14.

96 Cf. Boden, "Cold War Economics," 122; Lorenzini, "Comecon," 185.

97 Cf. Boden, "Cold War Economics," 117, 119.

98 See Philip Muehlenbeck, *Czechoslovakia in Africa, 1945–1968* (New York: Palgrave Macmillan, 2016), chapter 3.

99 See Sergey Mazov, *A Distant Front in the Cold War: The USSR in West Africa and the Congo, 1956–1964* (Washington, DC: Woodrow Wilson Center Press; Stanford, CA: Stanford University Press, 2010); Lise A. Namikas, *Battleground Africa: Cold War in the Congo, 1960–1965* (Washington, DC: Woodrow Wilson Center Press; Stanford, CA: Stanford University Press, 2013).

100 Cf. Ryan Irwin, "Sovereignty in the Congo Crisis," in James and Leake, eds., *Decolonization*, 203–218, 205–207.

101 Cf. Iandolo, "The Rise and Fall," 695–697.

102 Cf. Kanet, "Vier Jahrzehnte," 61.

103 Cf. Iandolo, "The Rise and Fall," 689, 694.

104 Cf. Rudner, "East European Aid," 11–12; Kanet, "Vier Jahrzehnte," 56.

105 Cf. Hilger, "Building a Socialist Elite?" 270, 278.

106 Cf. Eric Burton, "Socialisms in Development: Revolution, Divergence and Crisis, 1917–1991," *Journal für Entwicklungspolitik* 33.3 (2017): 4–20, 12.

107 Cf. Hilger, "Building a Socialist Elite?" 264, 275, 272.

108 Cf. Constantin Katsakioris, "Soviet Lessons for Arab Modernization: Soviet Educational Aid towards Arab Countries after 1956," *Journal of Modern European History* 8.1 (2010): 85–106; Hilger, "Building a Socialist Elite?" 276–278.

109 Cf. Benjamin Siegel, "'Fantastic Quantities of Food Grains': Cold War Visions and Agrarian Fantasies in Independent India," in James and Leake, eds., *Decolonization*, 21–42.

110 Cf. Andreas Hilger, "Revolutionsideologie, Systemkonkurrenz oder Entwicklungspolitik: Sowjetisch-indische Wirtschaftsbeziehungen in Chruschtschows Kaltem Krieg," *Archiv für Sozialgeschichte* 48 (2008): 389–410; Unger, *Entwicklungspfade*, 182–211.

111 Cf. Padma Desai, *The Bokaro Steel Plant: A Study of Soviet Economic Assistance* (Amsterdam: North Holland Publishing Company, 1972); Merrill, *Bread and the Ballot*, 131–134, 158–159, 176–177, 200–301; Unger, *Entwicklungspfade*, 157.

112 Cf. Jeffrey F. Taffet, *Foreign Aid as Foreign Policy: The Alliance for Progress in Latin America* (New York: Taylor and Francis, 2007), chapter 1; Kimber Charles Pearce, *Rostow, Kennedy, and the Rhetoric of Foreign Aid* (East Lansing: Michigan State University Press, 2001), 20–27.

113 Cf. Lancaster, *Foreign Aid*, 69.

114 Cf. Frey, "Entwicklungspolitik," 301.

115 Cf. Taffet, *Foreign Aid*, 7–8.

116 Marc Frey, "The Limits of Modernization: American Development Assistance and Southeast Asian Resistance during the 1950s," *Comparativ* 19.4 (2009): 44–60, 51.

117 Cf. ibid., 5.

118 Cf. Wood, *From Marshall Plan to Debt Crisis*, 196; Sayward, *The United Nations*, 94–95; Jolly et al., *UN Contributions*, 85–86.

Chapter 6

1 On the origins of the idea of self-help, see Sinha, "Lineages," 67.

2 Cf. Sackley, "The Village," 492; Immerwahr, *Thinking Small*, 56–61.

3 Cf. Eckert, "Regulating the Social," 486.

4   See Arthur F. Raper, *Rural Development in Action: The Comprehensive Experiment at Comilla, East Pakistan* (Ithaca, NY: Cornell University Press, 1970).

5   Cf. Harvey M. Choldin, "Urban Cooperatives at Comilla, Pakistan: A Case Study of Local-Level Development," *Economic Development and Cultural Change* 16.2, part 1 (1968): 189–218, 190–191.

6   Cf. Harvey M. Choldin, "An Organizational Analysis of Rural Development Projects at Comilla, East Pakistan," *Economic Development and Cultural Change* 20.4 (1972): 671–690, 675–676 (quote 675).

7   Ibid., 678.

8   See Rodgers, *Atlantic Crossings*, chapter 8.

9   See, among others, Matthew Hull, "Democratic Technologies of Speech: From WWII America to Postcolonial Delhi," *Journal of Linguistic Anthropology* 20.2 (2010): 257–282; Corinna R. Unger, "Family Planning—A Rational Choice? The Influence of Systems Approaches, Behavioralism, and Rational Choice on Mid-Twentieth-Century Family Planning Programs," in Hartmann and Unger, eds., *A World of Populations*, 58–82, 65–66; David Kuchenbuch, "A Laboratory of Anarchy? The London Pioneer Health Centre and the Experimentalisation of the Social, 1935–1950," *Journal of Modern European History* 13.4 (2015): 480–498.

10 Sackley, "The Village," 489.

11 Cf. ibid., 493. Also see Kapur, Lewis, and Webb, *The World Bank*, vol. 1, 220.

12 Cited in Robertson, *The Malthusian Moment*, 94.

13 See Immerwahr, *Thinking Small*, chapter 5.

14 See Elizabeth Cobbs Hoffman, *All You Need is Love: The Peace Corps and the Spirit of the 1960s* (Cambridge, MA: Harvard University Press, 1998).

15 Cf. Sheyda Jahanbani, "One Global War on Poverty: The Johnson Administration Fights Poverty at Home and Abroad, 1964–1968," in Francis J. Gavin and Mark Atwood Lawrence, eds., *Beyond the Cold War: Lyndon Johnson and the New Global Challenges of the 1960s* (New York: Oxford University Press, 2014), 97–117, 99–100.

16 Cited in Jahanbani, "One Global War," 102.

17 Cf. ibid., 99; Immerwahr, *Thinking Small*, 138–150. Many community development approaches included family planning measures. Here, too, did American experiences with foreign assistance have a domestic counterpart, with African American and Hispanic women with large families being considered as backward as women in Africa. See Anne Overbeck, *"Mothering the Race": Discourses on Reproductive Rights of African-American Women in the 20th Century*. PhD dissertation, University of Münster, 2017, chapter 5.

18 Cf. Sackley, "The Village," 490–493; Nick Cullather, *The Hungry World: America's Cold War Battle against Poverty in Asia* (Cambridge, MA: Harvard University Press, 2010), 77–80.

19 On Ladejinsky, see Linklater, *Owning the Earth*, 311–316; Frey, *Dekolonisierung*, 265–267; Cullather, *The Hungry World*, 94–107; Unger, *Entwicklungspfade*, 36–37.

20 Wolf Ladejinsky, "Too Late to Save Asia?" [1950] in Louis J. Walinsky, ed., *Agrarian Reform as Unfinished Business: The Selected Papers of Wolf Ladejinsky* (New York: Oxford University Press, 1977), 130–135, 131–132.

21 Cf. Anna Rossi-Doria, "Il movimento contadino nel secondo dopoguerra in Calabria," in Franco Bonelli, Guido Crainz, and Anna Rossi-Doria, eds., *La fine dei contadini e l'industrializzazione del mezzogiorno* (Catanzaro: Rubbettino, 1999), 91–108, 99.

22 Cf. Ginsborg, *A History*, 60–63, 73–79, 106–108.

23 Cf. G. Massullo, "La riforma agraria," in Piero Bevilaqua, ed., *Storia dell'agricoltura italiana in età contemporanea*, vol. 3 (Venezia: Marsilio, 1991), 509–542; Ginsborg, *A History*, 122–133.

24 Cf. Grazia Sciacchitano, "Rural Development and Changing Labour Relations in Italy and Spain in the 1950s and 1960s," *Comparativ* 27.2 (2017): 35–53.

25 See Immerwahr, *Thinking Small*, chapter 3; Unger, *Entwicklungspfade*, 42–74; Cullather, *The Hungry World*, chapter 3.

26 Cf. Tim Hanstad et al., "Learning from Old and New Approaches to Land Reform in India," in Hans P. Binswanger-Mkhize, Camille Bourguignon, and Rogier Van Den Brink, eds., *Agricultural Land Redistribution: Toward Greater Consensus* (Washington, DC: World Bank, 2009), 241–263.

27 See, for example, Foreign Operations Administration, *A Selected Bibliography on Community Development* (Washington, DC: Foreign Operations Administration, 1955). Also see Immerwahr, *Thinking Small*, 55.

28 Cf. Robertson, *The Malthusian Moment*, 102–103.

29 See Morris Szeftel, "Sir William Arthur Lewis," in Simon, ed., *Fifty Key Thinkers*, 144–149; Tignor, *W. Arthur Lewis*.

30 Cf. Tignor, *W. Arthur Lewis*, 62; Sieberg, *Colonial Development*, 506–510.

31 Cf. Sieberg, *Colonial Development*, 546–549.

32 See Tignor, *W. Arthur Lewis*, chapters 1 and 2; Hodge, *Triumph*, 266–267.

33 W. Arthur Lewis, "Economic Development with Unlimited Resources," *Manchester School* 22.2 (1954): 139–191. For a slightly different, but related interpretation, see Julius Herman Boeke, *Economics and Economic Policy in Dualistic Societies as Exemplified by Indonesia* (New York: Institute of Pacific Relations, 1953).

34 Cf. Cooper, *Decolonization*, 379; Tignor, *W. Arthur Lewis*, chapter 3.

35 Cf. John M. Staatz and Carl K. Eicher, "Agricultural Development Ideas in Historical Perspective," in Carl K. Eicher and John M. Staatz, eds., *International Agricultural Development*, 3rd ed. (Baltimore: Johns Hopkins University Press, 1998 (1984)), 8–38, 11–12; Cristóbal Kay, "Development Strategies and Rural Development: Exploring Synergies, Eradicating Poverty," *Journal of Peasant Studies* 36.1 (2009): 103–137, 109.

36 Bruce F. Johnston and John W. Mellor, "The Role of Agriculture in Economic Development," *American Economic Review* 51 (1961): 566–593.

37 William H. Nicholls, "Agricultural Policy: The Place of Agriculture in Economic Development," in Kenneth Berrill, ed., *Economic Development with Special Reference to East Asia* (London: Palgrave Macmillan, 1964), 336–375.

38 Cf. Adelman, "Fallacies," 109.

39 Theodore W. Schultz, *Transforming Traditional Agriculture* (New Haven, CT: Yale University Press, 1964).

40 See Céline Pessis, "The Tractor as a Tool of Development? The Mythologies and Legacies of Mechanised Tropical Agriculture in French Africa, 1944–1956," in Hodge, Hödl, and Kopf, eds., *Developing Africa*, 179–203.

41 Cf. Pharo, "Entrepreneurship," 60–61, 65–68, 73–76 (quote 75).

42 On the Freedom from Hunger campaign, see Salvatici, *Nel nome degli altri*, 265–272; Staples, *The Birth of Development*, 105–109; Kevin O'Sullivan, "'A Global Nervous System': The Rise and Rise of European Humanitarian NGOs," in Frey, Kunkel, and Unger, eds., *International Organizations*, 196–219, 202–205.

43 Cf. Staples, *The Birth of Development*, 107–112.

44 Cf. Ruth Jachertz, "'To Keep Food Out of Politics': The UN Food and Agriculture Organization," in Frey, Kunkel, and Unger, eds., *International Organizations*, 75–100, 87–88.

45 See Karin Bugow, "The BIMAS Project in Java, Indonesia, 1968–1970: An Example of a Close Public Private Partnership in the Green Revolution." Unpublished manuscript, 2017.

46 See, for example, Rempe, "Entangled Industrialization," 247.

47 Cf. Unger, *Entwicklungspfade*, 98–99.

48 Cf. Staples, *The Birth of Development*, 183.

49 On Borlaug see Katie Willis, "Norman Borlaug," in Simon, ed., *Fifty Key Thinkers*, 45–50.

50 Warren Weaver and J. George Harrar, "Research on Rice," October 21, 1954. Appendix I to Minutes of Board Meeting, November 30–December 1, 1954. RAC, RF, RG 3, Series 915, Box 3, Folder 23, 3. Italics in the original. Also see Robert S. Anderson, Edwin Levy, and Barrie M. Morrison, *Rice Science and Development Politics: Research Strategies and IRRI's Technologies Confront Asian Diversity (1950–1980)* (Oxford: Clarendon Press, 1991), 26–42.

51 See Anderson, Levy, and Morrison, *Rice Science*, 47–50; Cullather, *The Hungry World*, chapter 6.

52 Ford Foundation, "The International Rice Research Institute. Information Paper," December 1969. RAC, Ford Foundation (FF), Report 002810, 2.

53 Ford Foundation, "The Rockefeller-Ford International Agricultural Research Institutes." Information Paper, December 1967. RAC, FF, Report 002869.

54 See Randolph Barker and Robert W. Herdt with Beth Rose, *The Rice Economy of Asia* (Washington, DC: Resources for the Future, 1985), 62–65.

55 Ann Quinn, "RF Grants in the Philippines, 1958–1990," *Rockefeller Archive Newsletter* (2006): 10–12, 11.

56 Nick Cullather, "Miracles of Modernization: The Green Revolution and the Apotheosis of Technology," *Diplomatic History* 28.2 (2004): 227–254; Simon Toner, "The Life and Death of Our Republic: Modernization, Agricultural Development, and the Peasantry in the Mekong Delta in the Long 1970s," in James and Leake, eds., *Decolonization*, 43–61.

57 Cf. Francine R. Frankel, *India's Green Revolution: Economic Gains and Political Costs* (Princeton, NJ: Princeton University Press, 1971), 7–8; A. K. Chakravarti, "Green Revolution in India," *Annals of the Association of American Geographers* 63.3 (1973): 319–330; Pierre Spitz, "The Green Revolution Re-Examined in India," in Bernhard Glaeser, ed., *The Green Revolution Re-Visited: Critique and Alternatives* (London: Allen & Unwin, 1987), 56–75.

58 Carroll P. Streeter, *A Partnership to Improve Food Production in India: A Special Report from the Rockefeller Foundation* (New York: The Rockefeller Foundation, 1969), 3–4. For a contemporary evaluation of IADP's effects, see Uttar Pradesh Agricultural University, *Changing Agriculture and Rural Life in a Region of Northern India: A Study of Progressive Farmers in Northwestern*

Uttar Pradesh during 1967/8, vol. 1 (Patnagar: U. P. Agricultural University, 1969), 209–210.

59 See Streeter, *A Partnership.*

60 Cf. Jenny Springer, "State Power and Agricultural Transformation in Tamil Nadu," in Arun Agrawal and K. Sivaramakrishnan, eds., *Agrarian Environments: Resources, Representation, and Rule in India* (Durham: Duke University Press, 2000), 86–106, 103. Similarly, see Nitish Jha, "Barriers to the Diffusion of Agricultural Knowledge: A Balinese Case Study," in Jeffrey H. Cohen and Norbert Dannhaeuser, eds., *Economic Development: An Anthropological Approach* (Walnut Creek, CA: Altamira Press, 2002), 87–106; Akhil Gupta, *Postcolonial Developments: Agriculture in the Making of Modern India* (Durham: Duke University Press, 2003 (1998)), 9, 196–197, 203.

61 Cf. Frankel, *India's Green Revolution*, 191–203. Also see Barker, Herdt, and Rose, *The Rice Economy*, chapter 10.

62 Cf. Lancaster, *Foreign Aid*, 36.

63 E. F. Schumacher, *Small Is Beautiful: Economics as if People Mattered* (New York: Harper & Row, 1973). On Schumacher, see Tony Binns, "E. F. (Fritz) Schumacher," in Simon, ed., *Fifty Key Thinkers*, 218–223.

64 Cf. Arndt, *Economic Development*, 97; Stephen Macekura, *Of Limits and Growth: The Rise of Global Sustainable Development in the Twentieth Century* (New York: Cambridge University Press, 2015), 138–139, 149.

65 Rockefeller Foundation, "The Rockefeller Foundation Conquest of Hunger Program," December 1974. Prepared for the meeting of the Board of Trustees of the Rockefeller Foundation. RAC, RF, RG 3.2, Series 900, Box 39, Folder 207.

66 Cf. Sieberg, *Colonial Development*, 577–586.

67 Cf. Hodge and Hödl, "Introduction," 11.

68 See, among others, Esther Möller, *Orte der Zivilisierungsmission: Französische Schulen im Libanon, 1909–1943* (Göttingen: Vandenhoeck & Ruprecht, 2013).

69 Cf. Zimmerman, *Alabama in Africa*, 45–52; Hodge, *Triumph*, 129.

70 Quoted in Zimmerman, *Alabama in Africa*, 48. Also see ibid., 139.

71 Cf. Hodge, *Triumph*, 129–130.

72 See Charles W. Hayford, *To the People: James Yen and Village China* (New York: Columbia University Press, 1990).

73 Cf. Sieberg, *Colonial Development*, 647.

74 Cf. Hodge, *Triumph*, 192–193.

75 Cf. Sieberg, *Colonial Development*, 644–648; Hodge, *Triumph*, 192.

76 See John Hills, John Ditch, and Howard Glennerster, eds., *Beveridge and Social Security* (Oxford: Clarendon Press, 1994); Lees, *The Solidarities of Strangers* 343; Hodge, *Triumph*, 197–198.

77 Cited in Helleiner, *Forgotten Foundations*, 210.

78 Cf. Skinner, "Who Knew the Minds of the People?" 311. Also see Kate Skinner, "'It Brought Some Kind of Neatness to Mankind': Mass Literacy, Community Development and Democracy in 1950s Asante," *Africa* 79.4 (2009): 479–499, 479.

79 Cf. Skinner, "Who Knew the Minds of the People?" 299.

80 Cf. Sieberg, *Colonial Development*, 644–648.

81 Cf. Eckert, "Regulating the Social," 470–471; Hodge, *Triumph*, 12–15.

82 Cf. Lohrmann, *Voices*, 221–222, 224, 226; Crawford Young, "Imperial Endings and Small States: Disorderly Decolonization for the Netherlands,

Belgium, and Portugal," in Bandeira Jerónimo and Costa Pinto, eds., *The Ends of European Colonial Empires*, 101–125, 112.

83 See Huber, "Planning Education." Also see Arndt, *Economic Development*, 66–68.

84 See, among others, Srirupa Roy, *Beyond Belief: India and the Politics of Postcolonial Nationalism* (Durham: Duke University Press, 2007).

85 Cf. Skinner, "Who Knew the Minds of the People?" 301–302, 304–305.

86 See Poul Duedahl, ed., *The History of UNESCO: Global Actions and Impact* (Basingstoke: Palgrave Macmillan, 2016), part 3.

87 The following is based on Corinna R. Unger, "The United States, Decolonization, and the Education of Third World Elites," in Dülffer and Frey, eds., *Elites*, 241–261.

88 See Gary R. Hess, "Waging the Cold War in the Third World: The Foundations and the Challenges of Development," in Lawrence J. Friedman and Mark D. McGarvie, eds., *Charity, Philanthropy, and Civility in American History* (Cambridge: Cambridge University Press, 2003), 319–339, 327; Edward H. Berman, "American Philanthropy and African Education: Toward an Analysis," *African Studies Review* 20.1 (1977): 71–85, 76–80.

89 Cf. Carnegie Corporation, "First Memorandum on Commonwealth Program for the Period Ahead," September 18, 1963. Columbia University Libraries (CUL), Rare Books and Manuscript Library (RBML), Carnegie Corporation of New York (CCNY), Series I.D, Box 4, Folder 7. Also see Berman, "American Philanthropy," 78.

90 Cf. Carnegie Corporation, "For Agenda," September 29, 1960. CUL, RBML, CCNY, Series III.A, Box 384, Folder 3.

91 Carnegie Corporation, "First Memorandum."

92 Cf. Hess, "Waging the Cold War," 214–219; Robert F. Arnove, "Foundations and the Transfer of Knowledge," in idem, ed., *Philanthropy and Cultural Imperialism: The Foundations at Home and Abroad* (Boston, MA: G. K. Hall, 1980), 305–330, 307.

93 Cf. Amrith, "Internationalising Health," 257.

94 Cf. Corinne A. Pernet, "Between Entanglements and Dependencies: Food, Nutrition, and National Development at the Central American Institute of Nutrition (INCAP)," in Frey, Kunkel, and Unger, eds., *International Organizations*, 101–125, 106–107.

95 Cf. ibid., 112–117.

96 Roland Popp, "An Application of Modernization Theory during the Cold War? The Case of Pahlavi Iran," *International History Review* 30.1 (2008): 76–98, 79.

97 Cf. Mohan Rao, *From Population Control to Reproductive Rights: Malthusian Arithmetic* (New Delhi: Sage, 2004), 24–26.

98 Cf. Annika Berg, "A Suitable Country: The Relationship between Sweden's Interwar Population Policy and Family Planning in Postindependence India," *Berichte zur Wissenschaftsgeschichte* 33.3 (2010): 297–320; Sunniva Engh, "From Northern Feminists to Southern Women: Scandinavian Aid to India," in Pharo and Pohle Fraser, eds., *The Aid Rush*, vol. 1, 253–283.

99 See Heinrich Hartmann and Corinna R. Unger, "Family, Sexuality, and Gender," in The Population Knowledge Network, ed., *Twentieth Century Population Thinking*, 115–141; Corinna R. Unger, "The Making of the Small Family Norm in post-1947 India," *Contemporanea* 18.3 (2015): 483–488.

100 Robertson, *The Malthusian Moment*, 68. Also see Simon Szreter, "The Idea of Demographic Transition and the Study of Fertility Change: A Critical Intellectual History," *Population and Development Review* 19.4 (1993): 659–701.

101 See Matthew Connelly, "Taking Off the Cold War Lens: Visions of North-South Conflict during the Algerian War for Independence," *American Historical Review* 105.3 (2000): 739–769, 755–756.

102 Cf. Sayward, *The United Nations*, 80.

103 Cf. Majeed Khan, "Population Control: A Two-Year Rural Action Experience," *Demography* 1.1 (1964): 126–129, 129. Also see Unger, "Family Planning," 67–68.

104 Cited in Dörnemann, "Seeing Population," 207.

105 Cf. Sarah Stockwell, "Exporting Britishness: Decolonization in Africa, the British State and its Clients," in Bandeira Jerónimo and Costa Pinto, eds., *The Ends of European Colonial Empires*, 148–177.

106 Cf. Dörnemann, "Seeing Population," 208.

107 Cf. ibid., 211–212.

108 Cited in Robertson, *The Malthusian Moment*, 101.

109 Cf. ibid., 86–88, 97–102.

110 Cf. Matthew Connelly, *Fatal Misconception: The Struggle to Control World Population* (Cambridge, MA: Belknap Press of Harvard University Press, 2008), chapter 6; Engh, "From Northern Feminists," 267–268.

111 Cf. Engh, "From Northern Feminists," 269–280.

112 Cf. Beusekom and Hodgson, "Lessons Learned?" 29–30; K. Sivaramakrishnan and Arun Agrawal, "Regional Modernities in Stories and Practices of Development," in K. Sivaramakrishnan and Arun Agrawal, eds., *Regional Modernities: The Cultural Politics of Development in India* (Stanford, CA: Stanford University Press, 2003), 1–61, 28–30.

113 See, among others, Gupta, *Postcolonial Developments*; Tania Murray Li, *The Will to Improve: Governmentality, Development, and the Practice of Politics* (Durham: Duke University Press, 2007); David Mosse, *Cultivating Development: An Ethnography of Aid Policy and Practice* (London: Pluto Press, 2005).

Chapter 7

1 See Gregg A. Brazinksy, *Winning the Third World: Sino-American Rivalry during the Cold War* (Chapel Hill: University of North Carolina Press, 2017), 93–105, 129–131, chapter 9.

2 Cf. Burton, "Socialisms," 12.

3 Cf. Frey, "Entwicklungspolitik," 302; Lancaster, *Foreign Aid*, 31–32.

4 Cf. Giuliano Garavini, "Completing Decolonization: The 1973 'Oil Shock' and the Struggle for Economic Rights," *International History Review* 33.3 (2011): 473–487, 477.

5 Cf. Wood, *From Marshall Plan to Debt Crisis*, 76; Tarp, "Aid," 34; Lancaster, *Foreign Aid*, 35; Sharma, *Robert McNamara's Other War*, 82.

6 Cf. Iandolo, "The Rise and Fall," 699–703; Lorenzini, "Comecon," 186.

7   See Nunan, *Humanitarian Invasion*, chapter 4.

8   Cf. Lorenzini, "Comecon," 183–199, 185–186.

9   Cf. Burton, "Socialisms," 11; Byrne, *Mecca of Revolution*, chapter 2; Berthold Unfried, "A Cuban Cycle of Developmental Socialism? Cubans and East Germans in the Socialist World System," *Journal für Entwicklungspolitik* 33.3 (2017): 69–90, 76–77; Christine Hatzky, *Cubans in Angola: South-South Cooperation and Transfer of Knowledge, 1976–1991* (Madison: University of Wisconsin Press, 2015).

10 Cf. Lorenzini, "Comecon," 188.

11 Cf. Kanet, "Vier Jahrzehnte," 51–52; Lorenzini, "Comecon," 189.

12 Cf. Rudner, "East European Aid," 15–16.

13 Cf. Johanna Bockman, *Markets in the Name of Socialism: The Left-Wing Origins of Neoliberalism* (Stanford, CA: Stanford University Press, 2011), 100–104; Vladimir Unkovski-Korica, *The Economic Struggle for Power in Tito's Yugoslavia: From World War II to Non-Alignment* (London: I. B. Tauris, 2016), chapter 3. Also see Byrne, *Mecca of Revolution*, 165–166, 204–205.

14 Cf. Lancaster, *Foreign Aid*, 34–35; Angela Romano, "Shaping Pan-European Cooperation in the 1970s: Soviet Initiatives and the EEC-Nine's Response," in Claudia Hiepel, ed., *Europe in a Globalising World: Global Challenges and European Responses in the "Long" 1970s* (Baden-Baden: Nomos, 2014), 27–48.

15 Cf. Lorenzini, "Comecon," 187.

16 Cf. William Glenn Gray, *Germany's Cold War: The Global Campaign to Isolate East Germany, 1949–1969* (Chapel Hill: University of North Carolina Press, 2003), 218.

17 Cf. Lorenzini, "Comecon," 191–192.

18 Cf. Wood, *From Marshall Plan to Debt Crisis*, 72.

19 See, among others, Thomas Davies, *NGOs: A New History of Transnational Civil Society* (New York: Oxford University Press, 2014), 141–152. Also see Lancaster, *Foreign Aid*, 36–39; Macekura, *Of Limits and Growth*, 152–155.

20 Cf. Lancaster, *Foreign Aid*, 36; O'Sullivan, "A Global Nervous System," 210.

21 See, among others, Peter Willetts, ed., *"The Conscience of the World": The Influence of Non-Governmental Organizations in the UN System* (Washington, DC: Brookings Institution, 1996).

22 Schmidt and Pharo, "Introduction," 392.

23 Cf. Lorenzini, "Comecon," 186.

24 Cf. Schmidt and Pharo, "Introduction," 392. On GATT, see Francine McKenzie, "Free Trade and Freedom to Trade: Exports, Markets and the Development Challenge to GATT, 1948–1968," in Frey, Kunkel, and Unger, eds., *International Organizations*, 150–170.

25 See Johanna Bockman, "Socialist Globalization against Capitalist Neocolonialism: The Economic Ideas behind the New International Economic Order," *Humanity* 6.1 (2015): 109–128, 112–118.

26 Cited in Daniel J. Whelan, "'Under the Aegis of Man': The Right to Development and the Origins of the New International Economic Order," *Humanity* 6.1 (2015): 93–108, 94.

27 Cf. John Shaw, "Hans Wolfgang Singer," in Simon, ed., *Fifty Key Thinkers*, 242–247.

28 On Prebisch, see Cristóbal Kay, "Raúl Prebisch," in Simon, ed., *Fifty Key Thinkers*, 199–205.

29 Cf. Andrés Rivarola Puntigliano and Örjan Appelqvist, "Prebisch and Myrdal: Development Economics in the Core and on the Periphery," *Journal of Global History* 6 (2011): 29–52, 33–34; Speich Chassé, *Die Erfindung des Bruttosozialprodukts*, 169–170.

30 Cf. Friedrich List, *Das nationale System der politischen Ökonomie* (Stuttgart: J. G. Cotta'scher Verlag, 1841). On List see Eugen Wendler, *Friedrich List (1789–1846): A Visionary Economist with Social Responsibility* (Berlin: Springer, 2015).

31 Cf. Puntigliano and Appelqvist, "Prebisch and Myrdal," 39–42, 45–46; Arndt, *Economic Development*, 79–81; Sayward, *The United Nations*, 97–98.

32 Andre Gunder Frank, "The Development of Underdevelopment" [1969], in J. Timmons and Amy Hite, *From Modernization to Globalization: Perspectives on Development and Social Change* (Malden, MA: Blackwell, 2000), 159–168, 160. Also see Andre Gunder Frank, *Capitalism and Development in Latin America: Historical Studies of Chile and Brazil* (New York: Monthly Review Press, 1967).

33 On Frank's development thinking, see Michael Watts, "Andre Gunder Frank," in Simon, ed., *Fifty Key Thinkers*, 90–96.

34 See Byrne, *Mecca of Revolution*.

35 Cf. Giuliano Garavini, "From Boumedienomics to Reaganomics: Algeria, OPEC, and the International Struggle for Economic Equality," *Humanity* 6.1 (2015): 79–92.

36 See Jürgen Dinkel, "'Third World Begins to Flex its Muscles': The Non-Aligned Movement and the North-South-Conflict during the 1970s," in Sandra Bott et al., eds., *Neutrality and Neutralism in the Global Cold War: The Non-Aligned Movement in the East-West Conflict* (New York: Routledge, 2016), 108–123; Helleiner, *Forgotten Foundations*, 273–276; Arndt, *Economic Development*, 80–81; Sayward, *The United Nations*, 107–109.

37 United Nations General Assembly, "Declaration on the Establishment of a New International Economic Order," May 1, 1974, http://www.un-documents.net/s6r3201.htm (accessed December 4, 2016). Also see Nils Gilman, "The New International Economic Order: A Re-introduction," *Humanity* 6.1 (2015): 1–16, 3.

38 Cf. Kevin O'Sullivan, "Between Internationalism and Empire: Ireland, the 'Like-Minded' Group, and the Search for a New International Order, 1974–82," *The International History Review* 37.5 (2015): 1083–1101.

39 The 1 percent goal was also called for in the Pearson Report (named after former Canadian Prime Minister Lester Pearson (1897–1972)) of 1969, which had been commissioned by the World Bank. Cf. Tomlinson, "The Commonwealth," 428.

40 Cf. Maul, *Human Rights*, 229–230.

41 Cf. Lancaster, *Foreign Aid*, 40.

42 See Sharma, *Robert McNamara's Other War*, 91–95. Also see Daniel T. Rodgers, *Age of Fracture* (Cambridge, MA: Belknap Press of Harvard University Press, 2011), chapter 2; Thomas Borstelmann, *The 1970s: A New Global History from Civil Rights to Economic Inequality* (Princeton, NJ: Princeton University Press, 2012), chapter 3.

43 See, for example, Christina Klein, "Musicals and Modernization: Rodgers and Hammerstein's The King and I," in Engerman et al., eds., *Staging Growth*, 129–162.

44 Ester Boserup, "The Economics of Polygamy," [1970] in Chari and Corbridge, eds., *The Development Reader*, 232–240, 239.

45 On Boserup, see Vandana Desai, "Ester Boserup," in Simon, ed., *Fifty Key Thinkers*, 50–55; Sayward, *The United Nations*, 110–111.

46 Sayward, *The United Nations*, 111.

47 Cf. ibid., 74, 111–112.

48 Cited in ibid., 74.

49 Cf. Dienabou Barry, "Women and Development in the Dutch Cooperation Program in the Office du Niger, 1978–97." Unpublished manuscript, 2017.

50 Diane Elson, *Male Bias in the Development Process* (Manchester: Manchester University Press, 1985). On Elson, see Sylvia Chant, "Diane Elson," in Simon, ed., *Fifty Key Thinkers*, 84–90.

51 Cf. Barry, "Women and Development."

52 Cf. Macekura, *Of Limits and Growth*, 143–148; Arndt, *Economic Development*, 108–109.

53 Rachel Carson, *Silent Spring* (Boston, MA: Houghton Mifflin, 1962). Also see Lawrence Culver, Christof Mauch, and Katie Ritson, eds., "Rachel Carson's *Silent Spring*: Encounters and Legacies," *RCC Perspectives* 7 (2012), http://www.environmentandsociety.org/sites/default/files/rcc_issue7_web-3.pdf (accessed June 21, 2017); Macekura, *Of Limits and Growth*, 99–100.

54 Cf. David Zierler, *The Invention of Ecocide: Agent Orange, Vietnam, and the Scientists Who Changed the Way We Think about the Environment* (Athens: University of Georgia Press, 2011).

55 Cf. Henry Bernstein and Terence J. Byrnes, "From Peasant Studies to Agrarian Change," *Journal of Agrarian Change* 1 (2001): 1–56, 2–6.

56 James C. Scott, *The Moral Economy of the Peasant: Rebellion and Subsistence in Southeast Asia* (New Haven, CT: Yale University Press, 1976).

57 Cf. Corinna R. Unger, "Agrarwissenschaftliche Expertise und ländliche Modernisierungsstrategien in der internationalen Entwicklungspolitik, 1920er bis 1980er Jahre," *Geschichte und Gesellschaft* 41 (2015): 552–579, 573.

58 See Dipesh Chakrabarty, "Subaltern Studies and Postcolonial Historiography," *Nepantla* 1.1 (2000): 9–32; Georg G. Iggers and Q. Edward Wang, *A Global History of Modern Historiography* (Harlow: Pearson, 2008), 281–290.

59 See Giuliano Garavini, "The Colonies Strike Back: The Impact of the Third World on Western Europe, 1968–1975," *Contemporary European History* 16.3 (2007): 299–319, 302–305; Samantha Christiansen and Zachary A. Scarlett, eds., *The Third World in the Global 1960s* (New York: Berghahn, 2013); Robert Gildea, "European Radicals and the 'Third World': Imagined Solidarities and Radical Networks," *Cultural & Social History* 8.4 (2011): 449–471; Quinn Slobodian, *Foreign Front: Third World Politics in Sixties West Germany* (Durham: Duke University Press, 2012), chapter 2; Monica Kalt, *Tiermondismus in der Schweiz der 1960er und 1970er Jahre: Von der Barmherzigkeit zur Solidarität* (Bern: Peter Lang, 2010); Acker, *Volkswagen*, 236–261.

60 Cf. Lorenzini, "Comecon," 186–187.

61 See Wood, *From Marshall Plan to Debt Crisis*, chapter 6; Frey, "Entwicklungspolitik," 310; Adelman, "Fallacies," 114; Sharma, *Robert McNamara's Other War*, 132–136.

62 See Charles S. Maier, "'Malaise': The Crisis of Capitalism in the 1970s," in Niall Ferguson et al., eds., *The Shock of the Global: The 1970s in Perspective* (Cambridge, MA: Belknap Press of Harvard University Press, 2010), 25–48.

63 Cf. Hodge, *Triumph*, 272–273.

64 Cf. Lancaster, *Foreign Aid*, 41.

65 Cf. Sharma, *Robert McNamara's Other War*, 29–30, 43–45, 51–52; Louis Galambos and David Milobsky, "Organizing and Reorganizing the World Bank, 1946–1972: A Comparative Perspective," *Business History Review* 69.2 (1995): 156–190.

66 Cf. Adelman, "Fallacies," 110; Sharma, *Robert McNamara's Other War*, 54–58.

67 Cf. Maul, *Human Rights*, 250–254.

68 See Nancy H. Kwak, *A World of Homeowners: American Power and the Politics of Housing Aid* (Chicago: Chicago University Press, 2016). Also see Sharma, *Robert McNamara's Other War*, 64–65.

69 Gunnar Myrdal, *Asian Drama: An Inquiry into the Poverty of Nations*, 3 vols. (New York: Twentieth Century Fund, 1968); Paul R. Ehrlich, *The Population Bomb* (New York: Ballantine Books, 1968). On Myrdal, see Sarah Radcliffe, "Gunnar Myrdal," in Simon, ed., *Fifty Key Thinkers*, 181–187. On Ehrlich, see Robertson, *The Malthusian Moment*, 150–151.

70 Alex Inkeles, Moses Abramovitz, and Tibor Scitovsky, "Economic Growth and its Discontents," *Bulletin of the American Academy of Arts and Sciences* 27.1 (1973): 11–27, 26.

71 See Sabrina Kirschner, *From Clean Cities to Green Cities: The Beginnings of Urban Environmental Management in the 1970s*. PhD dissertation project, Bundeswehr University Munich.

72 Cf. Unger, *Entwicklungspfade*, 244–269.

73 See Ford Foundation, *Women, Poverty and Livelihoods: The Ford Foundation 1952–2002* (New Delhi: Ford Foundation, 2002), 15–16; Daniel W. Crowell, *The SEWA Movement and Rural Development: The Banaskantha and Kutch Experience* (New Delhi: SAGE, 2003); Martha C. Nussbaum, *Women and Human Development: The Capabilities Approach* (Cambridge: Cambridge University Press, 2000), 53, 67.

74 See Tazul Islam, *Microcredit and Poverty Alleviation* (Aldershot: Ashgate, 2007); Aminur Rahman, *Women and Microcredit in Rural Bangladesh: Anthropological Study of the Rhetoric and Realities of Grameen Bank Lending* (Boulder, CO: Westview Press, 2001).

75 Cf. Verena Kröss, "The World Bank's Move toward Rural Development." Unpublished manuscript, 2017. Also see Frank Ellis and Stephen Biggs, "Evolving Themes in Rural Development 1950s–2000s," *Development Policy Review* 19 (2001): 437–448.

76 Michael Lipton, *Why Poor People Stay Poor: A Study of Urban Bias in World Development* (London: Temple Smith, 1977). On Lipton, see John Harris, "Michael Lipton," in Simon, ed., *Fifty Key Thinkers*, 149–155.

77 Cf. Chari and Corbridge, *The Development Reader*, 241; Kay, "Development Strategies," 110.

78 Cf. Macekura, *Of Limits and Growth*, 153; Sharma, *Robert McNamara's Other War*, 64.

79 Amrith, "Internationalising Health," 261.

80 Staatz and Eicher, "Agricultural Development Ideas," 16.

81 Hodge, *Triumph*, 271. Also see Sharma, *Robert McNamara's Other War*, 117–124.

82 Cf. Hodge, *Triumph*, 271–272; Hodge, "British Colonial Expertise," 39–42.

83 Martha C. Nussbaum, *Creating Capabilities: The Human Development Approach* (Cambridge, MA: Harvard University Press, 2011).

84 Martha C. Nussbaum and Amartya Sen, *The Quality of Life* (Oxford: Oxford University Press, 1993); Sen, *Development as Freedom*. On Sen, see Stuart Corbridge, "Amartya Kumar Sen," in Simon, ed., *Fifty Key Thinkers*, 230–236.

85 Paul Streeten, *First Things First: Meeting Basic Human Needs in Developing Countries* (Oxford: Oxford University Press, 1982).

86 See R. Subramanian, "Introduction," in R. Subramanian, ed., *Rural Development: An Inside Look at Problems and Prospects* (New Delhi: Yatan Publications, 1988), xi–xv; K. C. Alexander, "IRDP and Eradication of Poverty," in ibid., 20–46. Also see Gerald E. Sussman, *The Challenge of Integrated Rural Development in India: A Policy and Management Perspective* (Boulder, CO: Westview Press, 1982).

87 Cf. Wood, *From Marshall Plan to Debt Crisis*, 196–197, 199–202.

88 Cf. Gilman, "The New International Economic Order," 7–8.

Chapter 8

1   Cf. Centre for Global Negotiations, "The Brandt Equation: 21st Century Blueprint for the New Global Economy," http://www.brandt21forum.info/About_BrandtCommission.htm (accessed August 8, 2017).

2   Cf. Frey, "Entwicklungspolitik," 298.

3   Cited in Jolly et al., *UN Contributions*, 9.

4   Sharma, *Robert McNamara's Other War*, 113.

5   Cf. Lancaster, *Foreign Aid*, 35–36.

6   See Sharma, *Robert McNamara's Other War*, chapter 7.

7   Cf. Lancaster, *Foreign Aid*, 44; Sharma, *Robert McNamara's Other War*, 155.

8   See Damien Cahill, Lindy Edwards, and Frank Stilwell, eds., *Neoliberalism: Beyond the Free Market* (Cheltenham: Edward Elgar, 2012); Philipp Mirowski and Dieter Plehwe, eds., *The Road from Mount Pelerin: The Making of the Neoliberal Thought Collective* (Cambridge, MA: Harvard University Press, 2009); Rodgers, *Age of Fracture*, chapter 2.

9   See Juliet Johnson, *Priests of Prosperity: How Central Bankers Transformed the Postcommunist World* (Ithaca, NY: Cornell University Press, 2016); Bockman, *Markets*, chapter 7.

10 John Williams, "Democracy and the 'Washington Consensus,'" [1993] in Chari and Corbridge, eds., *The Development Reader*, 288–296. Also see Narcís Serra and Joseph E. Stiglitz, eds., *The Washington Consensus Reconsidered: Toward a New Global Governance* (New York: Oxford University Press, 2008).

11 Cf. Vanni Pettinà and Artemy M. Kalinovsky, "From Countryside to Factory: Industrialisation, Social Mobility, and Neoliberalism in Soviet Central Asia and Mexico," *Journal für Entwicklungspolitik* 33.3 (2017): 91–118, 108–109.

12 Raewyn Connell and Nour Dados, "Where in the World does Neoliberalism Come From? The Market Agenda in Southern Perspective," *Theory and Society* 43 (2014): 117–138, 122. Italics in the original.

13 Cf. Connell and Dados, "Where in the World," 130–131.

14 See Eun Mee Kim, ed., *Four Asian Tigers: Economic Development and the Global Political Economy* (Wagon Lane: Emerald, 1998).

15 Cf. Pettinà and Kalinovsky, "From Countryside to Factory," 100–102; Bockman, *Markets*; Johanna Bockman and Gil Eyal, "Eastern Europe as a Laboratory for Economic Knowledge: The Transnational Roots of Neoliberalism," *American Journal of Sociology* 108.2 (2002): 310–352, 325–331.

16 See, for example, Kathleen D. McCarthy, "From Government to Grassroots Reform: The Ford Foundation's Population Programs in South Asia, 1959–1981," *Voluntas* 6.3 (1995): 292–316.

17 Cf. O'Sullivan, "A Global Nervous System," 209–210.

18 See Philipp Pattberg et al., eds., *Public-Private Partnerships for Sustainable Development: Emergence, Influence, and Legitimacy* (Cheltenham: Edward Elgar, 2012); Macekura, *Of Limits and Growth*, chapter 5.

19 Cf. Macekura, *Of Limits and Growth*, 103–104; Glenda Sluga, "Capitalists and Climate," *Humanity*, November 6, 2017, http://humanityjournal.org/blog/capitalists-and-climate/ (accessed December 4, 2017). On forerunners of international environmental efforts, see Anna-Katharina Wöbse, *Weltnaturschutz: Umweltdiplomatie in Völkerbund und Vereinten Nationen, 1920–1950* (Frankfurt am Main: Campus, 2012).

20 Donella H. Meadows et al., *The Limits to Growth: A Report for the Club of Rome's Project on the Predicament of Mankind* (New York: Universe Books, 1972). Also see Ugo Bardi, *The Limits to Growth Revisited* (New York: Springer, 2011); Sluga, "Capitalists."

21 Cited in Macekura, *Of Limits and Growth*, 113–114.

22 Cf. Sayward, *The United Nations*, 105–107.

23 Cited in Macekura, *Of Limits and Growth*, 252.

24 Cf. ibid., 222–223, 277.

25 Cf. Kanet, "Vier Jahrzehnte," 56, 58.

26 Jeffrey D. Sachs, *The End of Poverty: Economic Possibilities for Our Time* (New York: Penguin, 2005).

27 William Easterly, *The White Man's Burden: Why the West's Efforts to Aid the Rest Have Done So Much Ill and So Little Good* (New York: Penguin, 2006).

28 Dambisa Moyo, *Dead Aid: Why Aid Is Not Working and How There Is Another Way for Africa* (New York: Farrar Straus Giroux, 2009).

29 Cf. Lancaster, *Foreign Aid*, 46–49.

30 Cf. United Nations Development Program, "Human Development Index (HDI)," http://hdr.undp.org/en/content/human-development-index-hdi (accessed August 17, 2017).

31 Jolly et al., *UN Contributions*, 13.

32 Cf. Jan Pronk, "Collateral Damage or Calculated Default? The Millennium Development Goals and the Politics of Globalisation," in Max Spoor, ed., *Globalisation, Poverty and Conflict: A Critical "Development" Reader* (Dordrecht: Kluwer, 2004), 9–33, 9.

33 Oxford Poverty and Human Development Initiative, "Missing Dimensions," http://www.ophi.org.uk/research/missing-dimensions/ (accessed December 16, 2016).

34 Cf. Jocelyn Mercado, "Buen Vivir: A New Era of Great Social Change," https://www.pachamama.org/blog/buen-vivir-new-era-great-social-change (accessed July 20, 2017); Friedbert Ottacher and Thomas Vogel,

Entwicklungszusammenarbeit im Umbruch: Bilanz—Kritik—Perspektiven. Eine Einführung (Frankfurt am Main: Brandes & Apsel, 2016), 39.

35 Cf. Marc Becker, "Ecuador's 'Buen Vivir' Socialism," in Roger Burbach, Michael Fox, and Federico Fuentes, eds., *Latin America's Turbulent Transitions: The Future of Twenty-First Century Socialism* (New York: Zed Books, 2013), 99–113.

36 See Giacomo D'Alisa, Federico Demaria, and Giorgos Kallis, eds., *Degrowth: A Vocabulary for a New Era* (Abindgon: Routledge, 2016).

37 Research & Degrowth, "Definition," https://degrowth.org/definition-2/ (accessed July 20, 2017).

38 Most famously, Thomas Piketty, *The Economics of Inequality* (Cambridge, MA: Harvard University Press, 2015). Also see Heather Boushey, J. Bradford DeLong, and Marshall Steinbaum, eds., *After Piketty: The Agenda for Economics and Inequality* (Cambridge, MA: Harvard University Press, 2017).

39 Cf. Mikaela Gavas, "Global Security or Poverty Eradication: The Politics of the European Union's Development Assistance," *Briefings, Review of African Political Economy* 34.111 (2007): 186–193, 190–193.

40 Cf. Lewis Rasmussen, "Waging War on Daily Terrors: The Use of Development Assistance to Counter Violent Extremism and Combat Terrorism," *Brown Journal of World Affairs* 21.2 (2015): 72–93, 77–78.

41 See Charles Piot, *Nostalgia for the Future: West Africa after the Cold War* (Chicago: University of Chicago Press, 2010), 133–162; Tania Murray Li, *Land's End: Capitalist Relations on an Indigenous Frontier* (Durham: Duke University Press, 2014); Julia Elyachar, *Markets of Dispossession: NGOs, Economic Development, and the State in Cairo* (Durham: Duke University Press, 2005).

Chapter 9

1 See J. Peter Pham, "Germany's 'Marshall Plan' for Africa," *Atlantic Council*, January 23, 2017, http://www.atlanticcouncil.org/blogs/new-atlanticist/germany-s-marshall-plan-for-africa (accessed May 31, 2017); Wolf Poulet, "Ein Marshall-Plan löst Afrikas Probleme nicht," *Frankfurter Allgemeine Zeitung*, January 31, 2017, http://www.faz.net/aktuell/politik/ausland/entwicklungshilfe-ein-marshall-plan-loest-afrikas-probleme-nicht-14677751.html (accessed May 31, 2017).

2 Cf. European Parliamentary Research Service, "The EU's New Approach to Funding Peace and Security," March 20, 2017, http://www.europarl.europa.eu/RegData/etudes/BRIE/2016/589858/EPRS_BRI(2016)589858_EN.pdf (accessed May 31, 2017).

3 Cf. Bryant Harris, Robbie Gramer, and Emily Tamkin, "The End of Foreign Aid As We Know It," *Foreign Policy*, April 24, 2017, http://foreignpolicy.com/2017/04/24/u-s-agency-for-international-development-foreign-aid-state-department-trump-slash-foreign-funding/ (accessed May 31, 2017); Andrew Natsios, "What Trump's Foreign Aid Budget Means for the Rest of the World," *The Atlantic*, April 4, 2017, https://www.theatlantic.com/politics/

archive/2017/04/what-trumps-foreign-aid-budget-means-to-the-rest-of-the-world/521553/ (accessed May 31, 2017).

4 "Frankfurter Erklärung: Freiwilliges Bekenntnis zur Umsetzung einer gemeinsamen Nachhaltigkeitsinitiative am Finanzplatz Frankfurt am Main," May 23, 2017, http://deutsche-boerse.com/blob/3031312/f6861f886db9bee721ec6431b602b39b/data/Frankfurter_Erklaerung-1.pdf (accessed May 31, 2017).

5 Adelman, "Fallacies," 130.

6 Cf. James L. Brain, "The Uluguru Land Usage Scheme: Success and Failure," *The Journal of Developing Areas* 14 (1980): 175–190, 175.

7 See Michael Woolcock, Simon Szreter and Vijayendra Rao, "How and Why History Matters for Development Policy," in C. A. Bayly et al., eds., *History, Historians and Development Policy: A Necessary Dialogue* (Manchester: Manchester University Press, 2011), 3–38, 12–13; David Hall-Matthews, "Can Historians Assist Development Policy-making, or Just Highlight its Faults?," in ibid., 169–174; John N. Borton, "Improving the Use of History by the International Humanitarian Sector," *European Review of History* 23.1–2 (2016): 193–209.

8 Inkeles, Abramovitz, and Scitovsky, "Economic Growth and its Discontents," 27.

BIBLIOGRAPHY

Archival documents

Rockefeller Foundation, "Food as a Possible Field of Interest for the Rockefeller Foundation: Collected Memoranda," November 4, 1943 (900 PRO Food 1). Rockefeller Archive Center (RAC), Rockefeller Foundation (RF), Record Group (RG) 3.2, Series 900, Box 39, Folder 207.

Rockefeller Foundation, "The Rockefeller Foundation Conquest of Hunger Program," December 1974. Prepared for the meeting of the Board of Trustees of the Rockefeller Foundation. RAC, RF, RG 3.2, Series 900, Box 39, Folder 207.

Warren Weaver, "The World Food Problem, Agriculture, and the Rockefeller Foundation," June 21, 1951. RAC, RF, RG 3, series 915, Box 3, Folder 23.

Warren Weaver and J. George Harrar, "Research on Rice," October 21, 1954. Appendix I to Minutes of Board Meeting, November 30–December 1, 1954. RAC, RF, RG 3, Series 915, Box 3, Folder 23.

Ford Foundation, "The International Rice Research Institute. Information Paper," December 1969. RAC, Ford Foundation (FF), Report 002810.

Ford Foundation, "The Rockefeller-Ford International Agricultural Research Institutes." Information Paper, December 1967. RAC, FF, Report 002869.

Carnegie Corporation, "First Memorandum on Commonwealth Program for the Period Ahead," September 18, 1963. Columbia University Libraries (CUL), Rare Books and Manuscript Library (RBML), Carnegie Corporation of New York (CCNY), Series I.D, Box 4, Folder 7.

Carnegie Corporation, "For Agenda," September 29, 1960. CUL, RBML, CCNY, Series III.A, Box 384, Folder 3.

Carnegie Corporation, "First Memorandum on Commonwealth Program for the Period Ahead," September 18, 1963. CUL, RBML, CCNY, Series I.D, Box 4, Folder 7.

Primary literature

Benham, Frederic, *The Colombo Plan and Other Essays* (London: Oxford University Press, 1956).

Black, Eugene R., "The World Bank at Work," *Foreign Affairs* 30.3 (1952): 402–411.

Boeke, Julius Herman, *Economics and Economic Policy in Dualistic Societies as Exemplified by Indonesia* (New York: Institute of Pacific Relations, 1953).

Boserup, Ester, "The Economics of Polygamy," [1970] in Chari and Corbridge, eds., *The Development Reader*, 232–240.

Bowles, Gordon T., "Point Four and Improved Standards of Living," *Annals of the American Academy of Political and Social Science* 268 (1950): 140–147.

Brandt, Karl, "The Economic Objectives of F.A.O., Point IV, and the Colombo Plan,"in *Proceedings of the Eight International Conference of Agricultural Economists* (London: Oxford University Press, 1953), 117–133.

Carson, Rachel, *Silent Spring* (Boston, MA: Houghton Mifflin, 1962).

Davis, Kingsley, "The Unpredicted Pattern of Population Change," *Annals of the American Academy of Political and Social Science* 305 (1956): 53–59.

Easterly, William, *The White Man's Burden: Why the West's Efforts to Aid the Rest Have Done So Much Ill and So Little Good* (New York: Penguin, 2006).

Ehrlich, Paul R., *The Population Bomb* (New York: Ballantine Books, 1968).

Elliott, William Yandell, "Prospects for 'Personal Freedom and Happiness for All Mankind,'" *Annals of the America Academy of Political and Social Science* 268 (1950): 173–182.

Elson, Diane, *Male Bias in the Development Process* (Manchester: Manchester University Press, 1985).

Engels, Friedrich, *The Condition of the Working Class in England in 1844. With a Preface Written in 1892* (London: George Allen & Unwin, 1892).

Foreign Operations Administration, *A Selected Bibliography on Community Development* (Washington, DC: Foreign Operations Administration, 1955).

Frank, Andre Gunder, *Capitalism and Development in Latin America: Historical Studies of Chile and Brazil* (New York: Monthly Review Press, 1967).

Frank, Andre Gunder, "The Development of Underdevelopment" [1969], in J. Timmons and Amy Hite, *From Modernization to Globalization: Perspectives on Development and Social Change* (Malden, MA: Blackwell, 2000), 159–168.

Gates, Bill, "Why I Would Raise Chickens," *Gates Notes*, June 7, 2016, https://www.gatesnotes.com/Development/Why-I-Would-Raise-Chickens.

Gates, Melinda, "The Small Animal That's Making a Big Difference for Women in the Developing World," https://medium.com/bill-melinda-gates-foundation/the-small-animal-thats-making-a-big-difference-for-women-in-the-developingworld-15d31dca2cc2#.3h3q5313j.

Gerschenkron, Alexander, "Economic Backwardness in Historical Perspective," in B. F. Hoselitz, ed., *The Progress of Underdeveloped Areas* (Chicago: University of Chicago Press, 1962), 3–29.

Hakim, George, "Point Four—The Need and the Impact," *Annals of the American Academy of Political and Social Science* 270 (1950): 68–73.

Hirschman, Albert O., *Development Projects Observed* (Washington, DC: Brookings Institution, 1967).

Hirschman, Albert O., *The Strategy of Economic Development* (New Haven, CT: Yale University Press, 1958).

Hoskins, Halford L., "Point Four with Reference to the Middle East," *Annals of the America Academy of Political and Social Science* 268 (1950): 85–95.

Inkeles, Alex, Moses Abramovitz, and Tibor Scitovsky, "Economic Growth and its Discontents," *Bulletin of the American Academy of Arts and Sciences* 27.1 (1973): 11–27.

Inkeles, Alex, "Participant Citizenship in Six Developing Countries," *American Political Science Review* 63.4 (1969): 1120–1141.

Johnston, Bruce F., and John W. Mellor, "The Role of Agriculture in Economic Development," *American Economic Review* 51 (1961): 566–593.

Kalijarvi, Thorsten V., "Point Four in the Contemporary Setting," *Annals of the America Academy of Political and Social Science* 268 (1950): 1–8.

Khan, Majeed, "Population Control: A Two-Year Rural Action Experience," *Demography* 1.1 (1964): 126–129.

Ladejinsky, Wolf, "Too Late to Save Asia?" [1950] in Louis J. Walinsky, ed., *Agrarian Reform as Unfinished Business: The Selected Papers of Wolf Ladejinsky* (New York: Oxford University Press, 1977), 130–135.

Lewis, W. Arthur, "Economic Development with Unlimited Resources," *Manchester School* 22.2 (1954): 139–191.

Lipton, Michael, *Why Poor People Stay Poor: A Study of Urban Bias in World Development* (London: Temple Smith, 1977).

List, Friedrich, *Das nationale System der politischen Ökonomie* (Stuttgart: J. G. Cotta'scher Verlag, 1841).

Lugard, Frederick J. D., *The Dual Mandate in British Tropical Africa* (Edinburgh: W. Blackwood and Sons, 1922).

McKay, Vernon, "Needs and Opportunities in Africa," *Annals of the American Academy of Political and Social Science* 268 (1950): 75–84.

Meadows, Donella H. et al., *The Limits to Growth: A Report for the Club of Rome's Project on the Predicament of Mankind* (New York: Universe Books, 1972).

Millikan, Max F., and Walt W. Rostow, "Notes on Foreign Economic Policy" [1954]. Re-printed in Christopher Simpson, ed., *Universities and Empire: Money and Politics in the Social Sciences during the Cold War* (New York: The New Press, 1998), 39–55.

Moyo, Dambisa, *Dead Aid: Why Aid Is Not Working and How There Is Another Way for Africa* (New York: Farrar Straus Giroux, 2009).

Myrdal, Gunnar, *Asian Drama: An Inquiry into the Poverty of Nations*, 3 vols. (New York: Twentieth Century Fund, 1968).

Nicholls, William H., "Agricultural Policy: The Place of Agriculture in Economic Development," in Kenneth Berrill, ed., *Economic Development with Special Reference to East Asia* (London: Palgrave Macmillan, 1964), 336–375.

Pan, Chia Lin, "Demographic Aspects of Underdeveloped Countries," *Annals of the America Academy of Political and Social Science* 270 (1950): 42–50.

Piquet, Howard S., "Point Four and World Production," *Annals of the American Academy of Political and Social Science* 268 (1950): 148–159.

Rose, John, "Needs and Resources of the Brave New World," *Annals of the American Academy of Political and Social Science* 268 (1950): 9–21.

Rosenstein-Rodan, Paul N., "Problems of Industrialisation of Eastern and South-Eastern Europe," *Economic Journal* 53 (1943): 202–211.

Rostow, Walt W., *The Stages of Economic Growth: A Non-Communist Manifesto* (Cambridge: Cambridge University Press, 1960).

Sachs, Jeffrey D., *The End of Poverty: Economic Possibilities for Our Time* (New York: Penguin, 2005).

Schultz, Theodore W., *The Economic Value of Education* (New York: Columbia University Press, 1963).

Schultz, Theodore W., "Investment in Human Capital," *American Economic Review* 51.1 (1961): 1–17.

Schultz, Theodore W., *Transforming Traditional Agriculture* (New Haven, CT: Yale University Press, 1964).

Schumacher, E. F., *Small Is Beautiful: Economics as if People Mattered* (New York: Harper & Row, 1973).

Scott, James C., *The Moral Economy of the Peasant: Rebellion and Subsistence in Southeast Asia* (New Haven, CT: Yale University Press, 1976).

Sperling, Jan Bodo, *The Human Dimension of Technical Assistance: The German Experience of Rourkela* (Ithaca, NY: Cornell University Press, 1969).

Sperling, Jan Bodo, *Die Rourkela-Deutschen* (Stuttgart: Deutsche Verlagsanstalt, 1965).

Streeten, Paul, *First Things First: Meeting Basic Human Needs in Developing Countries* (Oxford: Oxford University Press, 1982).

Streeter, Carroll P., *A Partnership to Improve Food Production in India: A Special Report from the Rockefeller Foundation* (New York: The Rockefeller Foundation, 1969).

Taylor, Frederick W., *The Principles of Scientific Management* (New York: Harper & Brothers, 1911).

Thorp, Willard L., "The Objectives of Point Four," *Annals of the American Academy of Political and Social Science* 268 (1950): 22–26.

Truman, Harry S., "The Fourth Point in President Truman's Inaugural Address, January 20, 1949", *Annals of the American Academy of Political and Social Science* 268 (1950): 183.

Truman, Harry S., "The President's Message to the Congress on 'Point Four Legislation,'" *Annals of the American Academy of Political and Social Science* 268 (1950): 184–187.

United Nations General Assembly, "Declaration on the Establishment of a New International Economic Order," May 1, 1974, http://www.un-documents.net/s6r3201.htm.

Uttar Pradesh Agricultural University, *Changing Agriculture and Rural Life in a Region of Northern India: A* Study *of Progressive Farmers in Northwestern Uttar Pradesh during 1967/8*, vol. 1 (Patnagar: U. P. Agricultural University, 1969).

Valeo, Francis R., "Point Four Problems in the Far East," *Annals of the America Academy of Political and Social Science* 268 (1950): 104–111.

Warburg, James P., "A New Look at the Economic Challenge," *Annals of the American Academy of Political and Social Science* 270 (1950): 22–34.

Secondary literature

Acemoglu, Daron, and James A. Robinson, *Why Nations Fail: The Origins of Power, Prosperity, and Poverty* (New York: Crown Publishers, 2012).

Acker, Antoine, *Volkswagen in the Amazon: The Tragedy of Global Development in Modern Brazil* (Cambridge: Cambridge University Press, 2017).

Adelman, Irma, "Fallacies in Development Theory and Their Implications for Policy," in Meier and Stiglitz, eds., *Frontiers of Development*, 103–134.

Adelman, Jeremy, *Worldly Philosopher: The Odyssey of Albert O. Hirschman* (Princeton, NJ: Princeton University Press, 2013).

Ahlberg, Kristin L., *Transplanting the Great Society: Lyndon Johnson and Food Aid* (Columbia: University of Missouri Press, 2008).

Alacevich, Michele, "Not a Knowledge Bank: The Divided History of Development Economics and Development Organization," *Social Science History* 40 (2016): 627–656.

Alacevich, Michele, *The Political Economy of the World Bank: The Early Years* (Stanford, CA: Stanford Economics and Finance and the World Bank, 2009).

Alacevich, Michele, "Postwar Development in the Italian Mezzogiorno: Analyses and policies," *Journal of Modern Italian Studies* 18.1 (2013): 90–112.

Alexander, K. C., "IRDP and Eradication of Poverty," in Subramanian, ed., *Rural Development*, 20–46.

Allen, Robert C., *Farm to Factory: A Reinterpretation of the Soviet Industrial Revolution* (Princeton, NJ: Princeton University Press, 2003).

Ambler, Charles, "Alcohol, Racial Segregation and Popular Politics in Northern Rhodesia," [1990] in Le Sueur, ed., *The Decolonization Reader*, 341–357.

Amrith, Sunil S., "Internationalising Health in the Twentieth Century," in Glenda Sluga and Patricia Clavin, eds., *Internationalisms: A Twentieth-Century History* (Cambridge: Cambridge University Press, 2017), 245–264.

Anderson, Robert S., Edwin Levy, and Barrie M. Morrison, *Rice Science and Development Politics: Research Strategies and IRRI's Technologies Confront Asian Diversity (1950–1980)* (Oxford: Clarendon Press, 1991).

Applebaum, Ann, *Red Famine: Stalin's War on Ukraine* (New York: Doubleday, 2017).

Arens, Esther Helena, "Multilateral Institution-Building and National Interest: Dutch Development Policy in the 1960s," *Contemporary European History* 12.4 (2003): 457–472.

Arndt, Heinz W., *Economic Development: The History of an Idea* (Chicago: University of Chicago Press, 1987).

Arnove, Robert F., "Foundations and the Transfer of Knowledge," in idem, ed., *Philanthropy and Cultural Imperialism: The Foundations at Home and Abroad* (Boston, MA: G. K. Hall, 1980), 305–330.

Austin, Gareth, "Reciprocal Comparison and African History: Tackling Conceptual Eurocentrism in the Study of Africa's Economic Past," *African Studies Review* 50.3 (2007): 1–28.

Bamba, Abou B., "Triangulating a Modernization Experiment: The United States, France and the Making of the Kossou Project in Central Ivory Coast," *Journal of Modern European History* 8.1 (2010): 66–83.

Bandeira Jéronimo, Miguel, *The "Civilizing Mission" of Portuguese Colonialism (c. 1830–1970)* (London: Palgrave Macmillan, 2015).

Bandeira Jerónimo, Miguel, and António Costa Pinto, eds., *The Ends of Colonial Empires: Cases and Comparisons* (Basingstoke: Palgrave Macmillan, 2015).

Bandeira Jéronimo, Miguel, and José Pedro Monteiro, eds., *Internationalism, Imperialism and the Formation of the Contemporary World: The Pasts of the Present* (Basingstoke: Palgrave Macmillan, 2017).

Bandeira Jéronimo, Miguel, "Rural (In)Securities: Resettlement, Control, and 'Development' in Angola (1960s–1970s)," *Comparativ* 27.2 (2017): 75–97.

Bardi, Ugo, *The Limits to Growth Revisited* (New York: Springer, 2011).

Barker, Randolph, and Robert W. Herdt with Beth Rose, *The Rice Economy of Asia* (Washington, DC: Resources for the Future, 1985).

Barrett, Christopher D., and Daniel G. Maxwell, *Food Aid After Fifty Years: Recasting its Role* (Abingdon: Routledge, 2005).

Barry, Dienabou, "Women and Development in the Dutch Cooperation Program in the Office du Niger, 1978–97." Unpublished manuscript, 2017.

Barth, Volker, and Roland Cvetkovski, eds., *Imperial Co-operation and Transfer, 1870–1930* (London: Bloomsbury, 2015).

Bates, Robert, *Beyond the Miracle of the Market: The Political Economy of Agrarian Development in Kenya* (Cambridge: Cambridge University Press, 1989).

Bayly, C. A., et al., eds., *History, Historians and Development Policy: A Necessary Dialogue* (Manchester: Manchester University Press, 2011).

Becker, Marc, "Ecuador's 'Buen Vivir' Socialism," in Roger Burbach, Michael Fox, and Federico Fuentes, eds., *Latin America's Turbulent Transitions: The Future of Twenty-First Century Socialism* (New York: Zed Books, 2013), 99–113.

Beinart, William, "Soil Erosion, Conservationism, and Ideas about Development: A Southern African Exploration, 1900–1960," *Journal of Southern African Studies* 11.1 (1984): 52–83.

Berg, Annika, "A Suitable Country: The Relationship between Sweden's Interwar Population Policy and Family Planning in Postindependence India," *Berichte zur Wissenschaftsgeschichte* 33.3 (2010): 297–320.

Berman, Edward H., "American Philanthropy and African Education: Toward an Analysis," *African Studies Review* 20.1 (1977): 71–85.

Bernstein, Henry, and Terence J. Byrnes, "From Peasant Studies to Agrarian Change," *Journal of Agrarian Change* 1 (2001): 1–56.

Bhattacharya, Sanjoy, and Benjamin Zachariah, "'A Great Destiny': The British Colonial State and the Advertisement of Post-War Reconstruction in India, 1942–1945," *South Asia Research* 19.1 (1999): 71–100.

Binns, Tony, "E. F. (Fritz) Schumacher," in Simon, ed., *Fifty Key Thinkers*, 218–223.

Bluche, Lorraine, and Kiran Klaus Patel, "Der Europäer als Bauer: Das Motiv des bäuerlichen Familienbetriebs in Westeuropa nach 1945," in Lorraine Bluche, Veronika Lipphardt and Kiran Klaus Patel, eds., *Der Europäer—ein Konstrukt: Wissensbestände, Diskurse, Praktiken* (Göttingen: Wallstein, 2009), 135–157.

Bockman, Johanna, and Gil Eyal, "Eastern Europe as a Laboratory for Economic Knowledge: The Transnational Roots of Neoliberalism," *American Journal of Sociology* 108.2 (2002): 310–352.

Bockman, Johanna, *Markets in the Name of Socialism: The Left-Wing Origins of Neoliberalism* (Stanford, CA: Stanford University Press, 2011).

Bockman, Johanna, "Socialist Globalization against Capitalist Neocolonialism: The Economic Ideas behind the New International Economic Order," *Humanity* 6.1 (2015): 109–128.

Boden, Ragna, "Cold War Economics: Soviet Aid to Indonesia," *Journal of Cold War Studies* 10.3 (2008): 110–128.

Borgwardt, Elizabeth, *A New Deal for the World: America's Vision for Human Rights* (Cambridge, MA: Belknap Press of Harvard University Press, 2005).

Borowy, Iris, *Coming to Terms with World Health: The League of Nations Health Organisation, 1921–1946* (Frankfurt am Main: Peter Lang, 2009).

Borstelmann, Thomas, *The 1970s: A New Global History from Civil Rights to Economic Inequality* (Princeton, NJ: Princeton University Press, 2012).

Borton, John N., "Improving the Use of History by the International Humanitarian Sector," *European Review of History/Revue européenne d'histoire* 23.1–2 (2016): 193–209.

Bossuat, Gérard, "French Development Aid and Co-operation under de Gaulle," *Contemporary European History* 12.4 (2003): 431–456.

Boushey, Heather, J. Bradford DeLong, and Marshall Steinbaum, eds., *After Piketty: The Agenda for Economics and Inequality* (Cambridge, MA: Harvard University Press, 2017).

Brain, James L., "The Uluguru Land Usage Scheme: Success and Failure," *The Journal of Developing Areas* 14 (1980): 175–190.

Brazinsky, Gregg A., *Winning the Third World: Sino-American Rivalry during the Cold War* (Chapel Hill: University of North Carolina Press, 2017).

Brine, Jenny, *Comecon: The Rise and Fall of an Internationalist Socialist Organization* (Oxford: Clio Press, 1992).

Brohman, John, "Albert O. Hirschman," in Simon, ed., *Fifty Key Thinkers*, 126–132.

Brown, Judith, *Nehru: A Political Life* (New Haven, CT: Yale University Press, 2003).

Browne, Stephen, *The United Nations Development Programme and System* (Abingdon: Routledge, 2011).

Bruisch, Katja, *Als das Dorf noch Zukunft war: Agrarismus und Expertise zwischen Zarenreich und Sowjetunion* (Köln: Böhlau, 2014).

Brundage, Anthony, *The English Poor Laws, 1700–1930* (Basingstoke: Palgrave Macmillan, 2002).

Bruno, Karl, "An Experiment in Ethiopia: The Chilalo Agricultural Development Unit and Swedish Development Aid to Haile Selassie's Ethiopia, 1964–1974," *Comparativ* 27.2 (2017): 54–74.

Bugow, Karin, "The BIMAS Project in Java, Indonesia, 1968–1970: An Example of a Close Public Private Partnership in the Green Revolution." Unpublished manuscript, 2017.

Büschel, Hubertus, and Daniel Speich, eds., *Entwicklungswelten: Globalgeschichte der Entwicklungszusammenarbeit* (Frankfurt am Main: Campus, 2009).

Büschel, Hubertus, *Hilfe zur Selbsthilfe: Deutsche Entwicklungsarbeit in Afrika, 1960–1975* (Frankfurt am Main: Campus, 2014).

Burleigh, Michael, *Germany Turns Eastwards: A Study of Ostforschung in the Third Reich* (New York: Macmillan, 2002).

Burton, Andrew, and Michael Jennings, "Introduction: The Emperor's New Clothes? Continuities in Governance in Late Colonial and Early Postcolonial East Africa," *The International Journal of African Historical Studies* 40.1 (2007): 1–25.

Burton, Eric, "Socialisms in Development: Revolution, Divergence and Crisis, 1917–1991," *Journal für Entwicklungspolitik* 33.3 (2017): 4–20.

Bussière, Éric, et al., eds., *The Bank of the European Union: The EIB, 1958–2008* (Luxembourg: European Investment Bank, 2008).

Byrne, Jeffrey James, *Mecca of the Revolution: Algeria, Decolonization, and the Third World Order* (Oxford: Oxford University Press, 2016).

Cahill, Damien, Lindy Edwards, and Frank Stilwell, eds., *Neoliberalism: Beyond the Free Market* (Cheltenham: Edward Elgar, 2012).

Calandri, Elena, "Italy's Foreign Assistance Policy," *Contemporary European History* 12.4 (2003): 509–525.

Caprotti, Federico, *Mussolini's Cities: Internal Colonialism in Italy, 1930–1939* (Amherst: Cambria Press, 2007).

Castelo, Cláudia, "Developing 'Portuguese Africa' in Late Colonialism: Confronting Discourses," in Hodge, Hödl, and Kopf, eds., *Developing Africa*, 63–86.

Çelik, Semih, "Between History of Humanitarianism and Humanitarianization of History: A Discussion on Ottoman Help for the Victims of the Great Irish Famine, 1845–1852," *WerkstattGeschichte* 68 (2015): 13–28.

Centre for Global Negotiations, "The Brandt Equation: 21st Century Blueprint for the New Global Economy," http://www.brandt21forum.info/About_BrandtCommission.htm.

Centre for the Study of Developing Societies, http://www.csds.in/history.

Chakravarti, A. K., "Green Revolution in India," *Annals of the Association of American Geographers* 63.3 (1973): 319–330.

Chakrabarty, Dipesh, "Subaltern Studies and Postcolonial Historiography," *Nepantla* 1.1 (2000): 9–32.

Chant, Sylvia, "Diane Elson," in Simon, ed., *Fifty Key Thinkers*, 84–90.

Chari, Sharad, and Stuart Corbridge, eds., *The Development Reader* (Abingdon: Routledge, 2008).

Chatterjee, Partha, "The National State," in Partha Chatterjee, *The Partha Chatterjee Omnibus* (New Delhi: Oxford University Press, 1999), 200–219.

Chickering, Roger, and Stig Förster, eds., *Great War, Total War: Combat and Mobilization on the Western Front, 1914–1918* (Washington, DC: German Historical Institute; New York: Cambridge University Press, 2000).

Choldin, Harvey M., "An Organizational Analysis of Rural Development Projects at Comilla, East Pakistan," *Economic Development and Cultural Change* 20.4 (1972): 671–690.

Choldin, Harvey M., "Urban Cooperatives at Comilla, Pakistan: A Case Study of Local-Level Development," *Economic Development and Cultural Change* 16.2, part 1 (1968): 189–218.

Chopra, Preeti, *A Joint Enterprise: Indian Elites and the Making of Bombay* (Minneapolis: University of Minnesota Press, 2011).

Christiansen, Samantha, and Zachary A. Scarlett, eds., *The Third World in the Global 1960s* (New York: Berghahn, 2013).

Clavin, Patricia, *Securing the World Economy: The Reinvention of the League of Nations, 1920–1946* (Oxford: Oxford University Press, 2013).

Coghe, Samuël, and Alexandra Widmer, "Colonial Demography: Discourses, Rationalities, Methods," in The Population Knowledge Network, ed., *Twentieth Century Population Thinking*, 37–64.

Coghe, Samuël, "Reordering Colonial Society: Model Villages and Social Planning in Rural Angola, 1920–45," *Journal of Contemporary History* 52.1 (2017): 16–44.

Conklin, Alice L., *A Mission to Civilize: The Republican Idea of Empire in France and West Africa, 1895–1930* (Berkeley: University of California Press, 1997).

Conquest, Robert, *The Harvest of Sorrow: Soviet Collectivization and the Terror-Famine* (New York: Oxford University Press, 1986).

Connell, Raewyn, and Nour Dados, "Where in the World Does Neoliberalism Come From? The Market Agenda in Southern Perspective," *Theory and Society* 43 (2014): 117–138.

Connelly, Matthew, *Fatal Misconception: The Struggle to Control World Population* (Cambridge, MA: Belknap Press of Harvard University Press, 2008).

Connelly, Matthew, "Taking Off the Cold War Lens: Visions of North-South Conflict during the Algerian War for Independence," *American Historical Review* 105.3 (2000): 739–769.

Conrad, Sebastian, "'Eingeborenenpolitik' in Kolonie und Metropole: 'Erziehung zur Arbeit' in Ostafrika und Ostwestfalen," in Sebastian Conrad and Jürgen Osterhammel, eds., *Das Kaiserreich transnational: Deutschland in der Welt 1871–1944* (Göttingen: Vandenhoeck & Ruprecht, 2004), 107–128.

Cooper, Frederick, *Citizenship between Empire and Nation: Remaking France and French Africa, 1945–1960* (Princeton, NJ: Princeton University Press, 2014).

Cooper, Frederick, *Decolonization and African Society: The Labor Question in French and British Africa* (Cambridge: Cambridge University Press, 1996).

Cooper, Frederick, "Development, Modernization, and the Social Sciences in the Era of Decolonization: The Examples of British and French Africa," [2004] in Bandeira Jerónimo and Costa Pinto, eds., *The Ends of Colonial Empires*, 15–50.

Cooper, Frederick, "Possibility and Constraint: African Independence in Historical Perspective," *Journal of African History* 49 (2008): 167–196.

Cooper, Frederick, "Reconstructing Empire in British and French Africa," *Past & Present* 210, Supplement 6 (2011): 196–210.

Cooper, Frederick, "Writing the History of Development," *Journal of Modern European History* 8.1 (2010): 5–23.

Corbridge, Stuart, "Amartya Kumar Sen," in Simon, ed., *Fifty Key Thinkers*, 230–236.

Couperus, Stefan, Vincent Lagendijk, and Liesbeth van de Grift, eds., "Experimental Spaces—Planning in High Modernity," *Journal of Modern European History* 13.4 (special issue) (2015).

Cowen, Michael, and Robert Shenton, "The Invention of Development," in Jonathan Crush, ed., *Power of Development* (London: Routledge, 1996), 27–43.

Crowell, Daniel W., *The SEWA Movement and Rural Development: The Banaskantha and Kutch Experience* (New Delhi: SAGE, 2003).

Cueto, Marcus, ed., *Missionaries of Science: The Rockefeller Foundation and Latin America* (Bloomington: Indiana University Press, 1994).

Cullather, Nick, "Bomb Them Back to the Stone Age: An Etymology," *History News Network*, October 6, 2006, http://historynewsnetwork.org/article/30347.

Cullather, Nick, "The Foreign Policy of the Calorie," *American Historical Review* 112.2 (2007): 337–364.

Cullather, Nick, *The Hungry World: America's Cold War Battle against Poverty in Asia* (Cambridge, MA: Harvard University Press, 2010).

Cullather, Nick, "Miracles of Modernization: The Green Revolution and the Apotheosis of Technology," *Diplomatic History* 28.2 (2004): 227–254.

Culver, Lawrence, Christof Mauch, and Katie Ritson, eds., "Rachel Carson's *Silent Spring*: Encounters and Legacies," *RCC Perspectives* 7 (2012), http://www.environmentandsociety.org/sites/default/files/rcc_issue7_web-3.pdf.

D'Alisa, Giacomo, Federico Demaria, and Giorgos Kallis, eds., *Degrowth: A Vocabulary for a New Era* (Abindgon: Routledge, 2016).

D'Antone, Leandra, "L'interesse straordinario' per il Mezzogiorno (1943–1960)," *Meridiana* 24 (1995): 17–64.

Das Gupta, Amit, "Development by Consortia: International Donors and the Development of India, Pakistan, Indonesia and Turkey in the 1960s," *Comparativ* 4.19 (2009): 96–111.

Das Gupta, Amit, *Handel, Hilfe, Hallstein-Doktrin: Die bundesdeutsche Südasienpolitik unter Adenauer und Erhard, 1949 bis 1966* (Husum: Matthiesen, 2004).

Davenport-Hines, Richard, *Universal Man: The Seven Lives of John Maynard Keynes* (London: Basic Books, 2015).

David-Fox, Michael, *Showcasing the Great Experiment: Cultural Diplomacy and Western Visitors to the Soviet Union, 1921–1941* (Oxford: Oxford University Press, 2012).

Davies, R. W., *Soviet Economic Development from Lenin to Khrushchev* (Cambridge: Cambridge University Press, 1998).

Davies, R. W., and Stephen G. Wheatcroft, *The Years of Hunger: Soviet Agriculture, 1931–1933* (Basingstoke: Palgrave Macmillan, 2004).

Davies, Thomas, *NGOs: A New History of Transnational Civil Society* (New York: Oxford University Press, 2014).

Davis, Muriam Haleh, "Restaging *Mise en Valeur*: 'Postwar Imperialism' and the Plan de Constantine," *Review of Middle East Studies* 44.2 (2010): 176–186.

Desai, Padma, *The Bokaro Steel Plant: A Study of Soviet Economic Assistance* (Amsterdam: North Holland Publishing Company, 1972).

Desai, Vandana, "Ester Boserup," in Simon, ed., *Fifty Key Thinkers*, 50–55.

Diallo Cô-Trung, Marina, *La Compagnie générale des oléagineux tropicaux en Casamance. Autopsie d'une opération de mise en valeur coloniale (1948–1962)* (Paris: Karthala, 1998).

Diamond, Jared M., *Guns, Germs, and Steel: The Fates of Human Societies* (New York: W. W. Norton, 1997).

Dimier, Véronique, "Bringing the Neo-Patrimonial State Back to Europe: French Decolonization and the Making of the European Development Aid Policy," *Archiv für Sozialgeschichte* 48 (2008): 433–457.

Dimier, Véronique, *The Invention of a European Development Bureaucracy: Recycling Empire* (Basingstoke: Palgrave Macmillan, 2014).

Dinkel, Jürgen, "'Third World Begins to Flex its Muscles': The Non-Aligned Movement and the North-South-Conflict during the 1970s," in Sandra Bott et al., eds., *Neutrality and Neutralism in the Global Cold War: The Non-Aligned Movement in the East-West Conflict* (New York: Routledge, 2016), 108–123.

Dörnemann, Maria, "Seeing Population as a Problem: Influences of the Construction of Population Knowledge on Kenyan Politics (1940s to 1980s)," in Hartmann and Unger, eds., *A World of Populations*, 201–221.

Dragomir, Elena, "The Creation of the Council for Mutual Economic Assistance as Seen from the Romanian Archives," *Historical Research* 88.240 (2015): 355–380.

Duedahl, Poul, ed., *The History of UNESCO: Global Actions and Impact* (Basingstoke: Palgrave Macmillan, 2016).

Dülffer, Jost, and Marc Frey, eds., *Elites and Decolonization in the Twentieth Century* (Basingstoke: Palgrave Macmillan, 2011).

Dyroff, Stefan, "Minority Rights and Humanitarianism: The International Campaign for the Ukrainians in Poland, 1930–1931," *Journal of Modern European History* 12.2 (2014): 216–230.

Eckert, Andreas, "Julius Nyerere, Tanzanian Elites, and the Project of African Socialism," in Dülffer and Frey, eds., *Elites*, 216–240.

Eckert, Andreas, "Regulating the Social: Social Security, Social Welfare and the State in Late Colonial Tanzania," *Journal of African History* 45.3 (2004): 467–489.

Edgar, Adrienne Lynn, *Tribal Nation: The Making of Soviet Turkmenistan* (Princeton, NJ: Princeton University Press, 2004).

Ekbladh, David, *The Great American Mission: Modernization and the Construction of an American World Order* (Princeton, NJ: Princeton University Press, 2010).

Ekbladh, David, "'Mr. TVA': Grass-Roots Development, David Lilienthal, and the Rise and Fall of the Tennessee Valley Authority as a Symbol for U.S. Overseas Development, 1933–1973," *Diplomatic History* 26.3 (2002): 335–374.

Ellis, Frank, and Stephen Biggs, "Evolving Themes in Rural Development 1950s–2000s," *Development Policy Review* 19 (2001): 437–448.

Elmer, Sara, "Postkoloniale Erschließung ferner Länder? Die erste Schweizer Nepalmission und die Anfänge der technischen Hilfe an unterentwickelte Länder," in Patricia Purtschert, Barbara Lüthi, and Francesca Falk, eds., *Postkoloniale Schweiz: Formen und Folgen eines Kolonialismus ohne Kolonien*, 2nd ed. (Bielefeld: transcript, 2013), 245–266.

Elyachar, Julia, *Markets of Disposession: NGOs, Economic Development, and the State in Cairo* (Durham: Duke University Press, 2005).

Engerman, David C., *Modernization from the Other Shore: American Intellectuals and the Romance of Russian Development* (Cambridge, MA: Harvard University Press, 2003).

Engerman, David C., "The Second World's Third World," *Kritika* 12.1 (2011): 183–211.

Engerman, David C., et al., eds., *Staging Growth: Modernization, Development, and the Global Cold War* (Amherst: University of Massachusetts Press, 2003).

Engerman, David C., "West Meets East: The Center for International Studies and Indian Economic Development," in Engerman et al., eds., *Staging Growth*, 199–223.

Engh, Sunniva, "From Northern Feminists to Southern Women: Scandinavian Aid to India," in Pharo and Pohle Fraser, eds., *The Aid Rush*, vol. 1, 253–283.

Escobar, Arturo, *Encountering Development: The Making and Unmaking of the Third World* (Princeton, NJ: Princeton University Press, 1995).

European Parliamentary Research Service, "The EU's New Approach to Funding Peace and Security," March 20, 2017, http://www.europarl.europa.eu/RegData/etudes/BRIE/2016/589858/EPRS_BRI(2016)589858_EN.pdf.

European Review of History/Revue européenne d'histoire 22.6 (2015): 855–970.

"Experimental Spaces – Planning in High Modernity" in *Journal of Modern European History* 13.4 (2015).

Fairhead, James, and Melissa Leach, "Desiccation and Domination: Science and Struggles over Environment and Development in Colonial Guinea," *The Journal of African History* 41.1 (2000): 34–54.

Feichtinger, Moritz, "'A Great Reformatory': Social Planning and Strategic Resettlement in Late Colonial Kenya and Algeria, 1952–63," *Journal of Contemporary History* 52.1 (2017): 45–72.

Ferguson, James, *The Anti-Politics Machine: "Development," Depoliticization, and Bureaucratic Power in Lesotho* (Minneapolis: University of Minnesota Press, 1994).

Fernández Pietros, Lourenzo, Juan Pan-Montojo, and Miguel Cabo, eds., *Agriculture in the Age of Fascism: Authoritarian Technocracy and Rural Modernization, 1922–1945* (Turnhout: Brepols, 2014).

Fieldhouse, David, "Decolonization, Development, and Dependence: A Survey of Changing Attitudes," in Prosser Gifford and Wm. Roger Louis, eds., *The Transfer of Power in Africa: Decolonization 1940–1960* (New Haven, CT: Yale University Press, 1982), 483–514.

Fitzpatrick, Sheila, *Stalin's Peasants: Resistance and Survival in the Russian Village after Collectivization* (Oxford: Oxford University Press, 1994).

Ford Foundation, *Women, Poverty and Livelihoods: The Ford Foundation 1952–2002* (New Delhi: Ford Foundation, 2002).

Frankel, Francine R., *India's Green Revolution: Economic Gains and Political Costs* (Princeton, NJ: Princeton University Press, 1971).

"Frankfurter Erklärung: Freiwilliges Bekenntnis zur Umsetzung einer gemeinsamen Nachhaltigkeitsinitiative am Finanzplatz Frankfurt am Main," May 23, 2017, http://deutsche-boerse.com/blob/3031312/f6861f886db9bee721ec6431b602b39b/data/Frankfurter_Erklaerung-1.pdf.

Frey, Marc, "Control, Legitimacy, and the Securing of Interests: European Development Policy in South-east Asia from the Late Colonial Period to the Early 1960s," *Contemporary European History* 12.4 (2003): 395–412.

Frey, Marc, *Dekolonisierung in Südostasien: Die Vereinigten Staaten und die Auflösung der europäischen Kolonialreiche* (München: Oldenbourg, 2006).

Frey, Marc, "Doctrines and Practices of Agrarian Development: The Case of the Office du Niger in Mali," *Comparativ* 27.2 (2017): 15–34.

Frey, Marc, "Entwicklungspolitik," in Jost Dülffer and Wilfried Loth, eds., *Dimensionen internationaler Geschichte* (München: Oldenbourg, 2012), 293–312.

Frey, Marc, Sönke Kunkel, and Corinna R. Unger, eds., *International Organizations and Development, 1945–1990* (Basingstoke: Palgrave Macmillan, 2014).

Frey, Marc, "The Limits of Modernization: American Development Assistance and Southeast Asian Resistance during the 1950s," *Comparativ* 19.4 (2009): 44–60.

Frey, Marc, and Corinna R. Unger, "The World Bank and Agrarian Development, 1945 to the 1990s." Unpublished manuscript, 2013.

Frey, Marc, and Sönke Kunkel, "Writing the History of Development: A Review of Recent Literature," *Contemporary European History* 20.2 (2011): 215–232.

Fuller, Mia, *Moderns Abroad: Architecture, Cities and Italian Imperialism* (Abingdon: Routledge, 2007).

Galambos, Louis, and David Milobsky, "Organizing and Reorganizing the World Bank, 1946–1972: A Comparative Perspective," *Business History Review* 69.2 (1995): 156–190.

Garavini, Giuliano, "The Colonies Strike Back: The Impact of the Third World on Western Europe, 1968–1975," *Contemporary European History* 16.3 (2007): 299–319.

Garavini, Giuliano, "Completing Decolonization: The 1973 'Oil Shock' and the Struggle for Economic Rights," *International History Review* 33.3 (2011): 473–487.

Garavini, Giuliano, "The *Eurafrica Factor*: European Community Development Policy (1957–1992)," in Ulrich Krotz, Kiran Klaus Patel, and Federico Romero, eds., *The History of EC Foreign Relations, 1957–1992*. Forthcoming.

Garavini, Giuliano, "From Boumedienomics to Reaganomics: Algeria, OPEC, and the International Struggle for Economic Equality," *Humanity* 6.1 (2015): 79–92.

Gaudier, Maryse, "The International Institute for Labour Studies: Its Research Function, Activities and Publications 1960–2001," http://www.ilo.org/wcmsp5/groups/public/—dgreports/—inst/documents/genericdocument/wcms_192540.pdf.

Gavas, Mikaela, "Global Security or Poverty Eradication: The Politics of the European Union's Development Assistance," *Briefings, Review of African Political Economy* 34.111 (2007): 186–193.

Gerhard, Gesine, "The Modernization Dilemma: Agrarian Policies in Nazi Germany," in Fernández Pietros, Pan-Montojo, and Cabo, eds., *Agriculture*, 139–155.

Geyer, Michael, "Ein Vorbote des Wohlfahrtsstaates: Die Kriegsopferversorgung in Frankreich, Deutschland und Großbritannien nach dem Ersten Weltkrieg," *Geschichte und Gesellschaft* 9.2 (1983): 230–277.

Gildea, Robert, "European Radicals and the 'Third World': Imagined Solidarities and Radical Networks," *Cultural & Social History* 8.4 (2011): 449–471.

Gilman, Nils, *Mandarins of the Future: Modernization Theory in Cold War America* (Baltimore: Johns Hopkins University Press, 2003).

Gilman, Nils, "The New International Economic Order: A Re-introduction," *Humanity* 6.1 (2015): 1–16.

Ginio, Ruth, "Vichy Rule in French West Africa: Prelude to Decolonization?" *French Colonial History* 4 (2003): 205–226.

Ginsborg, Paul, *A History of Contemporary Italy: Society and Politics, 1943–1988* (London: Penguin, 1990).

Giustozzi, Antonio, and Artemy Kalinovsky, *Missionaries of Modernity: Advisory Missions and the Struggle for Hegemony in Afghanistan and Beyond* (London: Hurst & Company, 2016).

Glagow, Manfred, Wilfried Gotsch, and Andreas Stucke, *Das Bundesministerium für Wirtschaftliche Zusammenarbeit (BMZ): Entstehungszusammenhang, Personalstruktur, Steuerungsfähigkeit* (Pfaffenweiler: Centaurus-Verlagsgesellschaft, 1989).

Go, Julian, *American Empire and the Politics of Meaning: Elite Political Cultures in the Philippines and Puerto Rico during U.S. Colonialism* (Durham: Duke University Press, 2008).

Goebel, Michael, *Anti-Imperial Metropolis: Interwar Paris and the Seeds of Third World Nationalism* (New York: Cambridge University Press, 2015).

Gold, Jennifer, "The Reconfiguration of Scientific Career Networks in the Late Colonial Period: The Case of the Food and Agriculture Organization and the British Colonial Forestry Service," in Brett Bennett and Joseph Hodge, eds., *Science and Empire: Knowledge and Networks of Science across the British Empire, 1800–1970* (Basingstoke: Palgrave Macmillan, 2011), 297–320.

Goscha, Christopher E., and Christian Ostermann, eds., *Connecting Histories: Decolonization and the Cold War in Southeast Asia, 1945–1962* (Washington, DC: Woodrow Wilson Center Press; Stanford, CA: Stanford University Press, 2009).

Grabas, Christian, "Planning the Economic Miracle? Industrial Policy in Italy between Boom and Crisis, 1950–1975," in Nützenadel and Grabas, eds., *Industrial Policy*, 134–183.

"Graduate Institute of International and Development Studies," https://en.wikipedia.org/wiki/Graduate_Institute_of_International_and_Development_Studies.

Graevenitz, Fritz Georg von, *Argument Europa: Internationalismus in der globalen Agrarkrise der Zwischenkriegszeit (1927–1937)* (Frankfurt am Main: Campus, 2017).

Grando, Stefano, and Gianluca Volpi, "Backwardness, Modernization, Propaganda: Agrarian Policies and Rural Representations in the Italian Fascist Regime," in Fernández Pietros, Pan-Montojo, and Cabo, eds., *Agriculture*, 43–83.

Gray, William Glenn, *Germany's Cold War: The Global Campaign to Isolate East Germany, 1949–1969* (Chapel Hill: University of North Carolina Press, 2003).

Grote, Hendrik, "Von der Entwicklungshilfe zur Entwicklungspolitik: Voraussetzungen, Strukturen und Mentalitäten der bundesdeutschen Entwicklungshilfe, 1949–1961," *Vorgänge* 43.2 (2004): 24–35.

Gupta, Akhil, *Postcolonial Developments: Agriculture in the Making of Modern India* (Durham: Duke University Press, 2003 (1998)).

Gwynne, Robert, "Alexander Gerschenkron," in Simon, ed., *Fifty Key Thinkers*, 116–121.

Haefele, Mark H., "Walt Rostow's Stages of Economic Growth: Ideas and Action," in Engerman et al., eds., *Staging Growth*, 81–103.

Hall-Matthews, David, "Can Historians Assist Development Policy-making, or Just Highlight its Faults?" in Bayly et al., eds., *History*, 169–174.

Hampf, Michaela M., and Simone Müller-Pohl, eds., *Global Communication Electric: Business, News and Politics in the World of Telegraphy* (Frankfurt am Main: Campus, 2013).

Hansen, Peo, and Stefan Jonsson, "Building Eurafrica: Reviving Colonialism through European Integration, 1920–1960," in Kalypso Nicolaïdis et al., eds., *Echoes of Empire: Memory, Identity and Colonial Legacies* (London: I. B. Tauris, 2015), 209–226.

Hanstad, Tim, et al., "Learning from Old and New Approaches to Land Reform in India," in Hans P. Binswanger-Mkhize, Camille Bourguignon, and Rogier Van Den Brink, eds., *Agricultural Land Redistribution: Toward Greater Consensus* (Washington, DC: World Bank, 2009), 241–263.

Harris, Bryant, Robbie Gramer, and Emily Tamkin, "The End of Foreign Aid As We Know It," *Foreign Policy*, April 24, 2017, http://foreignpolicy.com/2017/04/24/u-s-agency-for-international-development-foreign-aid-state-department-trump-slash-foreign-funding/.

Harris, John, "Michael Lipton," in Simon, ed., *Fifty Key Thinkers*, 149–155.

Hartmann, Heinrich, and Corinna R. Unger, "Family, Sexuality, and Gender," in The Population Knowledge Network, ed., *Twentieth Century Population Thinking*, 115–141.

Hartmann, Heinrich, and Corinna R. Unger, eds., *A World of Populations: Transnational Perspectives on Demography in the Twentieth Century* (New York: Berghahn Books, 2014).

Harwood, Jonathan, "Peasant Friendly Plant Breeding and the Early Years of the Green Revolution in Mexico," *Agricultural History* 83.3 (2009): 384–410.

Hatzky, Christine, *Cubans in Angola: South-South Cooperation and Transfer of Knowledge, 1976–1991* (Madison: University of Wisconsin Press, 2015).

Hayford, Charles W., *To the People: James Yen and Village China* (New York: Columbia University Press, 1990).

Hein, Bastian, *Die Westdeutschen und die Dritte Welt: Entwicklungspolitik und Entwicklungsdienste zwischen Reform und Revolte* (München: Oldenbourg, 2005).

Heinemann, Isabel, and Patrick Wagner, eds., *Wissenschaft, Planung, Vertreibung: Der Generalplan Ost der Nationalsozialisten* (Stuttgart: Steiner, 2006).

Helleiner, Eric, *Forgotten Foundations of Bretton Woods: International Development and the Making of the Postwar Order* (Ithaca, NY: Cornell University Press, 2014).

Hess, Gary R., "Waging the Cold War in the Third World: The Foundations and the Challenges of Development," in Lawrence J. Friedman and Mark D. McGarvie, eds., *Charity, Philanthropy, and Civility in American History* (Cambridge: Cambridge University Press, 2003), 319–339.

Hilger, Andreas, "Building a Socialist Elite? Khrushchev's Soviet Union and Elite Formation in India," in Dülffer and Frey, eds., *Elites*, 262–286.

Hilger, Andreas, "Revolutionsideologie, Systemkonkurrenz oder Entwicklungspolitik: Sowjetisch-indische Wirtschaftsbeziehungen in Chruschtschows Kaltem Krieg," *Archiv für Sozialgeschichte* 48 (2008): 389–410.

Hills, John, John Ditch, and Howard Glennerster, eds., *Beveridge and Social Security* (Oxford: Clarendon Press, 1994).

Hobsbawm, Eric, *The Age of Extremes: A History of the World, 1914–1991* (New York: Pantheon Books, 1994).

Hochschild, Adam, *King Leopold's Ghost: A Story of Greed, Terror, and Heroism in Colonial Africa* (New York: Houghton Mifflin, 1999).

Hodge, Joseph M., "British Colonial Expertise: Post-Colonial Careering and the Early History of International Development," *Journal of Modern European History* 8.1 (2010): 24–46.

Hodge, Joseph M., Gerald Hödl, and Martina Kopf, eds., *Developing Africa: Concepts and Practices in Twentieth-Century Colonialism* (Manchester: Manchester University Press, 2014).

Hodge, Joseph M., and Gerald Hödl, "Introduction," in Hodge, Hödl, and Kopf, eds., *Developing Africa*, 1–34.

Hodge, Joseph M., "On the Historiography of Development (Part 1: The First Wave)," *Humanity* 6.3 (2015): 429–463.

Hodge, Joseph M., *Triumph of the Expert: Agrarian Doctrines of Development and the Legacies of British Colonialism* (Athens: Ohio University Press, 2007).

Hodge, Joseph M., "Writing the History of Development (Part 2: Wider, Longer, Deeper)," *Humanity* 7.1 (2016): 125–174.

Hodgson, Dorothy L., "Taking Stock: State Control, Ethnic Identity and Pastoralist Development in Tanganyika, 1948–1958," *Journal of African History* 41 (2000): 58–78.

Hoffmann, David L., *Stalinist Values: The Cultural Norms of Soviet Modernity, 1917–1941* (Ithaca, NY: Cornell University Press, 2003).

Hoffman, Elizabeth Cobbs, *All You Need is Love: The Peace Corps and the Spirit of the 1960s* (Cambridge, MA: Harvard University Press, 1998).

Holm, Michael, *The Marshall Plan: A New Deal for Europe* (Abingdon: Routledge, 2016).

Huber, Valeska, "Planning Education and Manpower in the Middle East, 1950s–60s," *Journal of Contemporary History* 52.1 (2017): 95–117.

Hübner, Stefan, "Muscular Christianity and the Western Civilizing Mission: Elwood S. Brown, the YMCA, and the Idea of the Far Eastern Championship Games," *Diplomatic History* 39.3 (2015): 532–557.

Hull, Matthew, "Democratic Technologies of Speech: From WWII America to Postcolonial Delhi," *Journal of Linguistic Anthropology* 20.2 (2010): 257–282.

Iandolo, Alessandro, "The Rise and Fall of the 'Soviet Model of Development' in West Africa, 1957–64," *Cold War History* 12.4 (2012): 683–704.

Iggers, Georg G., and Q. Edward Wang, *A Global History of Modern Historiography* (Harlow: Pearson, 2008).

Ikenberry, G. John, *After Victory: Institutions, Strategic Restraint, and the Rebuilding of Order after Major Wars* (Princeton, NJ: Princeton University Press, 2000).

Immerwahr, Daniel, *Thinking Small: The United States and the Lure of Community Development* (Cambridge, MA: Harvard University Press, 2015).

Iordachi, Constantin, and Arnd Bauernkämper, eds., *The Collectivization of Agriculture in Communist Eastern Europe: Comparison and Entanglements* (Budapest: Central European University Press, 2014).

Irwin, Ryan, "Sovereignty in the Congo Crisis," in James and Leake, eds., *Decolonization*, 203–218.

Islam, Tazul, *Microcredit and Poverty Alleviation* (Aldershot: Ashgate, 2007).

Jachertz, Ruth, and Alexander Nützenadel, "Coping with Hunger? Visions of a Global Food System, 1930–1960," *Journal of Global History* 6 (2011): 99–119.

Jachertz, Ruth, "'To Keep Food Out of Politics': The UN Food and Agriculture Organization," in Frey, Kunkel, and Unger, eds., *International Organizations*, 75–100.

Jahanbani, Sheyda, "One Global War on Poverty: The Johnson Administration Fights Poverty at Home and Abroad, 1964–1968," in Francis J. Gavin and Mark Atwood Lawrence, eds., *Beyond the Cold War: Lyndon Johnson and the New Global Challenges of the 1960s* (New York: Oxford University Press, 2014), 97–117.

James, Leslie, and Elisabeth Leake, eds., *Decolonization and the Cold War: Negotiating Independence* (London: Bloomsbury, 2015).

Jennings, Michael, "'A Very Real War': Popular Participation in Development in Tanzania during the 1950s & 1960s," *International Journal of African Historical Studies* 40.1 (2007): 71–95.

Jha, Nitish, "Barriers to the Diffusion of Agricultural Knowledge: A Balinese Case Study," in Jeffrey H. Cohen and Norbert Dannhaeuser, eds., *Economic Development: An Anthropological Approach* (Walnut Creek, CA: Altamira Press, 2002), 87–106.

Johnson, Juliet, *Priests of Prosperity: How Central Bankers Transformed the Postcommunist World* (Ithaca, NY: Cornell University Press, 2016).

Jolly, Richard, et al., *UN Contributions to Development Thinking and Practice* (Bloomington: Indiana University Press, 2004).

Kalinovsky, Artemy M., "Not Some British Colony in Africa: The Politics of Decolonization and Modernization in Soviet Central Asia, 1955–1964," *Ab Imperio* 2 (2013): 191–222.

Kalt, Monica, *Tiermondismus in der Schweiz der 1960er und 1970er Jahre: Von der Barmherzigkeit zur Solidarität* (Bern: Peter Lang, 2010).

Kanet, Roger E., "Vier Jahrzehnte sowjetische Wirtschaftshilfe," in Bernd Greiner, Christian Th. Müller, and Claudia Weber, eds., *Ökonomie im Kalten Krieg* (Hamburg: Hamburger Edition, 2010), 45–62.

Kapur, Devesh, John P. Lewis, and Richard Webb, *The World Bank: Its First Half-Century*, 2 vols. (Washington, DC: Brookings Institution Press, 1997).

Katsakioris, Constantin, "Soviet Lessons for Arab Modernization: Soviet Educational Aid towards Arab Countries after 1956," *Journal of Modern European History* 8.1 (2010): 85–106.

Kay, Cristóbal, "Development Strategies and Rural Development: Exploring Synergies, Eradicating Poverty," *Journal of Peasant Studies* 36.1 (2009): 103–137.

Kay, Cristóbal, "Raúl Prebisch," in Simon, ed., *Fifty Key Thinkers*, 199–205.

Kelemen, Paul, "Planning for Africa: The British Labour Party's Colonial Development Policy, 1920–1964," *Journal of Agrarian Change* 7.1 (2007): 76–98.

Kent, John, "The United States and the Decolonization of Black Africa, 1945–63," in Ryan and Pungong, eds., *The United States*, 168–187.

Khan, Yasmin, *India at War: The Subcontinent and the Second World War* (New York: Oxford University Press, 2015).

Khilnani, Sunil, *The Idea of India* (New York: Farrar Straus Giroux, 1999).

Kim, Eun Mee, ed., *Four Asian Tigers: Economic Development and the Global Political Economy* (Wagon Lane: Emerald, 1998).

Kirschner, Sabrina, *From Clean Cities to Green Cities: The Beginnings of Urban Environmental Management in the 1970s*. PhD dissertation project, Bundeswehr University Munich.

Klein, Christina, "Musicals and Modernization: Rodgers and Hammerstein's The King and I," in Engerman et al., eds., *Staging Growth*, 129–162.

Knudsen, Ann-Christina L., "Ideas, Welfare, and Values: The Framing of the Common Agricultural Policy in the 1960s," in Patel, ed., *Fertile Ground*, 61–78.

Kotkin, Stephen, *Magnetic Mountain: Stalinism as a Civilization* (Berkeley: University of California Press, 1995).

Kott, Sandrine, and Joëlle Droux, eds., *Globalizing Social Rights: The International Labor Organization and Beyond* (Basingstoke: Palgrave Macmillan, 2013).

Kramer, Paul A., *The Blood of Government: Race, Empire, the United States, and the Philippines* (Chapel Hill: University of North Carolina Press, 2006).

Krige, John, *Sharing Knowledge, Shaping Europe: US Technological Collaboration and Nonproliferation* (Cambridge, MA: MIT Press, 2016).

Kröss, Verena, "The World Bank's Move toward Rural Development." Unpublished manuscript, 2017.

Kuchenbuch, David, "A Laboratory of Anarchy? The London Pioneer Health Centre and the Experimentalisation of the Social, 1935–1950," *Journal of Modern European History* 13.4 (2015): 480–498.

Kundrus, Birthe, "Colonialism, Imperialism, National Socialism: How Imperial Was the Third Reich," in Bradley Naranch and Geoff Eley, eds., *German Colonialism in a Global Age* (Durham: Duke University Press, 2014), 330–346.

Kwak, Nancy H., *A World of Homeowners: American Power and the Politics of Housing Aid* (Chicago: Chicago University Press, 2016).

Labanca, Nicola, "Italian Colonial Internment," in Ruth Ben-Ghiat and Mia Fuller, eds., *Italian Colonialism* (Basingstoke: Palgrave Macmillan, 2005), 27–36.

Lämmert, Stephanie, *Finding the Right Words: Languages of Litigation in Shambaa Native Courts in Tanganyika, c. 1925–1960*. PhD dissertation, European University Institute, 2017.

Lagendijk, Vincent, "The Structure of Power: The UNECE and East-West Electricity Connections, 1947–1975," *Comparativ* 24.1 (2014): 50–65.

Lancaster, Carol, *Foreign Aid: Diplomacy, Development, Domestic Politics* (Chicago: University of Chicago Press, 2008).

Landes, David S., *The Wealth and Poverty of Nations: Why Some Are So Rich and Some Are So Poor* (New York: W. W. Norton, 1998).

Laron, Guy, *Origins of the Suez Crisis: Postwar Development Diplomacy and the Struggle over Third World Industrialization, 1945–1956* (Washington, DC: Woodrow Wilson Center Press; Baltimore: Johns Hopkins University Press, 2013).

Latham, Michael E., "Ideology, Social Science, and Destiny: Modernization and the Kennedy-Era Alliance for Progress," *Diplomatic History* 22.2 (1998): 199–229.

Latham, Michael E. Latham, "Modernization," in Theodore M. Porter and Dorothy Ross, eds., *The Modern Social Sciences* (Cambridge: Cambridge University Press, 2003), 721–734.

Latham, Michael E., *Modernization as Ideology: American Social Science and "Nation Building" in the Kennedy Era* (Chapel Hill: University of North Carolina Press, 2000).

Laqua, Daniel, "Inside the Humanitarian Cloud: Causes and Motivations to Help Friends and Strangers," *Journal of Modern European History* 12.2 (2014): 175–185.

Le Sueur, James D., ed., *The Decolonization Reader* (New York: Routledge, 2003).

Lees, Lynn Hollen, *The Solidarities of Strangers: The English Poor Laws and the People, 1700–1948* (Cambridge: Cambridge University Press, 1998).

Li, Tania Murray, *Land's End: Capitalist Relations on an Indigenous Frontier* (Durham: Duke University Press, 2014).

Li, Tania Murray, *The Will to Improve: Governmentality, Development, and the Practice of Politics* (Durham: Duke University Press, 2007).

Li, Yannan, "Red Cross Society in Imperial China, 1904–1912: A Historical Analysis," *Voluntas* 27.5 (2016): 2274–2291.

Linklater, Andro, *Owning the Earth: The Transforming History of Land Ownership* (New York: Bloomsbury, 2013).

Lipartito, Kenneth, "Reassembling the Economic: New Departures in Historical Materialism," *American Historical Review* 121.1 (2016): 101–139.

Lohrmann, Ullrich, *Voices from Tanganyika: Great Britain, the United Nations and the Decolonization of a Trust Territory, 1946–1961* (Berlin: Lit, 2007).

Lorenzini, Sara, "Ace in the Hole or Hole in the Pocket? The Italian *Mezzogiorno* and the Story of a Troubled Transition from Development Model to Development Donor," *Contemporary European History* (2016), doi: /10.1017/S0960777316000576.

Lorenzini, Sara, "Comecon and the South in the Years of *Détente*: A Study of East-South Economic Relations," *European Review of History* 21.2 (2014): 183–199.

Lorenzini, Sara, *Una strana guerra fredda: Lo sviluppo e le relazioni Nord-Sud* (Bologna: Il Mulino, 2017).

Louis, William Roger, and Ronald Robinson, "The Imperialism of Decolonization," [1994] in Le Sueur, ed., *The Decolonization Reader*, 49–79.

Low, D. A., and Alison Smith, eds., *History of East Africa*, 3 vols. (Oxford: Oxford University Press, 1976).

Low, D. A., and J. M. Lonsdale, "Introduction: Towards the New Order, 1945–1963," in Low and Smith, eds., *History of East Africa*, vol. 3, 1–63.

Lübke, Uwe, *Bedrohliche Nähe: Die USA und die nationalsozialistische Herausforderung in Lateinamerika, 1937–1945* (Stuttgart: Steiner, 2004).

Lumsdaine, David Halloran, *Moral Vision in International Politics: The Foreign Aid Regime, 1949–1989* (Princeton, NJ: Princeton University Press, 1993).

Macekura, Stephen, "The Point Four Program and U.S. International Development Policy," *Political Science Quarterly* 128.1 (2013): 127–160.

Macekura, Stephen, *Of Limits and Growth: The Rise of Global Sustainable Development in the Twentieth Century* (New York: Cambridge University Press, 2015).

Mai, Gunther, "Die Agrarische Transition: Agrarische Gesellschaften in Europa und die Herausforderungen der industriellen Moderne im 19. und 20. Jahrhundert," *Geschichte und Gesellschaft* 33.4 (2007): 471–514.

Maier, Charles S., "'Malaise': The Crisis of Capitalism in the 1970s," in Niall Ferguson et al., eds., *The Shock of the Global: The 1970s in Perspective* (Cambridge, MA: Belknap Press of Harvard University Press, 2010), 25–48.

Malinowski, Stephan, "Modernisierungskriege: Militärische Gewalt und koloniale Modernisierung im Algerienkrieg (1954–1962)," *Archiv für Sozialgeschichte* 48 (2008): 213–248.

Manela, Erez, "A Pox on Your Narrative: Writing Disease Control into Cold War History," *Diplomatic History* 34.2 (2010): 299–323.

Manela, Erez, *The Wilsonian Moment: Self-Determination and the International Origins of Anticolonial Nationalism* (Oxford: Oxford University Press, 2007).

Manjapra, Kris, *Age of Entanglement: German and Indian Intellectuals across Empire* (Cambridge, MA: Harvard University Press, 2014).

Mann, Michael, "'Torchbearers Upon the Path of Progress': Britain's Ideology of a 'Moral and Material Progress' in India," in Harald Fischer-Tiné and Michael Mann, eds., *Colonialism as Civilizing Mission: Cultural Ideology in British India* (London: Anthem Press, 2004), 1–26.

Mar, Tracey Banivanua, *Decolonisation and the Pacific: Indigenous Globalisation and the Ends of Empire* (Cambridge: Cambridge University Press, 2016).

Marung, Steffi, "A 'Leninian Moment'? Soviet Africanists and the Interpretation of the October Revolution, 1950s–1970s," *Journal für Entwicklungspolitik* 33.3 (2017): 21–48.

Mason, Edward, and Robert Asher, *The World Bank since Bretton Woods* (Washington, DC: Brookings Institution, 1973).

Massullo, G., "La riforma agraria," in Piero Bevilaqua, ed., *Storia dell'agricoltura italiana in età contemporanea*, vol. 3 (Venezia: Marsilio, 1991), 509–542.

Maul, Daniel, "'Help Them Move the ILO Way': The International Labor Organization and the Modernization Discourse in the Era of Decolonization and the Cold War," *Diplomatic History* 33.3 (2009): 387–404.

Maul, Daniel, *Human Rights, Development and Decolonization: The International Labour Organization, 1940–70* (Basingstoke: Palgrave Macmillan, 2012).

Maul, Daniel Roger, "The Rise of a Humanitarian Superpower: American NGOs and International Relief, 1917–1945," in Bandeira Jerónimo and Monteiro, eds., *Internationalism*, 127–146.

Mazov, Sergey, *A Distant Front in the Cold War: The USSR in West Africa and the Congo, 1956–1964* (Washington, DC: Woodrow Wilson Center Press; Stanford, CA: Stanford University Press, 2010).

McCarthy, Kathleen D., "From Government to Grassroots Reform: The Ford Foundation's Population Programs in South Asia, 1959–1981," *Voluntas* 6.3 (1995): 292–316.

McKenzie, Francine, "Free Trade and Freedom to Trade: Exports, Markets and the Development Challenge to GATT, 1948–1968," in Frey, Kunkel, and Unger, eds., *International Organizations*, 150–170.

McMahon, Robert J., *The Cold War on the Periphery: The United States, India, and Pakistan* (New York: Columbia University Press, 1994).

McWilliam, Michael, "The Managed Economy: Agricultural Change, Development, and Finance in Kenya," in Low and Smith, eds., *History of East Africa*, vol. 3, 251–289.

Mercado, Jocelyn, "Buen Vivir: A New Era of Great Social Change," https://www.pachamama.org/blog/buen-vivir-new-era-great-social-change.

Merrill, Dennis, *Bread and the Ballot: The United States and India's Economic Development, 1947–1963* (Chapel Hill: University of North Carolina Press, 1990).

Milne, David, *America's Rasputin: Walt Rostow and the Vietnam War* (New York: Hill and Wang, 2008).

Mirowski, Philipp, and Dieter Plehwe, eds., *The Road from Mount Pelerin: The Making of the Neoliberal Thought Collective* (Cambridge, MA: Harvard University Press, 2009).

Möller, Esther, "Between Globalisation and Contestation: Humanity as a Polemical Concept Within the Red Cross and Red Crescent Movement," in Fabian Klose and Mirjam Thulin, eds., *Humanity: A History of European Concepts in Practice from the 16th Century to the Present* (Göttingen: Vandenhoeck & Ruprecht, 2016), 209–227.

Möller, Esther, *Orte der Zivilisierungsmission: Französische Schulen im Libanon, 1909–1943* (Göttingen: Vandenhoeck & Ruprecht, 2013).

Mokyr, Joel, *A Culture of Growth: The Origins of the Modern Economy* (Princeton, NJ: Princeton University Press, 2017).

Moon, Suzanne, *Technology and Ethical Idealism: A History of Development in the Netherlands East Indies* (Leiden: CNWS, 2007).

Morris, Jonathan, "Challenging Meridionalismo: Constructing a New History for Southern Italy," in Robert Lumley and Jonathan Morris, eds., *The New History of the Italian South: The Mezzogiorno Revisited* (Exeter: University of Exeter Press, 1997), 1–19.

Moser, Thomas, *Europäische Integration, Dekolonisation, Eurafrika: Eine historische Analyse über die Entstehungsbedingungen der eurafrikanischen Gemeinschaft von der Weltwirtschaftskrise zum Jaunde-Vertrag, 1929–1963* (Baden-Baden: Nomos, 2000).

Mosse, David, *Cultivating Development: An Ethnography of Aid Policy and Practice* (London: Pluto Press, 2005).

Moyo, Dambisa, *Dead Aid: Why Aid Is Not Working and How There Is Another Way for Africa* (New York: Farrar Straus Giroux, 2009).

Muehlenbeck, Philip, *Czechoslovakia in Africa, 1945–1968* (New York: Palgrave Macmillan, 2016).

Müller, Uwe, "Der RGW als Schlüssel zu einer transnationalen Wirtschaftsgeschichte des östlichen Europas in der zweiten Hälfte des 20. Jahrhunderts," *IWVWW—Berichte* (April–June 2015): 32–50.

Mukerjee, Madhusree, *Churchill's Secret War: The British Empire and the Ravaging of India during World War II* (New York: Basic Books, 2010).

Mukherjee, Janam, *Hungry Bengal: War, Famine, and the End of Empire* (New York: Oxford University Press, 2015).

Muschik, Eva-Maria, *Building States through International Development Assistance: The United Nations between Trusteeship and Self-Determination, 1945 to 1965*. PhD dissertation, New York University, 2016.

Myint, Hla, and Anne O. Krueger, "Economic Development," *Encyclopedia Britannica*, https://www.britannica.com/topic/economic-development.

Namikas, Lise A., *Battleground Africa: Cold War in the Congo, 1960–1965* (Washington, DC: Woodrow Wilson Center Press; Stanford: Stanford University Press, 2013).

Natsios, Andrew, "What Trump's Foreign Aid Budget Means for the Rest of the World," *The Atlantic*, April 4, 2017, https://www.theatlantic.com/politics/archive/2017/04/what-trumps-foreign-aid-budget-means-to-the-rest-of-the-world/521553/.

Nunan, Timothy, *Humanitarian Invasion: Global Development in Cold War Afghanistan* (New York: Cambridge University Press, 2016).

Nützenadel, Alexander, and Christian Grabas, eds., *Industrial Policy in Europe after 1945: Wealth, Power and Economic Development in the Cold War* (Basingstoke: Palgrave Macmillan 2014).

Nussbaum, Martha C., *Creating Capabilities: The Human Development Approach* (Cambridge, MA: Harvard University Press, 2011).

Nussbaum, Martha C., and Amartya Sen, *The Quality of Life* (Oxford: Oxford University Press, 1993).

Nussbaum, Martha C., *Women and Human Development: The Capabilities Approach* (Cambridge: Cambridge University Press, 2000).

O'Brien, Patrick, "Ten Years of Debate on the Origins of the Great Divergence," *Reviews in History* 1008 (2010), http://www.history.ac.uk/reviews/review/1008.

O'Sullivan, Kevin, "Between Internationalism and Empire: Ireland, the 'Like-Minded' Group, and the Search for a New International Order, 1974–82," *The International History Review* 37.5 (2015): 1083–1101.

O'Sullivan, Kevin, "'A Global Nervous System': The Rise and Rise of European Humanitarian NGOs," in Frey, Kunkel, and Unger, eds., *International Organizations*, 196–219.

Oberkrome, Willi, "National Socialist Blueprints for Rural Communities and their Resonance in Agrarian Society," in Martina Steber and Bernhard Gotto, eds., *Visions of Community in Nazi Germany: Social Engineering and Private Lives* (Oxford: Oxford University Press, 2014), 270–280.

Office of the Historian, Department of State, "USAID and PL 480, 1961–1969," https://history.state.gov/milestones/1961-1968/pl-480.

Olesen, Thorsten Borring, Helge Ø. Pharo, and Kristian Paaskesen, eds., *Saints and Sinners: Official Development Aid and its Dynamics in a Historical and Comparative Perspective* (Oslo: Akademika, 2013).

Orders, Paul, "'Adjusting to a New Period in World History': Franklin Roosevelt and European Colonialism," in Ryan and Pungong, eds., *The United States*, 63–84.

Osterhammel, Jürgen, "'The Great Work of Uplifting Mankind':
Zivilisierungsmission und Moderne," in Boris Barth and Jürgen Osterhammel,
eds., *Zivilisierungsmissionen: Imperiale Weltverbesserung seit dem 18.
Jahrhundert* (Konstanz: UVK Verlag, 2005), 363–425.

Ottacher, Friedbert, and Thomas Vogel, *Entwicklungszusammenarbeit im
Umbruch: Bilanz—Kritik—Perspektiven. Eine Einführung* (Frankfurt am Main:
Brandes & Apsel, 2016).

Overbeck, Anne, *"Mothering the Race": Discourses on Reproductive Rights of
African-American Women in the 20th Century*. PhD dissertation, University of
Münster, 2017.

Oxford Poverty and Human Development Initiative, "Missing Dimensions," http://
www.ophi.org.uk/research/missing-dimensions/.

Pan-Montojo, Juan, "International institutions and European agriculture: From
the IIA to the FAO," in Carin Martiin, Juan Pan-Montojo and Paul Brassley,
eds., *Agriculture in Capitalist Europe, 1945-1960: From food shortages to food
surpluses* (Abingdon: Routledge, 2016), 23-43.

Patel, Kiran Klaus, ed., *Fertile Ground for Europe? The History of European
Integration and the Common Agricultural Policy since 1945* (Baden-Baden:
Nomos, 2009).

Patel, Kiran Klaus, *New Deal: A Global History* (Princeton, NJ: Princeton
University Press, 2016).

Pattberg, Philipp et al., eds., *Public-Private Partnerships for Sustainable
Development: Emergence, Influence, and Legitimacy* (Cheltenham: Edward
Elgar, 2012).

Pearce, Kimber Charles, *Rostow, Kennedy, and the Rhetoric of Foreign Aid* (East
Lansing: Michigan State University Press, 2001).

Peet, Richard with Elaine Hartwick, *Theories of Development: Contentions,
Arguments, Alternatives* (New York: The Guilford Press, 2009).

Pedersen, Susan, *The Guardians: The League of Nations and the Crisis of Empire*
(Oxford: Oxford University Press, 2015).

Perkins, John H., *Geopolitics and the Green Revolution: Wheat, Genes, and the
Cold War* (New York: Oxford University Press, 1997).

Pernet, Corinne A., "Between Entanglements and Dependencies: Food, Nutrition, and
National Development at the Central American Institute of Nutrition (INCAP),"
in Frey, Kunkel, and Unger, eds., *International Organizations*, 101–125.

Pessis, Céline, "The Tractor as a Tool of Development? The Mythologies and
Legacies of Mechanised Tropical Agriculture in French Africa, 1944–1956," in
Hodge, Hödl, and Kopf, eds., *Developing Africa*, 179–203.

Petersson, Niels P., "'Großer Sprung nach vorn' oder 'natürliche Entwicklung'?
Zeitkonzepte der Entwicklungspolitik im 20. Jahrhundert," in Büschel and
Speich, eds., *Entwicklungswelten*, 89–111.

Pettinà, Vanni, and Artemy M. Kalinovsky, "From Countryside to Factory:
Industrialisation, Social Mobility, and Neoliberalism in Soviet Central Asia and
Mexico," *Journal für Entwicklungspolitik* 33.3 (2017): 91–118.

Pham, J. Peter, "Germany's 'Marshall Plan' for Africa," *Atlantic Council*, January
23, 2017, http://www.atlanticcouncil.org/blogs/new-atlanticist/germany-s-
marshall-plan-for-africa.

Pharo, Helge, and Monika Pohle Fraser, eds., *The Aid Rush: Aid Regimes in
Northern Europe during the Cold War*, 2 vols. (Oslo: Unipub, 2008).

Pharo, Helge, "Altruism, Security and the Impact of Oil: Norway's Foreign
    Economic Assistance Policy, 1958–1971," *Contemporary European History*
    12.4 (2003): 527–546.
Pharo, Helge Ø., "Entrepreneurship and Development Aid: The Case of the Indo-
    Norwegian Fisheries Project," in Pharo and Pohle Fraser, eds., *The Aid Rush*,
    vol. 2, 53–93.
Piketty, Thomas, *The Economics of Inequality* (Cambridge, MA: Harvard
    University Press, 2015).
Piot, Charles, *Nostalgia for the Future: West Africa after the Cold War* (Chicago:
    University of Chicago Press, 2010), 133–162.
Pironti, Pierluigi, "Post-war Welfare Policies (Version 1.1)," *1914–1918 Online:
    International Encyclopedia of the First World War* (2017), doi: 10.15463/
    ie1418.10358/1.1.
Pletsch, Carl E., "The Three Worlds, or the Division of Social Scientific Labour,
    Circa 1950–1975," *Comparative Studies in Society and History* 23 (1981):
    565–590.
Pomeranz, Kenneth, *The Great Divergence: China, Europe, and the Making of the
    Modern World* (Princeton, NJ: Princeton University Press, 2000).
Popp, Roland, "An Application of Modernization Theory during the Cold
    War? The Case of Pahlavi Iran," *International History Review* 30.1 (2008):
    76–98.
The Population Knowledge Network, ed., *Twentieth Century Population Thinking:
    A Critical Reader in Primary Sources* (Abingdon: Routledge, 2016).
Potì, Giorgio, *Imperial Violence, Anti-Colonial Nationalism and International
    Society: The Politics of Revolt across Mediterranean Empires, 1919–1927*. PhD
    dissertation, European University Institute, 2016.
Poulet, Wolf, "Ein Marshall-Plan löst Afrikas Probleme nicht," *Frankfurter
    Allgemeine Zeitung*, January 31, 2017, http://www.faz.net/aktuell/politik/
    ausland/entwicklungshilfe-ein-marshall-plan-loest-afrikas-probleme-
    nicht-14677751.html.
Pronk, Jan, "Collateral Damage or Calculated Default? The Millennium
    Development Goals and the Politics of Globalisation," in Max Spoor, ed.,
    Globalisation, Poverty and Conflict: A Critical 'Development' Reader
    (Dordrecht: Kluwer, 2004), 9–33.
Pungong, Victor, "The United States and the International Trusteeship System," in
    Ryan and Pungong, eds., *The United States*, 85–101.
Purtschert, Patricia, and Harald Fischer-Tiné, eds., *Colonial Switzerland: Rethinking
    Colonialism from the Margins* (Basingstoke: Palgrave Macmillan, 2015).
Quinn, Ann, "RF Grants in the Philippines, 1958–1990," *Rockefeller Archive
    Newsletter* (2006): 10–12.
Rao, Mohan, *From Population Control to Reproductive Rights: Malthusian
    Arithmetic* (New Delhi: Sage, 2004).
Radcliffe, Sarah, "Gunnar Myrdal," in Simon, ed., *Fifty Key Thinkers*, 181–187.
Rahman, Aminur, *Women and Microcredit in Rural Bangladesh: Anthropological
    Study of the Rhetoric and Realities of Grameen Bank Lending* (Boulder, CO:
    Westview Press, 2001).
Raper, Arthur F., *Rural Development in Action: The Comprehensive Experiment at
    Comilla, East Pakistan* (Ithaca, NY: Cornell University Press, 1970).

Rasmussen, Lewis, "Waging War on Daily Terrors: The Use of Development Assistance to Counter Violent Extremism and Combat Terrorism," *Brown Journal of World Affairs* 21.2 (2015): 72–93.

Rassweiler, Anne D., *The Generation of Power: The History of Dneprostroi* (New York: Oxford University Press, 1988).

Rayward, W. Boyd, ed., *Information Beyond Borders: International Cultural and Intellectual Exchange in the Belle Èpoque* (Farnham: Ashgate, 2014).

Reinhard, Wolfgang, *Die Unterwerfung der Welt: Globalgeschichte der europäischen Expansion, 1415–2015* (München: Beck, 2016).

Reinisch, Jessica, "Internationalism in Relief: The Birth (and Death) of UNRRA," *Past & Present* 210.6 (2011): 258–289.

Rempe, Martin, "Airy Promises: Senegal and the EEC's Common Agricultural Policy in the Nineteen-Sixties," in Patel, ed., *Fertile Ground*, 221–240.

Rempe, Martin, "Decolonization by Europeanization? The Early EEC and the Transformation of French-African Relations," *KFG Working Paper Series* 27 (May 2011), http://www.polsoz.fu-berlin.de/en/v/transformeurope/publications/working_paper/WP_27_Rempe.pdf.

Rempe, Martin, "Entangled Industrialization: The EEC and Industrial Development in Francophone West Africa," in Nützenadel and Grabas, eds., *Industrial Policy*, 236–255.

Research & Degrowth, "Definition," https://degrowth.org/definition-2/.

Ribi Forclaz, Amalia, "Agriculture, American Expertise, and the Quest for Global Data: Leon Estabrook and the First World Agricultural Census of 1930," *Journal of Global History* 11.1 (2016): 44–65.

Ribi Forclaz, Amalia, *Humanitarian Imperialism: The Politics of Anti-Slavery Activism, 1880–1940* (Oxford: Oxford University Press, 2015).

Ribi Forclaz, Amalia, "A New Target for International Social Reform: The International Labour Organisation and Working and Living Conditions in Agriculture in the Interwar Years," *Journal of Contemporary European History* 20.3 (2011): 307–329.

Rice, Louisa, "Between Empire and Nation: Francophone West African Students and Decolonization," *Atlantic Studies* 10.1 (2013): 131–147.

Rivarola Puntigliano, Andrés, and Örjan Appelqvist, "Prebisch and Myrdal: Development Economics in the Core and on the Periphery," *Journal of Global History* 6 (2011): 29–52.

Rizzo, Matteo, "What Was Left of the Groundnut Scheme? Development Disaster and Labour Market in Southern Tanganyika, 1946–1952," *Journal of Agrarian Change* 6.2 (2006): 205–238.

Robertson, Thomas, *The Malthusian Moment: Global Population Growth and the Birth of American Environmentalism* (New Brunswick, NJ: Rutgers University Press, 2012).

Robin, Ron, *The Making of the Cold War Enemy: Culture and Politics in the Military-Intellectual Complex* (Princeton, NJ: Princeton University Press, 2001).

Rodgers, Daniel T., *Age of Fracture* (Cambridge, MA: Belknap Press of Harvard University Press, 2011).

Rodgers, Daniel T., *Atlantic Crossings: Social Politics in a Progressive Age* (Cambridge, MA: Belknap Press of Harvard University Press, 1998).

Rodogno, Davide, *Against Massacre: Humanitarian Interventions in the Ottoman Empire, 1815–1914: The Emergence of a European Concept and International Practice* (Princeton, NJ: Princeton University Press, 2012).

Romano, Angela, "Shaping Pan-European Cooperation in the 1970s: Soviet Initiatives and the EEC-Nine's Response," in Claudia Hiepel, ed., *Europe in a Globalising World: Global Challenges and European Responses* Rosenstein *in the "Long" 1970s* (Baden-Baden: Nomos, 2014), 27–48.

Rossi-Doria, Anna, "Il movimento contadino nel secondo dopoguerra in Calabria," in Franco Bonelli, Guido Crainz, and Anna Rossi-Doria, eds., *La fine dei contadini e l'industrializzazione del mezzogiorno* (Catanzaro: Rubbettino, 1999), 91–108.

Roy, Srirupa, *Beyond Belief: India and the Politics of Postcolonial Nationalism* (Durham: Duke University Press, 2007).

Roy, Tirthankar, "Geography or Politics? Regional Inequality in Colonial India," 2013, http://economics.yale.edu/sites/default/files/roy_paper_09_13.pdf.

Rudner, Martin, "East European Aid to Asian Developing Countries: The Legacy of the Communist Era," *Modern Asian Studies* 30.1 (1996): 1–28.

Ryan, David, and Victor Pungong, eds., *The United States and Decolonization: Power and Freedom* (New York: Palgrave Macmillan, 2000).

Ryan, David, "By Way of Introduction: The United States, Decolonization and the World System," in Ryan and Pungong, eds., *The United States*, 1–23.

Sachs, Wolfgang, ed., *The Development Dictionary* (London: Zen Books, 1992).

Sackley, Nicole, "The Village as Cold War Site: Experts, Development, and the History of Rural Reconstruction," *Journal of Global History* 6 (2011): 481–504.

Salvatici, Silvia, *Nel nome degli altri: Storia dell'umanitarismo internazionale* (Bologna: Il Mulino, 2015).

Sayward, Amy L., *The United Nations in International History* (London: Bloomsbury, 2017).

Schaefer, Bernd, "Socialist Modernization in Vietnam: The East German Approach, 1976–89," in Slobodian, ed., *Comrades of Color*, 95–116.

Schain, Martin, ed., *The Marshall Plan: Fifty Years After* (Basingstoke: Palgrave Macmillan, 2001).

Schivelbusch, Wolfgang, *Three New Deals: Reflections on Roosevelt's America, Mussolini's Italy, and Hitler's Germany, 1933–1939* (New York: Metropolitan Books, 2006).

Schmelzer, Matthias, *The Hegemony of Growth: The OECD and the Making of the Economic Growth Paradigm* (Cambridge: Cambridge University Press, 2016).

Schmidt, Heide-Irene, and Helge Pharo, "Introduction," *Contemporary European History* 12.4 (2003): 387–394.

Schmidt, Heide-Irene, "Pushed to the Front: The Foreign Assistance Policy of the Federal Republic of Germany, 1958–1971," *Contemporary European History* 12.4 (2003): 473–507.

Schneider, Jane, ed., *Italy's "Southern Question": Orientalism in One Country* (Oxford: Berg, 1998).

Schneider, Leander, "Colonial Legacies and Postcolonial Authoritarianism in Tanzania: Connects and Disconnects," *African Studies Review* 49.1 (2006): 93–118.

Schneider, Leander, *Government of Development: Peasants and Politicians in Postcolonial Tanzania* (Bloomington: Indiana University Press, 2014).

Schneider, W. H., ed., *Rockefeller Philanthropy and Modern Biomedicine: International Initiatives from World War One to the Cold War* (Bloomington: Indiana University Press, 2002).

Schuknecht, Rohland, *British Colonial Development Policy after the Second World War: The Case of Sukumaland, Tanganyika* (Berlin: Lit, 2010).

Schultz, Helga, and Angela Harre, eds., *Bauerngesellschaften auf dem Weg in die Moderne: Agrarismus in Ostmitteleuropa 1880 bis 1960* (Wiesbaden: Harrassowitz, 2010).

Sciacchitano, Grazia, "Rural Development and Changing Labour Relations in Italy and Spain in the 1950s and 1960s," *Comparativ* 27.2 (2017): 35–53.

Scott, James C., *Seeing Like a State: How Certain Schemes to Improve the Human Condition Have Failed* (New Haven, CT: Yale University Press, 1998).

Sen, Amartya, *Development as Freedom* (Oxford: Clarendon Press, 1999).

Sen, Amartya, "What Is Development About?" in Gerald M. Meier and Joseph E. Stiglitz, eds., *Frontiers of Development Economics: The Future in Perspective* (Oxford: World Bank and Oxford University Press, 2000), 506–513.

Serra, Narcís, and Joseph E. Stiglitz, eds., *The Washington Consensus Reconsidered: Toward a New Global Governance* (New York: Oxford University Press, 2008).

Sessions, Jennifer E., *By Sword and Plow: France and the Conquest of Algeria* (Ithaca, NY: Cornell University Press, 2011).

Sharma, Patrick A., *Robert McNamara's Other War: The World Bank and International Development* (Philadelphia: University of Pennsylvania Press, 2017).

Shaw, John, "Hans Wolfgang Singer," in Simon, ed., *Fifty Key Thinkers*, 242–247.

Sherman, Taylor C., "From 'Grow More Food' to 'Miss a Meal': Hunger, Development, and the Limits of Post-Colonial Nationalism in India, 1947–1957," *South Asia* 36.4 (2013): 571–588.

Sherman, Taylor C., William Gould, and Sarah Ansari, "Introduction," in Taylor C. Sherman, William Gould, and Sarah Ansari, eds., *From Subjects to Citizens: Society and the Everyday State in India and Pakistan, 1947–1970* (New Delhi: Cambridge University Press, 2014), 1–9.

Shipway, Martin, *Decolonization and its Impact: A Comparative Approach to the End of the Colonial Empires* (Malden, MA: Blackwell Publishing, 2008).

Sieberg, Herward, *Colonial Development: Die Grundlegung moderner Entwicklungspolitik durch Großbritannien, 1919–1949* (Stuttgart: Steiner, 1985).

Siegel, Benjamin, "'Fantastic Quantities of Food Grains': Cold War Visions and Agrarian Fantasies in Independent India," in James and Leake, eds., *Decolonization*, 21–42.

Silverman, Dan P., *Hitler's Economy: Nazi Work Creation Programs, 1933–1936* (Cambridge, MA: Harvard University Press, 1998).

Simon, David, ed., *Fifty Key Thinkers on Development* (Abingdon: Routledge, 2006).

Sinclair, Guy Fiti, "International Social Reform and the Invention of Development," *SSRN* (September 1, 2016), http://dx.doi.org/10.2139/ssrn.2842441.

Singh, Rana P. B., "Mohandas (Mahatma) Gandhi," in Simon, ed., *Fifty Key Thinkers*, 106–111.

Sinha, Subir, "Lineages of the Developmentalist State: Transnationality and Village India, 1900–1965," *Comparative Studies in Society and History* 50.1 (2008): 57–90.

Sivaramakrishnan, K., and Arun Agrawal, "Regional Modernities in Stories and
    Practices of Development," in K. Sivaramakrishnan and Arun Agrawal, eds.,
    Regional Modernities: The Cultural Politics of Development in India (Stanford,
    CA: Stanford University Press, 2003), 1–61.
Skidelsky, Robert, *John Maynard Keynes (1883–1946): Economist, Philosopher,
    Statesmen* (New York: Penguin, 2005).
Skinner, Kate, "'It Brought Some Kind of Neatness to Mankind': Mass Literacy,
    Community Development and Democracy in 1950s Asante," *Africa* 79.4
    (2009): 479–499.
Skinner, Kate, "Who Knew the Minds of the People? Specialist Knowledge and
    Developmentalist Authoritarianism in Postcolonial Ghana," *Journal of Imperial
    and Commonwealth History* 39.2 (2011): 297–323.
Slobodian, Quinn, ed., *Comrades of Color: East Germany in the Cold War World*
    (New York: Berghahn Books, 2015).
Slobodian, Quinn, *Foreign Front: Third World Politics in Sixties West Germany*
    (Durham: Duke University Press, 2012).
Sluga, Glenda, "Capitalists and Climate," *Humanity*, November 6, 2017, http://
    humanityjournal.org/blog/capitalists-and-climate/.
Sluga, Glenda, *Internationalism in the Age of Nationalism* (Philadelphia: University
    of Pennsylvania Press, 2013).
Speek, Sven, "Ecological Concepts of Development? The Case of Colonial
    Zambia," in Hodge, Hödl, and Kopf, eds., *Developing Africa*, 133–154.
Speich Chassé, Daniel, *Die Erfindung des Bruttosozialprodukts: Globale
    Ungleichheit in der Wissensgeschichte der Ökonomie* (Göttingen: Vandenhoeck
    & Ruprecht, 2013).
Speich, Daniel, "The Kenyan Style of 'African Socialism': Developmental
    Knowledge Claims and the Explanatory Limits of the Cold War," *Diplomatic
    History* 33.3 (2009): 449–466.
Speich Chassé, Daniel, "Towards a Global History of the Marshall Plan: European
    Post-war Reconstruction and the Rise of Development Economic Expertise," in
    Nützenadel and Grabas, eds., *Industrial Policy*, 187–212.
Spitz, Pierre, "The Green Revolution Re-Examined in India," in Bernhard Glaeser,
    ed., *The Green Revolution Re-Visited: Critique and Alternatives* (London: Allen
    & Unwin, 1987), 56–75.
Springer, Jenny, "State Power and Agricultural Transformation in Tamil Nadu,"
    in Arun Agrawal and K. Sivaramakrishnan, eds., *Agrarian Environments:
    Resources, Representation, and Rule in India* (Durham: Duke University Press,
    2000), 86–106.
Staatz, John M., and Carl K. Eicher, "Agricultural Development Ideas in Historical
    Perspective," in Carl K. Eicher and John M. Staatz, eds., *International
    Agricultural Development*, 3rd ed. (Baltimore: Johns Hopkins University Press,
    1998 (1984)), 8–38.
Stanard, Matthew G., *Selling the Congo: A History of European Pro-Empire
    Propaganda and the Making of Belgian Imperialism* (Lincoln: University of
    Nebraska Press, 2011).
Staples, Amy L. S., *The Birth of Development: How the World Bank, Food and
    Agriculture Organization, and World Health Organization Changed the World,
    1945–1965* (Kent, OH: Kent State University Press, 2006).

Stockwell, Sarah, "Exporting Britishness: Decolonization in Africa, the British State and its Clients," in Bandeira Jerónimo and Costa Pinto, eds., *The Ends of European Colonial Empires*, 148–177.

Stokke, Olav, *The UN and Development: From Aid to Cooperation* (Bloomington: University of Indiana Press, 2009).

Straus, Kenneth M., *Factory and Community in Stalin's Russia: The Making of an Industrial Working Class* (Pittsburgh, PA: Pittsburgh University Press, 1997).

Subramanian, Ajantha, *Shorelines: Space and Rights in South Asia* (Stanford, CA: Stanford University Press, 2009).

Subramanian, R., "Introduction," in R. Subramanian, ed., *Rural Development: An Inside Look at Problems and Prospects* (New Delhi: Yatan Publications, 1988), xi–xv.

Sum, Anna Barbara, "Widerspruch als Prinzip: Nachruf auf Albert O. Hirschman (7 April 1915–10 Dezember 2012)," *Geschichte und Gesellschaft* 39.1 (2013): 125–138.

Sussman, Gerald E., *The Challenge of Integrated Rural Development in India: A Policy and Management Perspective* (Boulder, CO: Westview Press, 1982).

Szeftel, Morris, "Sir William Arthur Lewis," in Simon, ed., *Fifty Key Thinkers*, 144–149.

Szreter, Simon, "The Idea of Demographic Transition and the Study of Fertility Change: A Critical Intellectual History," *Population and Development Review* 19.4 (1993): 659–701.

Taffet, Jeffrey F., *Foreign Aid as Foreign Policy: The Alliance for Progress in Latin America* (New York: Taylor and Francis, 2007).

Tarp, Finn, "Aid, Growth, and Development," in George Mavrotas, ed., *Foreign Aid for Development: Issues, Challenges, and the New Agenda* (New York: Oxford University Press, 2010), 20–53.

Taylor, Keith, *The Political Ideas of the Utopian Socialists* (Abingdon: Routledge, 1982).

Teichmann, Christian, "Canals, Cotton, and the Limits of De-colonization in Soviet Uzbekistan, 1924–1941," *Central Asian Survey* 26.4 (2007): 499–519.

Teichmann, Christian, "Cultivating the Periphery: Bolshevik Civilizing Missions and Colonialism in Soviet Central Asia," *Comparativ* 19.1 (2009): 34–52.

Teichmann, Christian, *Macht der Unordnung: Stalins Herrschaft in Zentralasien, 1920–1950* (Hamburg: Hamburger Edition, 2016).

Terretta, Meredith, "Cameroonian Nationalists Go Global: From Forest *Maquis* to a Pan-African Accra," *Journal of African History* 51.2 (2010): 189–212.

Terretta, Meredith, "'We Had Been Fooled into Thinking that the UN Watches over the Entire World': Human Rights, UN Trust Territories, and Africa's Decolonization," *Human Rights Quarterly* 34.2 (2012): 329–360.

Thompson, Elizabeth, *Colonial Citizens: Republican Rights, Paternal Privilege, and Gender in French Syria and Lebanon* (New York: Columbia University Press, 2000).

Tignor, Robert L., *W. Arthur Lewis and the Birth of Development Economics* (Princeton, NJ: Princeton University Press, 2006).

Tilley, Helen, *Africa as a Living Laboratory: Empire, Development, and the Problem of Scientific Knowledge, 1870–1950* (Chicago: University of Chicago Press, 2011).

Tischler, Julia, *Light and Power for a Multiracial Nation: The Kariba Dam Scheme in the Central African Federation* (Basingstoke: Palgrave Macmillan, 2013).

Tischler, Julia, "Resisting Modernisation? Two African Responses to the Kariba Dam Scheme in the Central African Federation," *Comparativ* 21.1 (2011): 60–75.

Tomlinson, B. R., "What Was the Third World?" *Journal of Contemporary History* 38.2 (2003): 307–321.

Tomlinson, Jim, "The Commonwealth, the Balance of Payments and the Politics of International Poverty: British Aid Policy, 1958–1971," *Contemporary European History* 12.4 (2003): 413–429.

Toner, Simon, "The Life and Death of Our Republic: Modernization, Agricultural Development, and the Peasantry in the Mekong Delta in the Long 1970s," in James and Leake, eds., *Decolonization*, 43–61.

Tooze, Adam, *The Deluge: The Great War and the Remaking of Global Order, 1916–1931* (London: Allen Lane, 2014).

Tooze, Adam, *The Wages of Destruction: The Making and Breaking of the Nazi Economy* (London: Allen Lane, 2006).

Trentin, Massimiliano, "Modernization as State-Building: The Two Germanys in Syria, 1963–1972," *Diplomatic History* 33.3 (2009): 487–505.

Unfried, Berthold, "A Cuban Cycle of Developmental Socialism? Cubans and East Germans in the Socialist World System," *Journal für Entwicklungspolitik* 33.3 (2017): 69–90.

Unger, Corinna R., "Agrarwissenschaftliche Expertise und ländliche Modernisierungsstrategien in der internationalen Entwicklungspolitik, 1920er bis 1980er Jahre," *Geschichte und Gesellschaft* 41 (2015): 552–579.

Unger, Corinna R., "The Decolonization of Development: Rural Development in India Before and After 1947," in Bandeira Jéronimo and Monteiro, eds., *Internationalism*, 253–278.

Unger, Corinna R., *Entwicklungspfade in Indien: Eine internationale Geschichte, 1947–1980* (Göttingen: Wallstein, 2015).

Unger, Corinna R., "Export und Entwicklung: Westliche Wirtschaftsinteressen in Indien im Kontext der Dekolonisation und des Kalten Krieges," *Jahrbuch für Wirtschaftsgeschichte/Economic History Yearbook* 1 (2012): 69–86.

Unger, Corinna R., "Family Planning—A Rational Choice? The Influence of Systems Approaches, Behavioralism, and Rational Choice on Mid-Twentieth-Century Family Planning Programs," in Hartmann and Unger, eds., *A World of Populations*, 58–82.

Unger, Corinna R., "Histories of Development and Modernization: Findings, Reflections, Future Research," *H-Soz-u-Kult*, September 12, 2010, http://hsozkult.geschichte.hu-berlin.de/forum/2010-12-001.

Unger, Corinna R., "The Making of the Small Family Norm in post-1947 India," *Contemporanea* 18.3 (2015): 483–488.

Unger, Corinna R., "The United States, Decolonization, and the Education of Third World Elites," in Dülffer and Frey, eds., *Elites*, 241–261.

United Nations Development Program, "Human Development Index (HDI)," http://hdr.undp.org/en/content/human-development-index-hdi.

Unkovski-Korica, Vladimir, *The Economic Struggle for Power in Tito's Yugoslavia: From World War II to Non-Alignment* (London: I. B. Tauris, 2016).

Vahsen, Urban, *Eurafrikanische Entwicklungskooperation: Die Assoziierungspolitik der EWG gegenüber dem subsaharischen Afrika in den 1960er Jahren* (Stuttgart: Steiner, 2010).

Van Beusekom, Monica M., "Disjunctures in Theory and Practice: Making Sense of Change in Agricultural Development at the Office du Niger, 1920–60," *Journal of African History* 41.1 (2000): 79–99.

Van Beusekom, Monica M., and Dorothy L. Hodgson, "Lessons Learned? Development Experiences in the Late Colonial Period," *Journal of African History* 41 (2000): 29–33.

Van de Grift, Liesbeth, "'On New Land a New Society': Internal Colonisation in the Netherlands, 1918–1940," *Contemporary European History* 22.4 (2013): 609–626.

Van Laak, Dirk, "Detours around Africa: The Connection between Developing Colonies and Integrating Europe," in Alexander Badenoch and Andreas Fischer, eds., *Materializing Europe: Transnational Infrastructures and the Project of Europe* (Basingstoke: Palgrave Macmillan, 2010), 27–43.

Van Meurs, Wim, "Demokratie oder Sozialismus? Bauernparteien in Südosteuropa um die Jahrhundertwende als Träger der Demokratisierung. Eine Skizze," *Archiv für Sozialgeschichte* 53 (2013): 93–112.

Vincent, James, "Bolivia Rejects 'Offensive' Chicken Donation from Bill Gates," *The Verge*, June 16, 2016, http://www.theverge.com/2016/6/16/11952200/bill-gates-bolivia-chickens-refused.

Viola, Lynn, *Peasant Rebels under Stalin: Collectivization and the Culture of Peasant Resistance* (Oxford: Oxford University Press, 1996).

Vivier, Nadine, ed., *The Golden Age of State Enquiries: Rural Enquiries in the Nineteenth Century. From Fact Gathering to Political Instrument* (Turnhout: Brepols, 2014).

Watts, Michael, "Andre Gunder Frank," in Simon, ed., *Fifty Key Thinkers*, 90–96.

Webster, David, "Development Advisors in a Time of Cold War and Decolonization: The United Nations Technical Assistance Administration, 1950–59," *Journal of Global History* 6 (2011): 249–272.

Weinstein, Barbara, "Developing Inequality," *American Historical Review* 113.1 (2008): 1–18.

Wendler, Eugen, *Friedrich List (1789–1846): A Visionary Economist with Social Responsibility* (Berlin: Springer, 2015).

Westad, Odd Arne, *The Global Cold War: Third World Interventions and the Making of Our Times* (New York: Cambridge University Press, 2005).

Whelan, Daniel J., "'Under the Aegis of Man': The Right to Development and the Origins of the New International Economic Order," *Humanity* 6.1 (2015): 93–108.

Wieters, Heike, "Of Heartfelt Charity and Billion Dollar Enterprise: From Postwar Relief to Europe to Humanitarian Relief to 'Everywhere'—CARE, Inc., in Search of a New Mission," in Frey, Kunkel, and Unger, eds., *International Organizations*, 220–239.

Willetts, Peter, ed., '*The Conscience of the World': The Influence of Non-Governmental Organizations in the UN System* (Washington, DC: Brookings Institution, 1996).

Williams, John, "Democracy and the 'Washington Consensus,'" [1993] in Chari and Corbridge, eds., *The Development Reader*, 288–296.

Willis, Katie, "Norman Borlaug," in Simon, ed., *Fifty Key Thinkers*, 45–50.

Wöbse, Anna-Katharina, *Weltnaturschutz: Umweltdiplomatie in Völkerbund und Vereinten Nationen, 1920–1950* (Frankfurt am Main: Campus, 2012).

Wong, Bin, *China Transformed: Historical Change and the Limits of the European Experience* (Ithaca, NY: Cornell University Press, 1997).

Wood, Robert E., *From Marshall Plan to Debt Crisis: Foreign Aid and Development Choices in the World Economy* (Berkeley: University of California Press, 1986).

Woolcock, Michael, Simon Szreter and Vijayendra Rao, "How and Why History Matters for Development Policy," in Bayly et al., eds., *History*, 3–38.

Worby, Eric, "'Discipline without Oppression': Sequence, Timing and Marginality in Southern Rhodesia's Post-War Development Regime," *The Journal of African History* 41.1 (2000): 101–125.

Young, Crawford, "Imperial Endings and Small States: Disorderly Decolonization for the Netherlands, Belgium, and Portugal," in Bandeira Jerónimo and Costa Pinto, eds., *The Ends of European Colonial Empires*, 101–125.

Zachariah, Benjamin, *Developing India: An Intellectual and Social History* (New Delhi: Oxford University Press, 2005).

Zanasi, Margherita, "Exporting Development: The League of Nations and Republican China," *Comparative Studies in Society and History* 49.1 (2007): 143–169.

Zeller, Thomas, *Driving Germany: The Landscape of the German Autobahn, 1930–1970* (New York: Berghahn Books, 2007).

Zierler, David, *The Invention of Ecocide: Agent Orange, Vietnam, and the Scientists Who Changed the Way We Think about the Environment* (Athens: University of Georgia Press, 2011).

Zimmerer, Jürgen, *From Windhoek to Auschwitz: On the Relationship between Colonialism and the Holocaust* (Abingdon: Routledge, 2018).

Zimmerman, Andrew, *Alabama in Africa: Booker T. Washington, the German Empire, and the Globalization of the New South* (Princeton, NJ: Princeton University Press, 2012).

Zürcher, Lukas, "'So fanden wir auf der Karte diesen kleinen Staat': Globale Positionierung und lokale Entwicklungsfantasien der Schweiz in Rwanda in den 1960er Jahren," in Büschel and Speich, eds., *Entwicklungswelten*, 275–309.

INDEX